W9-BOC-223

MAYOR

The City in the Twenty-First Century

Eugenie L. Birch and Susan M. Wachter, Series Editors

A complete list of books in the series is available from the publisher.

MAYOR

The Best Job in Politics

Michael A. Nutter

PENN

University of Pennsylvania Press
Philadelphia

Copyright © 2018 Michael A. Nutter

All images in the gallery between pages 68 and 69 are copyright © City of
Philadelphia. Photos by Kait Privitera and Mitchell Leff.

All rights reserved. Except for brief quotations used for purposes of review
or scholarly citation, none of this book may be reproduced in any form
by any means without written permission from the publisher.

Published by
University of Pennsylvania Press
Philadelphia, Pennsylvania 19104-4112
www.upenn.edu/pennpress

Printed in the United States of America on acid-free paper
10 9 8 7 6 5 4 3 2 1

A Cataloging-in-Publication record is available from the Library of Congress
ISBN 978-0-8122-5002-2

To my mom, Catalina; my dad, Basil; my sister, Renee; and my grandmother, Edythe, thank you always for the love, support, and encouragement to be a good man.

To Councilman John C. Anderson, Obra S. Kernodle III, Congressman William H. Gray III, and committee people of the Fifty-Second Ward, thank you for your inspiration, leadership, and mentorship—you made me a better man.

To Lisa, Olivia, and Christian, thank you for making me the best husband, father, and public servant I could ever hope to be.

This book is dedicated to the incredible citizens of Philadelphia who cared about me and gave me a chance to lead our great city, the Sisters of the Immaculate Heart of Mary at the Transfiguration of Our Lord School, the Jesuits and lay teachers at Saint Joseph's Preparatory High School who taught me to be a man for others, the faculty and staff at the University of Pennsylvania and the Wharton School, all of my classmates throughout my education, my incredible City Council staff, the tremendously talented leaders of my mayoral administration, the fine public servants of the City of Philadelphia, and public servants across America. Thank you for what you do every day.

CONTENTS

~

PART THREE

A photo gallery appears between pages 68 and 69.

PROLOGUE

~

The Best Job in Politics

In 1975, when I was an undergraduate at the University of Pennsylvania, I commandeered a large Deer Park water jug from somewhere on the campus. Every night, I'd empty my pockets and put the change in that jug, and after I graduated, wherever I moved, I always took that jug with me. By 1988, the water jug contained a fair amount of change. When I was first running for City Council in the 1987 election in Philadelphia, my car had died, and after I'd lost the election, I turned that jug upside down every day to get quarters so that I could scrape together the money to catch the SEPTA (Southeastern Pennsylvania Transportation Authority) bus and elevated train to work.

That was in 1988. Twenty years later, on January 7, 2008, I was standing on the stage at the Academy of Music at Broad and Locust Streets in Philadelphia, being sworn in as the ninety-eighth mayor of my hometown. The road was long, and there were many events and happenings, in between. And I didn't take the journey by myself.

This is a story, and a political autobiography, about commitment and perseverance, about the passion and desire to serve. If you enter the world of public service for the right reasons, it's the most incredible feeling that you will ever have. You will never make a lot of money in public service. Most of the people who try to make money in politics (government) end up going to jail. But there is something entirely unique about the opportunity, every day, to make somebody else's life better. It's a feeling that you can perhaps get in some other professions, but I know that it happens in this one. I would contend that being the mayor is the best job in politics, and possibly the best job in America.

⁓

Mayoring involves many paradoxes. Being mayor is a lonely business, and leadership of a city can be a very lonely place. At the end of the day, you're the ultimate decision maker, at least within your realm. To be sure, there are external factors and influences in city government: there are other nearby local governments, and state and federal governments with which you have to build relationships and interact. Cities generally are a political subdivision of their respective states. There can be a lot of tension between and among cities and their respective states, and between states and the federal government, depending on the policies and programs that are being proposed at any given time. But, for the most part, cities are allowed to operate autonomously. Many have home rule, and as mayor you are pretty much out there on your own. As mayor, just about all the bucks do actually stop at your desk. That doesn't necessarily mean, unfortunately, that the actual, financial bucks stop at your desk—but the problems, issues, and challenges all end up there. And, quite honestly, whether or not you have any control over the problems or issues in question, you're the mayor, so it all becomes your responsibility on some level.

At the same time, the mayor's office is the position that I believe is closest to the people and to their real lives and experiences. It's unlikely that you'll be able to chat on the streets with the president, a senator, or even a state legislator, but anyone in Philadelphia might have stopped me to talk at the supermarket or found me at Woody's barbershop in Wynnefield once every two weeks.

A lot of people depend on you on a daily basis. There is a weightiness to the mayor's office. The other political offices are certainly weighty, as well—being governor is an incredible responsibility, as is being the president of the United States. But people are sometimes not entirely sure what the governor may be doing at any moment, and I don't mean that disrespectfully toward the governor in any state. It's just that the gubernatorial position is usually a little more removed and distant from the people. Most presidents, of course, look at Washington, DC, as the place where they function and operate—although apparently not President Trump. As I write this in 2017, we mostly know where the president is but rarely know what he's doing. While some people consider both governor and president to be "higher" offices than mayor—and they are indisputably different offices—there is no office as close to the people as being in charge of a city. People understand intuitively the mayor's position more than other political offices, so while it may at times feel lonely, it is also a much more visible one, and you are rarely alone. People know where you are, and usually want to be near you.

When you as a citizen wake up in the morning and turn on your faucet, you have started your daily relationship with your local government and the mayor. You have an expectation that water—and potable, clean water—will come out of that faucet. When you step outside, you expect that the streetlights and traffic signals will work. Your roads on your drive to work in the morning will be decently paved. When you put your trashcan out on your trash day, you expect that it will magically be emptied by the time you come home. When you call 911, you expect a trained, respectful call taker will help you, and then a first responder will appear. When you take your children to a recreation center, there will be equipment such as basketballs and soccer nets, and in good condition. That is all city government. And that is the work of mayoring—an ongoing exchange between larger government policies, including the budgets that fund them, and a daily engagement with and in the lives of citizens.

As mayor, you can accomplish tangible things. I don't know the party affiliations of many other mayors in my acquaintance, because the problems and issues that we share are all the same and are often very remote from party dicta or ideologies. When he was mayor of New York, Fiorello LaGuardia famously said that "there is no Democratic or Republican way of cleaning the streets." Being mayor is where politics hits the road—literally. You remove snow, pick up trash, deal with climate events, and repair potholes. It's where the action is. But you can also apply your core values, principles, and vision to make a measurable improvement in your city and many communities.

During my eight years in office I learned another paradox in the work of mayoring. The buck stops with you, and it's a singular experience in that regard, yet it's a collective experience that you absolutely must do with a team of leaders and that absolutely involves communication across many different constituencies, neighborhoods, and audiences. When I look back on my mayoring years and at video clips from press conferences, I notice one striking thing: I am almost never, ever standing alone. I believe in "team."

Being mayor is one elected position, but it's not a singular operation. It is a very personal experience, but you have to do it in concert with a host of other people to communicate a message that will resound across the city, region, and state.

MAYOR

One of the constant themes in the chapters that follow is the relationship among the concepts of leadership, communication, and community. Leadership is about bringing people together in shared values for various common goals. It's about expanding the tent. You can only conduct the business of mayoring well if you communicate, support transparency, and create as big a tent for your constituents and goals as you can.

PART ONE

CHAPTER 1

~

Where'd You Go to High School?

Philadelphians take great pride in their community and their neighborhoods. I don't know if this is true of other places because I've never lived anywhere else—I was born, raised, and educated, and created all of my trouble, in Philadelphia. It's not the only place that I've ever been, but it is my hometown. I know that many cities claim this title, but we truly are a "city of neighborhoods." If you meet a Philadelphian somewhere outside of Philadelphia, there are really only two questions that get asked. First, What's your name? and second, Where'd you go to high school? That second question gives you an answer key to just about everything else you want or need to know.

I grew up at 5519 Larchwood Avenue. My parents moved into the Larchwood Avenue house—a classic, West Philadelphia row house with four bedrooms—in 1956. A year later, when I was born, Philadelphia's industrial and manufacturing decline was already underway. The city's population was highest in 1950, and then began to fall as the suburbs grew. Industries and warehouses were leaving the city and unemployment rose, but the high school graduation rate in West Philadelphia did not. My family was the third African American family on our block in

1956. By the time I was around ten years old, there were probably about three white families left on our block, so the neighborhood experienced a pretty rapid turnover. In a "white flight" fueled in part by much easier availability of mortgages for whites, the demographic changed dramatically as whites began to populate the suburbs around Philadelphia. Between 1950 and 1960, Philadelphia's African American, Latino, and Asian American population increased by 41 percent while its European American population declined by 13 percent. These changes, as well as the degree of racial isolation, were particularly pronounced in North and West Philadelphia, where I lived.

The neighborhood was a middle middle-class place—people were working, but nobody had much money. There was a black-owned grocery store on one end of the block, a white-owned butcher shop, a drug store, and a barber shop on the other end. There were a few bars, too. Every one of the corner properties had a business in it, and these were really the anchors of the neighborhood. Even after the neighborhood changed demographically, many of the non–African American business people stayed, and the mix helped maintain the liveliness of the neighborhood. Larchwood was what we would now refer to as a "mixed use" community, before its time. Larchwood Avenue was a fairly large, two-lane street with parking on both sides, and we played in the street a lot—football, king block, tops, half-ball (stick ball), and other games. The street furnished access to a hospital, so it would never be completely closed off, but we managed play between the cars coming up and down the street anyway. There were some challenging times with gangs and young people and violence in the 1960s and 1970s, but I never felt unsafe on my street.

I believe that a neighborhood and its values often define who we are. Neighbors on my street performed "community service" before that was a term of art. Saturday was the informal neighborhood cleanup day. Most of us had chores. I'd wash down the porch, the steps, and the sidewalk every Saturday before I could play, and a lot of my neighbors were out doing the same thing. It feels as if we had huge snowstorms when I was a kid, or perhaps it was just because I was little. But when I took over the shoveling duties from my father, it was never enough just to do the small part of the sidewalk in front of our house. My father insisted that I shovel all the way to the end of the block, to make a path for the seniors and elderly. I'd help carry groceries or assist older neighbors across the street—we all did that. It was that kind of neighborhood.

The value of respect was very important. This was still an era when any adult on the block was fully empowered and authorized to tell any child to stop doing something. Everybody knew everybody, so there was no running or hiding. My mother had always told me not to walk in the street. One day, when a neighbor was sweeping the sidewalk, I walked in the street to avoid her sweeping, and I got a good talking to when I returned home because one of the neighbors had immediately told my mother what I had done!

The basic rule from my mother did not require that I have a watch, a sundial, or a smartphone: Catalina's rule was that we had to be on the steps when the street lights come on— and it didn't necessarily have to be our own steps, but the steps of somebody she knew.

My mom worked for Bell Telephone and my father, Basil, worked for pharmaceutical companies, or sometimes was a plumber, or sometimes didn't work at all. I have a younger sister, Renee, and my grandmother Edythe lived with us. My mother is a twin, and her sister was married to a fireman, from Engine 11 in South Philly, who worked at the only station where African Americans could work at the time. Her brother Bill, my uncle, went into the military, so my mother was the last one out of the house, and her mother was apparently part of the marriage package.

Politics was not my family business. We were not a deeply political family, and there wasn't a great deal of political discussion at the dinner table. Parents in the neighborhood were very focused on school and education. Certainly, though, there was some degree of talk about current events and what was going on with this or that elected official in the city.

Although politics was not our family's stock and trade, I loved American history and government. I had an incredible history teacher at St. Joe's Prep, Mr. Jerry Taylor, and I always liked the subject. The Watergate hearings were going on one summer during my teens, and I probably knew more about Watergate than any adult around. I watched them as much as I could on our new color television in the living room. I'm not sure why the hearings fascinated me so much. These hearings just seemed to make government, politics, and American history come to life. I was also a little nervous about the Vietnam War draft at this time, too, although the war was winding down, and I remember the barrel and the balls for the draft lottery going around and around. But I found Richard Nixon to be an intriguing character for some reason—such a tangled story of his attempt to cover up shady activity and his lack of honesty with the American public. This made an indelible impression on me about honesty and transparency in government. I had learned about US history in school, and then this drama and slice of history was playing out on television. I think you'd have to go back to the McCarthy House Un-American Activities Committee trials in the 1950s for something comparably riveting, and I don't think in our times we've seen that level of focus, dedication, and indefatigable commitment of elected public officials to our democracy, on either side of the aisle. It captivated me. I knew this was serious.

Many Philadelphians attend their neighborhood high school, but I went to St. Joseph's Preparatory High School at Seventeenth and Girard, in North Philadelphia. It is the Jesuit high school in Philadelphia, and one of our best schools still today. I had friends in both public and private schools, and we didn't distinguish much between them. I'd developed an interest in going to military school, partly because I enjoyed a television show on Sundays about kids at a military school, and the back pages of the *Philadelphia Inquirer* magazine in my childhood would advertise schools such as the Valley Forge and Bordentown military academies. I'd interviewed at both of those schools when my seventh grade teacher, Sister Maureen James, said, "You don't really want to go to a military school, you want to go to St. Joe's." I'd never heard of the Prep, but Sister Maureen was very convincing, and my parents agreed. So I took the summer prep courses and the admissions test, and was admitted for high school.

To get to St. Josephs from my home at Fifty-Fifth and Larchwood, I had to take three different forms of transportation on SEPTA to North Philadelphia—the #56 bus, the El, and either the #2 bus from Center City on Sixteenth Street, or the Broad Street Subway. I was not on the track team, but there was a lot of gang war activity in Philadelphia in the 1970s, and in those years I would ask myself every day, "How fast do I feel I can run?" whether from Broad Street or from Sixteenth Street, to get to Seventeenth and Girard. Frank Rizzo was mayor of Philadelphia at this time, and there were a lot of police–community relations issues in addition to the gang activity. Gangs were identified by streets—the Moon gang, the Barbary Coast, Stiles, or Seybert Street gangs, and so on. There was a lot of concern about traveling and getting around, and navigating gang turf, but mostly no one really bothered the prep school guys wearing jackets and ties.

One of the things I learned early on and firsthand is that the resident of the White House at any given moment makes a huge difference in a city and in our lives. After the 1976 election, Jimmy Carter was president. Actually, he was the first presidential candidate I ever voted for, as I turned eighteen in 1975. President Carter appointed a National Commission on Student Financial Assistance and made college access and affordability a priority. The Middle Income Assistance Acts expanded what we know as the Pell Grant program and subsidized interest on guaranteed student loans. As a consequence of priorities in the White House and legislation in Washington, DC, financial aid skyrocketed for young Americans in my community and all others. My recollection is that every year there was more aid, and colleges had more students of color.

In the aftermath of the riots and other civil rights movements of the 1960s, colleges and universities were also actively, aggressively looking for African American, Latino, and other minority students. All of the parents on Larchwood Avenue were focused on their children going to college, although pretty much none of our parents had gone to college themselves. This was their almost single-minded goal and commitment. The message, reinforced from parents to neighbors to nuns in the schools, was to keep your record clean and stay out of trouble, because then you can go to college. And college was the gateway to a better life. That happened for my cohort of friends, those my age and anyone maybe three or four years older. These older kids we referred to as our "oldheads," the ones that we looked up to and were occasionally invited to hang out or play in a game with. They were also often our informal mentors.

Virtually everyone on my block in the 1970s went to college. After the 1980 election and the change in presidency to Ronald Reagan, there was a precipitous drop in financial aid for students and especially for students of color, and a precipitous drop in the number of African Americans, Latinos, and other minorities going to college. But in 1975, minorities were highly recruited, and financial aid forged a path for first-generation and lower-income students. That year, I was admitted to the University of Pennsylvania as a biomedical engineering student in the School of Engineering.

CHAPTER 2

⁓

How Chemistry 101 and a Disco Changed My Life

I have to confess that if I had visited the University of Pennsylvania campus as many times as a student as I did during my eight-year tenure as mayor of Philadelphia, who knows what my future might have been. I might not have been the best or most diligent student, but I had a big ambition, to be a doctor. I wanted to help people.

I came to the University of Pennsylvania from a high school with only 180 seniors in my class, and I went to my first chemistry class at Penn in a Roman-style classroom, with descending stairs and a professor who seemed very far away, a distant speck. The first class was packed—every seat was taken and there were students sitting on the floor and in the aisles.

But Chemistry 101 changed my life forever because it was pretty clear after failing my first few tests that I probably was not going to be a doctor, and it was time to move on. By midsemester in that class, the jam-packed aisles were only a memory: you could sit anywhere you wanted. There were plenty of seats in that chemistry class, that semester.

I graduated in 1979 from the Wharton School, which is the University of Pennsylvania's business school. Wharton, founded in 1881, was the first collegiate school of business in the world, and it's one of the most prestigious. How I got to Wharton, however, was a longer saga that, in some ways, first put me on a path to my political future.

It began with my decision to drop that chemistry class. I had several sound reasons for doing this. First, it was clear to me that I was going to fail that course. Second, I'd never intended to be a practicing doctor. I wanted to be an entrepreneur doctor and learn medicine so that I could open a medical devices company and sell and manufacture new products to and for doctors. But I theorized that I had to know and understand medicine in order to create that business. So, in that first course and first semester, I was trying to protect my GPA, and wanted to withdraw before I got an F for the class. Finally, and perhaps most importantly, I remember gazing at the periodic table of elements one day in class and realizing, "I just don't care enough about this. I'm not going to be a doctor."

I decided to apply to the Wharton School, on the erroneous assumption that since I was already a student at University of Pennsylvania, I could easily transfer to the business school. My application was rejected, because I hadn't taken and completed four courses once I withdrew from chemistry. Not only did I not get into Wharton, I attracted unwanted attention from the School of Engineering. They wrote me that they noticed I'd tried to transfer to Wharton, and if I did that again and was rejected, they'd kick me out of the engineering school as well. Welcome to the Ivy League, Mr. Nutter!

When I came back to school in January 1976, I hedged my bets. I applied to Wharton for a second time and also to the School of Arts and Sciences. Wharton rejected me a second time, but the Arts and Sciences school admitted me.

I started taking business and economics courses and decided to be an economics major. But I had a disastrous sophomore year. I had started a job, and was not paying attention or studying nearly enough. I told my mother that college wasn't going well for me and that I enjoyed work more than school. She said what I thought at the time was a very profound thing: I had swum to the middle of the pool, and I now needed to decide if I would go back to where I started or swim to the other side.

I decided to swim to the other side. I charted out my next few years, and thought about how to get my GPA up and get into Wharton. I was taking six courses a semester to catch up, and also working long hours. By May 1979 I was six courses short of graduation. At this point I'd gotten to know the Wharton School undergraduate dean fairly well and had spent a fair amount of time at the dean's office. The conversation I now had with the dean was in some respects my first political deal. I proposed to him that I very much wanted to transfer to his school, that I had six courses to complete, and I needed to finish now, in the summer of 1979. I needed special permission from the dean to take three summer courses per semester instead of the maximum of two. The dean agreed—I'd need to get a certain average for all of my summer courses, and if I did, he would approve my transfer to Wharton. I took classes that I needed to take based on the major requirements. I had also calculated for each course what I thought I would or could get grade-wise, estimated any margin of error or slippage, and proceeded to do what I needed to do. I fulfilled the dean's challenge, our deal was good, and I kept up my part of the bargain.

This meant that almost as I was walking out the door of the University of Pennsylvania, I was finally walking in the door of the Wharton School—from which I did formally graduate, in August 1979.

My collegiate odyssey taught me some valuable lessons, not the least of which concerned persistence and tenacity; knowing, understanding, and playing by the rules; and ways to push the envelope and succeed. Most importantly, I learned how to think, not only through the classroom work, but also through the long, torturous process of figuring out my own path through college and life.

—

Just as I was switching my focus from pre-med to the business school and navigating my way through the Penn and Wharton requirements, I was also getting lured into politics indirectly, through the front door of a disco. This transformation and transition was occurring at the same time, in 1976 and my sophomore year of college.

I had come to Penn with my best friend from high school, Robert Bynum, while our other great friend from high school, Chris Hannum, went to Amherst College. Both guys are still my best friends today. Robert and I lived in the quad our freshman year, and in our sophomore year we lived in high-rise East, one of the high-rises known only as East, North, and South at the time. They were fairly grim and nondescript. To some, they resembled Eastern European architecture. We moved off campus after our sophomore year, and this begins the story of how I answered the call to public service. The summer between freshman and sophomore year, Robert's father, Ben Bynum, closed one of his nightclubs, the well-known Cadillac Club. Some of the very best talent of the day had performed there—Billy Paul, Lou Rawls, Aretha Franklin, and many others. Ben Bynum, a music industry innovator, having caught the disco music wave coming from Europe, turned it into a disco. Robert and I worked there starting in the summer of 1976, right after it opened.

The Impulse Discotheque, as the old club was renamed, sat at the corner of Broad and Germantown Streets, in North Philadelphia. This was the first black-owned disco in Philadelphia. It catered to an older, thirty-plus, upscale clientele. It was situated close to Chuck's Place, Dwight's Bar-B-Que, Sid Booker's Stinger La Pointe—with the best fried shrimp in America—and Prince's Total Exerience Club. The black owners of these bars and clubs employed mostly black people and attracted a mostly black clientele. This was important to me and to my growth and development. The Impulse was one of the hottest clubs in its time and held the top spot for clubs/discos for decades. Many clubs had come and gone during that time, but the Impulse always stayed hot, with great music and DJs, and an upscale clientele.

My first few months of work in the disco coincided with a significant movement toward black empowerment in Philadelphia's political structure, led by John White Sr. More black candidates were running for office, running and winning, running and losing. They included Charlie Bowser, John White Jr., John Anderson, Marian Tasco, David Richardson, Dwight Evans, Bill Gray, Augusta Clark, and Hardy Williams, to name a few.

In that summer of 1976, and in subsequent years, many elected officials—black and white, but primarily the black establishment—had fundraisers, events, and activities at the Impulse club. I met a lot of people there. After I graduated from Wharton in 1979, I realized that I needed to find a more substantial job and applied to three places: Bell Telephone, Xerox, and IBM. In early 1980 I started at Xerox while I was still working as a DJ known as "Mix Master Mike" and assistant manager at the Impulse—two full-time jobs. Xerox had a wonderful training program, but after twenty-one months I was shocked that they didn't see the wisdom of catapulting me to a senior vice president position already, and I resigned—but not before I wrote an epic, five-page resignation letter, circulated to all the managers, that detailed all of my thoughts on Xerox's shortcomings. As a result of this letter I was invited out to regional headquarters to talk about my concerns, and was offered a raise and a promotion to a job three grades higher, but my response was to be shocked that they thought I was only after money, and I rejected their offer. For someone with all of twenty-one months of work experience I had a great deal of confidence and hubris—or, I just didn't know any better!

I continued my work at the disco instead, and there I was absorbing politics by osmosis, and eavesdropping on the workings and conversations of the emerging black political establishment in Philadelphia. I was curious, and intrigued by what I heard and saw. Eventually, by 1981, Robert and I, who had been initiated into politics informally day in and day out at the Impulse disco, found our way down to city hall, and started going to City Council meetings.

These meetings are free and open to the public, and I had my daytime hours free after my Xerox protest resignation. The most immediate inspiration for going to a City Council meeting was that Robert and I fancied ourselves future real estate moguls, and we had a plan to buy properties at sheriff's sales, rehab them, and sell them, to develop a portfolio. We thought the council meetings might provide additional useful information about how the city government worked. The sheriff's sales seemed like a sketchy process, however, so we decided it wasn't the business for us. But interesting things were happening at the council meetings, nonetheless. I would recommend that citizens try to attend a City Council meeting or two, if they can. In our case, Robert and I recognized a lot of council members from the Impulse club, where they were having fundraisers and parties.

One day I walked into the office of one of the elected officials that I met at the disco, Councilman John White Jr. His father, John White Sr., was a leader of the Black Political Forum.

"This political thing is kind of interesting," I said, "but I don't really know that much about it. How would I get involved?"

After we talked for a while he asked me, "Where do you live?"

"The Wynnefield section of Philadelphia," I responded.

"Oh! Right next door is one of my best friends who lives in Wynnefield and he's looking to recruit some folks to get involved in his political organization. Go next door, tell him I sent you, and you guys should talk."

I didn't know who he was talking about. His name was John C. Anderson, and he was a member at-large in his first term on the City Council. Anderson had a long family history in Philadelphia. His father was a prominent African American Episcopalian priest, and his mother was the matriarch of the family. There were three boys in the family: his younger brother, Louis, had died and his other brother, Jesse, was also a pastor. John C. Anderson was a very articulate, smart, and tremendously handsome man. He was also gay, which was unknown to many at this time in the early 1980s. As progressive as our values are in 2017, that same spirit was not the norm in Philadelphia in the early 1980s. A few people knew about Anderson's identity but most people did not, and as I started working with him, I would see the strain of holding that secret. From time to time, he was also threatened with outing and blackmail that would have damaged if not ruined his career in that era, so I saw the effects of that coercion, too.

I was a stranger to Anderson, but in December 1981, I knocked on his office door. Others have said that I don't lack for confidence, but I'm sure I was a bit nervous. Although I didn't even know what Anderson looked like, I was used to meeting new people and political figures all the time, from my work at the club. Anderson was in; I explained who I was to his staff, and he actually saw me. We chatted and he asked me exactly where I lived. At the time I was living in these wonderful apartments down on Conshohocken Avenue in the Wynnefield Heights neighborhood of Philadelphia. The bilevel apartment was all the rage at the time, and Robert and I lived in one on top of a Chinese restaurant right by a Pathmark supermarket and the ABC Channel 6 TV station. Our building housed a young, up-and-coming crowd, while the other two apartment buildings in the area were largely senior citizens. After this conversation I started volunteering in Anderson's office.

Anderson was running for ward leader, which is a neighborhood position, and the Democratic Party and the Republican Party each have leaders who comprise the local party leadership. The ward leader is responsible for helping to get out the vote on election day, distributing literature, shuffling a candidate's volunteers and resources from one location to another as needed, and being a liaison. When it's not election season, they might do things such as organize neighborhood events or cleanups, or put residents with problems in touch with their City Council member. Philadelphia is divided into sixty-nine wards, and each one has a ward leader. I lived in the Fifty-Second Ward, and Anderson needed ward committee people who were pledged to his candidacy and would support him. The committee person is the lowest elected office in the city. The ward committee is mostly responsible for voter registration and turnout in the ward, and choosing the ward leader. I happened to live in a division where they were looking for someone. So I ran for committee person to help my new friend, the councilman, become ward leader.

At this point, Marian Tasco became something of a "political mother" to me, as she has to so many other aspiring political candidates. I can think of no stronger, more politically astute and enjoyable political figure. Marian supported me early on when I was starting out as a committee person, and played a major role in my subsequent campaigns, including my candidacy for City Council in 1987 and beyond. No single person in Philadelphia, perhaps with the exception of Congressman Bill Gray, has helped, supported, encouraged, advised, and more forcefully supported more candidates for office than Marian Tasco.

I ran against an older woman, Lillian Levinski, who had been in office for probably about twenty years, in a division where many of the people on the voter registration records had dates of birth such as February 3, 1898, or March 20, 1901. In other words, it was a slightly older population—and I was just about to turn twenty-five in 1982, about a month after the election. I figured I had some challenges. But I worked hard and I campaigned.

Ms. Levinski beat me by 282 to 48, or somewhere in that neighborhood. But this was a first run. I ran again, and I did a little better. And then I deployed some of my Penn training and knowledge: I created this complex chart and regression analysis and figured out that if I kept running, I could beat her in about forty years at the pace I was going.

So I made maybe my first important political decision: I moved.

CHAPTER 3

~

Why Run?

I had been watching Councilman John Anderson's public service from
the time we met in 1981, through the 1982 ward leader race, and into
his reelection campaign of 1983 (ward elections at the time were held
every two years in Philadelphia). Anderson asked if I would be his campaign manager, and at first I declined, because I think it's really important in life that you know what you don't know—and I knew nothing
about managing a political campaign. But Anderson and his team, Obra
Kernodle III and Saul Shorr, persuaded me. I wanted to be helpful, I
wanted to be involved, and I came to realize, of course, that I had a lot
of free time and they would not have to pay me very much because I
didn't know very much. But mostly, I agreed because I was interested in
politics, and I wanted to support him.

I've lived in Philadelphia all my life, but Anderson took me to new
places across this city—to neighborhoods and institutions that I'd
never seen, and I met folks that I'd never heard of, didn't understand,
or know anything about. Before this point, my world in Philadelphia
for much of my life had often been no more than three or four blocks
around my house. Going to high school at the Prep did take me to North

Philadelphia, but I was a West Philadelphia guy my whole life, and had almost no incentive or reason to travel even to other parts of the city—this was not unusual. Why would I go to those places? I wasn't going to shop there, I didn't know anyone there, and in some cases they were not welcoming neighborhoods for African Americans. My neighborhood was my comfort zone, but with Anderson running for an at-large, citywide position, we went everywhere in the city. And, everywhere we went, people loved him.

Even more than that affection for him, I really saw the impact that Councilman John C. Anderson had on other people. They looked to him to lead, to stand up, to speak out, and to pass legislation. Through this campaign I started to better understand "power," but not power for the sake of power. Rather, I mean the impact that a person can have on others' lives through public service. This insight resonated with some of my earlier, altruistic motivations to enter the medical field. John was effective in his service for a variety of reasons. He was a risk taker, creative, bold, and kind. He was impatient about progress and cared very passionately about justice. Anderson took on the big challenges and was keenly attuned to the plight of others. He could have a short temper, but it was always sparked by his quest for excellence.

In the meantime, Mayor Green announced on election day in November 1982 that he was not running for reelection. The next day, the African American managing director for the city government, W. Wilson Goode Sr., resigned his office and announced that he was running for mayor.

Philadelphia had yet to elect a black mayor. State Senator Hardy Williams, who had helped to found the Black Political Forum in 1967 and had been the first African American varsity basketball player at Penn State, ran for mayor in 1971. Charlie Bowser had run in 1975. Bowser was a dynamic, energetic lawyer and community activist who fought against racism in Philadelphia for years and was known as a brilliant trial lawyer. So, there had been a couple attempts already to become that first African American mayor of Philadelphia. Everyone thought that Wilson Goode was poised, finally, to achieve this distinction. Goode came from a family of tenant farmers in Seabord, North Carolina, and had moved to Philadelphia early in his life. His political career began as the manager of Hardy Williams's unsuccessful 1971 mayoral bid, and his subsequent position as the first African American commissioner of the Public Utility Commission. Goode really built a following and made himself visible as the managing director, so that by 1983 he had endorsements from all but two ward leaders and most of the unions.

The mayor's primary race was a headliner, between Goode and Frank Rizzo. Rizzo was a controversial and polarizing figure in Philadelphia politics, and one of the last examples of the old urban machine politics in the Democratic Party. He was from South Philadelphia and had risen through the police department to become police commissioner. He became a touchstone in the 1967 mayor's race between Jim Tate and Arlen Spector, when Tate was repeatedly asked if he would keep Frank Rizzo as police commissioner if elected. In fact, this was among the first campaigns in which police commissioners became prominent and politically important in mayoral elections. Tate won the 1967 election but was term limited, so Rizzo ran and won in 1971.

His tenure was a fearful time for African Americans in Philadelphia, as Rizzo had confrontations with the black community and the Black Panthers, and his administration was marked by incidents of police brutality, in addition to controversies around cronyism, massive tax hikes, and corruption. Among other issues, Rizzo had botched the huge bicentennial celebration in 1976 by calling in the National Guard and making people afraid to come to the city for the festivities. He tried to change the city charter to run for a third term, and was the target of a recall effort. The City Council was becoming more engaged and activist during Rizzo's term, which created a great deal of antagonism between the mayor's office and the council. The mayoral legacy can be long lasting, far beyond a couple terms of office: Philadelphia is to some extent still dealing with the vestiges of Rizzo's time as mayor, through union work rules that he implemented in the 1970s that were incorporated thereafter and are very difficult to undo.

By 1983, Rizzo wanted to stage a political comeback, running against Goode, so this election was vitally important to the city of Philadelphia. It was a serendipitous time for Philadelphia to elect its first African American mayor. We were on the same election cycle as Chicago, where Harold Washington had become the first African American mayor of that city. Tom Bradley had become the first African American mayor of Los Angeles starting in 1973, so the ceiling on black mayors in major, large cities—there had already been a few in medium-sized cities—was beginning to crack.

And Goode had a lot of qualities that made him an obvious choice for the city's first African American mayor, and seemed the clear opposite of Rizzo. First, the city had reached a breaking point with Rizzo and was eager for change. Rizzo was tied to the past and corruption, and Goode was new and clean cut; where Rizzo was a polarizing, divisive figure, Goode cobbled together a formidable coalition, a true rainbow, of Philadelphians who were black, white, and Latino and who came from many different backgrounds.

The entire City Council was running at the same time, and there were fifty-six other candidates for the at-large council position. John Anderson and I were running all over the city on the campaign. We had a lot of fun together, though. With Anderson, during the campaign, I went to my first Penn Relays, the oldest track and field competition in the United States, which has a carnival atmosphere. We were slated to do several events that day, and John decided that we'd only go to the relays and give ourselves a break from the relentless pace. On election day Wilson Goode won the Democratic nomination for mayor, and Anderson came in first out of fifty-seven candidates, which had nothing to do with me or my nonexistent campaign management experience. It was all him: his record, campaigning acumen, and his ability to communicate and connect with people.

On that night in May 1983, at twenty-five years old, I made a decision that this is what I wanted to do with my life. I wanted to serve. I wanted to be a public servant. This came more like an epiphany than a gradual realization. I was enjoying what I was doing. I loved working on the campaign and seeing the positive impact that Anderson had with his work, but this was the first campaign I had ever worked on, and this was my first experience of election night victory, albeit vicariously. I was in a room alone for a moment, and as I sat there feeling the sweet joy of winning I said to myself, "This is what I want to do."

Over the course of that summer, Anderson and I made plans for the next cycle of elections, four years later, in 1987. We strategized that I should run for City Council in the district race. In Philadelphia, there are seventeen members of the City Council. The city has ten council districts, with one city council representative each, and seven members at-large. Anderson was an at-large councilman, so I didn't want to be in that race because theoretically I would be running against him. We decided that I should run in the Fourth District, where I lived. The district included Wynnefield, Overbrook, West Philly down to Market Street and Fifty-Fourth, Roxborough, Manayunk, and East Falls. I used to say of the Fourth District, to recall a popular movie, that "a river runs through it." The Schuylkill River cuts the district in half. West Philly, Wynnefield, Overbrook, and two public housing developments are on one side of the district, and on the other, neighborhoods such as East Falls, Manayunk, North Philadelphia Roxborough, and two public housing developments, as well as a fair amount of green space. On the east side of the district, even in the early 1980s, there were English Tudor homes worth anywhere from $300,000 to $500,000. The Fourth District was majority white, but it was changing in the 1980s because of West Philadelphia, Wynnefield, and Overbrook.

Just five months after John and I devised this plan, and a month before election day, Councilman Anderson died. He had been in and out of the hospital over the summer, and had a persistent cough. In September, he was back in the hospital. I saw him a couple of times there, the last time just a few days before he passed away. He was in great spirits that Thursday. But on Monday, when my phone rang, I knew what I'd be told. Two deaths have had a huge personal impact on me: my grandmother Edythe, and John Anderson. I realized that his staff would be as devastated as I was, so I went to the office, and this was the first time that I ever spoke to the news media.

Anderson's funeral was held at his father's church, and it was a typical political funeral, attended by family, real friends, and the political poseurs and faux friends who show up for all of these funerals. The funeral itself was a very difficult lesson for me in how the political universe operates. People engaged with me, or not, in a very different way now that my guy was dead and I was at the bottom of the political pecking order. I was at a loss: to have been attached to someone so beloved and then to have this suddenly end, and to become, overnight, a nonperson in the world of Philadelphia politics.

Anderson's death left a vacancy on the City Council and on the general election ballot in November, of course. Under these circumstances, the Democratic Party gets to replace the person—and the party replaced Anderson with someone who was the complete opposite of the social progressive politics that Anderson stood for. This happened because the replacement, Francis X. Rafferty, was the chair of the public property committee, and in 1983, the City of Philadelphia, like many other big cities, was trying to figure out cable television. Cable TV fell under the purview of the public property committee. The mayor's office and the City Council were at an impasse over cable TV. The mayor wanted one cable company for the entire city, and the City Council wanted to carve the city into four cable franchise areas. They also insisted that one franchise be African American or a minority-owned company. A battle was raging over the franchising of Area 2, between two African American cable TV companies.

The Democratic powers that be wanted support for one of these franchises over the other, and the council would have a vote on each of these four cable districts. The cable franchises had to be approved by the city, and that legislation ran through the public property committee, of which Rafferty was the chair. He had just lost the primary as an incumbent, and was going to be out of office, but the council needed his vote to prevail on the cable TV franchise. So they filled Anderson's vacant seat with Rafferty, with what appears to have been some kind of an understanding or a commitment concerning his vote related to a cable television franchise in this one contested area of the city.

Politically, ideologically, and temperamentally, Rafferty could not have been more different from Anderson. I was shocked and disillusioned by the decision. This was a hard, hard, lesson for me to learn, at twenty-six years old. The political decision making followed a calculus of narrow self-interest and short-term strategic horse trading that seemed so contrary to the impulses and spirit that Anderson embodied and that had drawn me into the political scene in the first place.

In any case it seemed that I was suddenly out of politics, because my guy had died and I had entered the business with him. He was my mentor and my political muse. He was why I had gotten into Philadelphia politics. Apparently my aspirations and ambitions for public office were over. So in January 1984, I went back to a friend of Councilman Anderson, Malcolmn Pryor, who owned an investment banking firm, got my Series 7 and Series 63 securities licenses, and began working in finance.

But then in the summer of 1984, a bizarre series of events indirectly drew me back in to politics. Another at-large city councilman, Al Pearlman, had been diagnosed with terminal cancer. He asked his ex-wife to bring his gun to the hospital—where he subsequently shot and killed himself. He was fifty-four. The *Philadelphia Inquirer* remembered Pearlman as a "self-made man with Rizzo's tough style." This shocking turn of events also had political consequences for Philadelphia: It created a vacancy in the city council at-large ranks.

After the cable TV–driven appointment of Anderson's replacement, Mayor Goode had promised a friend of Councilman Anderson that if ever there were a vacancy during his term, he would make sure that he got appointed by the party. He kept his word, and Angel Ortiz became the Democratic nominee to fill the seat of the deceased councilman Pearlman. Ortiz and John had been very close friends, and Ortiz asked me to manage his special election campaign in the 1984 general election. I did so with the understanding that I'd probably only stay with him for about a year, because I had my plan to run for City Council in 1987 as Anderson and I had decided in 1983. So I was his chief of staff and legislative assistant. This is the unusual turn of events that brought me back into the political game, and I wasn't leaving any time soon!

I left Councilman Ortiz toward the end of 1985 to go work on Ed Rendell's election for governor in 1986, and to run for ward committee person. I won my first elected office in 1986, after losing in 1982 and 1984. I was back in the game!

CHAPTER 4

~

Aren't You on City Council?
What Are You Going to Do About That?

I ran for City Council in 1987 according to the plan that I had developed with Councilman Anderson, against an incumbent named Ann Land. She'd been in office for about six years, and had been a member of Philadelphia's Democratic establishment for some time. Earlier in her life she had campaigned for John F. Kennedy. I lost this election by 1,882 votes. Not that I think about it very much! It was a close race, and it was just the two of us. In this first race, in 1987, the Fourth District was majority white by 55 percent. But in the ensuing years it would be closer to a 50–50 split. During my first campaign I knocked on ten thousand doors. I introduced myself. I put my face on posters, and people wondered why I would do this in the eastern part of the district, which was overwhelmingly white. I explained that the Fourth District needed to know who I was, and voters there seemed to appreciate my honesty. In the 1987 campaign Roxborough was 95 percent white, and I got 17 percent of the vote. Four years later in 1991, I would get 34 percent, and in 1995, 64 percent of that vote.

I vowed on the night that I lost in 1987 to run again in four years. Meanwhile I went back to the investment banking firm where I'd been working. The firm's owner had been a good friend of Councilman Anderson and appreciated my commitment to public service, but he would gently remind me that I could make a lot more money in investment banking. I worked there for three years, came back in the 1991 election, and won.

From the start, I planned to be a pretty active legislator. I had grown up through the City Council process, and I genuinely liked the council. When I joined I knew many of the members from my work with John Anderson, although not necessarily that well.

I had a tremendous team to support me while serving on the City Council. Debra Brown was the first person I asked to work in my City Council office. After I won the election, and not knowing Debra's exact address, I went back to the block where I thought she lived and knocked on doors until I found her, and offered her a job. Unquestionably loyal, a tremendously hard worker, and a good person, she had a bird's-eye view on all that happened, from the City Council to the mayor's office. Debra is also special because she shares my daughter Olivia's birthday! I first met Bobby Johnson because he was a longtime friend of John Anderson and his family, and based on that relationship and friendship he joined my council office, working mainly in the district office in Wynnefield, and then joining my mayoral administration. Bobby is just an all-around good man—low key, fun, highly reliable, and a good friend to many. Wadell Ridley's daughter and my daughter attended daycare together, and we have been friends a long time, through many battles. Wadell was part of my office, and, along with Steve Jones, was involved in all of the political campaigns and activities. I turned to Arlene Petruzzelli when I was looking for someone to run my district office in the Twenty-First Ward, which includes Roxborough and Manayunk. The ward leader had recommended her, and Arlene was hard charging, funny, and down to earth—a wonderful and sweet woman, who died a number of years ago after retiring from my office. She worked tirelessly to help and serve anyone, at any time, until the work was done. Mary Turtle took Arlene's place after she retired and moved to Florida, and was known for speaking her mind on behalf of constituents. She very effectively managed the often complicated relationships in this part of the city, with its numerous civic organizations, and also came on board for my mayoral administration.

The council president assigns members their budget, staff, and offices, so for this reason and many others it's an enormously powerful role, at least in Philadelphia. Your budget, desk, and even the chance to have your office painted are all determined by the council president. Obviously, it behooved me to try to maintain a positive relationship with the president, but we had a rocky start. The City Council president, future mayor John Street, had supported my opponent during the election, so we had a straight and frank talk about that issue. I told him I hadn't appreciated his support of my opponent; he told me he hadn't appreciated some of my criticism of him during the campaign, and we left it at that. Political life goes on.

At the start of my first term I was already known to be pretty independent. I tried to get along with folks and not be unpleasant, but I had some strongly held views about certain things, and there was a limit to the amount that I was going to compromise on those views. On the one hand, nobody passes council legislation on their own. You need eight and sometimes eleven other members to make that happen, and friendships and relationships are vital to getting there. On the other hand, I didn't go to city hall to be popular—I went there to get stuff done and make decisions.

Generally, if a fellow council member had supported me and asked for my support on legislation around which I didn't have particularly strongly held beliefs, then I would be inclined to listen, and support the legislation if it made sense for my constituents. But on legislation that touched my strong or core beliefs, I let fellow council members know that I would make my decision early on about whether I was for or against the legislation. I would tell sponsors of the legislation that I supported, "You don't need to waste time calling me anymore, because I'm for this." And I would tell sponsors of the legislation that I opposed, "You don't need to waste time calling me anymore, because I'm against this."

So unless they devised something so incredible, so spectacular, like anything beyond what I could imagine, they were, truly, wasting their political time. We could have ten meetings, we could have one meeting, and the outcome would be the same.

Some other City Council members had more angst around their decision making. I would advise them to resolve it, make a decision, and the sun will come up tomorrow. They would let members torment them with meetings and endless phone calls to woo their vote. As for myself, when I passed someone who wanted my vote in the halls, I would tell them "I'm good, I haven't changed my mind. How are you today?"

—

I ended up tackling some big issues very early on. My first big initiative on the City Council stemmed from concerns about the relationship between police and the community. There had been a couple of scandals here and there, and citizens beaten and roughed up, so I pieced together legislation to create an independent police advisory commission. I was not, and I still am not, antipolice. I support good police officers, but I'm also certainly pro-community. I think we need a forum or a place where good community people and good police officers can meet, get to know each other, and develop respect.

I introduced this highly controversial piece of legislation right out of the gate, when I was all of eight months into the job, in September 1992. It provoked a significant fight with new mayor Ed Rendell, who emphatically rejected the commission idea. He was a former prosecutor and didn't want to ruin his relationships with the police. Ed and I were friends, but I was committed to doing this work. He vetoed the bill and the council subsequently overrode his veto, 12 to 5.

Also during my first term, my new colleague and former boss, Angel Ortiz, had put forward legislation to give benefits to same-sex domestic partners of city employees. This legislation would only have applied to public employees, and it only provided for domestic partnership benefits—things such as health insurance benefits, a right to transfer property to the partner without fees, and the ability to assign a pension to a same-sex partner. We didn't have the authority to do anything about same-sex marriage—that's a state issue—but this would provide some similar benefits of marriage to city employees, at least.

The domestic partnership bill was being proposed about the same time as my police commission legislation. And I have to confess that I was not as supportive of that legislation at the time as I should have been, because the council president was supporting my police advisory commission and opposed the domestic partnership legislation, and wanted me to do the same, as an informal quid pro quo for his support of my legislation. This was an early lesson in my rookie term on the kind of horse trading that can occur, and the pressure that relationships can exert on legislative decisions on the council.

The police commission happened, and domestic partnership benefits did not, and I held myself somewhat responsible for that. It stuck with me that I had unfinished business. I was reelected to the council in 1995. I decided that I needed to remedy and make up for what I had not done in 1993 on the domestic partnership issues. I wrote three pieces of legislation in 1999 on those issues—and council president Street was furious about it. We had been working together on several things, and he knew that I knew that he was adamantly opposed to domestic partnership benefits, so I think from his perspective, he probably thought I was being disloyal if not presumptuous to write and introduce these three pieces of legislation.

From my perspective, I had to some extent retrained my mind, values, and judgement around the matter, and I felt that I was revisiting an issue that I should have supported years earlier. Far from being premature, the legislation, to me, seemed many years overdue. Street and I had some blowout conversations around this issue, and it is among the one or two factors that opened a huge rift between us.

There were numerous hearings around the domestic partnership legislation, and people would come to city hall and say the ugliest things imaginable about domestic partners, same-sex couples, and the LGBT community.

This legislation would be a meaningful step toward fairness, on its own terms, but it's also true that local government policies are often the leading edge or inspiration for changes in the private sector. As a council member I believed that government, in many instances, should lead the charge on issues of equity, fairness, justice, and rights, and propel the private sector forward. In this case, I knew that the council would hear from the private sector that they were a little nervous about the government establishment of domestic partnership benefits, because then they would start hearing from their own employees. This raised the stakes on the legislation, and likewise the political battle and furor surrounding it.

In 1997 and 1998, it was already obvious that Street was probably going to run for mayor in 1999. In part I argued the legislation's case to him by pointing out, "You have your personal position, everyone knows that you don't support this legislation. Why not get it over with now, and you won't have to campaign on or around it in 1999 or revisit it as mayor?"

With seventeen members we needed nine to pass the legislation, and it was a challenge to find those nine. Eventually, all three pieces passed. Ultimately, one bill passed 9–8, so we didn't have much on the margins. There was absolutely no room for political error. Rendell was still the mayor at this point, and he was eager to get the legislation passed and cleared out of the council. As legislation, the domestic partnership provisions worked well, and I'm especially proud that I had a hand in their passage.

My major City Council accomplishment in 2000 was to introduce the first legislation on a smoking ban in the city. That legislation actually began with my daughter, Olivia. She was five years old in 2000, and Lisa, my wife, was out of town. Lisa was a consultant and traveled a fair amount, so rather than torture our daughter by trying to prepare a perhaps inedible meal at home, we went out for dinner at a city restaurant.

We were sitting and chatting at the table, and Olivia was drawing. She looks up and says, "Daddy, that man over there is smoking."

I replied, "Well yes, people do that sometimes."

She goes back to her drawing and then she says, "Well, does he know that can kill him?"

And I said, "Well yeah, he probably does, but, you know, he's an adult."

Olivia returns to her drawing. Suddenly she says, "Well, aren't you on City Council? What are you going to do about that?"

So much for a quiet evening with my daughter!

I started doing research on smoking bans in other large cities; in particular, New York City was in the process of developing this sort of legislation. During this exploratory phase, Katherine Gajewski, an extremely smart and creative policy mind, started working with me as a consultant around the smoking ban legislation. She was a relentless driving force in the messaging, outreach, and advocacy around the issue (eventually, she joined my City Council staff, and would serve as the chief sustainability officer in my administration, leading Philadelphia to become internationally recognized in this area). After I'd done a fairly substantial amount of research on secondhand smoke, and waded through many denials from the tobacco industry about its dangers—just as they had earlier denied that cigarettes were addictive and unhealthy—I introduced a piece of legislation in 2000 for a smoking ban that went nowhere. There was great consternation that the world would end, the economy would tank, and people would lose their jobs.

While New York continued to refine and upgrade their smoking ban to make it even more stringent and encompassing, I kept making amendments and talking to my colleagues, but many were unyielding in their opposition. The tobacco industry was nowhere to be heard, but rest assured that they were behind the scenes, stealthily trying to undermine the legislation. As part of the big tobacco settlement, the large tobacco companies had to release millions of pages of documents. I went through a fair amount of that material since it was publicly available, and found a few documents that indicated that there was actually a significant amount of collusion between the tobacco industry and the liquor industry. I buried my council colleagues with this kind of information and more, but in this particular case I don't think the information and data mattered as much to the legislation's ultimate success as two other things.

First, New York had really accelerated its efforts to ban smoking in public spaces, and council members got to see the effects of the ban firsthand one year. Along with business people, community leaders, and well-propertied folks in Philadelphia, many council members attend an event sponsored by a hundred-year-old organization called the Pennsylvania Society. It was started by bankers and railroad barons, who would have their staffs and top salesmen up to New York around Christmas time each year, to congratulate them, celebrate, and take orders for the next year. The society still exists, and New York City is the only place where almost all of Pennsylvania's leaders can agree to spend a weekend together. By this time, in 2004, the smoking ban was in full effect in New York, and City Council members and business leaders experienced the benefits of a smoke-free environment. They went to what had always been a packed, smoke-filled basement bar, and found that it was still packed and thriving—but no longer smoke filled. It was the same story throughout New York City. The sky had not fallen on the hospitality and restaurant sector of the economy. To the contrary, places were still packed, but now had breathable air.

The second factor was New Jersey. A lot of Philadelphians vacation on the Jersey shore and, when New Jersey passed smoke-free legislation, we were virtually surrounded by states and cities that had done this kind of work.

I have to jump forward a few years for the end of the smoking ban story. It was during my last council session ever, in June 2006, when Councilman Frank DiCicco came over to me and said, "You know we should really take a look at the [smoking ban] legislation."

"Well, what do you think of it?" I replied.

And he said, "You know, if x, y, or z provisions were in there, I could probably support it."

"Well Frank, absolutely. We amended those things into the legislation a while back. They're already in there."

I showed him the latest version of the legislation. We looked at each other, and he said, "Okay. Let's do it."

We came back into the chamber and went to the council president, Anna Verna. Now, this bill had been sitting on the calendar for four years, literally, with no action. But in this moment the council president asked us, "Are you going to run with the smoking ban?" And I said yes. And she said, "Okay, we'll see what happens." She knew that I never would have come to her unless I had the votes. I'd been working on this thing for too many years. The smoking ban bill squeaked by that day, 9–8. Then there was dead silence in the room. Everyone was stunned and thinking, "Did that just happen? Did we just vote on that? Did that just pass?"

As it turned out, the smoking ban was one of the last bills of my City Council career, because I would resign two weeks later to run for mayor.

I called home after the bill passed, and by this point, Olivia was eleven—this just shows you how long the political gestation can be for a good idea, since she had been five when we had that dinner together in the smoke-filled restaurant!

I told her, "Daddy had a really good day today. Do you remember a bunch of years ago when you were talking about the man smoking? You know I've been working on that smoking ban, and it passed today!"

And she said, "Oh. Okay, well that's nice. So let me tell you about my day." So much for historic moments for eleven-year olds!

CHAPTER 5

~

Fifth in a Five-Way Race

In 2003, I was in my fourth term on the City Council. The general election for mayor that year was going to be a rematch between John Street and Sam Katz. They had run against each other the first time in 1999, where in one of the closest elections in Philadelphia mayoral history, John Street beat Sam Katz by about 9,400 votes. Generally speaking, if you win the Democratic primary in Philadelphia, unless you are subsequently indicted *and* convicted, you should go on to get sworn in to office. By 2007, we had what was probably a 5–1 Democratic to Republican ratio, and by 2017 it was about a 7–1 registration edge. That first race between Street and Katz in 1999, however, was very different. There was a lot of controversy, and the final vote was extremely close. Street had been a controversial figure, mostly because of actions he had taken, statements he'd made, and personal financial issues involving money allegedly owed to the city-owned gas works. There had also been two publicly financed major stadium deals and projects during his years in office as council president, and big deals and projects tend to create big controversy.

Now, four years later, we had a rematch race and it was an especially contentious and nasty one.

A month before the general election, on October 7, 2003, a listening device was found in the mayor's office. There was what the *Philadelphia Inquirer* called a "static of innuendo and speculation" as to the origins of such a listening device, and many assumed that it was political shenanigans that somehow may have involved the Sam Katz campaign. Speculation continued for a couple of days, until the FBI made an extremely unusual announcement. I think that if you want to come back as someone, you really want to come back as a spokesperson for the FBI. All they ever seem to say is, "We cannot confirm or deny that there is an investigation." It's an incredible job. But this time was different. The FBI announced that the Katz campaign had not put the listening device in the mayor's office; rather, they had. The FBI presented evidence to a federal judge with enough information—because you can only place a listening device if a federal judge signs off on it—that there may in fact have been criminal activity taking place in the mayor's office. Somehow the device was found, in the ceiling. It was never revealed how it was found, but it was. It hadn't captured much of anything, because it hadn't been there that long.

To be clear, not at this time or any subsequent time was Mayor Street ever charged with anything related to this investigation. But of course, this being Philadelphia, where political gossip, emotions, and drama run high, there was abundant speculation and meager information. To me, the announcements and developments suggested that almost anything was possible in this administration. Other things that had happened in the first four years of Street's term had kindled an environment in Philadelphia that raised some serious ethical concerns about how decisions were made regarding contracts and campaign contributions.

Philadelphians were suspicious of the FBI's timing, as well. An *Inquirer* column argued that "the bad coincidences and negative publicity attending Mayor Street's campaign for re-election—his bad political luck . . . surpasses anything I've seen in many years of covering this city." The revelation had "cast an unfair cloud over the mayor's campaign," the column asserted, and the FBI owed it to the city to make clear "whether the mayor is or is not a target of an investigation."

As a City Council member, I responded to the accumulating evidence of corruption and ethical violations by working with colleagues to pass campaign finance reform legislation. Councilman W. Wilson Goode Jr., son of the former mayor, put forward legislation immediately after the November 2003 election that for the first time put campaign contribution rules in place for city elections, and I strongly supported this legislation. The Street administration was adamantly opposed to it, but we passed it anyway, with a veto-proof majority, and the rules went into effect. The following year I drafted legislation that covered more in-depth campaign finance reform, procurement, and contracting reform. I firmly believe that the ethics and anticorruption pieces of legislation passed in these subsequent years only because there was so much criminal and corrupt activity going down that it made it exceedingly difficult for my council colleagues *not* to vote for them, even though some were demonstrably uncomfortable with the legislation. In this environment of both corruption and reform, I was beginning to be perceived as one of the public officials leading that charge on reform. This would prove significant when I ran for mayor.

Less than a year later, on June 29, 2004, the US Attorney's Office for the eastern district and the FBI, working jointly, charged twelve people with various levels of criminal activity and public corruption. They included Ron White, who was Mayor Street's chief fundraiser and close personal friend, and Corey Kemp, the thirty-five-year-old city treasurer who basically came under the control of Ron White. It was revealed in this federal indictment that White had carte blanche to tell Kemp who to do business with, knock out bids, and put other people in. Kemp was also indicted for smaller corruption involving Super Bowl tickets, free flights on planes, and even the construction of a deck on the back of his house.

Both were federally charged. White died before trial, and Kemp was convicted and spent ten years in federal prison. He was released in 2016. To reiterate, the charges or convictions never included Mayor Street. But federal agents were trying to figure out why the mayor and Ron White would always have person-to-person rather than phone conversations. This would appear to be the reason that they didn't tap the mayor's phone.

This environment of corruption in and around city hall was an embarrassment to the city of Philadelphia, and sometimes reminded me of my days watching the Watergate hearings. Even more embarrassing was the outlandish defense by many Democrats that the investigations were all a plot concocted by then vice president Dick Cheney and then president George W. Bush to bring down a black Democratic mayor in Philadelphia, in order to win Pennsylvania in 2004. There was, as they say, "no truth in that lie" at all, and it shamelessly exploited the city's disdain for Bush and the notion of Cheney as his loyal, evil genius. Even so, by playing on emotions about the Republican White House and conspiracy theories invented out of whole cloth, new voters were galvanized to turn out and the community surged to protect Street, who now looked like a besieged, victimized underdog. Former president Clinton commented about the campaign and Street: "They've made him downright charismatic overnight." Street ended up winning by some eighty-five thousand votes in 2003, after his first, extremely close win in 1999.

The Bush-Cheney conspiracy theory nonsense, coupled with the fact that a listening device would be placed in the mayor's office and the quantity of charges (eventually another ten people were indicted for other reasons) for a variety of scandals, was nudging me toward a momentous decision. I was reelected to the City Council for a fourth term, but two issues convinced me that I should start thinking about running for mayor, in what I would characterize as a quixotic campaign for mayor in 2007.

The first big issue was the corruption around city hall. The second was the growing crime and violence problem in Philadelphia. In most other major cities, crime was going down, but violent crime and shootings in Philadelphia had actually gone up from 2002 to 2005, and there was no particular plan to do anything about it. Mayor Street had implemented a plan in 2002, just in time for election season, called the "Safe Streets" program. Some people nicknamed it, more realistically, the "Save Street" program. It was largely theater, and not a serious plan to tackle crime and make the city safer. Street paid massive overtime for police officers and put them out on the corners, where some of them, literally, would sit and relax in lawn chairs. Street started the program in the summer of 2002, in the lead-up to the big 2003 election, and ended the program precipitously, a couple of days after his election victory. In the primary season, there were crime reductions, but at a huge cost in police overtime.

Now, it's not unusual in mayoring to make political hay out of public safety issues, but it became increasingly obvious to me that Philadelphia had no meaningful or effective plans to tackle the disturbing countertrend of rising homicide rates when other cities were making improvements in this area. At one point in these years, the police commissioner stated bluntly that he, and we, simply did not know what to do to address crime. But I thought that we could do something about this, and, with the right plan, we could reduce the homicide rate in a reasonable period of time.

So the two big campaign issues for me in a 2007 mayoral race would be corruption and crime, crime and corruption. And I started to think about where I was in my life in 2005. I was in my fourth term in City Council, in my late forties, married to my wife Lisa for fourteen years, with two kids, age twenty-two and ten, living in Wynnefield. You learn a lot about people in politics, and in my City Council career I saw colleagues who fretted and worried about getting reelected. My attitude was that if you do your job, more times than not, you'll get reelected. But if you get to the point where you think your job is keeping your job, rather than thinking your job is to *do* your job, then that's a sad place to be. I simply couldn't allow myself to get to that point. I loved this work. But at the same time, I was now seriously contemplating quitting my council job to pursue another job that, on paper, I stood absolutely, positively no chance of winning.

Every mayor who has run for reelection in Philadelphia since the home rule charter of 1951 has been reelected. So, even though it's a four-year term, it's de facto more like an eight-year term. I'm watching what's going on in Philadelphia, and I'm saying to myself that I think I can give more and do more, and wondering do I really want to sit on the City Council floor for another eight years and complain and groan about whatever the next mayor is doing or not doing? I was asking myself, if you think you're so smart, why don't you run? My attitude at the time was not some messianic belief that I was the only one who could save the city, or the only one who could run, but more modestly that I'm a public servant and I should step up.

And ultimately, I made a decision that only one of two things could happen: Either I'm going to win, and that would be great, or I'm going to lose, and I'll never have to go to another community meeting again in my life, and I'll triple my salary overnight by returning to the private sector. As they say, no one's ever scored a touchdown from the sidelines. I decided it was time to run for mayor.

—

At this point, in early 2006, I thought that I should at least get some objective data, because politicians are never really as popular as they think they are. I had been active on the City Council with the smoking ban, and campaign finance and contract reform, and I'd been out there fighting all of these battles and getting all of this press. I assumed that I was somewhat well-known in Philadelphia. So I took a poll in May 2006, working with a nationally recognized pollster, Garin-Hart-Yang, a firm that does serious national work out of Washington, DC, and could conduct a rigorous poll, which we paid for out of my own campaign finances. Fred Yang is an incredible pollster, and when his first poll came back it told me that I'd be fifth in *any* five-way race, no matter who ran and regardless of what names they plugged in to the scenarios. Whatever the mixing and matching of potential candidates, I always had 12 percent.

Now, that was interesting. So I asked Fred what he thought after we went through the top lines and cross tabs, and sliced and diced and discussed the poll extensively. He concluded, "It's difficult, but not impossible. . . . The difference here with you is, no matter who is in the race, your 12 percent never moves. They never go anywhere else. You put different names in, but . . . your folks never moved. You have a rock-solid 12 percent."

We have a resign-to-run provision in Philadelphia. If you're in an office and run for any another office, then you have to resign, no matter what office you are seeking. The resignation was a major decision for me because the last thing Philadelphia needed was another unemployed black guy. In June 2006, a month after my poll, I announced that I was resigning from City Council. And the Saturday after the Fourth of July I announced that I was running for mayor of the City of Philadelphia. Me and my 12 percent. Me and my fifth-place-no-matter-who-runs ranking. This was going to be exciting.

CHAPTER 6

~

My Name Is Olivia Nutter
and This Is My Dad

Politics in Philly, at least, is a full contact sport. I announced that I was running for mayor from the porch of Diane Marshall's house on Parkside Avenue, in West Philadelphia, across from the Mann Center. "Almost twenty-five years ago I got involved in politics," I told the crowd,

> and I've loved every minute of it—working with people from different neighborhoods, working to understand what strong communities are all about, and taking the time to listen. . . . Because every voice should be heard. . . . There is something very special about public service. There is a special feeling you get when you know at the end of the day that you've really helped a person get something done. I've enjoyed my time in City Council, but as I have taken on more issues and more challenges and more leadership, I've had to think about my future and my service. . . . I came to one conclusion: in order to make real change . . . to provide strong, determined, and principled leadership for the whole city it's time for me to make

a decision. It's the same decision that Mayor Rendell and Mayor Street have all had to make, for their careers. . . . Let there be no more confusion, mystery or speculation. Listen well: today, as we stand here, I am now a candidate for mayor!

Everybody gets their day in the sunshine, and that was our day. I thought that I'd made a decent speech. About two hundred people came out for the announcement, and I got good press coverage. The media applauded some of my skills and accomplishments as a city council member—the *Philadelphia Inquirer* characterized me as a "budget wonk and a government reformer," who displayed "tough, lawyer-like questioning" at budget hearings. Others reflected that I had had a lot of good ideas and was a policy guy. But it's a shame, most all of these stories concluded, that I'd end up last in a five-way or ten-way race and didn't stand a chance.

The *Inquirer* quoted J. Whyatt Mondesire of the NAACP, who speculated, "Michael's biggest detriment probably is his lack of inside game. Even though Nutter is from Philadelphia and knows Philadelphia, he needs to get well-rooted in neighborhoods all the way down to the ward precinct level across the city in order to make a viable run." The *Inquirer* article underscored that I didn't seem to have the "inside game" that Mondesire mentioned. They noted my "tough campaign road ahead," as demonstrated by the fact that none of my City Council colleagues and just three ward leaders had attended my announcement. "One neighborhood family having a small reunion across the street from Nutter's event," the *Inquirer* continued, "didn't have the slightest interest in him, or his candidacy. 'I don't think he's crooked,' said 64-year-old Barbara Thorne of Olney as she seasoned barbequed spare ribs. 'I just don't think he's too cool.'"

Ouch. I took in all of this pessimism, but didn't agree with it. For one thing, I was the only announced candidate on that day. There were no other candidates yet, so I couldn't lose to myself. For another, I was sensing the frustration with the "inside game" and established political life in Philadelphia. The apparent detriment of not having deeply rooted political connections could turn out to be an advantage.

—

So I was off and running. A campaign is like a start-up business. It didn't exist before you showed up. You're the CEO and the product at the same time. A campaign is an organic entity that has its own life, and you have to build it up. You put together a bunch of different people who mostly don't know each other, or who do know each other and sometimes don't like each other, and you manage that as well as the tensions between finance and field operations, between those on payroll and those who are not. Initially, a campaign is a disorganized, chaotic situation, for which order and standards must be established. As a mayoral candidate you have an idea, a vision, some things you want to communicate, and you have to put together a team. A city politician can't rely just on family and friends, unless you have a really large family, which I don't.

We had a little office down at 123 South Broad Street. There were five or six of us in a 500-square-foot office. Eryn Santamoor was the first person on the campaign staff in that office on Broad Street. She served as the finance director and was primarily responsible for raising all of the money needed for the primary election. We had more and more volunteers coming to the office before long, however. So eventually we moved to 42 South 15th Street, which seemed like a huge space at the time. Through whatever means, a bit of our message was getting out there, and people were coming in who wanted to volunteer to augment my core campaign staff. A few aspects of my campaign and message were appealing to them. There is something about the underdog role that resonates, and in Philadelphia, in particular, we root for the underdog. Volunteers wanted something new and wanted to clean things up. I had a record for ethics, which people wanted. There was a lot of embarrassment at the time about corruption at city hall, and I think the indictments were a final straw. You never know in politics where the edge is—when citizens and voters will finally insist on change—but we had gone over that edge after 2003. I remember an older gentleman named Jim, who was one of those who came to volunteer. I'm not sure why he turned up, or where he came from in the city, but he was extremely consistent and dedicated, just like the other early volunteers who wanted to do something about ethics, crime, and corruption.

We had already brought on a political consultant team, led by Neil Oxman and his firm, the Campaign Group, from Philadelphia. I think of Neil as the mad genius of politics and political strategy. To date, Neil has directly helped to elect every mayor of Philadelphia since the mayoral race of 1983, with one exception. He has a unique style to help candidates understand that he knows more than they do about how to get elected (which happens to be *completely true*), and that if the candidate just does everything that he says, he or she is likely to win. His quiet manner takes a little getting used to, and many wish that he would speak up more and share his thoughts and advice more clearly. Neil was one of the first and only people who thought that I could actually win the Mayor's race.

Next we brought on a campaign manager, Bill Hyers, from New York City. Hyers oversaw possibly the most unlikely group of staff and volunteers ever assembled, for a campaign that no one believed could win. Bill's careful analysis of the people we had and their talents, and his development of our finance, field, and overall campaign strategy, was masterful. After Hyers, I started hiring more staff. I was putting together an organization, because you cannot do this by yourself. It doesn't matter who you are, how big you are, how much money you have, how smart you are, or how well positioned you are. *You need a team* to run. This is a large city. Philadelphia is 143 square miles, with 1.5 million residents. It takes a lot of communicating across large distances and neighborhoods to make a mayoral campaign happen. And so we started building an organization. *Organizations win elections.* I can't say that emphatically enough. It's not just the candidate.

An organization, by which I mean a bona fide, highly functioning campaign operation and a real field operation, is essential. There can be historical battles between these two groups, the finance dimensions and the field dimensions of a campaign. The finance arm of the organization typically wants all of the candidate's time to raise money, and the field arm responds that they actually get people to vote and mobilize. There is a lot of back and forth within any organization and jurisdictional battles over finance and field time.

To handle that, the organization needs a strong manager. Hyers kept things together when they might have fallen apart many times. He kept people who were often at odds working together through his leadership and management skills. It was incredible to see. When you watch a campaign, it is a window into the soul of how that candidate will govern. It really is your first indication of what they will be like in office. The candidate is the one constant between campaigning and governing. In the first six months after a successful candidate takes office, there can be a fair amount of shakeout and shifting around, as some individuals within an organization are good at the campaign dimension and simply cannot make the transition to governing. But there can be no substitution, shuffling out, or transformation of the elected candidate himself. President Trump, as Jeb Bush aptly commented, was a "chaos candidate," and now he's a chaos president. There is very little difference between the campaign and governance styles.

In addition to the campaign core that I've described, I had other dynamic, colorful, driven, and highly effective people on the campaign team. Dick Hayden, a friend and adviser for over thirty years, and Jay Goldstein, another longtime friend and adviser, comprised something like the good cop/bad cop duo of the campaign. In some ways Dick was the key to the whole operation. He was loyal, respected by everyone, dedicated, and focused. There would not have been a campaign without him. Anyone and everyone with a complaint, idea, or argument would reach out to him for advice and support, or to resolve the problem. I think of him as the architect of the campaign. Jay had been my main finance person from early in my City Council elections, and continued that role in the 2007 primary campaign. He was honest, trustworthy, and analytical.

Other old friends and advisers were part of the campaign ensemble. My friend John Saler is also known as a political historian for Philadelphia and Pennsylvania. He knows who ran for what and when, and how things turned out. He knows where the bodies are buried (he buried them!), and can deliver certain messages that need to be delivered to certain people in certain ways—all with a smile. My oldest political partner on the campaign was Steve Jones. We had started out as committee people together in our Wynnefield neighborhood, and he has been with me in every political election, at every level. At this writing he was serving as the ward chairman of the Fifty-Second Ward, where I serve as ward leader, but everyone knows that Steve is in charge of all ward business and activities. No one is more focused on working toward success, in any mission. Steve will get it done.

～

During my 2007 campaign, cell phones were still somewhat new. I think Myspace was still around, and I remember asking someone during the campaign what a "blog" was. The very idea that people who didn't really know each other could talk to each other was baffling. We brought on some experts, such as they existed then, to help us navigate this "space," wherever that space may have been. Since 2007, it would be no over-statement to say that social media and the 24/7 news cycle have pretty much changed everything about campaigning. You must manage social media, or social media will manage you.

However, I don't think that social media has supplanted the importance of traditional political organizations, even if it has shifted the contents of American politics dramatically. Campaigns still need the human touch, and strength in both fundraising and field operations.

On the campaign trail through Philly I talked about crime, corruption, jobs, and education. Those were the four fundamentals. Before campaign audiences I would often say, "I'm just an unemployed brother from West Philadelphia, trying to get a job." I was trying to keep it real!

Gradually other people announced their candidacies and eventually there were, as hypothesized, five of us in the race, and it was a very strong field of candidates. Tom Knox had an interesting personal story. He had joined the Navy after dropping out of high school, and acquired a GED. He became a multimillionaire through an insurance advisory firm and other entrepreneurial ventures in the 1980s. Congressman Bob Brady was another primary contender. He has been chairman of the Philadelphia Democratic Party since 1986, and a congressman for many years from the First District. Chaka Fattah was also a US representative from the Second District and on the Appropriations Committee. State representative Dwight Evans, the state House appropriations chair, rounded out the Democratic primary field. Before getting into politics Evans had been a teacher in the Philadelphia public school system and an Urban League community activist.

At a kind of impromptu, in-house campaign rally, I told my staff what I still believe to be true about a mayoral campaign: "I really appreciate you, being out here this afternoon," I began.

We made a lot of calls and a lot of you responded . . . and you're ready to join in. This is the heart and soul of what a campaign is all about, not only what happens here in this main office but in other offices we hope to have in other parts of the city, but having a ground operation, a field operation is really what elections are all about. It's where elections are won or lost. It's out in the field. It's not just what the candidate is doing; it's what enthusiastic workers are doing leading up to the election. If we do our work—there is no question what the result will be on election day. It's everything you do leading up to the day. When we wake up on May 15 we should already know what the outcome will be when the polls close later that night.

⏤

Generally, and this was true of my campaign as well, there wasn't a lot of door knocking in the early stages. Instead, there were mayoral forums and the task of creating a presence for myself in the city. This meant, for example, doing several transit stops most mornings, along the elevated train (El) and the Broad Street SEPTA subway. I would run all day and half the night. I'd start with transit stops in the morning, do meetings and fundraising all day, then go to a transit stop until rush hour was over. In March, we were sending people out in the field. Twenty, thirty, or forty volunteers on any given day knocked on doors and dropped literature, day in and day out. The campaign manager, using statistics and polling data, developed a field strategy, and most of our early field work occurred in West, Northwest, and South Philadelphia, and some parts of North Philadelphia.

That is what the volunteers did. As for myself, I spent a great deal of time raising money. After my rush hour transit stops ended, I'd retreat to do fundraising calls. This isn't at all unusual for mayoral candidates. It takes a lot of money to run for the mayor's office. And, by midcampaign, we had a growing staff and were running the equivalent of a small business. I was put on a regimen of four to five hours of "call time" a day. This meant that I went to a little back room of the operation, with people assigned to me who only did finance. Keri Salerno was my call time manager, as part of the finance team. Every day she gave me a stack of sheets from which I was to make my calls. This occurred four to five hours every day, Monday through Friday. Calls were timed, and I couldn't stay on the call for more than three minutes. I had daily, weekly, and monthly fundraising goals. In fact, Keri probably spent the most time with me as a candidate, and was implicitly responsible for the daily maintenance and upkeep of my psychological well-being, because of the daily rejection that I had to endure during those hours of fundraising calls.

There are very few people who actually enjoy making political fundraising phone calls, and those who do enjoy it most likely have some psychological problem! I approached fundraising almost as an out-of-body experience. I was watching someone else do this. I felt as if I was selling part of my soul, calling people that I didn't know and telling them that they will get nothing in return but public service. When it comes down to it, this is essentially begging—albeit at arm's length, but begging nonetheless. Whatever my feelings, there was no way to avoid this task, because I had built an operation—my start-up business. I had a payroll to meet. What I did or didn't do would affect people in the campaign and their pocketbooks. The campaign manager said to the campaign team, "If you like getting paid you will not interrupt call time, you will not stop him in the hallway, you will not engage in chitchat because every minute that he is not on the phone he is not raising money." Miraculously, no one ever really talked to me because, under the circumstances as described, they wanted me on the phone constantly.

Imagine trying to raise money when everyone knew that I was, literally, fifth in a five-way race. Yet we raised more money than all the other candidates by the end of 2006, with the exception of one: the self-funded Tom Knox. We affectionately referred to Tom as the Human ATM. Knox said he would spend roughly $10 million of his own money on the campaign. Going into 2007, however, we were actually leading on the money side among those who were just raising funds, even though candidate Evans had always been a better fundraiser than me in the past. The other candidates had always struggled to raise money in the past or didn't really to need to raise much for their previous elections.

With fundraising, I exhausted my family and friends quickly enough, and had to start calling a slew of people that I didn't know. My rule was that unless you were related to one of the other candidates, on their campaign finance team, or had some other strong relationship,

I would not let you get off the phone without giving me something. I might start at the maximum donation—we had campaign contribution limits for the first time in the city's history, and I understood them deeply, because I wrote them as a councilman. Then we could halve that amount, and then halve the half, and eventually I might get down to a request that they just give me $25. People gave me money sometimes just to get me off of the phone. What they didn't understand was that I was going to call them back in three weeks because we had everyone on a three-week rotation. If someone gave me $50, I'd call in three weeks and ask them for $100, then I'd call three weeks later and ask for $150. Because now the donor had made an investment—they wanted want me to win because they had invested in me.

One day in February, I made five hours of calls, and not a single person answered my call. I left messages, and my call time manager Keri was dreading that next day because she would have to tell me first that no one had returned any of my calls from the previous day, and then motivate me to make new calls that day. But I made another four to five hours of calls—a mayoral campaign is a grind sometimes, and you simply have to knock the tasks out, one by one.

Even with frustrating days like that, the money was, surprisingly, rolling in. Led by Eryn Santamoor, the finance staff and volunteers would raise over $4.6 million for the primary election, and achieve what was thought to be impossible: ultimately, we would out-fundraise all of the other candidates in the 2007 primary field—a stunning achievement for Eryn, the staff, and volunteers. My average donation may have been larger than Bernie Sanders's claim of $27. For events, we'd have different donation levels. A sponsor might be $1,000, a co-sponsor $500, and so on, in that range. But with a lot of events and a lot of phone calls, the donations of a few hundred dollars add up. Aside from making payroll, we needed money for the largest and most necessary cost: television ads.

⁓

The Philadelphia region is the fourth-largest television market in the country. It encompasses nineteen counties, 2,953,760 television households as of 2015, and includes portions of New Jersey and Delaware as well as Pennsylvania. Television ads were crucial to this and other primary elections. To give you a sense of the scale of advertisement: According to 2015 research by the University of Delaware's Center for Community Research & Service, in the final two months of the 2014 midterm election, citizens in the Philadelphia television market saw almost twelve thousand political ads, on which candidates had spent a total of $14.4 million. TV was especially important to the primary race in 2007, because, as hard as it is now to imagine an age before social media, we were campaigning largely in the pre-Twitter, pre-Facebook, and even pre-smartphone era.

Tom Knox went on TV in December 2006. He was at 2 percent, so he knew he needed more runway. But he spent hundreds of thousands of dollars from December to March on television, and had the airwaves all to himself. And then some of the other candidates came on. My contributors and supporters were calling and asking why we weren't on TV, and saying, "We're sending in this money and not seeing anything." In mayoral campaigns, everyone's got an opinion. Everyone.

For us, it came down to a math issue, pure and simple. In 2006, it cost about $300,000 a week to have serious television. There's no credit—you wire your money in by 5 P.M. on Tuesday, or your ads do not air. So the equation is, divide the amount of money you have by $300,000, and that tells you how many weeks of television you can do.

Of course you have to put some money aside for election day, payroll, literature, mailers, and other expenses.

We held our money in reserve for some time, because we made a decision that once we went on television, we weren't going off of television. The race was coming down to Tom Knox and the other candidates, and we knew that we could never match Knox dollar for dollar.

My strategy with television, and staying on once we went on, was that you have to do a certain amount of "breakthrough" messaging with any campaign. You also have to give people a consistent message. In an effort to save money, some candidates would go on and off television—they'd break through initially and thereafter get forgotten, because they had disappeared from the airwaves. Then they'd come back on television and have to reestablish their identity from the beginning. I wanted a consistent television presence and message, and I wanted to be seen all the time.

When we had adequate money to accomplish this and to stay on the air, we started with a series of ads in which I essentially said, "I'm not him." And the "him" was the incumbent mayor, John Street, who was not running, and was ineligible to run, for reelection. This was highly controversial. We were on pins and needles when we made the ad, and there was some negative reaction to it. But this kind of ad tapped into the tenebrous mood of the city. We knew voters were upset about the corruption issues and wanted change.

One of the fundamental rules in the political business is define yourself before someone does it for you. In these ads, my first definition of myself boiled down to "You may not know me that well, but I'm not him." This was controversial. Then we ran a second ad that said in essence "You may not like what I said in my first ad. If you don't, you should vote for someone else, because . . . I'm not him."

We ran ten ads in that year in the primary, and in late March we came out with the only ad that anyone ever remembers. It features our daughter, Olivia, who says, "My name is Olivia Nutter, and this is my dad. This is the house my dad grew up in in west Philadelphia. This is our dog. My dad's pretty cool for an old guy. This is where I go to middle school. My dad is the only Democrat running for mayor with a child in the public schools. I know he wants to make the city better and safer. My dad's pretty busy these days, but he still finds time to take me to school." Olivia was twelve at the time, she was beautiful, and the ad told a great story in thirty seconds. This ad is still on YouTube today, the "Nutter ad with Olivia."

The germ of the idea for the ad began when I started writing some copy, not that that was my forte or business, but I did sense that there was a need for some further definition of who I was, so I wanted to do something that spoke to families and about my family. Originally, I wrote this copy for a piece of campaign literature, and then I thought that it might work best as some kind of video, so I sent it over to the Campaign Group and we batted around some ideas. The quiet operator at the Campaign Group, J. J. Balaban, ended up writing the dialogue and script, and we talked to the filmmaker and then found the locations—in our house, at her school, and in the car as I took my daughter to school. My daughter wisely maintained some editorial veto power for herself, and the production worked out well.

Even so, I didn't anticipate the impact of that ad. The "Olivia" ad all but erased the first two ads entirely. It shifted the story from "I'm not him" to "This is who I am." It's not an overstatement to say that this ad actually changed the course of the race. People started paying attention to our campaign. It ran for one week, concurrent with another ad that was much more dramatic because we were concerned that the ad with my daughter might be too trivial to the moment. The purpose of the "Olivia" ad was to define me. I'm not sure who or what the voters thought I was, but this ad told them: I grew up in a row house in West Philadelphia; I have a child in public school (the only candidate who could make that claim) and I drive her to school every day, which is true; she has friends, we have a dog, I have a family. Olivia apparently keeps her room nice—it looked especially good in the ad! My daughter conveyed that I actually really cared, and I want to make this city better. And no matter how busy I am running as a candidate, I still found time to take her to school. I wasn't just a nerdy, Ivy League guy, but a regular guy from West Philly who grew up in a row house. All of that meant something to the people. We put the pieces together, and this ad, thirty seconds long, conveyed the story—my story—much better than I had myself.

This ad touched voters in different ways. I had African American men who said to me, "Yes, I take my daughter to school every day, too." I had older African American women who would comment, "Your daughter is so cute, she reminds me of my baby girl." So Philadelphians took their own piece, and different pieces, from this ad. It meant different things to different people.

Our ads in the 2007 campaign, and especially the "Olivia" ad, were critically acclaimed. The series of them won the Pollie Awards for 2007, the equivalent of an Oscar for political campaigns. Before he became mayor, Kasim Reed of Atlanta saw the "Olivia" ad and said, "Whoever produced that ad, I want them working on my campaign." The first two ads or the last seven, people didn't care about or remember all that well—but ad #3, with my daughter, was exceptional.

In addition to television ads, the other major campaign outreach consisted of candidate forums. There were seventy candidate forums in the primary election of 2007. I participated in sixty-eight of them. One I missed because my brother-in-law had died, and the other because I was filming another commercial. There comes a time in every campaign when every candidate has their speech and their responses to predictable questions, and even though the candidates are competitors, we know just what the others are going to say and we know each other's positions intimately. Toward the end of the campaign, I'm confident that we were all tired of hearing the other four, and, ultimately, tired of hearing ourselves. I know that I was, at least.

The sustainability community was probably the most organized group during the 2007 election. So much so that by the end of the campaign season, every candidate had become a green candidate. I think they dramatically influenced the election, and this is a key example of how citizens who write letters, send emails, and organize around local issues can make a difference in a city. Midway through that campaign, the sustainability community was so organized and had held so many forums that candidates realized pretty quickly this is a serious issue and these folks are going to have influence in this election. It's about being engaged, showing up, letting your voice be heard, and reminding people like me that I work for you.

You know that you're making movement in a campaign when the other candidates start paying attention to you. After the commercial with my daughter and tireless forum participation, our own internal polling indicated that I had moved from fifth to fourth, and then suddenly an independent poll came out that said I was in second place. Somebody released the poll—we had nothing to do with it and hadn't commissioned it—and it confirmed that I was closing in. Other data had the race as a virtual dead heat between Knox and myself. One of our ads even said explicitly, "It's a dead heat." These polls, on the heels of the "Olivia" ad, really took us into an entirely new territory in the campaign. We got more volunteers, and more money, and suddenly the fundraising calls became easier.

In the last two weeks, we actually had people calling the campaign and asking if we were still accepting donations and taking money. Momentum is huge in mayoral politics. Knox and I had pulled away from the rest of the pack, and the positive news from the polls catalyzed more of everything—money, volunteers, resources, attention, and even negative attacks from the other candidates, which are really good political news in disguise. As a candidate, when you start attracting fire from opponents, it means that you're in range of victory. I had taken some strong positions on public safety as a councilman, and these became fodder for some of the negative attacks in the final weeks of the campaign.

Our own polling shortly after the independent poll also told us I was many people's second choice. I wasn't their first choice, because I was originally fifth in a five-way race, and people didn't want to waste their vote. But when the independent poll validated that I was in second, voters realized that I could actually win, and, if they voted for me, I probably would.

In the home stretch, I continued to talk about the issues: corruption, crime, jobs, education, and sustainability. What you do before the election should tell you what's going to happen on election night. Our pollster out of Washington, DC, told us two weeks before election day that I was going to win by thirteen points. On election night, the results came in almost exactly as Fred predicted. I won by twelve points. I did that by starting with my rock solid 12 percent. Philadelphia is a very heavily Democratic city, so if you win the Democratic primary and, as I said, if you don't get indicted *and* convicted, more than likely you will be elected mayor in the fall. And I would go on to get 83 percent of the vote in the general election.

I thought about where this journey had started—the Impulse nightclub, my time with John Anderson, and all of the people that I had met on the streets while campaigning. The primary election night was emotional for me. So many people had had an impact on my life, and taught me lessons that had culminated in this moment. I found myself remembering my high school football coach, Gamp Pellegrini. When I was fifteen and my family was going through difficult times and turmoil, he was the most constant, biggest male figure in my life. We all loved and hated him, every day, but many of the things he taught me stayed with me. He was a no-excuses person, and he imparted that value to me. He created some of the moments in my early life that built confidence. And I recalled the Philadelphia Outward Bound program I had created with two friends. Part of the program was a tightrope walk. Everyone is harnessed, but the tightrope is high above the ground. The exercise is about trusting the equipment, trusting each other, and self-esteem. When I walked that tightrope, I stood there at the start for what seemed like a very long time. The challenge really was about simply taking the first step. A lot of moments from our personal histories and life experiences build confidence and skills. They had all culminated, for me, in this moment.

Becoming mayor was about perseverance, tenacity, and positioning. Winston Churchill said that "nothing in the world can take the place of perseverance." After this evening I reflected that there was no reason for any of this to have happened in my life. I never thought it would happen; I had no plan for it to happen; but by moving forward through the years with my own commitment to serve in place, this is where I had arrived.

My improbable and unanticipated victory is also a lesson in the importance of timing and positioning. I sometimes draw on basketball metaphors when I'm trying to encourage or motivate young people. I tell them, on the court, it's not always the tallest player who gets the rebound. It's the person who is in the best position. It's not where the ball is that matters, but where it is going next, and making sure that you are in that spot to get it, even if you're not the tallest. Thinking back on this race, I was well positioned by leadership, sponsorship, and support—and the timing was right for what I had to offer. I moved from my solid 12 percent to 83 percent because voters wanted change, they wanted reform, they wanted someone who actually knew the issues and knew the city. The one advantage that I had over the other four great candidates is that I had served in city government. My City Council experience distinguished me from the others. My most notable achievements as a councilman—campaign finance reform, the anticorruption measures, and the smoking ban—were momentous in their time. They were all big battles, all controversial, and all ultimately implemented successfully—and afterwards, the world was still spinning on its axis. For me personally, these council experiences helped me tremendously as I ran for mayor. I was running against two members of Congress, a state representative, and a businessman. I actually knew the issues and had been in the city political trenches, which was extremely helpful in an issues race. And this was definitely an issues race—as change elections often are.

~

One of the very greatest moments in being in elected to office, whether mayor, governor, or certainly president, is that inaugural speech. You only get one chance to give the first one. If you're lucky, you get a second one. In my inauguration speech that day, I told Philadelphians:

> We can choose to challenge the status quo that has been holding us back for much too long. We can choose to try new ideas and new approaches. We can choose to make a shared commitment to return this city to one of the greatest cities in the United States of America. The next chapter in this great city has yet to be written because we now have an opportunity to write it ourselves. To the law-abiding citizens in Philadelphia I say we are the great majority. To the law breakers, I say that you are in the small minority. This is our city, and we're taking the city back—every day . . . everybody . . . every neighborhood, everywhere in Philadelphia.

Then I had to make the transition from campaigning to governing, because it was all real now. I cannot tell you how nervous I was on that stage. I realized suddenly and with much greater force that I was about to become the mayor of the fifth largest city in the United States of America. The birthplace of freedom, liberty, and democracy. All mayors are special and all cities are great—but I do truly believe that there is something just a little extra special to be mayor of Philadelphia where, more than two hundred years ago, people really put their lives and fortunes at risk because they wanted something different, a different form of governance. People took serious risks to forge our political system and our country here. With our history and prominence, people actually pay attention to what happens here. We are not just a wonderful train station stop between those two other great cities of

Washington, DC, and New York. Philadelphia is the true birthplace of freedom, liberty, and democracy.

There is something special about this place, and I had to take that seriously. I didn't want to take myself too seriously, but I did take the work and the job and the people and the responsibility very seriously, as a sacred trust. So my hand was shaking as I was reciting the oath. I knew the oath, I'd read it many times, but it was with a nervousness and an awareness that when you are sworn in as mayor, your life and your family's life are about to change dramatically.

The moment of truth. I announce my run for mayor on Parkside
Avenue, in West Philadelphia, in July 2006, with Lisa, Olivia,
Steve Tones, Pastor Al Campbell and his wife Ruth.

Victory! Standing with my wife Lisa and daughter Olivia
after our win on election night, 2007.

I'm about to become the ninety-eighth mayor of my hometown, and was nervous as I recited the oath. The enormous responsibility, and trust, placed in my hands became real at that moment.

The first black mayor of Philadelphia and a mentor of mine, W. Wilson Goode Sr., congratulates the third black mayor.

Superintendent William Hite and the team talk education and schools. During my terms, the high school graduation rate rose from 53 percent to 68 percent.

After Amtrak train #188 derailed on May 12, 2015, in Philadelphia, the united effort and teamwork of several agencies was demonstrated in our daily walk to the press briefing.

I get inspiration from President Barack Obama . . .

. . . and encouragement from First Lady Michelle Obama.

Hillary Clinton has a sharp intellect and a generous spirit. She has become a good friend.

I talk with two of my favorite people in politics, Mayor
Mitch Landrieu and President Bill Clinton.

A chat with the most important person in Philadelphia, a young child.

A guy from West Philly talking to a guy from Brooklyn, Jay-Z, after he announced the Made in America Festival on the art museum steps.

I was honored to stand with Mayor Peter Feldmann in Frankfurt, Germany, our sister city, in July 2015. As mayor I also thought of myself as the ambassador for the city of Philadelphia.

Learning from a friend in Tel Aviv, Mayor Ron Huldai, in July 2015. There was no "mayor's school" to attend, but I learned and borrowed from other mayors all the time, and shared my best practices with them.

Education was a priority for me during my terms in office, and there was no better way to start the day than with kids in school.

Assisting a student at Hill Freedman Middle School, and hoping that I'm not messing up her project!

Congratulating new graduates from local colleges and universities
at the annual "Toss Your Caps" celebration.

Speaking to graduates at the school district's commencement ceremony.
I'm so proud of you all!

They did it; Lisa and I only helped. The "Philly Goes 2 College" walk
down Broad Street was part of a larger initiative to change the
community's thinking about going to college.

Throwing out the first pitch at the Philadelphia
Phillies home opener on March 31, 2008.

My eight years in office ended with a highlight—a visit to Philadelphia
from Pope Francis for the World Meeting of Families in 2015.

My wife Lisa—the only reason I won.

PART TWO

～

CHAPTER 7

Budgets and Roses

.

W hen I took office on January 7, 2008, Philadelphia had a million and a half people, but a population that had been declining since the 1960s. It was a large, old northeastern manufacturing city that was going through significant economic change. The year I took office, for example, almost 31 percent of employed people in Philadelphia worked in the education or medical sectors, not in manufacturing. Philadelphia has had a poverty rate over 20 percent for three decades, and it was certainly 24 percent or so when I first took office. The city's demographics were changing as well. Philadelphia in 2017 is a majority minority city with a growing Hispanic and Latino population, and that trend started before I took office.

And so it took, and still takes, a coalition campaign not only to run for office and be successful, but also to govern, in a twenty-first-century American city. Being mayor is a CEO job, in every respect. If I were delivering a talk at the University of Pennsylvania's Wharton School of Business, I would describe Philadelphia as about the 360th largest corporation in the United States of America, with $7.9 billion in revenues, twenty-eight thousand employees, and a million and a half shareholders. We have a variety of lines of business. We don't necessarily create jobs; we create opportunity. We create an environment that will allow entrepreneurs and business leaders to put people to work.

~

On day one, a new mayor has to make a pretty significant transition from candidate to elected official, from campaigning to governing. When I began my first term I knew that I had at least four years, and I had run on some basic elements. First and foremost, issues of corruption and integrity in government; public safety; education—in 2007, Philadelphia had a high school graduation rate of around 53 percent; and jobs. I did not run for mayor to be the caretaker of the status quo.

My first order of business was to fulfill a campaign promise: I had promised that on my first day in office I would declare a crime emergency in Philadelphia, and about an hour after the inauguration, over in the mayor's reception room after the swearing-in of cabinet officers and top staff members, I did just that, through an executive order. It directed our brand new police commissioner Charles Ramsey to immediately come up with a plan and a new strategy to fight crime in Philadelphia. And he had thirty days to put that plan together, because I wanted to incorporate his plan and any new spending it might require into my first budget.

Our plan for the crime emergency in Philadelphia had a few major components. We had twenty-three police districts in the city, and data analysis showed that 65 percent of all the murders in the city were in nine of those districts, so we wanted to adjust how we were allocating and using police resources. Second, we wanted more officers on foot patrol. Third, we were enthusiastic about hot spot policing. This means taking the crime data not just by district, but getting it down to a more granular level of block-by-block crime analysis within a district. The twenty-three police districts in the city are fairly large, and most homicides were occurring in a much more specific area no larger than a few blocks or streets within each of the nine districts. Additional funding was another component of the plan, as well as changes in police training, with an emphasis on communication and the tenets of community policing.

The city budget was another urgent matter of business in the first weeks. A new fiscal year budget under the city charter has to pass by the end of May of the current year. Budgets are usually submitted in February, and no later than March. Of course, I had no idea that a Great Recession was coming. Economists now conclude that the recession started in December 2007. I was elected in November 2007 and sworn in in January 2008. The timing was perfect! Not one memo, not one transition document, not a slip of paper or a note jotted on the back of an envelope, ever mentioned that we were about to go into the worst recession since the Great Depression. Of course, no one knew that at the time.

With both the city and I having no idea what was looming, I composed a budget. For a mayor, budgets are more than words and numbers on a sheet of paper. Budgets tell a story, and should be a reflection of a mayor's values and what he or she is committed to and trying to get done.

We released our budget on February 14. I had pushed the budget address back to give Commissioner Ramsey more time to prepare his crime reduction plans. As it happens I was giving my first budget address on Valentine's Day, and since these were all my former colleagues, and in the spirit of peace, love, and happiness between the mayor's office and the City Council, I gave each one of them a red rose.

In your first months of the year as the new mayor in Philadelphia you get to make two major presentations or speeches. The first, of course, is your inaugural address, in which you are delivering a message to the citizens of the city, to the people in the region, if not across the country, and to financial markets and other entities and people who pay attention to what goes on in cities. It is an important moment to signal intentions, and a major address. It should set the stage for what you want to do, at least for the next four years, and, if you're lucky, for the next eight.

Then there is your first budget address. I prefaced my comments on the budget by introducing myself as a mayor who was going to manage the city government as a public trust. I promised to be guided by "values of respect, integrity and service," and to see that my administration operated "under the guiding principles of efficiency, transparency, and accountability." The budget differed from those in the past, I said that day, because it was focusing on six areas: public safety, education, jobs and economic development, sustainable communities, ethics, and customer service. The budget would increase funding to the Police Department by $78 million over five years; expand emergency medical services with an additional $3.8 million; reopen the Office of Arts and Culture and support a director of sustainability; increase funding for Fairmount Park—at over ten thousand acres, one of America's largest urban green spaces—by $16.5 million over five years; shore up the weekly, single-stream recycling program across the city through $6.5 million to the Streets Department; and provide $4 million a year to the Community College of Philadelphia and $3 million a year for community health centers. At the same time the budget proposed to continue to cut wage and business taxes over the next five years, and to offset those cuts with an increase in parking lot taxes from 15 percent to 20 percent, among other things. We did not spend wildly, but we were making important investments to better serve our citizens.

I concluded by promising that we "will transmit this city not only, not less, but greater and more beautiful than it was transmitted to us." That line is the ending of the last sentence of the Athenian oath. I used this oath as a fundamental guide in my governance philosophy.

My budget speech was well received. "Nutter and his budget team have decided to confront a crisis that has been decades in the making," the *Inquirer* editorialized approvingly. "The mayor deserves credit for tackling an unsexy—but serious—problem [the wage tax] that past mayors have avoided. The rest of his first budget contains sound priorities [that] . . . should put the city's finances on more sound footing for decades to come." Things seemed pretty good, and revenues were coming in—and the dark cloud of the Great Recession was still a few months in the distance.

When you are mayor, keeping the long view in mind is vital. As a way of communicating priorities to citizens, the budget makes clear to all that you as mayor cannot fulfill all of your campaign promises in the first two weeks or two months in office. Those who try are usually not successful. Instead, good mayoring takes a measured approach, focused on a vision for the future, while delivering high-quality services daily.

I firmly believe that part of our problem with a lot of people in the business of politics is that they think about the world and they make plans in the context of two or four years or, if you're in the Senate, six-year cycles. Life and government really don't work that way. They do not unfold in finite terms but on a continuum. What you really should try to do—what you *must* do—at the inauguration and the first budget address, is establish priorities. What are we trying to get done, what are our commitments, what did we say we were going to do. A mayor can't do them all at the same time, and may not have the money to do them all, and may have to postpone some. And, in that case, how do you communicate to various constituencies who supported you, elected you, worked hard for you, and are committed to you, that you cannot immediately do the thing you committed to do for them, because you're committed to doing something more urgent first? Prioritizing resources and your time are critical components of governing.

⸺

This balancing requires a team, and we had a tremendous and remarkably persistent, steadfast team in office. As mayor, I thought more about how my people would work together, as a team, than their own individual luster or prestige, and I would advise that other new mayors do the same. My own team was so devoted to the idea of public service and getting stuff done that I would sometimes have to encourage them to do press releases or interviews to highlight their remarkable individual accomplishments. When my health commissioner Donald Schwarz was named Local Physician of the Year by the AMA, I asked him if he had done a press release and he replied that no, he hadn't thought of that. The team has to endorse your own vision, and you, as mayor, must ensure that you back them up with support and public acknowledgment.

Putting together a team initially can be a delicate process. After I won the primary, I still had to win the general election, but at the same time I had a pretty good sense that I would probably win in November, so it would have been a waste of time and very unwise to squander the time from May to November. It would also be unfair to city employees who were definitely not going to be asked to stay to withhold that information until December. People have families, and mortgages to pay, and I thought it best in the time between the primary and the general to tell them that they should get their résumés in order.

Conversely, I knew that I would have some vacancies to fill; namely, the previous police commissioner was going to leave, so I started thinking about that position right after the primary. I knew I'd need a social services head, and we had an interim health commissioner. So after the primary we pulled together a discreet transition team to start thinking about candidates for every department, in the hope that we could get to work immediately in my first term. Fortunately, I had been in Philadelphia government for many years and knew most of the current appointees and potential candidates. Or, unfortunately for some people, I had been in government for many years and knew a lot of them. I started quietly asking candidates if they might be interested in joining. Here, it pays to think ambitiously and innovatively, and to cast a wide net.

Don Schwarz, for example, was at the time in a high-six-figure, prestigious position as a pediatric physician at the Children's Hospital of Philadelphia, and nationally and internationally renowned. Everyone told me that he would "never come to government," and never take a job as commissioner. "Can I at least meet with him?" I remember asking one of my team. Don and I talked for two hours on a Sunday, and he accepted the job. I didn't ask him at the time why he did so, but had a chance to ask years later. Don told me that he had heard a speech I'd made on health issues, out on Civic Center Boulevard on the Penn campus, and he said to a friend that day, "If he asks me, I'll come into government." Sometimes you simply have to ask, boldly. I recruited other team members from the financial community, so casting a wide net in different directions is a good thing to try.

A couple of my priorities on the campaign trail were crime and corruption, and my team had powerful leaders on both fronts. Charles Ramsey was heading the police and public safety issues. Ramsey had been the chief of police in Washington, DC, since 1998 before he joined our team. During his time there, crime rates in Washington declined by about 40 percent. I've often referred to Chuck as the smartest hire I made in my administration. Commissioner Ramsey developed the new crime-fighting strategy for Philadelphia, reenergized the morale of the department and the brave men and women who serve in it, collaborated with other departments to realize a 31 percent reduction of homicides during his eight years as commissioner, and is the longest-serving police commissioner of the last thirty-five years. To tackle corruption I brought in two former federal prosecutors, Amy Kurland and Joan Markman, city inspector general and chief integrity officer, respectively, to deal with issues of government integrity and transparency. Both were former federal prosecutors who had worked together at the US Attorney's Office before joining my administration, and had been involved in high-profile anticorruption cases involving the Philadelphia government. Markman was the second chair in the city hall listening device case and Kurland had put a lot of people in jail in her previous life, working for the US Attorney's Office. The chief integrity officer was a brand new position. This was equivalent to the role of an internal compliance officer in the corporate community, and I really emphasized this new position early in my first term. In other words, the integrity officer would be our own internal oversight mechanism on how we made decisions, to ensure transparent and unbiased practices. The creation of this position stemmed directly from the 2003 scandals and the subsequent indictments. By creating a new position I wanted to convey my seriousness in tackling corruption and send an unmistakable message that this behavior was not going to be tolerated. As inspector general, Kurland was relentless in fighting waste, fraud, corruption, and abuse of the public trust, and is the longest-serving inspector general in Philadelphia city government history.

Both Kurland and Markman were fully authorized to do their jobs without regard for anything else going on in the government. They did not take any particular direction from me, and they had the authority to walk into any meeting, anytime and anywhere, to do their jobs. I allocated more money to the inspector general office as well.

We were trying to send a very clear message. Markman's Chief Integrity Office was next door to mine. You had to pass her office to get to my office. That was not because we ran out of office space. It was not because we didn't have anywhere else to put her. The office placement was a direct visual message about change. We're going to do things differently, and corruption would not be tolerated. That's the stance we tried to maintain during our entire eight years in office.

Markman and Kurland were co-workers and friends, so they spent a lot of time together. They did things such as visiting sanitation yards at 5:00 A.M. before the workforce went out. In one famous incident they were literally standing on the back of a sanitation vehicle trying to explain to our workforce that they really could not take tips on the job, and were roundly booed. Their larger project was to create public integrity officers (PIOs) in every department and agency, and the PIOs would work with their department heads and the two top integrity officers across the government. They held workshops, did informational mailings and regular ethics training, and monitored social media sites. Tragically, Joan died after a long battle with breast cancer in January 2015. She left a legacy of having changed the culture of corruption in Philadelphia city government. Together, Kurland and Markman restored meaningful levels of integrity for citizens.

After a few years, we had developed a program where if someone from the public did try to bribe or offer something to a public employee, and the employee turned them in or rebuffed the offer, they would automatically get a signed letter from me thanking them for doing what they did and for being a person of integrity. When we heard that a public servant had firmly rejected bribes or payoffs, I would recognize that good behavior. We created an integrity award program to give real recognition to people who had done a superior job in that area. Ethics, corruption, and similar issues are somewhat unique. Ethics and political integrity are not like filling a pothole, where you fill it up, put the asphalt in, and move on with your life. They're not one and done. Battles of integrity are ongoing and always imperfect. Inevitably, the next ethics culprit thinks they are a little smarter and will violate the rules. This kind of problem, and hence the work to correct it, is chronic and ongoing, and we had a consistent message in that regard.

Some people didn't get the message, and they got locked up. We would highlight some of the celebrated cases so that people understood that we were really paying attention to corruption and serious about it. For example, in July 2010 the *Inquirer* reported on Kelly Kaufmann Layre, an employee in Philadelphia's records department who had charged special clients as little as $5 in cash for traffic and other records that usually cost $25, and pocketed the money herself. This seemingly petty swindle cost the city cumulatively almost $600,000. Kurland got a tip on Layre's activities and investigated the case, and Layre was charged. "This should send a message," Kurland added, "that city employees must uphold the public trust at all times in their official duties."

Indeed, these stories reinforced a clear message. Look at what just happened to your co-worker, who is going to jail. Was it really worth it for $500 or $1,000? To lose your job, lose your pension, and go to jail? Because much of political corruption in cities is, quite simply, stupid. It is usually committed for comically low stakes. Suddenly, political corruption didn't seem like such a good or lucrative idea.

Other core team members and leaders included our chief of staff Clarence Armbrister, a college friend with extensive city and school district experience, who was the first African American male to hold the position. Clay was the leader of our team. He provided strategic direction and handled external communications with City Council and business leaders. Clay was authorized to speak on my behalf at all times. Known as the "air traffic controller" of my life, Denise Dixon is the longest-serving staff member of my political career and my postmayoral life. We have worked together for twenty-two years, and Denise has managed every aspect of my professional and personal appointments, logistics, and family-coordinated events and activities. Everett Gillison was the deputy mayor for public safety, and became the second chief of staff after Clay stepped down. Everett had all of the chief of staff duties, as well as the maintenance of his portfolio as deputy mayor for public safety. Camille Barnett, our first managing director, experienced tragedy the weekend before the inauguration. Camille's husband was killed in a car accident while the family was moving to their home in Philadelphia. His funeral was held in Washington, DC, the day after the inauguration, and many members of the administration attended it. Camille implemented the early stages of our reform measures before and during the Great Recession. My director of communications was Desiree Peterkin-Bell, who joined the term in the fall of 2010, after having worked in three previous mayoral administrations, including those of Michael Bloomberg in New York City and Cory Booker in Newark. In addition to being the director of communications, Desiree later became my city representative—a cabinet-level position. She developed the city communications strategy for us, and oversaw the planning of major city events, including writing the bid for and overseeing our successful application to host the 2016 Democratic National Convention.

Suzanne Beimiller started as a consultant for my administration's Greenworks Philadelphia sustainability plan, and then became my first deputy chief of staff, after Wendell Prichett, who later became provost at the University of Pennsylvania, with Clay and Everett, serving as interim chief of staff between their tenures. Her formidable skills meant that Suzanne was also assigned many special and difficult projects. She was followed as deputy by Tumar Alexander, whom I brought on to the team in my first month because of his unique skills of being able to get almost anything done, talk to and negotiate with virtually anyone, and his reputation as a "go to" guy. You may remember that I mentioned the impact of the sustainability community on the 2007 mayor's race. I committed at the first inauguration to make Philadelphia the #1 green city in America. This effort was led by Mark Alan Hughes, along with Laurie Actman and Katherine Gajewski, who later became chief sustainability officer. Their work produced Greenworks Philadelphia, our sustainability plan. On legislation and other major policy matters, I had my legislative director Julia Chapman, who was my legislative assistant in my council office, now at the helm as the principal liaison between the mayor's office and the City Council. Smart, focused, and thorough on the details, with an unyielding commitment to policy development and the improvement of people's lives, she fought for every component of my administration's policy and legislative agenda. Chapman was highly accomplished, and known for getting results.

My first "special assistant to the mayor" (SAM)—situated at a desk just outside of my office and functioning as a gatekeeper—was Jordan Schwartz, whom I had known and worked with since his teenage years. He'd volunteered in my City Council office when he was in college and helped on the mayoral campaign. He was sharp, funny, perceptive, and always on task—and, as with any skilled special assistant, he was a trustworthy confidant. He set a high standard for his successor as SAM, Luke Butler, who was originally from the United Kingdom. Luke was a great student of US and UK government and public policy, and had a delightful British accent. He was followed as SAM by Lauren Walker, a smart, well-grounded young person in the administration. Lauren was the first woman in this position since anyone could recall, and we worked very well together, always with a lot of laughter and humor. Finally, Jonathan Todd became the SAM after Lauren was recruited to another government position because of her talent. His predecessors formed a "SAM Club" to show him the ropes!

⁓

In this mayor's job you get to do some fun things—and you must do some heart-wrenching things. Within the scope of five weeks during my first months as mayor, I experienced both.

March 31, 2008, was the home opening day of baseball, and the Philadelphia Phillies played at Citizens Bank Park. I've done a lot of things in my life, but throwing the first pitch that day—the 60 feet and 6 inches from the mound to home plate, on opening day before a packed ball park—was one of the scariest, ever.

Philadelphians love to boo elected officials for no particular reason. But I was brand new, and had run on a wave of reform, and everybody was excited, and nice! The Phillies, through Mike Harris, gave me a jersey with my name on the back, number 08, for the year. I practiced for two weeks throwing a ball. I know how to throw, but this is a little different. I went to the ballpark twice to stand on the mound to get a feel for it, because the mound is elevated and I wanted to throw in a straight line. I didn't want to throw it in the dirt, and I didn't want it to go wild. After two weeks of practice, I was nervous as can be when I threw out that first pitch. But I threw a strike—no question about it. Chris Coste caught it, signed the ball, and said it was one of the best first pitches ever—an absolute dead strike.

But this is Philadelphia. What did people notice? Not my perfect strike, but another detail. You can't imagine how much criticism I got— for having my jersey tucked in. No one noticed my strike right down the center. No one noticed the wind up. No one noticed the pitch. They had no idea that I spent two weeks practicing or that I was so nervous. They did notice that I was a guy with his jersey tucked in. I went to Catholic school, where I always kept my shirt tucked in. I was just trying to be neat. Ball players do it! But they're ball players.

My advice is this: If you ever happen to be mayor, and you happen to have the opportunity to throw out the first pitch, never tuck your shirt in.

That opening game was a highlight of my first months, and a fun day. Saturday, May 3, 2008, was not. In fact it might well count as the worst single day in my career as mayor. On that day, I had a break between one event and another and happened to stop by my office in city hall. It's an easy place to get to, park, and jump out. When I arrived at my office I got a call from the police commissioner that a Philadelphia police officer had been shot, and that it was bad. No one had any more details than that. Sergeant Stephen Liczbinski had arrived at the scene of a bank robbery and was met by a person carrying an AK-47. The assailant shot Liczbinski with that AK-47, and his arm was nearly taken off by the blast.

The chief of staff, deputy mayor for public safety, police commissioner, managing director and I, and others, rushed over to the Temple University hospital where Liczbinski was being treated. The scene at the hospital was complete chaos, and this was my first personal experience with a police shooting. There was a room off of the emergency and trauma area with refreshments for family members, which also helped to shelter them from the frantic, heroic efforts to keep their loved one alive.

At some point that day, as we sat and waited in this anteroom, the doctor came in and explained that Sergeant Liczbinski's injuries were simply too severe and he had not survived. I saw firsthand the profound pain, experienced not only by the family but also the police officers when this happens. Men and women—fellow officers—were crying in the hallways, and outside of the hospital. Liczbinski had three children, Matt, Stephen, and Amber.

As mayor, there is nothing, absolutely nothing, that can prepare you for this moment. There's no conversation, there's no training, there's nothing you can read about that helps you to grapple with the gravity and severity of losing one of your officers in the line of duty. I didn't know Sergeant Liczbinski personally, but it was still so painful. This was one of my cops, one of our folks. I felt responsible and I had to fight within myself not to have real emotions on display. Because I had a responsibility—to the other officers, the family, and Philadelphians.

My job at that moment was to hug his wife and those children, who no longer had a father, and to console and support. People have so many conversations today about the police and the public, police misconduct and violence, and crime and justice. But I had an officer dead, and my world had just narrowed down to that one simple and tragic fact. I wasn't thinking about the calendar or other commitments or abstract debates concerning crime. I had a singular, laser focus on what I could possibly do to be supportive and empathetic.

I spoke to the media and called the sergeant's death a "tragedy for the city of Philadelphia." Eventually I commented, "that officer was assassinated on the streets of Philadelphia. People need to look in their hearts and minds about what happened. That's the kind of firepower our officers are up against"—guns that penetrate vehicles and leave them without protection. We need to ban assault weapons. We need to ban the high-capacity clips and magazines. We need serious background information, and a system upgrade. There is no reason for a civilian to have an automatic weapon. All eyes at the federal level are on the war on terror. The fact is, al Qaeda wouldn't have lasted a day in parts of Philadelphia. I had gangsters with .45s that would have run them out of town. I'm a big supporter of the Second Amendment. But I think I have a First Amendment right not to be shot.

The next task was to work with those officers and to prepare for what needed to be done next. Everyone will look to the mayor, the minute that you walk out of that hospital door. Having control of yourself is the most important thing, and having a level of responsibility. One of the suspects in the crime was dead, one was in custody, and the other one was on the loose. Catching the third suspect was the first priority. There was a manhunt, in which we coordinated with federal agencies and state agencies, to find this one individual.

In the midst of all this, on Monday, two days after the sergeant's death, a few officers thought that they might have a car with suspects in it, and they were captured on helicopter video dragging people out of the car and beating them. Now we had a new controversy. First, an officer killed and, next, officers beating up people who may or may not have been guilty of anything.

At this moment I had to run through the raindrops and not get wet. The city and officers were devastated by the shooting, and I had to be sympathetic to that, but also rebut and deflect a narrative that the police were out of control and raging on the streets because of what had happened Saturday. I had to convey firmly that I stand with the police, but that I can't stand with this kind of behavior.

Now, the sergeant's funeral was planned for Friday. In any police or paramilitary organization, any uniformed service, there are a lot of traditions. With ours, one of them is that we are driven to find and capture that person before the officer's funeral. The second is that when that person is captured, they will be handcuffed with the handcuffs of the deceased officer. That is our policy; that is our tradition; that is what we do as a sign of respect to someone who loses his or her life in the line of duty.

I enlisted the public's help. I mentioned at a press conference that there was a significant reward out on the street for the capture of this individual. At that press conference, over $100,000 had been raised already for information leading to the capture and conviction of this person, from city money, the Fraternal Order of Police, and other citizens. Using a variety of technologies, informants, and other techniques, Eric Floyd was captured on Thursday night in a vacant house out in southwest Philadelphia. And he was handcuffed by Sergeant Liczbinski's handcuffs. And the sergeant's funeral then took place that Friday.

There was a largely unspoken understanding among my team that after the funeral, we needed to deal with the Monday situation and the possible police misconduct in a much more direct fashion. We ended up in my office with the video of the incident, and we slowed it down as much as we could so that we could truly understand what each officer had done, and who was just standing there. We had to be tremendously fact-specific about each officer and their role in the incident in order to mete out appropriate discipline.

We went from the death on Saturday, to Monday's incident, to the capture of the last suspect, to the funeral, to the disposition of the

Monday events, in one tragic and complicated week. We learned something about our team through this, and about the importance of being fair and just to all sides.

In 2008, we lost four Philadelphia police officers killed in the line of duty, the most of any major city in the country that year. Tragically, Sergeant Liczbinski's death was the beginning of these tragic police officer deaths, not the end.

On February 13, 2009, John Pawlowski became the fifth Philadelphia police officer killed in the line of duty in the first fourteen months of my administration, and the first in the year 2009. He was a veteran officer; his wife was pregnant at the time and, unfortunately, he never lived to see his son, whose name is John.

When events like this happen, being mayor is about leadership, and it's about the inner strength of your team. And when we experienced challenge and controversy or tragedy, or even the many good things that happened in Philadelphia, it was never just about myself as the mayor. It was always about a team. It's about a group of individuals demonstrating leadership and also speaking to the public. The press conferences always took place right outside of the hospital after we had learned inside, all of us together, that an officer did not survive his or her wounds.

We lost, in our time, a total of eight officers, four firefighters, a gas company worker, and a fleet management employee during our eight years in office. As mayor, these are the most serious incidents—losing personnel, losing our brave men and women in blue, are some of the greatest challenges that mayors face all across the country. In Pittsburgh, in my time, three officers were killed in one incident. I went out to Pittsburgh to support the relatively new, young mayor there. It was his first experience with this tragedy, and I went out to help him through it.

MAYOR

~

Being mayor is not all budget spreadsheets. There's a profound human component to this work. I would describe being mayor as a roller-coaster of emotion. And on any given day, a lot of good things can happen that you're not anticipating, and a lot of bad things. Your job and responsibility is to keep a fairly even keel to provide leadership and support, encouragement, and uplift, while also trying to maintain some sanity for yourself. Because there will be human tragedies in any mayoral term, and in any city—and Philadelphia has had its share of them.

CHAPTER 8

—

The Last Call You Ever Want to Get

In late July 2008, I got a phone call from the chief of staff and the finance director, Rob Dubow. I'd known Rob from his previous service in the Rendell administration, and had hired him two days after the general election in November, to send a message to the business and financial community that my administration would make financial integrity a hallmark. Clay and Rob said that they needed to meet with me, and that it was important. Being in my first year and not knowing all of the things that I needed to know, I didn't realize that the last call you ever want to get is the chief of staff and the finance director saying they want to talk to you and it's important. If you ever find yourself in that position, run. Nothing good can come from that conversation. They are not coming to tell you that they found a billion dollars in the sofa.

We had passed the first budget with flying colors and made investments, but they had discovered something unusual in our tax collections. They weren't exactly sure what it was, but there was some kind of problem. In perfect hindsight, there was one early, leading indicator of the financial meltdown of the Great Recession even before this one: we noticed during my first year that the real estate transfer tax had dropped precipitously, but without even the wisp of a memo or a clue to the imminent disaster, we thought the transfer tax decline was just an anomaly. For now, we decided to monitor the unusual tax collection situation and figure out what was going on, and my staff agreed to update me in a couple of weeks. Which they did, in August.

"We actually have a serious problem," they told me. "There's something really bad going on. We're starting to run out of cash. We don't understand what's going on in the economy, our tax revenues have taken a sudden turn downward where in the spring they were going up, and we need to start making plans for reduction in service." We were talking about the prospect of the city actually running out of cash at some point.

On Thursday, September 11, 2008, I announced to the public that there were signs of serious fiscal distress. "The subprime mortgage debacle," I began, "is working its way through the economy, leaving wreckage in its wake." The economic problems had "now come to the front-door step of Philadelphia." I described that the city was facing at least a $450 million five-year plan deficit, but I knew that number would certainly grow. In this early speech, my team and I were already devising a more specific plan to handle this blindsiding debacle, but I wanted to reassure the city that we'd have one in place by the end of October. The first order of business, I said, "is what we're doing today. This is an open, transparent government," and we were letting Philadelphians know honestly what was going on. As for the next steps, "everything, everything is on the table, including scheduled tax cuts." It seemed important to comment on the process, and to warn citizens against taking seriously the "regular buzz" sure to emanate from the rumor mill. No cut or decision is true or official, I underscored, until my office announces it.

From the end of May, when the budget passed with flying colors, to September, a mere four months later, we were announcing a massive five-year plan deficit, out of nowhere. People were starting to wonder about our capacity to lead and manage money. They assumed that we were incompetent and stupid, or that we simply couldn't count. That was the view on September 11. That weekend, Lehman Brothers crashed and burned. And every single day the following week, some bank, some larger organization, crashed and was in financial straits if not a death spiral. The economy was in a free fall. As it turned out, Philadelphia just happened to be one of the first major cities in the country to react publicly to a financial catastrophe that reverberated globally and far beyond our particular city. Many more cities would follow. We were now in a full-blown recession.

In October, I updated citizens that we were facing what was now a $650 to $850 million five-year budget gap—and we knew that even *that* number would grow. We announced the measures we were going to take, but they were still somewhat general. In outline, they included cutting back on salaries, cutting back on services, and eliminating services altogether. I described that nonunion city employees would forego promised $1,100 bonuses, which would yield about $5 million in savings, and we would ask for a voluntary 5 percent reduction in budgets for elected officials. I promised more detail by the end of the month. When asked if this was the worst case scenario, I answered, "I would truly hesitate to say that we're looking at a worst case scenario, as each day seems to redefine that term."

While we were contending with a budget crisis, we also hosted presidential candidate Barack Obama to do four events on one day. The campaign rejected this number initially and explained that the most they ever did was two events on a day. We argued about that for a week, and prevailed. And so they gave us Senator Obama, who won Philadelphia, but did not win Pennsylvania, in the primary. He did four stops in different locations all across the city: 8 A.M. in North Philadelphia at Progress Plaza; later on in the morning at the Mayfair Diner; early in the afternoon up in Germantown; and the final stop was at Fifty-Second and Locust in West Philadelphia. There were forty thousand people out on Fifty-Second Street that day in October 2008.

President Obama is not only a historic president but also a great person to talk with—kind, inspirational, and passionate. He and First Lady Michelle Obama were tremendously kind and generous with their ideas, proposals, and collaborative efforts during the seven years of my mayoral service, which overlapped with his presidency. It was the thrill of my public service career to have served concomitantly with President Obama.

Looking back on it, I've come to refer to this as The Week. It's a snapshot of just how many different things can happen in the course of one single week as mayor of a large American city. The Phillies won the World Series on October 29, 2008. It's customary to have a celebratory parade within two days of the win; otherwise players scatter and you have no parade. That parade was on Friday, October 31, and two million people were there. Then election day was Tuesday, November 4. And two days later, on Thursday, November 6, I announced that the City of Philadelphia had in excess of a $1.4 billion five-year plan deficit. The first black guy in America becomes president—and I announce a $1.4 billion budget deficit. Way to go, Nutter!

To prepare the city for the budget disaster, we decided that I would hold eight public forums—which was probably not one of my best ideas in those first months but, at the same time, it was absolutely the right thing to do. You have to face the music as mayor: you can't hide, and if you expect to lead then you have to listen to the people. You can't cancel or skirt that process because it's going to be unpleasant. I also wanted to at least try to be heard, and to get my own message across. The first forum was three hours of the community screaming at us, mostly along the lines of we can't do the job, we're incompetent and we should resign, with a couple of questions tossed in here and there. After the first one I asked one of my staff, "Seven more of these? Whose idea was this?" only to be reminded, of course, that it was my idea. I would tell any mayor to grit their teeth if necessary but to do things like this: keeping the lines of communication open and straightforward in times of budget or other crises is irreplaceable, and lays the groundwork for trust, years down the road.

—

In the fall of 2008 my team and I did indulge in some gallows humor. We started thinking that perhaps there should be a recount of the election results? And perhaps we didn't really win? But it's a testament to my team of dedicated public servants that we all stuck together through the crisis, for which no life circumstances or career experiences could adequately prepare us.

If my October Great Recession speech was more about updating and observing the financial wreckage, along with some strategies to try to staunch the deficit, then my November 6, 2008, speech outlined more serious and concrete plans. This was a live television speech to explain the circumstances and some preliminary plans to the citizens. "The economic storm has arrived," I began, and has not spared the public sector. Most major cities were facing what I characterized, mildly, as "huge" budget gaps. They were "slamming on the brakes of spending," laying off employees, abolishing unfilled positions, and reducing services. Although we had started the fiscal year with a $119 million surplus, I told the public that we would need to take "bold action" now in a midyear revision of epic proportions, and would have to search beyond quick, one-time changes to do so. My team rejected across-the-board cuts as inherently unfair, and in my November blueprint I elaborated that we would measure every decision and program against our core values, with the goals of preserving programs that work, adjusting programs to actual needs, finding real and expedient efficiencies, collecting money owed to the city, rebalancing fees, and sharing the burden of sacrifice.

Then, the tough decision making began. This budget crisis set the tone, to some extent, for the next few years. Raising taxes and cutting services is not a particularly great combination. But we made a commitment that we were going to stabilize the government and be prepared for the recovery whenever that would happen; but, of course, we had no idea when the recovery would actually happen.

My team and I had a few options—all grim, none good. Nationally, by two years into the Great Recession, some seven hundred thousand public employees had lost their jobs. For Philadelphia, massive layoffs were always one option, and in some cities this did occur. I don't make any criticism of other places, since every city is different and its circumstances unique. I'm sure that there are things we did during the recession that other cities vowed not to do. But, for Philadelphia, we were very determined and in agreement that widespread layoffs were not the best approach. The idea that thousands of people would lose their jobs through no fault of their own but because of an economic cataclysm that they had had no role in creating was unacceptable to me.

Aside from these moral objections, we reasoned that if you decimate the internal, basic operations of your government and your agencies, when it is time to recover, you have nothing to recover with. That first year we also had negotiated one-year contracts with all of our unions, which was completely against convention. We didn't know a recession was coming. We just wanted one-year contracts because we were brand new and didn't know all of the things that we might want to do. That subsequently turned out to be a really great decision for many different reasons. If we had made the traditional three- or four-year contract agreements with our union workforce, there is no way in the world that we would have been able to pay for those contracts, given our financial situation. That would have led to massive layoffs of our workforce, which I didn't want to do in the first place. Having those one-year contracts in place put us in a situation of being able to negotiate just a year later, but now with the information that we were in a full-blown, worldwide economic recession.

Police and fire go through an arbitration process. My city solicitor, Shelley R. Smith, dealt with contract negotiations among dozens of other responsibilities as the lawyer for the city of Philadelphia. She oversaw an office of lawyers that would be comparable to one of the largest private law firms in the city. The nonuniformed unions go through a collective bargaining process (the latter is a process of negotiation between employers and employees, while the former is an agreement to allow a third party to resolve disputes and formulate a binding agreement). The police ended up with a contract. The arbitrator gave us a contract that had some of the reforms that we wanted, and raises for the police, so they were the first to have a multiyear contract. During all of my years as mayor, the police were always operating under a full contract. As a union leader, John McNesby was always the most honest and straightforward.

Fire was a different story. We had a contract with the fire department that we couldn't afford, and there was constant litigation. We could never reach agreement with our two AFSCME unions, as much as we wanted to. They ended up not having a contract for over six years because we could not reach agreement.

Virtually no one in the city got laid off, and they still had jobs, but they had no pay increase, and no step or longevity increases. Still, at least everyone was working, and they never went on strike. I think they understood that the public would never put up with that kind of action during a financial crisis, when we were simultaneously raising people's taxes almost every year and cutting their services. And many citizens not working for the government had lost their jobs, or health care, or even their homes. I did everything I could to make sure that never happened to my public employees, but there were some sacrifices to be made.

As part of our plan I cut my own pay, and that of everyone in the nonunion workforce in the executive branch, down to those making $50,000, with five mandatory unpaid furlough days for two years. I forgot to mention this to my wife. She was not amused to hear that on the news, given our household budget, but understood.

On November 6, I also announced that we would be reducing police overtime and leaving 200 positions vacant. We reduced overtime in the fire department as well and decommissioned 5 engine companies and 2 ladder companies. We had proposed to close 11 libraries (worst idea ever!), close 62 of 73 outdoor pools for the summer months, end residential street cleaning services, and cut back on resurfacing money.

I ended with a call for volunteers to help, for shared sacrifice, and with reassurances that Philadelphia was a "livable, walkable, affordable city," and we would "get through this turbulence. On the other side of this crisis, we'll be a stronger, more efficient government."

I believed that, too. But there were harder times to come. There came a point when we actually made a public announcement that we would stop payments to all city vendors—all the people who contract with the city to provide any number of services, from copying machines and faxes to transportation. This amounted to a massive cash conservation project. We were concerned that we would literally run out of cash, so we paid salaries, debt service, and emergencies, only. And for weeks, no city vendors got paid. But not one of them stopped providing service, and not one sued us. Not a one. I think this was indicative of just how bad things were, and our vendors' awareness of that, and of how terrible they would look after the recession if they had simply stopped servicing the city. We also reassured them that we were going to pay them, eventually. Not one vendor lost money through this arrangement, ultimately, but there is cash and then there is cash flow: they might have had serious cash flow problems that could not really be solved by even the most sincere promises of future payment. Vendors also continued to provide services because we constantly communicated our circumstance and situation, and I think we had developed a level of trust and honesty such that companies knew when things got better, they would participate on the other side.

In my November speech I said that this was a shared sacrifice and that everyone had to put something on the table. *Something.* But we wanted to keep our people working. We had to keep the government working, operating, and moving forward.

It wasn't until almost two and a half years later, in the summer and fall of 2011 going into 2012, that the financial crisis finally crested and leveled off, as I would describe it. We came to what I referred to as a new normal, but at least a stable normal.

To navigate the recession, my team and I drew on some of the lessons learned from the early 1990s, when Philadelphia faced some similar, although different, financial challenges. We borrowed some strategies from that crisis that helped us manage the one in 2008. Chief among them, communication and honesty. From the start, we chose honesty with Philadelphians. In public service, mayoring, and politics generally, this vital kind of communication is often undervalued and overlooked. Governance really is about the communication of big ideas and vision and, simultaneously, communication about the everyday details of urban life. Communication and its degree of candor shapes how citizens will hear and respond to the next crisis, or to the next announcement, and it becomes in this way a cumulative process of trust building. To *not* communicate, even or especially in the grips of serious crises, is to take a huge risk.

The challenge in 2008, of course, was to be honest—yet not so honest that I would damage the very entity I was trying to save. I couldn't go to the podium and say, "Things are so dire and terrible that I could barely get out of bed this morning," or "Things are hopeless and I suggest that you all move," although on any given day in the nadir of this crisis, either statement might have felt emotionally true to me. As a mayor, communication is a delicate balancing act of honesty and hope—but realistic hope. I always wanted to end the day on some level of an upbeat feeling. Philadelphians needed to believe that there was a future, a better day coming, and that we were building and preparing for it, years down the road, even in the midst of the crisis.

I rarely if ever allow myself to dream of what it would have been like that first term, and what we could have done, if we actually had money rather than deficits. For example, even though we didn't have all the dollars that we thought we were going to have, even though we didn't have all the resources that we needed, in that first year, even though I didn't hire the four hundred more police officers that I wanted because we ended up pushing back and eliminating two new classes of officers to save money, in our first year, we still had a 15 percent reduction in homicides in Philadelphia. Even though we cut the police department's overtime budget in the second budget, we had an 8 percent reduction in homicides in Philadelphia that second year.

This reduction in homicides happened despite the budget problems, and without any changes in gun laws at the time. And as a matter of fact, working with the City Council at that time we put forward some gun safety legislation earlier in my tenure as mayor, probably in the first two months of my tenure. On my hundredth day in office as mayor, I was sued by the NRA, which for me was one of the proudest moments of my entire political career.

The reduction in homicides had to do with a couple of factors. We had a brand new police commissioner, who put forward a new strategic plan to fight crime. We put more officers on foot patrol even though we did not increase the overall numbers of officers because we couldn't for financial reasons. In other words, we deployed the assets we had differently.

We engaged some new strategy, technology, and analysis. As mentioned previously, we'd discovered that 65 percent of the homicides in the city were occurring in only nine of the twenty-three police districts, and so we also had a redeployment of officers, obviously putting more officers where the activity was taking place, and more officers on foot patrol. Even without adding new personnel, we could more strategically redeploy the personnel we had.

We stimulated more engagement with citizens in terms of community policing. Finally, we tried to send a strong message that we were not going to tolerate this kind of nonsense without a significant response. We protected people's civil rights, but we were being very serious with the criminal element. We were much more aggressive in going after illegal guns on the street, and I think that combination of things certainly helped a great deal. I think the officers were also reenergized by a new administration and a new police commissioner—they had tremendous respect for Commissioner Ramsey. A serious reduction in a city's homicide rate comes from a variety of factors. There's never any one explanation for the numbers going down or up.

⁓

This was just the first year. But it gives you a sense of what the rest of the years were like. The pain, the anxiety, the fights, and the battles. Through it all, you still have to govern. You still have to "mayor," as a verb. It really is an action, more than an office or a person. By mayoring I mean that you have to pick up the trash, fill potholes, keep the water running and the lights on, deal with storms, hurricanes, celebrations, and, in my case, as you'll see, even an earthquake. There are so many different things that happen and that must function in the daily life of a city: Good, bad, everything in between. That's what mayoring is.

—

CHAPTER 9

Getting to the Brink of Plan C

In the summer and fall of 2009 we were feeling anxious, tense, and extremely worried about the city's finances. People talk about their preferred and first plan in life as Plan A, and their less preferred, fallback one as Plan B. Of course, the ideal and true Plan A would have been to have no Great Recession at all, and a $119 million surplus in place. Since that wasn't our reality, Plan A was the steps we had already taken back in the fall of 2008 to solve the first $450 million deficit. Plan B was the austere and painful salary cuts and suspension of payments to city vendors that we took to solve the next $1.4 billion five-year deficit problem. So, we had breezed past Plan A, and we had exhausted Plan B. We were now at Plan C. And it was a brutal plan, falling somewhere beyond cataclysmic and apocalyptic for Philadelphia. We would have to lay off over 3,000 public employees, including 900 police officers and nearly 300 firefighters. Every other agency in the city government would take pretty significant personnel cuts, as well. That's how bad things were.

We had one plausible option left. We were going to have to increase the sales tax in Philadelphia, which at the time was seven cents. We needed an increase to eight cents, but, as a city, we don't have the authority to raise the sales tax on our own. We also needed the state to pass legislation to allow us to delay a couple of payments into the city's pension fund, which we planned to pay back in full a couple of years later. We didn't have the authority to do this either. Without state legislation to authorize these two critical steps, I have no doubt but that some Philadelphians could have died from lack of basic services, from police to fire, to keep them safe.

We had been talking with the state general assembly for months. We'd actually already passed the budget, and had a press conference about it. The budget has to be passed by the end of May in Philadelphia. We were starting to run out of money. We held a press conference at the Second and Fifteenth Districts police headquarters on August 3, 2009, for one basic reason. By holding the press conference at the police station, we wanted to dramatize the severity of the situation.

This kind of press conference is the ultimate in public communication, and as mayor I had press secretaries and communications staff who understood the nuances of this kind of event. This press conference was a moment for them to shine. I had recruited Doug Oliver as my first press secretary, and he was the first African American man to hold that position. Doug was highly respected for his honesty with the press, and he understood strategic communications in the short and long run. After Doug left the position, the also highly respected veteran newsman Mark McDonald, who had covered the City Council for a long time, took over. Mark was thorough and a stickler for detail, which is one reason why he initially became my speech writer. He could translate my thoughts and voice into various messages, and was a powerful, dynamic force, working later with Director of Communications Desiree Peterkin-Bell when she joined the team in the fall of 2010.

The stakes couldn't be higher for Philadelphia at this particular press conference. With all of those officers lined up—and there were some firefighters and other public employees there as well—we were trying to convey the severity of the budget emergency, not only to the citizens, but also frankly to our larger viewing audience in Harrisburg, because every one of these clips from press conferences were now circulating through social media, YouTube, as well as television. So this budget press conference was being held not just for the citizens of Philadelphia but really for legislators in the surrounding suburbs who also have constituents who work in the City of Philadelphia—or, conversely, our constituents work in their towns, townships, and municipalities. This was a message to the state general assembly.

Technically, we were not asking the state legislators to raise taxes themselves, but only to authorize the city to do so. But in the political world, "authorization to raise taxes" and "raising taxes" is a distinction without a difference, a nuance that would be lost on upstate voters. Several state legislators feared that they'd have an opponent in the future who would attack them by alleging that they had raised taxes and, more contentiously, raised taxes to support Philadelphia. Lost in all the rhetoric, of course, was the fact that the taxes were being paid primarily by Philadelphians to save Philadelphia!

We were getting assailed not only by legislators but also by the public, and both groups found it hard to believe that our Plan C was anything more than political theater. Ironically, precisely because this option was so devastating and horrible, it was getting dismissed as hyperbole or an idle threat. So this press conference was high stakes for me and for the city. I had to speak to all of these apprehensive audiences and convey that this plan was both real and imminent. We gave a date sometime in September, on a Friday, on which we were going to have to send out the three thousand lay-off notices. And on Thursday, the day before that fateful date, at about 4:30 in the afternoon, in what was pretty much the eleventh-and-a-half hour, the general assembly of Pennsylvania finally passed the legislation that we needed. We had benefited from solid support from all city unions, which helped greatly, and we had tried to communicate honestly with legislators and the public. The legislation was immediately rushed over to the governor, who then signed it, and we made a big public announcement that Plan C, mercifully, had been averted. I was almost in tears as I made that announcement. We had saved the city of Philadelphia from a devastating outcome. I could not have been more proud of my entire team for their efforts in this success.

The three thousand lay-off notices were taken up to the Fire Academy and burned. I wasn't there personally to see this, but some of my staff were. To this day, no one knows whether they were personally on that lay-off list. We didn't want that information to leak out, as, of course, it would have had a pretty devastating impact on the morale of our public employees. But our employees, and everyone else, understood in the course of this process just how dire things had gotten in Philadelphia. Our public employees performed admirably under enormous financial and emotional pressure. They showed themselves to be model public servants.

⁓

The positive dividends of our decision making during the 2008/2009 financial and economic crisis were largely deferred, which is true of many mayoral decisions. Much of the energy and dynamism that's happening in Philadelphia today—its best bond rating in thirty years and its booming real estate investments—are the fruits of decisions and choices seeded years earlier during the abyss of the Great Recession.

Because of the measures we took, coming out of the recession we were one of the only big cities in America to have our bond rating upgraded, and in 2017 we have an A rating from all three agencies for the first time since the 1970s. Recession decisions set the stage of the "hot" city that Philly is today.

One of the great tragedies of politics today is its short-sightedness. As mayor, or as any elected public servant, it's good to come to grips with the fact that many of the things that you want to achieve—good things—will go unnoticed. Or, you won't get credit for them. Or, many will complain about them. Perhaps twenty years down the road your contribution will be acknowledged, and you'll be thanked. But if you're not willing to make that level of commitment and to personally sacrifice your own ego and any narcissism for the sake of deferred and often uncredited achievements and successes, then you should avoid public service and electoral politics. If you have a deep-seated need to be loved and admired every day, you shouldn't be in politics. You should go work at a pet shop. My motto was to manage for the present and prepare for the future.

As mayor, you don't pick your moments; the moments pick you. I would not have chosen to grapple with an economic meltdown as mayor, but I think I was in the right place at the right time, and if I was put here on this earth to do something, then maybe the management of this crisis was it.

As for lessons learned, first, try to pick a good time to run for office! Barring this prescience of pending disaster, it's important to remember your core values, and everything else can—and probably *will*—get negotiated. My core values for Philadelphia were distilled in the litmus test for any decision or action: will this make the city safer, smarter, more sustainable, and its neighborhoods and people healthier? As mayor you need to believe in something, care about something, and understand that your decisions will affect other people's lives, not only in the here and now, but years down the road. If not, then you'll be cavalier in your decision making or you'll follow the opinion of the last person you happened to talk to, because you lack your own core beliefs by which to navigate. Almost everything else can be negotiated, so long as it doesn't violate your fundamental personal principles.

For example, I had, literally, led a march to force a reduction in taxes while on the City Council in 2002. Subsequently, when I was mayor, from 2008 to 2010 during the recession, I raised taxes. It was a terrible conflict for me and it violated every economic, philosophical, and business belief that I had—but it was not a core personal value not to raise taxes, ever, and I was committed to paying our public employees, delivering city services, and not running out of cash.

You don't always, or even frequently, get to do what you *want* to do, but you can always do the things that you *have* to do well. You can do them competently, ethically, and in accordance with your core values.

~

CHAPTER 10

We're Not Running a Big Babysitting Service. We're Running a Big Government

Whatever our priorities and ongoing concerns about the global recession might have been, mayoring always throws out prosaic emergencies that need to be dealt with in the here-and-now and that preempt long-term worries and priorities. I don't think any other political office combines the attention to microlevel details—garbage dumpsters and potholes—with the macrolevel picture of, say, a global economic crisis, quite like the office of mayor. These prosaic emergencies are the "known unknowns" of any given year in an administration, and a common one is snow or dangerous weather.

It's arguably the case that mayors in large American cities get judged by their snow removal prowess as much as any other issue. It's one of the most tangible examples of competency and efficiency, or their opposites.

In December 2010, a significant snowstorm was on the way. We ended up with 23.8 inches of snow. At my initial press conference about the storm I told Philadelphians that this would be a snow emergency and we would do whatever it takes to clear the streets, "and you know what that means—parking. Any cars on snow emergency routes will be relocated." We like to talk about "relocating" vehicles, not "towing" them. In my later years, just to make sure the press was paying attention as well as the public, when we declared these kinds of events I would usually announce, "Your car will be relocated and then crushed." We found that that announcement helped to ensure about a 95 percent response rate by our citizens. I just wanted to make sure that people were paying attention!

This storm was going to coincide with a scheduled Philadelphia Eagles game against the Minnesota Vikings, which is of intense interest to many Philadelphians, including myself. I'm a big Eagles fan. As a mayor I had to be concerned about this, too. We were anticipating a pretty big storm, and the question was whether I was going to cancel the Eagles football game. The mayor actually has nothing to do with whether a football, basketball, baseball, hockey, soccer, or any other game gets canceled. That's an NFL or another league's decision. What we can do is provide the information that we think a fairly large storm is coming. The storm was going to hit that weekend, and there was no way in the world that we were going to be able to get the streets cleared and provide an environment where fans would be able to get to the game safely. So we had a press conference to share information about the weather, and our discussions with the Eagles, but it was not our call as to whether the game was played.

As it turns out the NFL heeded our advice and that game was canceled, and we did have a pretty big snowstorm. Actually, it was the third largest snowfall in recorded history in the city of Philadelphia. The game was rescheduled to the following Thursday, but unfortunately the Eagles lost that game 24 to 14, which had nothing to do with us, nor were we the agents who rescheduled the game. But, then again, the buck stops at the mayor's desk.

⁓

Public safety is always a challenge in our city. After we saw a 15 percent and 8 percent reduction in homicides in our first and second years, respectively, things plateaued in the next two years.

The reasons for this plateau are not entirely clear, and that ambiguity is typical for crime rates in most major US cities. We had made progress and reached a certain point, but since we had a fiscal crisis, we weren't able to hire as many officers or provide as much overtime hours as we would have liked ideally. Even so, and even if we had all the money for extra law enforcement support, homicide rates do tend to ebb and flow. Some of the underlying factors are beyond a mayor's complete control. In my first term, Philadelphia had already moved past the "drive-by" gang shooting phase of the drug wars, and most of the homicides were direct person-to-person, between people who knew each other and had personal conflicts over money, domestic issues, and things of that nature. My administration wanted to make pushing through the barrier of fewer than 300 homicides a year as our goal, but we couldn't hit that mark in our first years. We did come close, with 302 and 306 in the next two years, and, eventually, we saw a significant drop in the last three years of my eight years in office, and fell well below 300.

While some of the underlying issues of homicide are beyond a mayor's influence, other policies and decisions absolutely made a difference in getting below 300 homicides. We increased outdoor video surveillance cameras and text hotlines; we developed a closer relationship with community leaders and prioritized community policing; we placed a heavy emphasis on foot patrol; and in the later years we focused intensively on gangs and their interrelationships, especially through their use of social media.

Our homicide and shooting clearance rates went up, and that in turn built momentum. This is a crucial but almost always overlooked element in the public safety puzzle. As mayor, if you can get on a downward trajectory, most of the time, that trajectory will keep going and improve. You may have a blip or spike in one year, but your overall momentum and direction will be positive.

It's worth any and all effort, because you cannot have a great city, quite simply, if people don't feel safe. Tall buildings will get built and business conferences will be hosted, but the heart and soul of a city really is that sense of safety.

The triangulated relationship among the public, the police force, and the mayor's office can be a challenging one. When I was in office I felt that citizens wanted me to have one unequivocal and unconditional position on the police: I was either with them or against them. That is not feasible, prudent, or true. I tried to let police officers know in many ways that when they did their jobs correctly, I had their backs, 100 percent, and when they did not, they'd have a problem.

～

In 2011, we were also facing some new public safety challenges. The idea of flash mobs had emerged. Groups of teens would alert each other by smartphone and social media to gather spontaneously at a particular time and place in the city to perform some fun action, or some mischief, as a group. In some cases this meant people breaking out into song or pillow fights, and harmless antics of that nature. Unfortunately, we had some other, more serious challenges with young people in flash mobs. There was a particularly disturbing incident involving some young people in August 2011. A magazine editor who was walking with a friend to another friend's house, just a few blocks from her home, was confronted by a yelling group of teenagers—one as young as eleven—who grabbed her bag, punched her in the face, and knocked her to the ground. Her leg was so severely broken that her knee had to be held together by screws.

After this incident, I made a speech at the Mt. Carmel Baptist Church where I'm a member, which attracted a fair amount of attention and is in my opinion one of the best speeches I ever made as mayor. I would characterize this speech as a little bit of carrot and a whole lot more stick. I was proposing new programs and services but also taking a pretty aggressive posture toward our young people, and their parents.

I warned the congregation that my words would not be "PC." As for the flash mobs specifically, I said forcefully and unmistakably: "This nonsense must stop. It must stop. If you want to act like a butthead, your butt is going to get locked up. And if you want to act like an idiot, move. Move out of this city. We don't want you here anymore."

Then I turned to the parents. I told them bluntly, "Get your act together." Raise your own kids. Know where they are. I had a particular message for the fathers in the black community: "You're not a father just because you have a kid or two or three. That doesn't make you a father," I said. "A father is a person who's around to participate in a child's life. He's a teacher. Helps to guide and shape and mold that young person, someone for that young person to talk to, to share with—their ups and their downs, their fears, and their concerns." If you're not doing that, "you're what the girls call out in the street, 'That's my baby's daddy. That's my baby's daddy.' Don't be that."

I didn't hold back. "We have too many men making too many babies that they don't want to take care of, and then we end up dealing with your children. We're not running a big babysitting service. We're running a big government and a great city. Take care of your children—all of 'em."

Since I was in church I concluded in a religious vein: "The Immaculate Conception of our Lord Jesus Christ took place a long time ago," I said, "and it didn't happen here in Philadelphia. So every one of these kids has two parents who were around and participating at the time. They need to be around now. Ain't no Immaculate Conception happening up in here. Parents, you need to step up before we have to step to you."

The language in this speech is pretty significant, although I was in church, so I refrained from cursing. But it was pretty significant nonetheless. This speech preceded a press conference the next day where we were going to make announcements about expanded recreation programs and activities, but also to announce a citywide curfew targeted by age. We wanted parents to better understand that they are responsible for their children and that these are their children.

In city government we can be helpful, but we can't literally raise your kids. You have to step up as well. Sometimes as mayor you wear multiple hats. I was the elected mayor, but I was also, and still am, a parent. And here, in trying to have this discussion with our city's parents, I was perhaps more in my parent role and responsibility than my mayor's role. One of the local anchors introduced the story that evening on the news by saying, "Mayor Nutter goes off."

The next day I was much calmer. We had the press conference outside city hall with a large group of people with us from the Streets Department, the NAACP, the clergy, and many others. We also had people from what I sometimes referred to as the "fun departments," Parks, Recreation, and Libraries. Michael DeBerardinis oversaw these areas, and developed large projects, leveraging public and private funding sources, at recreation facilities and in the park system. "We need to remember," I said at this press conference, "that most of the young people are doing the right thing. They do not participate in random attacks on our citizens and visitors. Unfortunately there is a tiny minority of reckless fools who are engaged in violent acts across the city. They seem not to grasp the full consequences of their actions."

As mayor I also delivered a message to young people that they needed to take responsibility. "If you walk into somebody's office," I said, "with your hair uncombed and a pick in the back, and your shoes untied, and your pants half down, tattoos up and down your arms and on your neck, and you wonder why somebody won't hire you? They don't hire you 'cause you look like you're crazy!"

We announced that we were investing more money in summer programs and recreation programs, and expanding hours of operation at our recreation centers. We were continuing to invest in library services but also some new activities, especially on the weekends, for young people, in addition to the curfew announcement. That press conference was outside on the northwestern corner of city hall—and, as with most other occasions, I was with a variety of groups and organizations. But I was the person making various announcements and trying to set standards of individual conduct and responsibilities for our kids, parents, and community leaders. As I've said, mayoring is the loneliest teamwork that there is.

CHAPTER 11

~

Why Not a Tax on Cheesesteaks Instead of Soda?

A nother initiative that focused on Philadelphia's young people and their well-being was the protracted campaign to create a soda tax. Dr. Don Schwarz, our deputy mayor for health and opportunity and also the health commissioner, had been the physician in chief at the Children's Hospital of Philadelphia before he joined the government ranks. He came up with the idea that, for health and financial reasons, the city should propose a soda tax. To be accurate, this was not a "soda" tax but a sugar-sweetened beverage tax. We first proposed a tax of two cents per ounce of drink sweetened by sugar or a sugar substitute, to be paid by distributors, who we assumed in turn would pass the cost on to retailers and consumers. Baby formula, beverages that were more than 50 percent milk, and unsweetened drinks to which a consumer might request to have sugar added were exempted. When Dr. Schwarz had first suggested this, back in 2010, only Berkeley, California, had a soda tax. We love Berkeley, but no big city, no major city in the country, had proposed such a thing before. We may have been the first and largest city in the country to attempt a soda tax. And Philadelphians just love change. They absolutely, massively love change—just as long as things can stay the same! So this was a brand new, ambitious initiative in a city notoriously reluctant at times to embrace change.

Dr. Schwarz had made clear to us that we had a very serious public health problem. We had significant obesity and overweight rates for children and adults here in Philadelphia. In 2006, 21.7 percent of Philadelphia's school children, age five to eighteen, were obese, and 8.5 percent were severely obese. In 2010, half of the city population overall was at least overweight if not clinically obese.

I was asked about the soda tax on a local evening news show and explained that the excessive amount of sugar in sodas was a "significant public health issue," and the anchor who was doing the interview asked me, "Why tax sodas? Why not tax doughnuts, grease, French fries, or cheesesteaks?"

Cheesesteaks? Really? Even I would not have proposed that. I explained that the soda tax made sense because of "substitution availability—there were 100 percent juices, there's water, and milk," all of which can easily substitute for soda. Honestly, I know that no one in Philadelphia would think that a true cheesesteak has *any* substitute.

This was the initial introduction of the sugar-sweetened beverage tax in Philadelphia. Some of the money collected through this tax would go to health programs, and the rest was going to restore programs that we had cut in 2008 and 2009 with the recession-created budget crisis.

The soda tax was quite a challenge, however. The tax did not move forward in 2010. The City Council was very concerned about this particular initiative. There were some objections and opposition to the tax in the public and press as well. The *Philadelphia Inquirer* editorialized that although a good idea in theory, the tax would be "unfair to the poor," hitting "those who can least afford it the hardest," and would be "unlikely to improve the health of residents." They and others also questioned why the tax was levied on businesses and not at the point of sale, directly to consumers, where it would maximize incentives to change behavior (the tax on distributors, however, meant that we wouldn't need to seek approval from the state legislature, so it had that tactical aspect). Additionally the council was catching massive opposition from what we called Big Beverage, or Big Soda—the soda industry lobbying forces. They were contending with a phalanx of lobbyists from the American Beverage Association as well as opposition from the unions that represented truck drivers who delivered soda. In my opinion this issue was too important to put up for a vote when I knew that I didn't have the votes to win, and under no circumstances did I intend to bring a doomed soda tax up for a vote. That loss for us would have been a major victory for Big Soda. So there was no vote on this measure in 2010.

The soda tax returned in 2011 for the second time. By that point the city's budget had fairly well stabilized, but now the school district was in serious financial crisis. When we came back with the idea, we proposed that all of the money from the soda tax would go to fill budget gaps for the school district.

It did not go forward at this point, either. There are seventeen members of the City Council, and you need nine votes to pass a bill. I would say that for perhaps two minutes during the height of that debate, we had nine votes. That is, until one of the members stepped out of the then council president's office, got cornered by a Big Soda lobbyist, and that was the end of that. The soda tax did not move forward in my administration. Consequently, to save the schools financially, we raised property taxes instead.

However, it did pass in 2016, under a new administration with many new City Council members. I see that as the deferred fruition of a six-year-long effort here in the city, fraught with all kinds of controversy. When it did pass, there were six brand new City Council members who had never been through the fights, and a brand new mayor. They were also planning to fund great projects with the soda tax that were hard to oppose—things such as universal pre-K, parks and recreation, and a number of others. Interestingly, when the new administration introduced the measure in City Council, they used the exact same version of the bill that my administration used, literally copying the same bill, changing some dates, and increasing the proposed tax to three cents per ounce.

Even under these circumstances, the soda tax still saw massive opposition. There were dire prognostications: People were going to lose their jobs, companies were going to go out of business, this was going to be a disaster—all of the same horror stories. And the soda tax, which hasn't been in effect for long at this writing in 2017, was proposed at three cents and ended up at one-and-a-half cents, so a lot of compromise was involved in its passage.

The soda tax campaign reminds me of the smoke-free campaign that I started when I was on the City Council. That took six years. I introduced it in 2000 for the first time, and it didn't pass until 2006. The soda tax we proposed in 2010 essentially passed as basically the same bill in 2016. Call it the six-year rule!

A lot of factors determine which legislation will pass in a city government, and when. With the soda tax, the mayor and City Council members had changed since the tax was first proposed, and so had the landscape, both culturally and politically. Sodas were less popular by then because of public awareness and the cumulative effects of many ads we ran during my administration, with grant money we received from the CDC, about sugar-sweetened beverages. The CDC found that between 2009 and 2015, soda consumption had declined, especially among children, even without the soda tax. Among teens, soda consumption declined by 24 percent between 2007 and 2013.

The ads and public awareness had changed opinion and consumption to measurable degrees. Philadelphia had seen reductions in soda consumption even without the implementation of a sugar tax. People with more information from public health sources realized that without being against soda, they might want to cut down on their consumption. Instead of having two or three a day, maybe they'd have one, and back it up with some water. Maybe they would not have five a week, but only three. It all contributes. Doubtless, this created a more favorable political environment for soda legislation as well. Successful legislation in a city depends sometimes on a gradual spiral of cultural and social changes, which in turn alter the political landscape, which in turn can alter social and cultural conditions.

One of the lessons of mayoring, which the soda tax illustrates, is that sometimes you just have to wait, and you have to be patient. Sometimes it takes time for a message to come across, and you have to use a variety of methods, from ads to a tax. As mayor, you can't expect to fulfill every ambition in your first hundred days, or even your first administration. With some issues, you'll be seeding a project for success in a subsequent administration, and if we are all more concerned with the work than with the credit (as we should be), then things often work out fine.

~

My first term as mayor was characterized by tough times and equally tough decisions. My staff and I recognized early on that we were contending with a chaotic and destructive financial storm. We also recognized that this was our new normal, and we weren't going to complain or moan about it. Everyone had some resources, and we did the best we could with what we had to navigate and steer Philadelphia out of the storm. Remarkably, my core team stuck together, and most stayed on through the second term. Even though our short term was consumed by a crisis, our focus remained steadfastly on the long term, and taking steps to secure the future. We stayed focused.

My inspiration came from seeing improvements along the way, including improved high school graduation rates. Sometimes it's good to step back from time to time and celebrate the successes. My chief education officer, Lori Shorr, was the first person I met in the mayor's office with as mayor-elect on the Saturday before inauguration, and she spoke for me on all education policy, funding, and reform matters. Lori contributed to this improvement in the graduation rate.

During your first term as mayor, you learn on the job. In my time, there was no "mayor school" to attend. Although, one of the mayors whom I have long admired, Michael Bloomberg of New York City, is in essence creating something of a Mayor School at the new Bloomberg Harvard City Leadership Initiative. Mike Bloomberg has invested $32 million in helping to create the program, and they started some of their work in the summer of 2017. The Bloomberg Harvard school will be a vital training and educational opportunity for current and new mayors in the future.

I also learned informally from other mayors, either in general or around specific issues. When I began as mayor of Philadelphia I observed other mayors such as Joseph Riley in Charleston, South Carolina; Don Plusquellic, in Akron, Ohio; Jerry Abramson in Louisville, Kentucky; Antonio Villaraigosa in Los Angeles; and Kasim Reed in

Atlanta. There are a tremendous number of great leaders out there who are doing great mayoral work in their cities.

It would be a challenge to whittle the list for my own personal Mt. Rushmore of mayors. New York's mayor Michael Bloomberg would definitely be first on the list, which would also include Mayor Doug Palmer in Trenton, Mayor Shirley Clarke Franklin in Atlanta, Mayor Mitch Landrieu in New Orleans, Mayor Wellington Webb in Denver, and Mayor Richard M. Daley in Chicago. Michael Bloomberg has been a tremendous friend, generous supporter, and innovative leader of mayors across America, and internationally. Mayor Bloomberg was the first mayor I visited after winning the Democratic primary. He is the "World Mayor of Mayors." Mayor Daley is also a good friend and innovator, and was the second mayor I visited in August after my primary victory. Daley was especially focused on sustainability and "greening" Chicago, and I adopted many of his strategies in Philadelphia. Mitch Landrieu is my best current mayoral friend, and I admire him for his boldness in leadership, his willingness to speak truth to power, and his intense focus on violence reduction in the African American community. He has pulled together proposals to increase services to support citizens, provide jobs for young people, and reform policing that have improved community-police relations. Mayor Doug Palmer and I have been friends a long time, and he immediately became one of my mayoral mentors. He was the one who took the time to help me understand tangibly what a mayor does, and how a mayor takes action and demonstrates leadership. He also encouraged my interest in a leadership role in the US Conference of Mayors.

These mayors are all great in their own unique ways, but they also share characteristics that in my opinion define a good and effective mayor. They—and other successful mayors—are all generous with their time, talent, ideas, and resources. They are ambitious for success but also empathetic.

As mayors we borrowed and poached ideas from each other. We gave attribution, of course, but we freely drew on each other's ideas and innovations to improve our own leadership. I was always watching what was unfolding in other cities. For example, at the same time that the School District of Philadelphia was in the process of closing some of our underutilized schools, Mayor Rahm Emanuel was dealing with similar issues in Chicago. I was reading about and talking to Mayor Emanuel about some of the challenges that he was facing out there. I talked to Mayor Sly James in Kansas City, Missouri, who was also having flash mob challenges, when he called me to ask me about some of the things that we did to try to calm things down in Philadelphia.

When I was coming into the mayor's position, I learned by trial and error, and by the mistakes made and successes achieved.

And, sometimes, you just get flat-out lucky.

PART THREE

CHAPTER 12

~

There Was Never an Earthquake Here Before You Were Mayor

Every now and then you get something a little different as a mayor. This was unusual for Philadelphia: on August 23, 2011, we had an earthquake that measured 5.9 on the Richter scale. The earthquake didn't cause much damage, but an amusing political story emerged out of it.

I think it's safe to say that we had not had an earthquake in Philadelphia in an extremely long time. We get a lot of other things, and other crises, but we don't usually get earthquakes. Now, in 2011 I was also running for reelection, and I was facing off against my general election opponent, Republican Karen Brown, in a one-hour debate. This is campaign time, so all kinds of things get said. Brown was criticizing me that I hadn't done this and I hadn't done that and I hadn't done the other thing—and that was not surprising to me. You develop a thick skin as mayor, you deal with it, and this is what you have to expect in a campaign. But then Brown said: "You know, before he became mayor, we never had an earthquake in Philadelphia." The TV guys were as stunned as I was. Really, the moderator conveyed, Is *this* where we are going?

But I guess the buck stops at the mayor's office, on all things—including an earthquake, which was apparently my fault.

The next calamity, a less rare but still unusual hurricane, was much more serious. One of the most unheralded and vital positions in city government, and for a mayor, is the director of the Office of Emergency Management. It's one of those positions where as mayor you might not be exactly sure of what they're doing or how, but you're extremely glad that they're doing it. The "3 A.M. emergency phone call" to a mayor, governor, or president is a cliché of American politics, but people never ask, who is calling that leader at 3 A.M., and who is on the other end of the line? That person was already up and prepared to make the call. In the case of weather emergencies, the director of emergency management is the person on the other line.

In late August, our director informed me five days out that a potential major storm—the Category 3 hurricane Irene—was headed our way. And there is nothing like the emergency management of a weather crisis, as mayor of a large city, to underscore that the data on climate change is very real. Storms are getting more severe. As we experienced with hurricanes Harvey and Irma in August and September 2017.

In this case our preparation followed what had become, if not a routine, then at least a protocol, during my administration. It began with the Office of Emergency Management, located in the basement of a fire department administrative building, with several huge screens across one wall. The office gets data twenty-four hours a day, seven days a week, on what's going on around the city and from the National Weather Service.

After our own meetings to coordinate, the first of which took place in my office, we would meet to tell the public what was going on. With Irene and in other cases, we did this at least two to four days in advance of the storm. In the last years of my terms, we were using social media heavily to inform the public, along with radio and more traditional communications.

I conveyed as much accurate information and predictions as I could about Hurricane Irene. I told the city that we could expect "seven inches of rain and flooding of all rivers, creeks, and the Schuylkill, flash flooding in streets, storm gusts of forty to fifty miles an hour, and significant damage to trees, power lines, and infrastructure." That turned out to be fairly accurate. Because of the hurricane we declared a state of emergency in Philadelphia for the first time since 1986. At this press conference as with most others that concerned weather emergencies, an array of officials and team members flanked me. This serves to show that we knew what was going on, we had personnel and a plan, and these are the things you need to do to protect yourself. In terms of preparation, I used to joke that Philadelphia must be the French Toast capital of the world, because residents would go out and buy large quantities of eggs, milk, bread, and cinnamon in advance of storms.

My team and I thought it was best to give the public an inside view of how we were managing this hurricane and other storms, so we'd hold meetings and press conferences in the Office of Emergency Management. Viewers would see twenty agencies represented there and a beehive of activity, with people who were not going anywhere, working sixteen-hour shifts and eating pizza after pizza for dinners.

Philadelphia is often less affected by storms than its surrounding areas, owing to its lower geological placement, but the entire region looks to the mayor of any large city for information, and we share the same television markets. In these situations a mayor can also become a regional leader and spokesperson. I warned during Irene that "waters had already climbed to street-sign levels" in towns surrounding Philadelphia, with the water sending "couches, furniture, all kinds of stuff floating down the street." It was as blunt as I could be about the flooding severity.

It's a point of mayoral pride for me that we had established such a level of trust and credibility with the city that if we told people to stay home, then for the most part, they did. We were correct about 98 percent of the time in our weather predictions, and people came to expect accuracy from us.

Nationally, Hurricane Irene caused $16.6 billion in damage. Locally, the storm was tough on the city. Half a million people in the region were without power, 7 buildings collapsed, 400 trees fell, 20 roads were closed, and some SEPTA service was temporarily suspended due to flooding. But most importantly, we had no casualties in the city.

So, this rounded out my month of August 2011 as mayor. The flash mob speech was on August 8, we had an earthquake on August 23, and we had a hurricane on August 28. It was a somewhat busy month for us.

But again, through it all, these events and disasters required communication and sharing information with the public, and that is one element that all of these disparate events have in common. Over time we had actually established a level of trust with the citizens of Philadelphia through the financial crisis, snowstorms, and earthquakes, and by the constant communication and sharing of information. So when we told citizens to please stay off of the streets, they did. And not only were they safer, but it also allowed us to maintain public safety and get the recovery going. The other component of that message to stay home is really about the speed with which we can get the city back up and running. It's dramatically easier to do that safely when folks are not out on the street and not in their vehicles, and it gives us opportunity to get the city back in operating condition.

—

During this year of 2011, Philadelphia also had the emergence of its own Occupy movement, an offshoot of the Occupy Wall Street protest that had begun in mid-September 2011. The first Occupy protestors encamped in Zuccotti Park in New York City's Wall Street financial district. With their rallying cry, "We are the 99 percent," they intended to call attention to income disparity in the United States, joblessness, and the inordinate power of corporations in politics and society. From Zuccotti Park, the Occupy movement spread quickly to other cities, with their own improvised encampments, including Cleveland, Los Angeles, Seattle, Birmingham, Alabama, Boston, San Francisco, and Washington, DC, to name only a few. We had our own Occupy Philadelphia out on what was then called Dilworth Plaza and has now been transformed into Dilworth Park. The protestors were there for a few months, but things started to deteriorate pretty rapidly after that first month or so. We needed them to move. And so my team made the decision that not only were things deteriorating from the standpoint of living conditions but also—and we had told Occupy this at the beginning—we had planned a massive, $55 million transformation of Dilworth Plaza. All of the concrete and granite and the multilayer, multilevel staircasing were going to be transformed into a brand new Dilworth Park, with new access to public transportation. So we let the Occupiers know what was going on, right after Thanksgiving 2011, when I held a press conference about the protests.

"For the last fifty-one days," I said,

people from this region and beyond have demonstrated their strongly held views at Dilworth Plaza and on the streets of the city. Without a doubt, Occupy Philadelphia has created a handful of fiscal and operational challenges in the city. Free speech in a city is a real issue, and at times it's a real challenge, but from the start I directed every member of our senior team to look for ways to accommodate Occupy Philadelphia's desire to enact their free speech rights. This is the birthplace of our American democracy, and there should be no other response. Since October Occupy Philadelphia has been generally cooperative, providing us with advance notice of marches and demonstrations. In return, we have maintained open and regular communications with Occupy Philadelphia at every step along the way. The police department has also shown how to maintain public safety and demonstrate a spirit of cooperation. Occupy Philadelphia has also faced its own challenges in exercising what they call direct democracy. Public health and safety concerns are becoming evident as each day wore on.

I concluded that it was now time for the protestors to move on.

This press conference, however, was only part of the communication that we had maintained around the protests for weeks and weeks beforehand. We had met with Occupy before they even arrived. We'd been paying attention to the Occupy Wall Street movement in New York. We knew some of the people who were involved with the organization and some of their legal counsel, so they came to visit us.

I attended this meeting with our senior team, and we talked about the issues that they were concerned about, although we already had a pretty good idea of what those issues were. Prior to this meeting, we had made a very conscious decision that we were going to try to have a somewhat cooperative relationship with Occupy, and that there was no better place to model this cooperation than Philadelphia, the birthplace of freedom, liberty, democracy, and free speech. We offered Dilworth Plaza as the place where they could set up, right on the "front porch" of city hall.

"How long do you plan to be there?" I asked them at the end of the meeting.

"Until the change comes," they answered.

I replied, "Well, you know, I'm a government person so I need some parameters here. So, just tell me, when?"

"Well, we'll know it when it happens," they said.

Okay. It was not really the kind of answer that I sought, but it is what it is.

Two days later they showed up and set up camp. On that first night I went down and wandered through the encampment, just to see people and informally review the scene. A few folks recognized me, took photos, and posted them on social media. I got a few alarmed calls from my staff, wondering if I had been captured and kidnapped by the Occupy forces, and questioning what I was doing, wandering around the camp. "They're on our front porch," I responded, "and I'm just checking it out."

One day I was walking past a tent at the encampment, and I noticed that it was filled with laptops, computers, and every tech device imaginable. It looked like a tech convention in there. I realized that protestors were talking to other Occupy movements across the country. I reasoned that if the Occupy movements were communicating, then we mayors should be as well. I was a vice president in the U.S. Conference of Mayors, so I organized a conference call with twenty to thirty mayors across the country so we could update each other and to share best practices. We talked about how to handle the movement—although *handle* is not the most accurate word; rather, how to engage with this new organization and its issues and challenges, in urban parks and plazas and public spaces all across the country.

Things went fairly well and peacefully for several weeks, although Occupy was having their own challenges, early on. Initially they had told us that they didn't want assistance or interference by the government. But at one point they actually came to us to complain. They had set up tents, were cooking food, had people milling about and camping, but they were surprised, apparently, that the homeless community figured out that they could get three free meals a day over at Occupy Philadelphia on Dilworth Plaza. They complained to us that homeless people were coming. I said, in effect, they're part of the 99 percent and so these are your folks, and what do you want us to do about it? If you're there cooking three meals a day, what do you expect? And they agreed, and said, okay, we'll live with it.

Then, as a result, we had sanitation issues. The Occupy protestors were eating a lot of fresh foods and grains, and healthy stuff. And some of the homeless visitors perhaps weren't completely accustomed to a lot of fresh food in their diets, and the Plaza area—our "front porch!"— started to take on a certain pungent odor. There were some other safety, assault, and crime incidents. Ultimately it became clear that it was time for Occupy Philadelphia to go, or occupy some other location.

We needed to clear the site, and the unions who were going to build the new park—a project that would give jobs to a thousand people— decided that they were also part of the 99 percent. They began to show up at Occupy general assembly gatherings and chanting "We are the 99 percent," to communicate to the Occupy folks that they were impeding the jobs by which these union workers were taking care of themselves and their families. We gave the Occupy protestors two weeks' notice that they were going to have to move. We posted fliers, we had meetings, and we spread the word. The protestors knew that we were serious, and on the evening when we cleared Dilworth Plaza their ranks had thinned to perhaps only 25 percent of what they had been at their peak. We also knew through the Office of Emergency Management that it would be raining on the night in question, which meant that fewer people would be out at the camp, in any event. We tried to be as gentle about their removal as possible.

Nevertheless, viewers of the local evening news might have thought quite differently. "There were scores of arrests and some *dramatic moments*," a local news station intoned, as we cleared out Dilworth. "Police broke up protestors who had confronted them when they gathered outside of city hall this morning. One protestor was up in a tree. Others chanted."

I love TV news as much as the next person, but I'm not exactly sure what the "dramatic moments" were, because we were watching everything that was transpiring at Dilworth. I think the worst thing that happened that night was that one of the protestors apparently touched a police horse who got a little nervous and stepped on her foot. That was pretty much the sum total of the drama for the night. The person in the tree, that was a little bit of a challenge. The marching and protesting took place well into the night and early morning hours, but eventually Dilworth got cleared, the protest ended, and we moved on with our lives. About two days later it would appear as if Occupy Philadelphia had never been on Dilworth Plaza.

Philadelphia was seen as one of the leading cities for demonstrating how to deal with the Occupy movement, not just at the end, but during the course of the protests and even before they began. Police Commissioner Ramsey made several important and exemplary decisions about how to approach the protests. When Occupy first came to town, he put out an order that at every roll call, every day, in every police station, the First Amendment would be read to the officers assembled. This was to remind officers about who we are and what we're about as a police department and as a nation. The reading conveyed the clear message that so long as the protests were peaceful, they could continue.

Later, when Occupy staged demonstrations and marches, Commissioner Ramsey made the shrewd decision to hand-pick all of the officers who would be on the scene of these events, so that they weren't assigned randomly. It takes a lot to be an officer and do your job to protect people who are shouting insults and curses at you, and telling you that they hope you die, and that you and your family should f— off. This is not easy, and Ramsey's decision to think carefully about the officers with the right mindset, patience, temperament, and experience to handle fractious and sometimes verbally abusive protesters doubtless helped keep officers, protestors, and citizens all safe. The city, and certainly the Philadelphia Police Department, was complimented repeatedly on how it handled Occupy.

Locally, the *Philadelphia Inquirer* editorialized after the eviction that "appropriate tactics were used" and that "Ramsey's officers deserve praise for emptying the Plaza quickly, then stepping back while arm-in-arm Occupy marchers walked around Center City." Commissioner Ramsey agreed that officers "showed remarkable restraint and patience. They [the protestors] weren't exactly orderly. They were very confrontational."

I was even more gratified to read letters in the *Inquirer* from readers. "I do not recall being as proud" to be a Philadelphian, one wrote. "The right to peaceably assemble and the needs of the city were simultaneously protected." Another congratulated, "there was a dialogue between City Hall and Occupy Philadelphia throughout the protest, and respect for the Constitutional right to protest." Still another praised the "professionalism of the Philadelphia police force and their leadership. . . . Philadelphia has again shown how to best protect freedom and liberty."

The benefits of handling one kind of protest well as an administration can reverberate powerfully, and the lessons and small victories of mayoring are cumulative. When Philadelphia and the nation faced a series of officer-involved shootings and subsequent protests, we drew on the lessons learned during the Occupy protest. We imparted to citizens and officers that people have a right to protest, and that so long as the protests are peaceful, officers to the front, rear, and sides of protestors will be there to protect them.

—

The Occupy negotiations exemplify the importance, once again, of communication, which is perhaps the most constant and recurring theme of my experience as mayor, and the lessons learned about how to do the job effectively. As mayor, you work for the public, and you need to meet the public where they are. That is the job.

The forms of communication might have changed since 2008, but not the importance of it. Today there are a lot of ways both to communicate and to get information, from all of the social media sites to website portals. And there are still the old-fashioned town hall meetings. I'm not against town hall meetings—although when I scheduled eight of them in the middle of an economic crisis in my first term, as I've described, I shouldn't have expected that citizens were going to be happy at those town meetings. But the meetings are still informative and a viable tool. Those town hall meetings in particular reinforced several things that we thought we knew. At this writing in 2017, some congressional representatives have avoided holding town hall meetings in fear of having to confront their constituents angry over healthcare or other controversies, but in my opinion that is an abrogation of a public servant's most basic responsibility.

No matter how painful, awkward, or repetitive it might be to elicit comments online or to hold a town hall meeting—whatever the situation may be and whatever the mode of communication—it's vital to communicate, because then you can also start to analyze and go back to the early questions, start doing some data analytics to figure out if a particular issue is a really serious one for people and if it recurs. It should inform some of your decision making. You can't do everything the public wants to do. But you should at least be well aware of what's on the public's mind.

Communication goes both ways, of course. Transparency was very important to me, and I never wavered from the conviction that government should be transparent. People want to know that things are operating aboveboard. They want to know how you make decisions. Who's involved in that process? Are people getting jobs and contracts for the right reason? Or is it just the same old political horse trading?

As mayor I wanted to communicate not only to the public but also to the business community, rating agencies, and people across the country, if not around the world, that this is a place where you can come and do business. You will not be shaken down. You don't have to make contributions to particular campaigns. You don't have to know somebody. And you can see the people that you need to see in order to get your project done, to help you relocate, or whatever the case may be.

There had been concerns about transparency and honest communication in the prior administration, and whether those concerns were fact or perception, perception tends to become reality. If the perception has the quality of truth for people and it's what they are thinking, then that's how they're going to react and respond. I thought it was our job and responsibility as early on as possible to try and send a different kind of message. I think we were rewarded for that over the years.

As mayor, every day you have an opportunity to communicate a variety of messages, to break through all of the other noise that's out there and all the other stuff that's happening. I advise elected officials all the time that people do not pay nearly as much attention to us as any of us would like to think, because they have real lives. They have real things going on. And they actually spend very little time focused on or thinking about the things that we're talking about. And so it takes constant communication and a consistency of message to really catch the public's attention.

~

CHAPTER 13

A Cool and a Hot City:
Attracting the New and Retaining the Old

During my second term the face and geography of Philadelphia were changing. While I was in office we had the largest percent increase of millennial population of any major city in the United States. Our millennial population increased by 43 percent from 2005 to 2016. As I write this in the spring of 2017, there are about 25 to 30 cranes in the sky. From 2013 to 2015, 200 projects were completed, under construction, or in the planning phases in the city, representing $11.4 billion in value. There is anywhere from $10 to $12 billion of economic activity taking place in the city, and Philadelphia has achieved the urban ideal of being cool and hot at the same time. In 2007, Philadelphia was holding on to only about 28 percent to 29 percent of our nonnative college and university students. In 2015, that figure was about 49 percent. The number of new businesses and start-ups is tremendous. Taking all of this together—the level of construction going on in the city, the number of new businesses, the attraction of start-ups, and the number of young people staying here in the city after school—we see that these are dividends of an overarching strategy to communicate that this city is a place where you want to be. And, as I mentioned earlier, they are dividends, deferred, from tough decisions made during the depths of the Great Recession six years earlier.

Several things, ranging from image and outreach to the stodgier but absolutely vital reforms that scaffold economic growth, created this environment for Philadelphia's economic dynamism and development. At the helm of the effort, originally, was Andrew Altman, the first deputy mayor for economic development. Andrew developed our initial strategies in the first year of the administration. Alan Greenberger took his place in the second year, and served in that capacity for six years, after having been the executive director of the city planning commission. He had started in the private sector, where he was a partner in an architecture firm. As deputy mayor of economic development, Greenberger implemented many of Altman's plans and developed our overarching strategy for Philadelphia. He was responsible for much of the economic boom in the city after the Great Recession.

In terms of keeping in Philadelphia the talented young people educated at the city's universities, the key to retention is jobs, plain and simple. Not to disrespect other cities, but New York, Boston, and San Francisco are not the only places that a millennial can get a job and build a life. There are some great financial institutions here in the city if you're a business school student and want to pursue that path. Organizations such as Campus Philly and Graduate Philadelphia have done a better job at reaching out and enticing millennial freshmen and sophomores to choose the city, because as a mayor that's when you really need to grab them for those internships and connect them with companies that want to invest in them. The number of millennials has increased in Philadelphia because they can actually see a future in the city. Some have run up mom and dad's credit card for four years, graduated, had a party, and are ready for a job—and if we don't have jobs available, at that very moment, then they will take their Philadelphia-acquired education and go earn a living and pay taxes in some other city.

New York is still New York, of course, and I understand its lure. There are more jobs there, and a lot of a young person's friends might be moving there. But we did a better job with outreach during my time in office, and did it as early on in a college student's career as we could. Philadelphia has become more competitive with our salaries, amenities, and attractions.

Similarly, outreach to enhance the image and luster of Philadelphia to the start-up and business communities was also vital to economic development. I was criticized for doing a fair amount of national and international travel during my second term in office, after the recession had ended. I thought the travel was vital for development. I was not only the mayor of the city but its chief cheerleader, and that demanded that I make myself visible and circulate to elevate the city's profile and promote opportunities for start-ups. I focused a lot of that travel and effort in the tech community. We communicated what goes on at Penn and Drexel and Temple and St. Joe's, among other incubators of ideas and innovation in the city. It's a constant effort to communicate a message that this is a good government, in a vital city.

Then there are the less visible but absolutely indispensable pillars of economic development that demand a mayor's attention. For example, we had to fix the property assessment system so that it reflected the changing values of Philadelphia real estate. I hired Richard Negrin as the director of the Office of Property Assessment, to orchestrate this massive overhaul (eventually, Negrin became the managing director of the city, the second-highest position in city government under the Philadelphia home rule charter). Actually, I had been trying to fix the property assessment system since I was on the City Council, with no success. It had the terrible political trifecta of being broken, flawed, and corrupt. Knowing that to be true, I vowed as mayor to revisit the problem, as a fair and transparent tax system is another of the unglamorous foundations for the glamorous transformation of a city's skyline with new buildings, cool start-ups, and enterprise. The first and core problem was the Board of Revision of Taxes. This board was the judge, jury, and executioner for property tax bills in Philadelphia. They set the values of property, and they were the adjudicator if a citizen objected to their tax bill. This all-in-one system is not typical of other cities. Generally, it seems that Philadelphia is either the first or the last city to change something, and there is not much middle ground. In this case, we were the last to tackle the antiquated Board of Revision of Taxes.

Furthermore, Board of Revision of Taxes members were neither elected by citizen vote nor confirmed by the City Council. They were appointed by the Board of Judges, who were all elected. The board's appointees might not have reliably known much about taxes, but they did reliably know how to get through the Philadelphia political grindstone. There were corruption issues here, as well, around appointments.

My first task was to separate the two functions: to have a separate office of assessment and a separate appeals process for tax bills. Then I wanted to change the appointments system. We succeeded at the first task, but not the second.

We tried to do a couple things right after we fixed the property assessment system, including the Actual Value Initiative, in 2014. We wanted to address the fact that many poor people in parts of our city were paying more in taxes than they should have, and many higher-income property owners were paying less. There was a fair amount of groaning and fear around the Actual Value Initiative, and dire prognostications that everyone's property taxes would rise. We retorted simply that we wanted every property owner to pay their fair amount, and here as elsewhere toward the end of my second term, data and "big data" were playing a larger role in our decision making and communication.

In short, "big data" refers to huge data sets that might reveal trends and patterns, and that can be mined in new, previously unavailable ways through cutting-edge computer technologies. Big data is now being used across many sectors of society, from finance to crime to consumer marketing. With the Actual Value Initiative, I had the solid data to prove inequities in the tax bills, and I shared that data widely with the City Council and citizens. I said, some of you have been getting ripped off and some of you have been getting a tax break for upwards of twenty or thirty years, and not paying your fair share. When citizens understood these problems and saw the stark numbers, many were persuaded that the initiative would promote basic fairness in taxation.

In the end, we did fix the system, and after all was said and done, 70 percent of property owners saw their new tax bills either stay the same or go down, in contrast to opponents' predictions. In 2015, we had an extremely low 5 percent of taxpayers appeal their new rate, and no major lawsuits; in contrast, when Pittsburgh reformed their assessment system many years ago, they had a 30 percent appeal rate and a huge lawsuit.

With more equitable and accurate assessments, we also wanted to address the downside of economic growth that may cause gentrification. We were concerned that gentrification could potentially and literally push residents out of their homes because of the revaluation process. As with many aspects of mayoring, there was a flip side to economic dynamism. We had to think about the Philadelphians who

have been here in their neighborhoods for a long time and who sometimes live below the poverty line. During these years, my grandmother's
words and wisdom that you can be house rich and cash poor rang in
my head. In other words, the projected market value of your home has
nothing to do with your ability to pay your taxes. And so we created a
new program. It is really true that the government could not operate
without acronyms, so the program was called LOOP, for, Long-term
Owner-Occupied Program, and it was designed to help Philadelphians
stay in their homes and not get pushed out by higher property taxes
resulting from the revaluation. We already had a property tax freeze
program for senior citizens who met certain income thresholds. With
LOOP, their taxes basically wouldn't go up, no matter what else was
going on in their neighborhood.

We reasoned that people who were in their fifties, sixties, and
beyond, who had raised their families here, lived in their homes forever,
and done none of the fancy renovations that tend to elevate a house's
value, should not be priced out of their homes because they couldn't
pay tax bills and assessments that were rising on the tide of Philadelphia's economic revitalization. First, that's not who we are or the sort
of value that I wanted my administration to endorse; second, it's fun-
damentally unfair that the very families and citizens who were anchors
of the neighborhoods and kept them viable through the very lean and
tough times would now be driven out by the good times; and, third,
we could do something about this. LOOP helps to ensure that these
citizens won't be forced out of their homes because of tax assessments
and bills they can't pay.

Another foundational basis for Philadelphia's economic and business development was a revised, user-friendly zoning code. Admittedly,
a zoning code sounds about as exciting as paint drying, but it's the

nuts and bolts foundation of a city's business and real estate prospects, and its revision can be a fractious, controversial process. In 2011, in the midst of the Great Recession, we changed the zoning code for the first time in fifty years. At the time it was so byzantine and confusing that lawyers who charged roughly $400 to $600 an hour would have to get a builder or developer through the process. I would state, only half-jokingly, that developers ought to be able to complete and develop their projects in their own lifetimes. It's not something that they should be handing down to their children for them to finish.

To revise the code we borrowed models from other cities, and we also convened a commission. Notoriously in politics, commissions are known as the place where good ideas go to die, but that wasn't true with zoning reform. It was a serious commission, with a serious director and serious developers as well as community representatives.

The revision process took a couple of years, but we succeeded in making the code much more elegant, intuitive, and user friendly, and the City Council approved the new code. It clarified for developers as well as the community the criteria of what can be built, where. The new zoning code also provided for a neighborhood planning process that is still in place today. Every neighborhood would have its own neighborhood plan so people could see it and participate. We even created a citizens' engagement academy to encourage a better understanding between communities and city governments about how development decisions are made.

Every piece of ground in Philadelphia does not have to have a building on it, and every old building is not historic. Some are just old. On matters of zoning and building, mayors have to maintain a balance between these often competing issues. Generally, in any city, fault lines emerge between community people and neighborhoods, and developers. The community groups assumed that we were trying to give the city away to developers, and the developers felt that we were making it impossible from them to build or do anything in the city. Listening to the community, in this and other things, is essential. You need to be in touch with people out in neighborhoods, and listen to what they have to say.

But changes to Philadelphia's zoning code are also an example of a new emphasis in mayoring on using big data, more data-driven decision making, and evidence-based research. Nothing replaces the information I got as mayor from simply listening to citizens and gathering anecdotes. But toward the latter half of my eight years in office, there were a great many more discussions about data, big data, open source platforms, data releases, and about how to use data to solve problems. Increasingly, we made more decisions based on actual facts and data as opposed to anecdotal stories, or some sense of what I or others thought or felt based on experience, although there is still an important place for experience and history in decision making as well.

Looking back, changes in the zoning code involved the use of data-driven approaches, and the planning and zoning codes changes, in turn, have really been critical to the almost explosive growth in development in the city in the twenty-first century. We were asking, what are the demographics of a particular neighborhood? What are the income levels? What are the needs in that community? What are we doing about economic development? How many schools are in that neighborhood? What's the utilization rate at the local library? How many daycare centers are in this neighborhood? What's our programming at the Department of Recreation?

All of these changes—the outreach to graduates and entrepreneurial communities, zoning code reform, the rehabbing of the tax assessment system, the implementation of programs to offset the effects of tax revaluation for long-term residents who were elderly or cash poor, and the reduction of corruption in the tax and development process, coupled with the stabilization of government finances after the recession—sent strong signals to the development and real estate communities that they could actually get a project initiated and completed in Philadelphia. They really didn't have to know someone, or contribute to my campaign or to anyone else's campaign.

I made a major speech to the development community in which I said bluntly, to get a project started, to build your building, please don't come to me seeking my approval. Go to the City Planning Commission.

Meanwhile, to the employees of all the departments that touched or processed one part of a big project, I made clear that I wanted all of the departments working on the big project at the same time. I wasn't asking them to cut corners, but the main goal was efficient and expeditious work: do your job, review your part of the project, and get it off your desk. For years some employees had settled into a state of lethargy about their work, and part of the economic jump-start was to reanimate their sense that this work is important. I made a number of comments to public employees that they were not just mindlessly stamping pieces of paper. That application on their desk, I said, represents economic growth and jobs in the city. With the revenues generated by it, in turn, we can implement after-school programs and fund libraries. Do your job, do it well, and understand the tangible value that emerges out of what can sometimes feel like an intangible, rote process.

I would tell them, "When you drive down the street with your kids in the car, you can and should point to a building and say, I helped to build that."

CHAPTER 14

~

Tragedies, Frustrations, Accidents, and a Holy Visit

I believe it is almost inevitable that mayors of cities will be tested by entirely surprising and significant tragedies. On June 5, 2013, I was in my office at city hall, and someone came in and told me that there had been a building collapse at Twenty-Second and Market Streets, but we didn't have any details. It was between 9 and 10 that morning. Immediately, a group of us rushed out to Twenty-Second and Market, on the southeast corner, and we assembled diagonally across on the northwest corner of that site. Firefighters were still trying to get in the building, and still trying to get people out of the building when we arrived at the scene.

Six people died in that building. Thirteen people were injured to varying degrees. It was particularly painful to lose citizens, and at a very personal level the twenty-four-year-old daughter of our then city treasurer, Nancy Winkler, and the daughter's best friend were in that building as well.

I had asked Nancy to come into public service from the private sector, where she had been a financial expert. We were out there at the building site most of the day and into the night, and that night, they found her daughter and her daughter's best friend right next to each other in the rubble of that building. Nancy lived roughly four or five blocks north of that location. She'd been talking with her daughter that morning. I went to her house that evening, with a few others, to personally let her know that we had found her daughter and her friend. They had perished in that building.

It was certainly one of the toughest moments in my life, to have to tell the families that their child had died, and in such a horrific manner.

We had many press conferences at that location, and the tragedy was followed by a series of investigations and hearings. The cause of the disaster was quickly discerned. The building that had collapsed was a still-occupied Salvation Army, which stood next to two buildings that were in the process of being demolished. One of these buildings had an unstable wall, which fell on top of the occupied Salvation Army building and crushed it. It is a sad truth that these kinds of tragedies often catalyze serious and significant changes in policies and practices to ensure that they don't happen again. Just a few days after the building collapse, I issued an executive order to make changes in the building construction, inspection, and demolition standards that I could do myself, as mayor. Thereafter we convened an expert commission to review the process for construction and demolition in the city, and the City Council held their own hearings as well. Perhaps the most visible change in the landscape that emerged out of this process, poached directly from New York City, is the now-mandatory posting of large signs on every construction project in the city. They describe the completion date for the project, who is doing it, what it will be, and an emergency phone number.

Having to tell Nancy that her daughter Anne had died in the building collapse, and having to see Philadelphia through that tragedy in which five other citizens were killed, was one of my deepest sadnesses as mayor. All of that sorrow is seared into my mind and soul for the rest of my life. I drive past that site often, and relive those moments and days. As mayor, you really do feel responsible for everything.

One of my greatest frustrations as mayor was unexpected, and not at all something that I had campaigned on or anticipated. I don't generally use the term *frustration*. I think more often in terms of *challenges*. But the attempted sale of the Philadelphia Gas Works (PGW), which had failed by December 2014, would qualify as a frustration—or, more aptly, a saga. Looking back on my time as mayor, this emerges vividly as an example of the worst of politics and personalities, combined.

I had never campaigned for mayor on the idea of selling PGW. True, I didn't think that Philadelphia necessarily should own a gas company, which we have for about 180 years, and during my term as mayor we were the largest city in the country to own one. Rina Cutler, my outspoken, highly respected, and blunt deputy mayor for transportation and utilities, oversaw PGW as part of an extensive portfolio of responsibilities, ranging from SEPTA to the creation of bicycle lanes. But ownership of a gas company is not really a core service for the city. Although I had never campaigned on it, the idea of a PGW sale was certainly not new. It had come up in the Rendell and Street administrations. In 2013, circumstances were different, and more favorable for a sale. First, we were coming out of the recession and there was a lot of private sector money sitting on the sidelines, looking for opportunities. Second, the city pension fund was about 50 percent funded and needed an infusion of cash. Third, in my view, we really didn't need to be in the gas business. But perhaps the real issue was the fourth: who would buy a municipal entity, with a billion dollars of debt on its books? We didn't actually know how much this company was worth.

The problem was, we had never valued PGW. Nor did we know if anyone would actually want to buy it or how much they would pay. This potential sale was grounded in a lot of theory. So we decided at least to get an answer to both of these questions. We brought on a firm to give us advice and valuation, and to assess who could possibly buy PGW and for how much. In their report, our consultant Lazard concluded that the company was worth anywhere between $1.2 and $2 billion, and that there was indeed a market out there to pay this amount and run the company.

This report turned heads, and beliefs, on the City Council and with the unions. Before, I don't think anyone on the council thought that we were serious about the sale or that PGW would have great value. There was a great deal of fear around this potential sale. It made the relevant unions nervous, the business community confused, and the lawyers anxious.

With our report in hand we next pulled together a Request for Proposals to solicit legitimate potential buyers. After several months, we had an astonishing thirty-three letters of intent. Evidently, PGW held a lot of potential and appeal for the private sector, which wouldn't be limited to the sale of gas only in Philadelphia as we had been as a government entity. The company also offered huge infrastructure investment opportunities.

We winnowed the field down to six final bids, at which point each contender had to get more specific and granular, and fill out more forms for compliance. Since this was a private sector transaction, governed by due diligence and nondisclosure issues and agreements, we could never be as transparent as we wanted to be. Unions were able to produce a large amount of disinformation and misinformation, while my team and I had to remain silent, hamstrung as we were by privacy and nondisclosure regulations in the private sector.

Meanwhile, this was 2013, and rumors were swirling that I might be leaving to take a job in the Obama administration and continued speculating that success with this sale would catapult me to the next job. Personally, I don't know how you campaign around the sale of a gas company, but this was the perception. Some on the City Council didn't want to hand me this victory, and in any case a lot of skepticism and even disbelief had been sowed by rumors, silence, and misinformation. In retrospect I really wish I had been able to spend more time trying my best to convey the particulars and details, but I was limited by nondisclosure. Council members simultaneously complained that they had no information about this sale while some of their leaders had refused to sign the nondisclosure agreements that would have given them access to all of the information they wanted. That is how the private sector operates.

The council vowed to do their own research and produce their own report on this potential sale—at the cost of half a million dollars—but before they even reviewed or read their own report, they decided, unconditionally, that they would not take up the issue of the PGW sale at all, and it was politically dead.

The benefits of the PGW sale were for some people almost too perfect to be true, but they were true, nonetheless. The final buyer selected would have paid $1.86 billion, out of which the city would have netted a clear $500 million. Almost all of that profit would have gone into Philadelphia's pension fund, which would be 80 percent funded today, had that happened. Instead, the Philadelphia pension fund is still only about half funded. Among the other advantages of this sale, PGW employees would have had a three-year guaranteed no-lay-off clause, which the employees of PGW did not have at that time. And the private company was going to invest heavily in pipe and main replacement, which would have created more jobs. Furthermore, the company already had union employees, so they were comfortable working within a union environment and with other protections in place. The PGW sale was a fantastic deal, plain and simple. It had something for everyone.

A lot of really good people spent a really large amount of time working on a deal that would have been really great for Philadelphia. Mention PGW today to some of those same people, and they will sigh audibly or put their heads down on the table in despair. My character and inclination when I was mayor—and still today—is to treat people like adults. I provided information about the PGW sale and trusted them to draw conclusions—notwithstanding the fact that rules governing private sector transactions did prevent me from making as explicit or detailed a case in public as I might have, with City Council members who refused to sign nondisclosure agreements. Anyone should have been able to see that it was actually a good deal, all the way around. Of course, we were more involved in explaining and endorsing the sale than that, but the deal in many respects spoke for itself and sold itself. Or at least it should have.

Perhaps the biggest frustration for me was that the PGW sale broke down for reasons that had nothing to do with the actual transaction, but more to do with all of the other ancillary issues that can influence a mayor's tenure. It had to do with short-term thinking, local politics, and personalities. It got ensnared in concerns about who was going to win politically and who was not, and about which person didn't want this or that other person to score a big win. The Republican State House leader at the time characterized the deal's scuttling as a case of "pure parochialism," and I used similar language in my press release on the failure. I called the deal's demise a "big mistake and a massive failure in leadership," during which "small-minded, parochial, and often petty issues and interests" prevailed over the common good. The *Philadelphia Inquirer* editorial page editor opined that there was "no mystery" as to why City Council president Darrell Clarke had used the consultant's study to kill the sale. It was "an exercise in sheer power. . . . Clarke from the beginning showed his disdain for the proposal," the *Inquirer* wrote, "because he had not been included in its formulation." The column continued that the use of a costly report to nix the deal was a "tip of his hat to a way of doing business that Philadelphia has become infamous for," that "won't entice many companies to come to this town."

Being mayor, you learn that people will do what they do, and sometimes what they do doesn't make much sense to you. You learn to accept responsibility for your actions or inaction. Ultimately, even though I never ran on any platform concerning PGW, this incident is now used as an example of how I could not get my agenda through the City Council. Which is nonsense, and inaccurate. I got virtually everything that I ever sent up to the City Council completed—except for two items. One was the soda tax, and as I've explained, Philadelphia now does have one after we attempted it twice. The other was PGW.

Being mayor has to be about getting results, rather than getting credit. Just as the soda tax eventually succeeded, there have been some other successes, deferred. Progress in a city often has a long runway. These successes include the renovation and repair of Penn's Landing, our waterfront area at the Delaware River, to connect this riverfront back to Center City, a connection that the construction of I-95 had severed in the mid-1970s. We seeded the idea and started the process. We knew we weren't going to fully fix Penn's Landing, but we started the city on that path, and in 2017 the governor, the mayor, and the William Penn Foundation announced that they would be investing $225 million to complete the Penn's Landing project, including the creation of a civic space, a trail, and a cap over I-95 with several amenities. This is the culmination of some of the actions that we had initiated years earlier. Mayoring should always be less about credit and more about results, because you can't do everything, even in an eight-year tenure. Do your part, while you're there. Make the best of it. And then literally and figuratively walk off the stage—let the next mayor take over. Being mayor, especially if you have term limits, is like running a relay race. Run your best and fastest for your part, and then hand off the baton, get off the track, and let the next runner do their thing.

—

The building collapse was a stunning and painful tragedy in 2013; PGW was an unanticipated frustration in 2014; and the Amtrak rail crash in Philadelphia was an instructive calamity in 2015.

On May 12, 2015, Amtrak train #188, bound for New York City from Washington, DC, derailed in Port Richmond, a Philadelphia neighborhood. Eventually, investigators found that the train was traveling at just over 100 miles per hour in a zone of curved track with a 50 mph speed limit.

When you're mayor, you are on call twenty-four hours a day, seven days a week. Even on your days off, you are on. Anything can happen, as the Amtrak crash illustrates. I would always say that my schedule was an estimate of what might happen on any given day, but a lot of other things might take place, and you have to be responsive and in many instances *responsible*, whether you are directly or not. When I first arrived at the Amtrak crash scene I described it to the media as an "absolute, disastrous mess."

The days after the crash we did what I've now come to refer to as "the walk." We were all stationed in a nearby trailer. Every day for that week we made this walk, many times a day—from the trailer to the press staging area. By "we" I mean city officials, Amtrak representatives, the National Transportation Safety Board, the Federal Railway Administration, the Amtrak police, the Philadelphia police, the state police, and representatives from the governor's office. Occasionally, a City Council person would join us as well. The governor came out twice, and we had two US senators, members of Congress, and a number of others for that entire week. A calamity such as this is about the coordination of a large number of agencies and people, many of whom don't work for you or are accountable to some other authority.

And we probably had two or three press conferences a day, trying to explain to folks what had happened in the tragedy of Amtrak train #188. I learned some very important lessons about mayoring through this tragedy. First, if you don't have certain factual information, don't try to guess. Second, if you don't know what you're talking about, stop talking. Third, let the professionals explain the things that you're unfamiliar with or don't have all the details on. And last, stay calm and focused.

For example, the first question for roughly the first twenty-four to thirty-six hours or so was, how many people died? We weren't exactly sure. And in the first press conference, that night, we didn't even know how many people were on the train. There was no passenger manifest available to us for hours. This is a situation where if you don't have all the variables and you give just a couple of them, you leave the press and public to their own devices. They'll start figuring and calculating the math on their own. We never gave all the information. Not because we were purposefully trying to withhold it, but because we didn't know the complete answers and we did not want folks to start making assumptions about their loved ones.

That night, at the very first press gathering right after the crash occurred, I told the media, "We do not know what happened here. We are not going to speculate" about causes or casualties. And so until we had a full manifest and had accounted for every person on that train—and part of the problem was that that night some people had gone to the hospital and some people had gone home—we had no idea how many people had died or been injured. We had to track down all 243 people that we finally determined were on the train. Unfortunately, eight people died. But, amazingly, 235 survived.

We went down on the tracks right after the crash, in the pitch black night. Police and firefighters saved people's lives that night. They ran toward danger—they had no idea what they were facing. It could might have been a bomb, a terrorist attack; it could have involved something else entirely. They never hesitated, and they brought people out. When I arrived on the scene, people were literally walking past me who had just come off the train. "It's amazing," I commented. "I don't know how they did it." Some were bleeding, and some were in bad shape. Philadelphians rushed out of their homes to help. They brought towels and water and other things in a spontaneous response of caring and helping, but this was of course a national, potentially international incident. There was a large press presence from across the country behind the barricades of the accident, and some international press arrived a couple days into this incident.

We took all of this very seriously. I cancelled a large portion of the schedule for the week, because mayoral leadership requires that you show up. Leadership requires that you are on the scene. Leadership requires that you give as much information as you can that you know *for a fact* and can stand behind. And there was a lot of coordination.

This incident happened in Philadelphia, but it was not our incident, technically. Many of the passengers on that train were Philadelphians, but this aftermath was all under the jurisdiction of the National Transportation Safety Board. They immediately took jurisdiction, control, and responsibility. And so we had a morning meeting in a trailer on the street where we had briefings and discussions about what we were going to talk about and communicate that day. What was the message of the day? What were the multiple messages of the day? We wanted to make sure that we were not operating outside of those parameters, and so that there would be no surprises in the course of the day.

Amtrak did a spectacular job getting the railroad together, but at the city's insistence with Amtrak, there was a service that following Sunday because we thought it important to recognize the eight who died and the 235 that survived. We planned for a memorial service before train service resumed early that Monday morning around 6:00 A.M. with a train out of the Thirtieth Street Station. I went to Thirtieth Street that Monday morning and greeted all the passengers who were about to get on the resumed service going to New York or Boston that morning. I was trying to reassure them that things were safe, and better.

Which turns out to be much of what being mayor is about.

⁓

You could say that my eight years as mayor ended on a holy note— the holiest imaginable. In 2014 my administration had bid, successfully, to have Philadelphia host the 2016 Democratic convention. I had appointed Melanie Johnson as the Director of Big Events and Research, to research and decide which events the city should host and to learn from other cities' experiences with major events. Melanie's initial research led to Philadelphia's successful bid to host the NFL draft. But you don't bid to host the pope. He decides what he wants to do and where he wants to go. In early 2013 we had learned that the pope and the Vatican had selected Philadelphia as the very first city in the United States to host a World Meeting of Families. Our archbishop received a call from the Vatican one day, to share this news. He immediately called to let me know, and I replied, "That's great news. By the way, what is the World Meeting of Families?" I had a little catching up to do.

About a month after this announcement, Pope Benedict resigned, something that hadn't occurred for centuries, and subsequently Francis became pope. The World Meeting of Families, first held in 1994, is described as an event that combines prayer, lectures, and religious instruction, but it also has a rejuvenating, festival atmosphere. It was estimated that over half a million people would be in Philadelphia for the pope's visit, and some local businesses even offered pope-themed specials, with restaurants preparing food from Pope Francis's home country of Argentina. In exchange for hosting, the city was reimbursed for costs directly related to the papal visit, which largely went toward security costs.

The city received a tremendous amount of logistical support. This event was categorized as a federal national security special event. And, no disrespect intended, but it's also the case that our neighbors to the south and the north—Washington, DC, and New York City—somewhat jumped on the bandwagon of our Philadelphia event. The Speaker of the House at the time, upon learning that Pope Francis was coming to the United States, asked him to come and speak in Washington. And then there was, coincidentally, a UN meeting taking place, and the folks in New York asked him to come as well.

My biggest concern, predictably, was security and safety. Trying to guard the pope is a bit of a challenge. Pope Francis does not like security and does not like seeing security. He gets very upset when he sees that. On one of our visits to the Vatican to discuss logistics, events, and security, we talked with the gentleman who is personally responsible for the pope's safety.

"We've heard some things about the pope, that he doesn't like a whole lot of security—how do you deal with that?" I asked him.

"The Lord will protect him," his security person replied.

"We need a little more than that," I said. "I can appreciate that philosophy, 'when in Rome,' but in Philadelphia, we actually would like to be a little more proactive in our security."

We worked it all out, and the event was incredible, a truly great moment for the city of Philadelphia to shine. On Sunday afternoon the pope said mass for thousands and thousands of visitors on the Benjamin Franklin Parkway. We had what is estimated to be one of the largest crowds ever gathered in the city, with no significant logistical or security glitches. The papal visit elevated the city's standing in the country and the world. It was an incredible experience—and, personally, the highest of high notes on which to soon end my eight years in office.

~

United Cities of America

People often ask me what I'm most proud of, or what I think were my biggest failures as mayor. It depends on the person asking the question, whether they are curious about the biggest failure or the biggest success. The things I'm most proud of are actually the same two things that I wished I'd been able to do more of. So it's one coin with two sides, the greatest success and greatest regret.

First, I'm most proud of the significant reduction in Philadelphia homicides. There are people alive today because of some of the things that we did. At the inauguration I said that we needed a 30 to 50 percent reduction in homicides in three to five years. We had a 37 percent reduction in my sixth year. For the eight years of my administration, we had a 31 percent reduction in homicides in the City of Philadelphia overall.

Second, I'm most proud of the significant increase in high school graduation: It was 53 percent when I came into office and about 68 percent when I left. The other side of that success is the stubborn reality that there are still too many people being killed and shot, and there are still too many Philadelphians who haven't graduated from high school. I wanted an 80 percent high school graduation rate, and I only got to 68 percent. We made significant improvements in both of these critical areas, but I wanted more and better for my city and citizens.

Other accomplishments stand out in my mind. We began a process of reducing civilian fire deaths in the city. We reformed the troubled Department of Human Services, under the leadership of Anne Marie Ambrose, who implemented the nationally recognized Improving Outcomes for Children program. During her tenure, child deaths as well as out-of-home placements in Philadelphia were dramatically reduced. We had eight straight years of population growth, reversing about sixty years of decline. We had the largest percent increase of millennial population of any major city in the United States. Financially, we weathered the Great Recession, and our bond rating was as high as it had been in forty years.

The construction, the start-ups, and the economic growth all convey and communicate that this is a place where you want to be. Events, activities, and innovation happen here. It's a constant effort to communicate a message that this is a good government. There are high-quality people here. This is a serious place. We want to demonstrate respect. We know how to have fun.

We didn't achieve all of the things we wanted to in my administration, or single-handedly, but we certainly set the stage and built on the ideas and programs of other people to make them happen. And we passed on the baton of success, and challenges, to my successor.

~

Unlike my good friend Mayor Bloomberg of New York, I could not serve a third term as Philadelphia's mayor. But, if I had had a third term, then I would have spent even more of my time focused on the two issues of homicide reduction and graduation rates.

But in reality, both of those issues fall under the one much larger umbrella of urban poverty. I have been banging the same drum for many years, but problems in American cities such as Philadelphia really come down to lack of opportunity, literacy, skill sets, problems of incarceration and reentry, and health disparities. The discrete issues are much more complicated, because they are part of an urban dynamic. Philadelphia is a city with 1.5 million people, and nearly 500,000 of them are considered low-literate. We have an estimated 300,000 people who have a previous criminal record, and may find it difficult to get a job, even when they very much would like to. Today, Philadelphia still suffers from the highest poverty rate of any major city in the United States. Of the top ten cities, unfortunately, we are still number one. We've had a poverty rate of over 20 percent for more than thirty years. So the poverty problem was not caused by the recession, although the recession exacerbated it. It was engrained more deeply in the economy of our city. It's the one big thing that holds us back.

Our unemployment rate is certainly lower than it was during the recession, and things have gotten better on that front. We had more Philadelphians working in 2015 than in the previous fifteen years. I have more statistics like this than I know what to do with.

But, still, there is an unacceptable level of human suffering, misery, and anxiety in this city that is deeply embedded and that has what I refer to as a viselike grip on many of our people. It is intergenerational in nature and it is still holding the city back from its even greater potential. Not only does it hold Philadelphia back, but because of the interdependency of Philadelphia and its neighboring counties—Bucks, Chester, Delaware, and Montgomery counties—the human suffering here is actually having a negative effect regionally as well. When we do well, the suburbs do even better. They understand that, and that's why we try to create a lot of partnerships.

This is where the state and the federal government, the philanthropic community, the corporate community, the clergy community, and a number of others can play a very significant and dramatic but also long-term role. In fact, it is impossible for the city to make significant progress on poverty without involvement from these interests. Nor can any of a city's problems be reversed in the short term. In 2012 and 2013 we finally consolidated several agencies and came up with a plan to create Shared Prosperity Philadelphia, which is a plan to reduce poverty in the city in a much more coordinated fashion. And that still continues.

As mayor, you have to have a plan. Mayoring is really about setting goals, having an agenda, making plans, communicating constantly, governing transparently, and providing leadership. This is not like the television show *The West Wing*. It's not a series of encapsulated episodes where you have a problem, you convene several meetings, you have a commercial break, you come back, you fix it, wonderful music plays, and the "episode" is over.

Some days really end badly. Some things are left unresolved—chief among them, huge issues of race, income inequality, and poverty. Mayoring is a lot of responsibility as well as a lot of authority that you have to try to use wisely. That's what I tried to do for eight years as mayor of Philadelphia. I made a lot of decisions, made some mistakes, learned from them, made some other mistakes, learned from those. I tried not to make the same mistake twice. But no one gets it right all the time. I still believe in honesty in communication and laying out what you're trying to do. Acknowledge where you may have made a misstep. And then keep it moving. No one's ever been able to figure out how to fix yesterday. But you can do something about tomorrow.

—

Moving forward from 2017 and into the 2020s, these years are likely to be a test of the sovereignty of cities and home rule. These years will probably cause us to reevaluate the role of the federal government vis-à-vis cities. As I mentioned earlier, the inhabitant of the White House makes a difference in our cities. For example, I have great admiration for Bill and Hillary Clinton. I ran as a Clinton delegate in his 1992 presidential race, and attended my first inauguration in 1993 after he won. Our relationship developed over time while I was on the City Council, and even more so after I became mayor. Both Bill and Hillary Clinton had great generosity and are incredible leaders. They have become good friends of mine, and I admire their sharp intellects, deep compassion for others, and political skills. As president, Clinton cared about issues that affected American cities, and this made a difference in Philadelphia, and elsewhere.

I've been predicting that after the 2016 election, we will see the rise of the United Cities of America. There will be a number of conflicts with the federal level that test the authority of cities to set their own policies. For instance, although the definition is murky, "sanctuary cities" are those that refuse to share immigration status information with federal agencies or to have local police officers act like federal immigration control and enforcement agents. The Trump administration threatened in 2017 to withhold money from these sanctuary cities that do not comply with what they believe is policy or the law.

The federal budget itself, as proposed in 2017, is devastating for cities all across America, whether they are run by Democratic or

Republican mayors. The elimination of a variety of programs and funding sources for cities puts many of us in danger. But it is also sending a powerful if subtle message, to some extent, that cities may be on their own.

This means that mayors will have to look at other collaborations, relationships, public-private partnerships, the foundation community, the corporate community, and resources in the local environment. There is a lot of uncertainty about what cities are going to do and how they'll be affected by the current administration and some of their proposals.

In the meantime, however, mayors need to keep on mayoring. They still have to pick up the trash and fill potholes. Water's got to come out of the faucet; someone's got to respond to a 911 call. Cities are resilient and will figure this out—they have survived for thousands of years now—but I think there's going to be some pretty rough sledding ahead for the next couple years in America while this new arrangement, and this new environment, takes hold.

⁓

There's no public service like being mayor. I enjoyed my time tremendously. I spend my time now talking with other people, other mayors, other leaders—people who want to get into office or folks who have been in office for some time—about some of these challenges and opportunities.

Part of the work that I want to do going forward, and continue to do, is to focus on the issue of poverty, especially for Philadelphia but also for cities across the country. The federal government—and states, too, but especially the federal government—has a significant role to play in that regard, and it would really unlock much of the potential of our cities across America if the federal government would be more supportive and not do things and enact policies that plunge or entrench our people further into poverty.

Some people devote almost all of their working lives to being mayor. Joe Reilly of Charleston, South Carolina, was mayor for forty-three years, and I cannot even imagine being mayor of the same city for that long. For the rest of us—those of us who have mayored for four or eight years—there is life after mayoring, and one of the best examples of the continuation of commitment and dedication to public service in postmayoral life is Mayor W. Wilson Goode. He has further committed his life to the children of incarcerated parents, which is a continuation of his life work and service to the city, and now to the nation. His work comes from a place of deep authenticity, because he experienced the same thing as a child. His father had spent some time incarcerated, and he talks extensively about that.

When I look at what people have done after they've had this enormous responsibility, authority, and power, I give the following advice: Don't fall in love with the job, fall in love with the work. Fall in love with public service and the calling to service.

People often ask me if I miss being mayor. I loved it while I was there, but we have term limits, so I knew it wasn't going to last forever. What I miss the most are the people I worked with—the families, the stories, and watching people grow. As mayor, you have the authority to perform weddings. I've performed weddings for any number of my staff, who've gone on and had kids, bought houses, and gotten other jobs. Some have left public service, then come back to public service.

That's what I miss the most—that daily engagement of knowing that you have *one more opportunity, one more day* to try to make a difference in people's lives by the work you do. And it's thrilling and exciting—it's a rollercoaster of emotion. I could be reading to second graders at a quarter to nine in the morning and delivering remarks at the funeral of a friend at 11 o'clock that day. And everything else that could happen for the rest of the day.

Public service is a trust, a gift, and it is an honor to serve, whether you are elected or selected. And, if you ask me, being mayor *is* the best job in America.

HD
8039
.S86
U63
1994

$24.95

Sims, Patsy.

Cleveland Benjamin's
   dead.

W9-BOC

DATE			

400 S. STATE ST.   60605

BAKER & TAYLOR

Cleveland Benjamin's Dead

PATSY SIMS

Photographs by Mitchel L. Osborne

A
Struggle
for
Dignity
in
Louisiana's
Cane
Country

Cleveland Benjamin's Dead

The University of Georgia Press   *Athens and London*

Published in 1994 by the
University of Georgia Press
Athens, Georgia 30602
© 1981, 1994 by Patsy Sims
All rights reserved

Designed by Kathi L. Dailey
Set in Century Schoolbook by
Tseng Information Systems, Inc.
Printed and bound by Braun-Brumfield, Inc.
The paper in this book meets the guidelines for
permanence and durability of the Committee on
Production Guidelines for Book Longevity of the
Council on Library Resources.

Printed in the United States of America

98 97 96 95 94 C 5 4 3 2 1

Library of Congress Cataloging in Publication Data

Sims, Patsy.
    Cleveland Benjamin's dead : a struggle for dignity in
    Louisiana's cane country / Patsy Sims ; photographs by
    Mitchel L. Osborne. —
    Expanded ed.
        p.   cm.
    ISBN 0-8203-1581-8 (alk. paper)
    1. Sugar workers—Louisiana. I. Title.
HD8039.S86U63   1994
338.7′63361′09763—dc20   93-15731

British Library Cataloging in Publication Data available

An earlier edition of *Cleveland Benjamin's Dead: A Struggle for
Dignity in Louisiana's Cane Country* was published in 1981 by
Elsevier-Dutton Publishing Co., Inc., New York. "Lulu's Story"
and a portion of "On the Way to Rienzi" were published in
Southern Exposure, vol. 22, no. 1, Spring 1994.

The photograph of Gustave Rhodes on page 143 and the
photograph of Viola Freeman on page 4 of the insert © 1992 by
Mitchel Osborne/Southern Mutual Help Association. All other
photographs © 1992 by Mitchel L. Osborne.

CHICAGO PUBLIC LIBRARY
BUSINESS / SCIENCE / TECHNOLOGY
400 S. STATE ST.   60605

*To those who lived this story—the cane workers and
their families, the people involved in helping them,
and the growers—with appreciation and love and
with hope for a mutual understanding of and among
them all. And especially to Gustave and Huet, for
their courage.*

Our people are good people; our people are kind people.

Pray God some day kind people won't be poor.

Pray God some day a kid can eat.

—John Steinbeck, The Grapes of Wrath

Contents

Acknowledgments

This book could never have been possible without the many
people who willingly, and often lovingly, allowed me into their
homes and lives and world. I am grateful to them, and to the
many who provided valuable background material and insights
—especially Dr. Thomas Becnel, Sister Anne Catherine Bizalion,
Lorna Bourg, Sister Robertine Galvin, Hogan & Hartson law
firm, the late Frank Lapeyrolerie, Sister Imelda Maurer, the late
H. L. Mitchell, Henry Pelet, and Peter Schuck.

My thanks to Charles A. Ferguson, who first assigned me to
write about the cane workers; to the Times-Picayune Publishing Company, for permission to use material from the resulting
series; to G. E. Arnold and Ronald LeBoeuf, the photographers
who accompanied me on that venture, and to Mitchel L. Osborne,
whose fondness and feelings for the people and the land are reflected in the photographs herein.

I am especially grateful to my agent, Ellen Levine, and to my
editor, Nancy Holmes, and the University of Georgia Press for

making this expanded edition possible; to Roy Reed, who encouraged me to write the original book; to my former agent Mel Berger for sharing my vision and hope that this material would become a book in the first place; to my editors for the first edition, Elizabeth Backman, Roxanne Henderson, and Paul DeAngelis; to Iris Day, for her sensitivity for words, feelings, rhythm, and a writer's weary bones and head and spirit; to Father Vincent O'Connell, Philip Larson, and Dottie Vann, for advice on the manuscript; and, as always, to Bob Cashdollar for enduring yet another deadline.

Introduction

In late November 1972, when I first traveled to Louisiana's cane
country, little had changed since sugar was first brought to
Louisiana in 1751. Little, except the tractors and giant harvesters that dotted the fields. Year after year the tall green
cane would shoot up, lining highways and dirt roads and hiding
behind it the mostly black fieldworkers and the paint-thirsty
shacks where their parents and their parents' parents had lived,
struggled, and died since the days of slavery. People living just
five miles up the road frequently did not know the workers were
there, virtually tied to the plantation, still calling the grower
"Boss" and the grower still calling them "Boy."

Life for a cane worker meant raising a family of six or eight
children on less than four thousand dollars a year, on a day-after-
day diet of beans and rice and little else, in a dilapidated house
that often had only a fireplace for heat and no indoor toilet or
running water. Many lived and died without learning to read or
write or count, without ever traveling the seventy-five or a hundred miles to New Orleans, without benefit of paid sick leave

or pensions, even without knowing what their income would be from one week to the next.

Under the Sugar Act of 1937 the United States Department of Agriculture held annual hearings to determine "fair and reasonable" wages for the workers, wages that for years inched up a dime an hour until, by the time the act expired in 1974, they had reached $2.50 for machine operators, $2.35 for handworkers. An even greater problem than the hourly wage was the lack of a guaranteed forty-hour work week. During the October-to-January harvest season—known as "grinding"—the workers would labor from sunup to sundown; the rest of the year they might have work only one or two days a week.

As far back as the 1874 strike on the Henry W. Minor Plantation near Houma, fieldworkers had tried to organize to improve their conditions. In the wake of "Kansas Fever," or "the Exodus of 1879," when mounting unrest drove more than ten thousand blacks out of the state, a broader-reaching series of strikes swept through cane country. Beginning on March 17, 1880, workers in St. Charles Parish walked out of the fields after growers turned down their demands for a wage increase from seventy-five cents to a dollar a day. Less than two weeks later, laborers in neighboring St. John the Baptist Parish made the same demand. Still later in the month, minor strikes were reported in Ascension, St. James, St. Bernard, Jefferson, and Plaquemines parishes. The disturbances ended without serious incident and with workers returning to the fields with no more benefits than they had when they started. Over the next six years, localized disturbances of lesser consequence erupted with still no gains.

All these were but a warm-up for what was to occur after the Knights of Labor moved into Louisiana in 1883. Described by historian William Ivy Hair as "one of the most ambitious and visionary associations in American labor history," the Knights endeavored to bring workers of all skills together into one large organization, regardless of color or sex—a platform that doubly angered the generally antiunion South. In 1886, their organizers spread out from New Orleans into the lower delta parishes, urging black fieldworkers to rally together for higher wages and payment in regular currency rather than the customary commissary script redeemable only at plantation stores. The move came after growers reduced wages for the next year to $.65 per day, without rations. For grinding, rates were to vary from $.75 to $1.15 per day for "first class" males; and for six hours of overtime night work, known as "a watch," the plantations would pay $.50. That August 1887, ten weeks before grinding, the Knights asked the Louisiana Sugar Planters' Association to meet to discuss wages for the approaching harvest. In October, after receiving no reply, the Knights sent a circular letter to planters in Iberia, Lafourche, St. Martin, St. Mary, and Terrebonne parishes informing them that they must meet the demands for higher wages by November 1, or face a strike. When growers again refused to concede, an estimated six to ten thousand workers struck.

On the first day of the walkout, a contingency of state militia arrived in Thibodaux, in Lafourche Parish, where members of the Sugar Planters' Association feared violence would follow their announcement that all strikers would have to vacate plantation housing. Ten days later, ten more companies and two batteries of state militia were ordered in, and at least one of the units brought along an early version of the machine gun to back up the militiamen assigned to carry out evictions.

During the first three weeks of the strike, several blacks and whites were killed or wounded, with each side blaming the other for the bloodshed. The situation became even more desperate on November 20 when a freeze threatened what growers had viewed as a near-record crop. By that point the militia had vacated the area, and in its place an armed band of white vigilantes gathered in Thibodaux, which had become a refuge for the evicted workers and their families. Shooting began on the night of November 22. When it ended at noon the next day, at least thirty blacks were dead; hundreds more were wounded—only two of them white. A newspaper reporter wrote of seeing even more bodies in nearby swamps. For a time there was talk of another black exodus, and at least one group did head for Mississippi in search of more humane conditions, but by the first of December most of the blacks were back in the fields. A year after the Thibodaux Massacre, strikes broke out in four parishes, but sixty-five years passed before there was another serious attempt to organize the fieldworkers.*

* For a fuller discussion of the Knights of Labor and the Thibodaux Massacre, see William Ivy Hair, *Bourbonism and Agrarian Protest: Louisiana Politics, 1877–1900* (Baton Rouge: Louisiana State University Press, 1969), pp. 152–53, 176–85; also, Thomas Becnel, *Labor, Church, and the Sugar Establishment: Louisiana, 1887–1976* (Baton Rouge: Louisiana State University Press, 1980), pp. 2–8.

That effort was led by the Southern Tenant Farmers' Union (STFU), which became interested in organizing sugar workers in 1937 and, along with envoys from Archbishop Joseph Francis Rummel of New Orleans, began showing up at the annual wage hearings to testify on their behalf. The actual organizing got under way in 1948, with H. L. Mitchell and members of his National Agricultural Workers' Union (the renamed STFU) first tackling dairy farmers and strawberry growers to establish an agricultural base before moving on to the workers behind what had become known as the "cane curtain."

The Catholic church's role in these efforts was considerable, with Archbishop Rummel providing financial backing and frequently acting as a go-between with the union and the growers. The prelate had established himself as an advocate for social justice in the mid-1930s after becoming archbishop of New Orleans. In 1939, he took an active role in the newly formed Catholic Committee of the South, a group of clergy and lay leaders dedicated to solving problems of labor-management relations, race relations, and social reform. That same year he called a special conference to explore industrial problems and created the Archdiocesan Social Action Committee to act as a liaison between the church and industry, selecting a young priest named Vincent O'Connell as chair.

The committee met with representatives of labor and management and eventually succeeded in organizing garbage workers, domestics, carpenters, and communications workers. Father O'Connell and the committee turned their attention to sugarcane workers after he learned of their plight during his temporary assignment to St. Peter's Church in Reserve, in the heart of cane country. Soon, he and several other priests were in the thick of things, speaking out against the injustices, opening their church halls and schools to organizing meetings, even—in the case of Father O'Connell—helping with the organizational efforts.

And so with aid of the clergy the National Agricultural Workers' Union finally chartered a local of sugar workers in 1953. In July of that year, union representatives sent letters to nine of the state's biggest producers asking them to enter into collective bargaining. After that and still another request to bargain were turned down, an estimated three thousand workers struck on October 12, 1953. But again the growers refused to budge, ignoring even Archbishop Rummel's appeals. Grinding was slowed but not stopped as the planters doggedly persisted with whatever workers they could muster. By early November the union was virtually out of money, and after the courts issued a temporary order forbidding sympathetic refinery workers from walking off their jobs in support of the fieldworkers, the organizers had no recourse but to end the strike. By November 10, the workers were back in the fields. In 1954, another effort to organize met with yet another failure.

Even with the union and the Catholic church behind them, the fieldworkers were impotent against the powerful growers. Neither the American Federation of Labor nor the Congress of Industrial Organizations would give H. L. Mitchell and his National Agricultural Workers' Union the financial support they needed to do the job, and even some of Archbishop Rummel's priests bucked his bidding on behalf of the workers. Thus the workers ground on in a servitude perpetuated decade after decade by regulations that shackled them to the growers and the land as surely as had slavery—regulations overseen first by the generals of the conquering federal armies and Freedmen's Bureaus and finally by the United States Department of Agriculture.*

And so it was that on July 9, 1971, the department came to Houma and staged its annual wage hearing. But that October, contrary to custom, the hourly rates were not announced at the start of grinding season. Not until late December did Agriculture Secretary Earl Butz report that the fieldworkers would receive a ten-cents-an-hour raise—effective January 10, 1972. By that date, however, the crop was in, and since rates traditionally dropped a dime an hour after harvest, workers remained at their 1970 pay scale. Butz blamed the delay in setting the wages on Phase 2 of President Richard Nixon's Economic Stabilization Act—better known as "The Freeze"—and refused to make the raise retroactive, reasoning that the growers should not be required to pay rates they did not know about when the work was performed. Partly because they lacked the education to express themselves, and partly because they feared the power-

*For a fuller discussion of the church's role in organizing cane workers, see Becnel, *Labor, Church, and the Sugar Establishment*.

ful growers, the workers complained to one another but not to outsiders. The growers, with the help of Nixon and Butz, had won again.

This time, however, the workers had an ally—the Southern Mutual Help Association (SMHA). Composed mostly of rural priests and nuns and college students, the small but fearless—and often-threatened—organization existed solely to help the workers. And so that summer, with SMHA's encouragement and backing, two workers—Huet Freeman and Gustave Rhodes—decided to sue Butz and the Department of Agriculture for the wages owed them and Louisiana's twelve thousand cane workers. They knew the risk. They could lose their jobs and their homes. But they also knew the time had come to stand up to the growers.

It was at this point that I arrived in cane country in late November 1972 to begin a series of articles on the fieldworkers for the New Orleans *States-Item,* an assignment that was to earn me the growers' wrath and deeply involve me in the lives of the workers and those dedicated to helping them. I had recently completed an eleven-part series on race relations in New Orleans, and I think the editor saw me as the logical person to tackle the assignment. I remember him telling me he didn't care how long I took or how much we spent. Such freedom was unheard of for a reporter, even one in my enviable position as "special assignment writer." It was understood that we were doing something special.

The initial plan was for one writer and one photographer to create a record of human conditions in the cane fields, somewhat as James Agee and Walker Evans had done with cotton tenant farmers in the late 1930s. But fearing a camera might call attention to our presence, the editors and I decided that I should make the first trips onto the plantations alone or with a contact from SMHA to avoid interference by the growers. Ultimately we decided that I would accompany instructors from SMHA's Plantation Adult Education Program, as one of them, until I secured the workers' trust.

Now, after twenty years of intimacy with the workers and their problems, it is difficult to look back and measure just what I knew then about the workers. I think, however, it would be safe to say I knew absolutely nothing, even though I had lived less than fifty miles away in New Orleans for twenty-three years. And I was not unique—few people knew of the workers and their desperate lives.

For more than three months their world became mine. I shared their joys and their crises, their births and deaths. I came to care deeply for them—and yes, I think the caring was mutual. After a while, as soon as my car pulled up, they would fly from their raw-wood shacks with open arms and news of a daughter's baby, a granny's passing. That period was a turning point in my own life: my writing, my interests, my concerns have never been the same.

I returned in 1974 and again in 1978 to expand the newspaper series into a book, each time finding a few changes, a few improvements. For the most part, however, the workers' plight was unchanged. The prospect of the book was a source of excitement and joy for the workers and me. Together we looked forward to the publication—to their names, their faces, their stories becoming a book. After the original publisher was sold to another house, however, the manuscript became enmeshed in the complications that so often accompany such mergers. Eventually I had to delete a hundred pages, and, at least for me, the book was never the same.

Then the University of Georgia Press expressed interest in restoring the cut material for a revised edition, and so, twenty years after my initial visit, I found myself back in cane country and back among the tapes and transcripts and notes that had been collecting dust in my basement. The journey was at once rewarding and frustrating. Once one has literally committed something to print, it is not easy to change even what one knows is flawed. And so I indulged in days, weeks, of what writer-teacher Janet Burroway might call comma shoving, rewriting a passage and the next day changing it back to what it was, and the day after that changing it yet again. Two complete chapters and many more pages, paragraphs, and sentences are restored here; other passages I decided, in the end, to leave out. But what seems to me of greater importance is that another generation of readers will be able to venture behind Louisiana's cane curtain.

Persons and Places

Mabel Freeman Williams	Huet's mother
Andrew Williams	Huet's stepfather; a retired fieldworker
Jessie Preston	Huet's grandfather; a retired fieldworker
Florida (Shug) Preston	Jessie's wife and Huet's grandmother
Joe (Peanut) Freeman	Huet's older brother; a former fieldworker who now lives in California
Gustave Rhodes	A cane worker on Elm Hall Plantation, near Napoleonville; president of the Southern Mutual Help Association's Plantation Adult Education Advisory Committee
Beverly Rhodes	Gustave's wife
Tim	Age twenty-one; away in the military
Hester (Cookie)	Age nineteen
Wanda	Age thirteen
Rodney	Age twelve
David	Age eleven
Matthew	Age ten
Charlene	Age eight

Cane Workers and Their Families

Because of the workers' fear of reprisal, many names have been changed.

Millard Barnes	A cane-cutter operator on Hard Times
Cleveland Benjamin	A tractor driver on Enola Plantation, near Napoleonville
Mrs. Moser Benjamin	Cleveland's mother

Tillman Dickinson	A retired fieldworker and Huet's neighbor on Hard Times
Willie Dowell	A tractor driver who lost his legs in an accident on Enola Plantation
Bertha Dowell	Willie's mother
Percy Green	A retired cane worker on Coulon Plantation, near Thibodaux
Fillmore Jones	A fieldworker on a plantation between Thibodaux and Napoleonville
Mattie Jones	Fillmore's wife
Eula	Age seventeen
Leroy	Age fifteen
Annie	Age fourteen
Joyce King Hadley	A community organizer for the Southern Mutual Help Association (SMHA) who once lived on Coulon Plantation with her family
Willie King	Joyce's grandfather; a retired worker living on Rienzi
Lulu King	Willie's wife and Joyce Hadley's grandmother
Golena King Wright	Adult children of Willie and Lulu King; also fieldworkers
Lois King	
Junius King	
Oliver King	
Turner King	
Lily Mae Smith	Wife of a white tractor driver on a plantation between Thibodaux and Napoleonville
Sister	Wife of a handyman on Levert-St. John Plantation, near St. Martinville
Moses West	A retired cane worker residing in an abandoned shack near Houma

Rosa West	Moses's wife
Pearlie	Age twenty-one
Jay	About age sixteen
Ida	About age fourteen
Elsie	A former fieldworker on Enterprise Plantation, near New Iberia
Jasper	Elsie's son; a fieldworker on Enterprise Plantation

Growers

Thomas H. Allen	General manager of Sterling, Inc.
John Vernon Caldwell	Owner of Coulon Plantation, near Thibodaux
Pete J. deGravelles, Jr.	A grower in St. Mary Parish; official spokesman and chairman of the American Sugar Cane League's Employees Relation Committee
J. P. Duhe II	A grower in the Jeanerette area
Murphy J. Foster	A grower in St. Mary Parish; son of a former Louisiana governor and U.S. senator
F. A. Graugnard, Jr.	A grower in St. James Parish; secretary of the American Sugar Cane League
William S. Patout, Jr.	Major owner of M. A. Patout and Son, which operates Enterprise Plantation and a sugar mill in the Jeanerette–New Iberia area; employer of Elsie and Jasper

Organizations

American Sugar Cane League	Composed of Louisiana growers

National Farm Labor Union, AFL	Renamed the National Agricultural Workers' Union during its attempt to organize cane workers during the 1940s and early 1950s; previously involved in California with grape and lettuce pickers
Southern Mutual Help Association	A small group of priests, nuns, and volunteers formed in 1969 to help cane workers and their families
Plantation Adult Education Program	An SMHA program headquartered in Thibodaux
Southdown Lands, Inc., and South Coast Corporation	Largest sugar growers in Louisiana and subsidiaries of out-of-state conglomerates

Workers' Allies

Sister Anne Catherine Bizalion	A Rural Dominican nun originally from France; executive director of the Southern Mutual Help Association
Millie Bordelon	Employee at area Neighborhood Service Center; daughter of a white small grower in the New Iberia area who befriended the fieldworkers
Lorna Bourg	SMHA's assistant director
Father Vincent O'Connell	Head of SMHA's Plantation Adult Education Program; active in attempting to unionize the fieldworkers in the 1940s
Rose Mae Broussard	Director of SMHA's health clinic in Franklin; active in early integrated community service programs
Bernard Broussard	Rosa Mae's husband

Elnora Mack Jo Ann Morris	Instructors for the Plantation Adult Education Program
Father Frank Ecimovich	SMHA's board president before growers pressured his religious order to transfer him to Arkansas
Henry Pelet	SMHA board member; sugar-mill worker in Labadieville, between Thibodaux and Napoleonville; president of Local P-1422, Amalgamated Meat Cutters and Butcher Workmen, which represented mill workers
Sister Robertine Galvin	Principal of St. Cecilia School in Broussard who became involved with helping the fieldworkers
Sister Mildred Leonard	A teacher at St. Cecilia School
Sister Imelda Maurer	A member of their religious order who joined Sister Robertine's efforts with the cane workers
Frances Bernard	Director of the Neighborhood Service Centers in Broussard, Long, Lafayette, Youngsville, and Milton
Curley Bernard	Frances's husband; a small farmer
Father Bill Crumley	A Holy Cross priest and supporter of the workers; board member of the Louisiana Council on Human Relations
Frank Lapeyrolerie	Son of a black cane farmer; helped organize fieldworkers in the late 1940s; SMHA board member
H. L. Mitchell Hank Hasiwar	Organizers with the National Agricultural Workers Union who attempted to unionize the fieldworkers in the late 1940s and early 1950s

Victor Bussie	President of Louisiana AFL-CIO
Peter Schuck	Attorney with Ralph Nader's Center for the Study of Responsive Law
John Ferren Arnold Johnson Philip Larson	Attorneys with Hogan & Hartson, the Washington law firm that represented the fieldworkers

Others

Earl Butz	Secretary of agriculture; principal defendant in the Freeman-Rhodes lawsuit
Archbishop Joseph Rummel	The late prelate of the Archdiocese of New Orleans; staunch behind-the-scenes supporter of the workers' efforts to organize a union
Bishop Robert Tracy	Bishop of Baton Rouge diocese
Bishop Maurice Schexnayder	Bishop of Lafayette diocese; member of a family of Louisiana growers
Bishop Gerard L. Frey	Bishop Schexnayder's successor
Monsignor John Kemps	Pastor of Sacred Heart Church in Broussard, part of the Lafayette diocese
Edwin E. Huddleson III	Attorney representing the U.S. Department of Agriculture and Secretary Earl Butz
Judge John H. Pratt	U.S. district court judge for the District of Columbia; presided over fieldworkers' suit
James Agnew Earle Gavett Marvin Gelles	Officials from the U.S. Department of Agriculture who presided over 1973 Houma wage hearing

Donald Heitman
William Ragsdale

Paul G. Borron   Attorney for the American Sugar
                                   Cane League

Dr. Joe R. Campbell   Agricultural economist at
                                   Louisiana State University; a
                                   principal witness for growers at
                                   annual wage hearing

The Setting

In 1972, cane country consisted of sixteen parishes (counties) concentrated in the southeastern portion of Louisiana. The book's action is centered in three areas: Thibodaux-Napoleonville, two small towns about 60 miles southwest of New Orleans on Bayou Lafourche; Lafayette–New Iberia (also known as Teche Country because of its proximity to Bayou Teche), about 150 miles west of New Orleans; and Houma, the setting for the wage hearings, home of numerous plantations, and headquarters for Southdown Lands, Inc., and its refinery. Houma is approximately 20 miles south of Thibodaux and 50 miles southwest of New Orleans.

Donaldsonville   Towns in the Thibodaux-
Dorseyville   Napoleonville area
Labadieville

Belle Alliance   Plantations in the Thibodaux-
Belle Rose   Napoleonville area
Coulon
Elm Hall
Enola
Hard Times
Little Texas
Magnolia
Orange Grove
Rienzi
St. Thomas
Wildwood

Broussard Franklin Jeanerette St. Martinville Youngsville	Towns in the Lafayette-New Iberia area
Bayside Enterprise Hope Katy Levert-St. John Maryland Oaklawn	Plantations in the Lafayette-New Iberia area
Belle Grove Crescent Farms Hollywood Iodine	Plantations in the Houma area
Reserve	A small town about an hour northwest of New Orleans; sugar-growing center and site of Godchaux-Henderson sugar refinery

Cleveland Benjamin's Dead

Grinding

Now the cutters hungrily ravaged the fields. Trailers and trucks raced up and down the roads to load and unload the cane. Twenty-four hours a day they hurried to the mill, lining up all the way to the big highway. The tireless mill belched smoke—sometimes white, sometimes gray—and at night its blazing lights invaded the dark. The drivers stood in twos and threes alongside their trucks and trailers, talking, lighting cigarettes, waiting turns for their cane to be weighed and unloaded. Giant claws reached into the trailers and trucks and grabbed the stalks, lowering them into special bins or onto storage piles that grew into hills and the hills into mountains, and then—almost as quickly—dwindled to hills and the hills to piles as the cane traveled through the mill. Inside, shredders and crushers pressed out the sweet juice and separated it from the fibrous stalk—bagasse, it's called. Then the juice journeyed through strainers and purifiers and evaporators until it emerged a thick syrup—molasses—and, after boiling and separating, became crystallized raw sugar ready for still another trip, by truck or trailer or train or barge, to the refinery.

1972

The cane cutter

The Death

The shouts traveled down the dirt road: *"Cleveland Benjamin jes' been kilt! Cleveland Benjamin jes' been kilt!"* Through the living quarters, past the faded green houses, faint, almost indistinguishable from the hum of distant tractors, the cries grew louder until they became words and then, like the man who shouted them, disappeared into the distance. Just those words. Over and over, rhythmically, a death knell accompanied by the rapid thud of feet hitting damp, packed earth, and then the banging of screen doors and more footsteps, on wood, as the people—women and children, mostly; the men were in the fields—hurried onto porches, into yards. Some exchanged words with the man, the tones more understandable than the words themselves; but most stood mute, their expressions changing to anguish when they heard, when they understood.

Overhead the sky was shrouded in gray, and a wind, warm for December, whipped through the tall cane which grew to the edge of the yards and stopped, abruptly, hemming in the people

and the houses like a curtain that had shut out time and tres-
passers. Eight houses huddled beside the road—dust in summer,
now turned to mud by endless days of rain. Behind them, on a
similar road, were nine more houses, each connected by a narrow path to an outhouse. And beyond that, cane stretched as far
as you could see. With the coming of the man, the sound of tractors was lost in a chorus of questions, pleas, shrieks, moans—at
once, yet not together, never blending: *Dead? Cleveland's dead?
Nooooooo! Oooooooh, Lawd—Gawd—Lawd! Jeeeeeeesus, Lawd
Jeeeeeeeeeesus! Have mercy!*

Beverly Rhodes and I were outside watching four hogs root-
ing in the mud when we heard the shouts. As we turned toward
them, toward the road and the gathering people, Beverly put her
hand to her mouth and gasped "When?" The man yelled back
"Jes' now!" and kept running, occasionally answering a question
but never stopping, never slowing, never altering his pace. We
glimpsed the horror on his face, and then he was past us, gone.
Beverly stepped back from the pen, stunned, silent, oblivious
to the grunting pigs and to me. Then, realizing I may not have
understood, she repeated, "Cleveland Benjamin jes' got killed.
Tractor turned over on him next plantation over." She spoke the
words slowly, lowly, all emotion wrung from them.

"The first week of grindin' a young man got both his legs burnt
off on that same plantation," she fretted. "Tractor turned over on
him an' caught fire. When they got him to the hospital, his legs
they be burnt so bad they had to cut 'em off. One boy got killed
right here on Elm Hall, the Williams boy. That was durin' the
time I was workin' in the fields, an' I was right there when he
got killed." We began walking toward the house, slowly, Beverly's
voice trailing off, then starting again. "It's a dangerous job. *Real*
dangerous. 'Specially now. The fields they be wet, an' that heavy
machine can easily turn over in that mud."

At thirty-eight, Beverly was a tall woman of large frame and
sturdy build with strong shoulders and eyes and chin—a woman
confidently growing into her role as matriarch, as family bul-
wark. Her still-smooth features bore promise of an even deeper
beauty, when a wrinkled patina would be etched by surviving
and by wisdom learned from living, not from books. She had been
cheerful when we met half an hour earlier, but now bewilderment, then worry moved across her face like storm clouds dark-

ening the land. Her husband, Gustave, was somewhere in the fields high on a cane cutter, a far more dangerous machine than a tractor. It could have been him. For seventeen years she had lived with the fear that he might lose an arm, a leg—*his life*—to the mammoth machine. The fear was as strong, as nagging, as real as her fear of the man they all called "Boss."

"When they first put Gustave on the cane cutter, they was the type he had a blade man an' he wouldn't have to get down," she said, still walking. "But since they got the Blue Boy, he have to work ever'thing by hisself. He have to cut the roads close to the ditch bank, an' sometime they cave in, an' oh! I be so afraid he'll turn over. Sometime other people done knocked off, an' if they don't have enough cane cut for the next mornin', he have to stay an' cut in the dark, an' I be so afraid he'll have a accident an' won't nobody be there."

Her pace quickened, past neat rows of cabbages, turnips, mustards, carrots, and shallots, which, come summer, would be replaced by okra, squash, snap beans, eggplant, and corn to feed the hogs. Nearby, dried ears from last season's crop were stored in a dilapidated shed, and charred food wrappers spilled from two rusted metal drums, littering the pathway to the house where she and Gustave and six of their seven children lived.

A black-and-orange cat stopped licking its paw to watch as we crossed the porch. Beverly opened the screened door and called, "*Cookie!* Oh, Cookie!"

A girl in her late teens appeared.

"Yessum?"

"You mind the others while Miss Patsy an' I go see Viola Freeman," Beverly told the girl. Then we got into my Volkswagen and backed onto the dirt road.

It was the end of my first week in cane country, a week I had spent interviewing black fieldworkers and their families for a series I was writing for the New Orleans *States-Item*. Originally Beverly had planned to introduce me to workers on other plantations, but now that purpose seemed secondary to reaching Hard Times to tell Viola Freeman about Cleveland Benjamin's death. The two women had known each other for years, as most plantation families did, but their friendship had strengthened since the previous summer when Gustave and Huet Freeman filed their lawsuit. After the men challenged Secretary Earl Butz and the

United States Department of Agriculture to retrieve wages the workers had been denied, many of those same workers, out of fear, had isolated the two families in much the same way the towering cane separated them from the outside world.

Leaving Elm Hall we were for a time shut in by cane, the dirt-and-gravel road seeming to meander on forever. Then a cluster of frame houses appeared in a distant clearing, and as we neared, I heard a bell clanging.

"Enola Plantation," Beverly said simply. "That's the bell to let ever'body know somethin's happened."

"The bell?"

"Same one they wakes the people with."

The clanging became slow, measured, a toll, then stopped as we approached the houses, one of them alive with people. "That's where Cleveland Benjamin lived, but we best not stop," Beverly said. "The foreman, he live across the road, an' he sometime throw white people off the place for fear they be tryin' to organize a union."

A half dozen women were sitting on the porch of Cleveland Benjamin's house, some on kitchen chairs, some on the steps. Nobody was crying. They were just sitting there staring at the dirt road.

The Labyrinth

*The network of dirt roads is not unlike the mazes used with
mice in psychology labs. If you don't make the right turn you
don't get out, and somehow the workers—most of them treated
not too unlike the field mice that scurry through the cane in
summer and flee to the shacks during grinding—never make
that turn.*

On Hard Times Plantation

We drove for a time past alternate patches of stubble and standing cane. In one field, already leveled by the cutter, a man in
work clothes moved up and down the rows, methodically touching a handful of flaming stalks to the felled cane. Flames soared
skyward as they burned away the leaves, the tops—the shucks.
The man laid down the torch and ambled to the side of the road
to watch. Soon the flames flickered, then died, leaving a field of
white smoke and, finally, naked black stalks ready for the mill.

From the car, Beverly and I watched before proceeding down
the road until we came to a railroad crossing and still another
dirt road, where Beverly said to turn. On the other side, a half
dozen brick-papered shacks hugged the road, sticking up like
warts on the land.

"This is Hard Times," she announced.

The settlement was as depressing as its name. Gray boards
showed through the tattered imitation-brick tar paper, and the
tin roofs were patched and rusty, the porches eaten away by time

and weather. Muddy tractor ruts separated the houses from the road, with an occasional plank from a torn-down shack straddling the puddles, connecting the two.

Women and children peeked through screen doors as we drove past a small, shed-size house and its larger neighbor. At the third house a woman stepped onto the porch and watched as Beverly and I approached. By the time we reached the house, six small girls of assorted sizes had gathered with her.

"This is Viola Freeman," Beverly said by way of introduction, "an' Patsy Sims. She's from New Orleans, from the newspaper."

Viola Freeman was a short, happy-looking woman of thirty. She wore a cotton shirt and slacks, and her hair was wound on pink curlers. She smiled shyly as the smallest child grinned, then buried her face between her mother's legs. Before Viola could speak, Beverly asked, "You hear about Cleveland Benjamin, 'bout him gettin' killed on a tractor?" The smile vanished as Beverly repeated the few details she had heard about the accident, the ones shouted by the man.

"He live by Willie Dowell," Viola said absently, her mind seemingly far away, perhaps in the fields with her husband, Huet.

Beverly answered, "Uh-huh."

"Oh, Lawd!" Viola cried, as if there was no more she, or anybody, could do. "My sister-in-law's husband he got killed on Elm Hall. He was back a the cart, an' he fell off an' got run over."

"You worry about Huet?" I asked.

"Yeah, I be thinkin' about him gettin' killed, gettin' hurt," she said as she led us into the house.

The living room was about twice the width of a sway-backed bed that was pushed to one side and covered with a faded red chenille spread. Near the door were a threadbare sofa and a dresser with family snapshots displayed on top. Children's clothes hung from a wire stretched across one corner, for there were no closets. The adjoining room was crowded with another double bed, a folded-up roll-away, a shabby couch, and a platform rocker. On the mantle of a fireplace no longer safe to use sat a spray gun for mosquitoes and a bottle of pine oil. The flowered wallpaper was rain stained, with large holes that exposed cracks in the outer walls and, beyond that, the brick-paper siding.

"I put that wallpaper up to make it look nice an' to keep the wind out," Viola said. "But the rats ate it, an' now they be after my clothes. We been puttin' down rat poisonin', but them rats are takin' over the house." She chuckled. "This house been here so long till a little wind come an' I be ready to get out, it shake so."

Daylight showed through gaps in the walls of the kitchen, and the ceiling was cardboard. The room was furnished with a stove, a refrigerator, a worktable, and a cabinet of odds-and-ends dishes, but no sink. A bowl filled with soapy water rested on top of a barrel near the back door.

"That's our face bowl," Viola said. "The water faucet's outdoors."

So was the toilet.

"That's where you get the water for your baths and everything?" I asked, looking into the yard at a hydrant sticking up through the mud and weeds.

She nodded. "Catch it, tote it in, heat it—do all that."

Viola had moved onto the plantation ten years earlier after she and Huet were married at his grandparents' house across the road. They had lived in one of the smaller shacks until their family outgrew it. Other relatives dwelt up and down the road: the grandparents, retired now; Huet's uncle; and two of Viola's brothers who, like her, had migrated from St. Francisville, just north of Baton Rouge, where her father had been a carpenter and worked cotton. She had quit school in eighth grade to help her parents provide her and her eight siblings with a life that was little better than what she had now on the plantation.

Back in the front room, I asked the women what they had thought when their husbands filed the lawsuit, and Beverly admitted she was afraid. "A lotta people were talkin' that they would throw us off the plantation," she said, "but I felt if they did we always could go to another one. Really, we had to do somethin'. But the people back here aren't a hundred percent behind us. When we have meetin's we can't get nobody to go. I guess they be afraid."

"What about the women—do they associate with you?" I asked.

"Not too much," Viola answered.

"Are you sort of by yourself?"

"That what it seem like to me."

Beverly added, "A couple men from the plantation called Gustave 'white mouth.' They say he be doin' what the white people at Southern Mutual Help Association told him to do."

Viola's six daughters had drifted into the room, and the tallest stood close beside her, waiting eagerly as though she had something important to say.

"Ann Marie had a birthday," Viola explained.

The girl grinned.

"How old were you?" I asked.

"Was ten." She ducked her chin, her eyes focused on the floor.

"What did you get for your birthday?"

The grin widened, but it was Viola who answered. "Her daddy, last year he brought her a big orange. She say, 'Daddy, all I want you to bring me is the same thing, a big orange.'"

"You didn't make her a cake?" Beverly said, surprised. "Awwwwww, Mama didn't make you a cake? Any my kids have a birthday I *have* to make 'em a cake, an' if I don't they get out there in the street an' tell ever'body." She laughed and Viola, embarrassed, offered, "I'm gonna make her a cake next week. See, that's when I make my groceries."

For the most part, that shopping list would be made up of staples like beans and rice—that's what the family ate, mostly. Even milk and juice for the kids were rare, and if it wasn't for food stamps and the coons and rabbits Huet was able to put on the table, Viola didn't know what she would do.

I asked, "Do you think you'll ever move off?"

"I hope so."

"Does your husband want to?"

"Yeah," she said softly, confidently. "He's talkin' about it."

"Have you ever been out of Louisiana?"

"Out of Louisiana? Not me, *no!*" She laughed gently. "I woulda like to when I was young, but I done got too old."

Beverly grew nostalgic. "Once I did; when my brother had a heart attack I went to see him in Georgia. But mostly jes' young men go outta state, to the service. Fieldworkers an' their families seldom get past Charity Hospital in New Orleans. Some never go to Baton Rouge even."

When Beverly and I were ready to leave, Viola and the girls walked us to the door. Down the road, a large man in khaki work clothes was standing on a porch. He waved, and Beverly waved back.

"That's Millard Barnes," she said. "You want to meet him?"

As we made our way through the mud and across the road

she called out, "You hear about Cleveland Benjamin?" The man limped to the edge of the porch, curious. "Tractor turned over an' killed him."

Millard Barnes creased his brow. "Oh no! That boy on the same plantation jes' lost his legs." He looked down at his own limbs. Even with the limp he was a sturdy man—his chest was broad, his face full, his hands large and strong. He shook his head, remembering. "It be fo'teen years since the tractor turned over, turned bottom up," he said. "It was on top a me but I didn't figure it was serious as it was. I was kinda young then, an' I jes' went along with the owner of the place. He's dead an' gone now, but he kep' on tellin' me about how 'You don't have to go to the doctor, man—you'll overcome it.'" Millard Barnes looked at me, explaining as much with his eyes as with his words. "He wanted me for grindin', you understand, an' I *wanted* to he'p him, so I limpt around an' worked. About eight years after that, it upsetted me an' I stayed in Charity Hospital fifty-eight days before I come out."

A woman and a boy of nine or ten stood in the doorway, listening but not entering the conversation as Millard Barnes continued. "I didn't put in no claim till after I fell sick. I went to Charity an' they took x-rays. First thing these people told me, 'Somethin' heavy done fell on you.' So now I got plastic intestines because a that accident."

"Do accidents scare you?" I asked.

He grew excited, his speech rapid. "Y'all passed that machine settin' down there off the road, that three-leg thing?" He pointed in the direction of a cane cutter pulled to the side of the road in the distance. "That's what I run, an' you *know* that enough to scare me."

A pickup truck pulled into the gravel driveway, and the driver —white, fortyish, wearing khakis—glared at Beverly and me, and then at Millard Barnes while the motor idled. Millard Barnes looked from the truck to us, nervously.

"This was my dinner break," he said, "I gotta go to the fields now."

He hurried down the steps and eased into the cab. The driver gunned the motor and the truck spun backward, slinging gravel and shattering the rear window of Millard Barnes's parked car as the truck sped off down the road. Millard Barnes's wife had not spoken during our conversation and she didn't now, not verbally, at least—only with her eyes, as if someone had torn her only Sunday dress.

Farther down the Road

An elderly man sat on a bench in front of the small shack next to the railroad tracks. His head snapped toward the sound of our car engine, and he hurried to his feet and motioned for us to pull over, to stop. He trudged toward the car and stuck his head through the window on Beverly's side. "I'm Tillman Dickinson," he said in a Cajun patois. "We gonna talk. I wanna talk to y'all."

He stepped back, childlike anticipation on his face, and watched, waited. When we opened the car doors, his face crinkled so that I could see four browning teeth—two uppers, two lowers. He was an average-sized man, slightly stooped, with bright eyes and a smile that overcame the facial lines carved by time and hard work. A billed cap covered his head, but his sparse mustache and the stubble on his chin were gray. Mud caked his clumsy shoes and baggy pants, yet he seemed not to notice as he urged us toward the shack.

"I work hyere," he said proudly. "I scrap cane an' I he'p 'em out.

When I don't feel like it, I don't—when I'm not able. I'm goin' on sixty-three."

"Were you born here?" I asked.

"Naw, I wadn't born hyere. I was born in Lafourche Parish, on the Cedar Plantation. I live there till a good while, but then I ramble a li'l bit." He chuckled, then turned his back and struggled across the yard, motioning for us to follow.

He had lived on one plantation or another all his days. His father, he said, had been a *farmer's* farmer, managing a piece of land for a man named Mr. Labadie. As for his grandfather, Tillman Dickinson had never known him.

"You live alone?" I asked.

"Yeah, all by myself," he said, gesturing toward the bench as he passed it. "I just settin' there 'cause it feel good an' I be lonesome inside alone."

Indoors, light from a side window formed a square on the worn floor of the dark kitchen. A battered coffeepot rested on a burner of the small gas stove, and next to it three blackened skillets hung from nails. Like the floor, the walls were made of crude gray boards, and the only color came from a fireplace that had been painted red.

"We don't use that now 'cause they don't want no fire hazard, see? So they connect a li'l heater hyere," he said. "Sometime it get col' but my heater warm me up. When it get *real* col' I put on plenty clothes an' get to the heater an' I be warm."

The old man walked to the vintage refrigerator. Rust had eaten through the enamel; nevertheless he patted it proudly. "Look hyere what I got! I'm gonna get another one, but I been havin' that so *long*. When them things first come out, the man—they call him Mr. Allen—he bought one an' put on my gall'ry, an' when I come in I seen that big box there an' he tell me, 'You need that.' So I took it an' it was a hundred an' thirty dollars." He pointed to the stove. "An' I paid a hundred an' thirty for that."

"You paid for it on time?" I asked.

"On time, but the quicker I would pay the better it be, idn't that right?" He chuckled smugly, then opened the refrigerator door and removed a coffee can. "This lard in hyere." He pointed to another coffee can. "There mo' lard, an' some mo' lard. I made that from hog fat. The butcher man come around an' sell me that hog fat." He pulled open the vegetable bin and showed off some smoked meat, stew bones, and a crumpled-up loaf of bread—the drawer's only contents. "If I have tobacco an' coffee I can make out awright," he insisted. "One good meal'll do me."

He slammed the door and started across the room, toward the doorway leading to the shack's other room. "It might be a li'l dirty but I clean it up today," he said. The walls and ceiling were lined with cardboard, and another useless fireplace stood idle. Neither the bed nor a folded-down sofa had sheets—only rumpled remains of spreads and blankets. Underneath the bed stood a slop jar.

"See what a pretty bed I have?" the old man said. "An' I got plenty covers." He craned his neck, inspecting the cardboard. "I put that up to keep the wind out the house," he said, then shifted his attention to a religious card tacked near the room's only window. "See that lovin' picture a Christ?" Beverly and I nodded. "My first religion was Catholic. Then I was Baptist. Now the Jehovah Witness—I don't go to their church but they come see me sometime, like you doin'."

He took a leaflet from the bed and thumbed through it, smiling.

"Can you read that?" I asked.

He looked up, confident. "Yeah, sho'. The—Happy—Wife—an' Mother," he read awkwardly, then stopped and glanced at us for approval, for encouragement. "If I had my glasses I could go a li'l further." He chuckled. "I got up into the fourth but I didn't get no further. I forget all that learnin' till I start readin' the Bible. The Bible—that's a *good* book. I increased my learnin' readin' it."

Later, on Elm Hall

Windows glowed in the dusk, and the air smelled of browning onions, simmering beans, and baking cornbread. The quarters, almost deserted earlier in the day, were filled with the sounds of children playing and heavy boots plodding through the mud. Brakes screeched, a car door slammed, and male voices exchanged good-byes. Then a brawny man stepped inside. Before Beverly could introduce me, he strode over. "Gustave Rhodes," he said, extending his right hand and then, discovering it was dirty, drawing it back. He examined his large hands, and his eyes traveled down to his muddy trousers and boots. He looked at me, embarrassed. "Lemme see can I wash up an' I'll be right back." As he turned to leave, Beverly stopped him. "You hear about Cleveland Benjamin?" Holding aside a cotton-print curtain that hung in the doorway, he mumbled, "Uh-huh, this is a shock, a real shock," and disappeared.

Beverly's eyes lingered on the curtain, her face reflecting concern. She had grown up in Napoleonville, a mile or two away on Bayou Lafourche. Her father had worked as a barber; her mother, as a cleaning woman. Yet she had known plantation life even before she married and moved onto Elm Hall. She had gone to school with the fieldworkers' children, visited their homes, played on the dirt roads and in the fields. And she was as familiar as they were with the sugarcane work cycle: March to July, cultivating, laying by, preparing some fields for harvest, others for planting; August to September, bending and stooping under the summer sun to plant next year's crop; October to January, long hours of grinding—from dark until dark—cutting the cane, getting it out of the fields and to the mills before it froze or soured; January to March, doing without when the cane was cut and the work over. The women were never spared, not even during childbearing, and so, like her grandmother, Beverly had been a "scrapper," using a curved cane knife to cut stray stalks missed by the harvester.

Now, she complained, "I feel bad when I see how tired my husband come home. Sometime he be so tired he can't do anything. He work sick a lotta times. Whenever he stay home, miss a day's work, he's gotta be very, very sick. Sometime he go to work with a headache an' he come home with that headache." Her indignation mounted. "I be angry with *all* of 'em because they could pay more, 'specially a big place like this. Last January, Gustave was laid up with the flu for three weeks, an' long as he didn't work he didn't get paid. If I wouldn't a been babysittin', I don't know what we woulda did. The company insurance don't pay for nothin' like that. Only time they pay is if you have a accident or some kinda sickness that's gonna last you two, three months."

She fingered the arm of the frayed velvet chair. It and a matching armchair, an iron bed, a cedar chest, a portable television, and a dresser furnished what served as both the living room and Beverly and Gustave's bedroom. Only the curtain separated it from the rest of the house. The linoleum was worn through to the wood in spots, yet the room was neat and clean. A simple bookcase held volumes of an encyclopedia bought one at a time at the supermarket.

Gustave returned carrying a kitchen chair and sat in it, tilted backward, his head resting against the wall. At thirty-nine, he was a large man molded by working in the fields since his early teens: His muscles were lean and hard, his hands calloused and scarred, his eyes bloodshot. His voice was soft, and when he spoke about the accident, his manner was gentle, almost shy.

"I feel bad, because I'm thinkin' if he turned over on this tractor we should be havin' more safety meetin's," he said. "The tractors are much, much faster than ten, fifteen years ago, an', well, I'm thinkin' the cane growers, they should be a little bit more stricter on the mens that operate them because it's too many things that happen like this."

He recalled two men who had been killed in recent years and four more who had been seriously injured in similar accidents. No telling how many others had suffered such fates on plantations too far removed for him to hear about. As he spoke, he rubbed his hands together, each feeling the other's roughness, the other's scars. The skin looked tough, and I wondered how many miles they had steered tractors and harvesters.

I asked, "How long have you worked in the fields?"

"When I was thirteen, after I come home from school I'd go out an' help my mother, take her place until I was able to work on my own," he said. "I was fourteen when I quit school an' was workin' full time."

Two of the Rhodeses' three boys listened intently, sometimes wide-eyed and serious, sometimes snickering. They were close in age and size and, I imagined, not much younger than their father had been when he began working in the fields.

"How do you feel about your sons working on the farm?" I asked.

"Continuin' as I'm doin'?" Gustave bit his bottom lip. "I can't see it. You might say it was a way a life I was born into. I work it, but I wouldn't want my children to stay in the same rut I'm in."

The smaller boy grinned, "I'd like it!" and giggled, but the other one shook his head vigorously. "Noooo, unh, unh!"

Gustave studied his sons. "Kids today won't take it, because like what my grandfather took my father wouldn't take, an' what my father took I won't take."

"So why do you stay?"

He sighed, then laughed. "That's the sixty-four-dollar question. When I was young I had the desire to leave, an' I did. I went to New Orleans, an' I stayed about a year an' came back. I jes' didn't like the town." Quickly he added, "I'm not ashamed of farm work because someone have to do it, but we jes' not gettin' treated right."

Shortly before I traveled to cane country, I had read about a preliminary injunction being handed down in Gustave's lawsuit by the federal district court in Washington. The judge, John H. Pratt, had ordered the Department of Agriculture to withhold its payment of subsidies to cane growers until the case was settled and to issue within thirty days a new wage scale for the 1971 harvest season. In the article, attorneys at Hogan & Hartson, the Washington law firm that had agreed to handle the workers' case gratis, estimated that back payments of fifty to seventy-five dollars per worker would collectively cost growers more than a million dollars.

Now, when I mentioned the injunction, Gustave brought his chair upright. "It's excitin' because this is somethin' we have been waitin' for, somethin' we been talkin' about, an' worked *hard* for. After Henry Pelet come by an' told me, I got Beverly an' the kids together an' had a little shoutin' for joy, sayin' this be what happen if you try hard. I believe within myself we've made a major step. We are on our way up."

He reassessed the news. "There's been hassles, but I'd do it all over again. The onliest thing, this time I would like to see more a the laborin' people understand an' realize what happenin' an' what *can* happen. We need to be organizin' among ourselves, an' *then* we be more stronger together."

"When did you file the lawsuit?" I asked.

"This past July, working with Father O'Connell and Sister Anne and Henry Pelet—the people with SMHA," he answered.

"Was it their idea? Did they encourage you to file?"

Gustave leaned forward, resting his forearms on his thighs. "This the way it happen. I went to testify with SMHA in Washington last March about how the wages be set. So, now, Father an' Sister Anne musta already talked it over before with a Peter Schuck, a lawyer there in Washington. An' I met him, an' he was sayin' the onliest way we might be able to get back our money was to file a suit. He say I'd have to get at least one or two more mens. Father an' Sister Anne said, 'You don't have to make the lawsuit, we'll get the necessary documents should you be willin', but it's up to you.' It wasn't a long time for me to make the decision because I knowed *then* if we was to get any money, if *anybody* in Louisiana was gonna change things, it would have to be a lawsuit. Long as a person are workin' an' nobody isn't sayin' anything, the grower figure we satisfied. Because even one senator said that the only thing the farm workers want is a glass a wine. This is *his* words, 'Give 'em a glass a wine an' a pack a cigarettes an' they's satisfied.'" Anger filled Gustave's voice. "He's a liar an' the truth ain't in him, because *I'm* a fieldworker an' the onliest thing I need is to take care a my family, an' I need my wife to feel she have a man."

A june bug buzzed around the bare bulb that dangled from a cord, dimly lighting the room and casting shadows on the walls. Gustave concentrated on the bug before he returned to the lawsuit. "Jes' about two years ago they came down an' set our wages, an' then they went back to Washington an' claim they jes' put it on the desk an' forgot about it. Then we was workin' in harvest. It was *way* up in November, November tenth, before we got the ten cents' raise. Then last year, when the president put the Freeze, it affected us instead a the growers. So when the suggestion come that we file the suit, I said this is the best thing to do."

"You came back and got Huet to go along with you?"

Gustave shook his head. "Not right away. I tried maybe thirty-five or forty people an' I was turned down, an' then it come to my mind about Huet Freeman. In sixty-nine we got a bus to go to Houma to the wage hearin's, an' Freeman was the onliest one to ride on the whole bus outside my family. So I went an' talked with him—not jes' me, but also a law student that was workin' with Southern Mutual. We told him by doin' something like this we both could be fired. Huet said to give him time to think about it. He wanted to talk it over with his wife. So he thought it over an' next day he say he would do it."

When I asked Gustave if he was afraid or if he had been threatened, he answered no. "But I have been ran off. They thought I was tryin' to organize, an' some a the growers even say their people are doin' fine. They didn't see why we should come around an' upset 'em so."

"*Are* they treated all right?"

He glanced around the room, at his home, admittedly better than most on the place, and shook his head. "On most farms they truly believe that Mistah Charlie pat John on the back an' say,

'John, you is a good workin' man'—an' this is all the hope the workers have. The grower give John this story—'Look what I'm doin' for you. I'm fixin' your house up for you. I'm givin' you land to plant. I give you a little bit more than the other fella givin' his man.'"

Gustave continued. "Really, I'm not tryin' to get the people off the farm. I'm tryin' to improve conditions. On some farms it's pitiful. Most the people have two rooms, an' they're young people with like five or six kids. I can't see how they live like that."

"Is the threat of the boss against fieldworkers organizing really as bad as most people say?" I asked. "Could you lose your job?"

Without hesitation he answered, "I could sure well lose my job if I had thirty people settin' in my livin' room sayin' 'Let's organize.' That's true in most cases if you jes' have one or two because the man will get rid a one man. He'll think, 'Well, he's wisin' up an' he's gonna be wisin' up someone else, so let's get rid a him an' then we can cower the rest of 'em down.'"

Gustave was not the first to experience the frustration of failing in his attempts. Nor was Henry Pelet, a white sugar-mill worker and president of his union local who had worked toward that goal since the 1940s and was largely responsible for recruiting Gustave to the cause. "I've been involved in gettin' people together for ten years, maybe a little longer," Gustave estimated. "But we really started tryin' to get better conditions for workin' people—really the first of it was in fifty-three."

"That was when the workers formed a union and struck up and down the bayou?"

"Yeah."

"Did you strike?"

"No, I left jes' before then to go to New Orleans. I wasn't involved, but my father was. I didn't have no interest in it because in my mind I had enough a the plantation. I figured the strike or the union wasn't gonna stop the cane knife or the shovel. I was thinkin' about survival. I don't know would I have used the term *survival* at that particular time. I probably woulda said, 'I wanta try an' do somethin' to better myself.' But, really, it was survival. I wanted to survive an' I didn't know how. But then I found there's more in life for me than jes' to try to provide for my own family. I want to involve myself. Jes' to put a little toehold here, a little fingerhold there, that this was where somebody was active in doin' somethin' for more than jes' themself. So now, since from about sixty-four through sixty-eight, we've really tried hard to get the people to go to one a the hearin's they have in Houma."

I asked if many workers were aware of the hearings held annually by the Department of Agriculture, and Gustave shook his head. "Really, before I was invited by Henry *I* didn't know these hearin's existed, an' if they did exist that I had the right to go. So then, I wanted some other people off the plantation to go with me, but always the black people had an excuse. Always it was to be like Sister Anne an' Miss Rose Mae Broussard an' Henry Pelet an' Father Frank. Always it was the white people to speak out, not the blacks."

He illustrated: "This last year we had maybe fifty from the Napoleonville area come to a meetin' at Masonic Hall—mens *an'* women—to let 'em know what was goin' on, what to expect when they got to Houma, that it was nothin' to jeopardize their job. Jes' to be there. An' we had another meetin' down in Freetown an' another one in Thibodaux. We wanted to see more black faces, people that work on the farm, settin' in an' listenin' to the people that was speakin' for them an' people that was speakin' against 'em. Well, it jes' didn't work. We had maybe thirty or thirty-five outta the hundred an' fifty that had showed up at the other meetin's."

Frustrated, he grappled aloud with the problem, with whether it was a matter of education or if the workers really were afraid. "If they'd only jes' stand up for what they think is right," he said. "I don't mean get out in the street an' rant an' rave. Nothin' like that. Jes' go to the right places an' let their voice be heard."

"What about the black ministers?" I asked. "Do they do anything to help?"

"No," he answered, disappointment, disillusionment in his voice, "they not too interested. The ministers could do so much, but they never turn to do nothin'."

The reason for the disinterest among black ministers was left unstated, but I was soon to learn from other sources that many black churches in cane country had been built and were still supported by white growers. If the black ministers were to side with the fieldworkers, this could—many of the preachers feared—jeopardize the contributions. And so they remained silent.

Gustave credited the recent injunction with playing a major

role in this year's twenty-five-cent raise—a drastic deviation from the usual ten cents given the workers.

"Now are you paid a dollar ninety-five an hour?" I asked.

"Two dollar," he corrected me. "South Coast pay a nickel higher than the minimum for machine operators."

"How much do you clear every two weeks, during a pay period? And isn't grinding a good time?"

"Yes, a *very* good time. I'm workin' some awfully long hours. Fourteen hours a day, seven days a week. Since the price raise I make about three hundred dollars ever' two weeks. Now I'm countin' in travelin' time. See, I'm workin' for the same company, but not here. I have to travel about a hundred an' thirty miles a day. My time starts when I leave the house until I get back here. Now this is only me. To get back to the whole group, they not quite makin' that much. They should be down to about two hundred dollars. Maybe two hundred twenty-five, for two weeks. They not workin' quite as long hours, an' the handworkers only makin' a dollar eighty. That's their minimum."

"You work like that *every* day from October through January?"

Gustave corrected me, "No, not *through* January. *Up to* January. Like durin' January, February, an' part a March—well, March they start fertilizin' the cane—but durin' January an' February there's not too much work. South Coast is one a the largest sugarcane industries, an' they try real hard. If you're able to make it, they'll give you five days. But's jes' if you're able to get out there an' break ice. Lotta times on other places they wouldn't have no work at all."

When I asked about his average paycheck after grinding, he answered, "A hundred an' twenty-five to a hundred an' thirty every two weeks, when the weather's good—from March to October. Not January an' February. Last January I was makin' somewhere in the neighborhood a ninety dollars ever' two weeks—at the most. I don't know what it'll be this year. I had some days the work was there but the weather was jes' too bad."

Restless now, Gustave offered to show me the rest of the house: two more bedrooms, each with two double beds, a kitchen, and an indoor bath—the only one in the quarters. Except in the living room, the walls were pockmarked where field mice had gnawed their way into the house. In the kitchen Beverly showed off a built-in sink and a washing machine.

"We bought 'em an' Gustave put 'em in," she boasted. "Ever'-thing we buy we have to pay on time. I jes' finished payin' for the washin' machine. They give you two years to pay for it. Twelve dollars a month."

But Gustave was proudest of his indoor toilet. "Plantation didn't give me that. *I* bought it an' I put it in."

I admired the shiny white toilet. "Can you remember the first time you ever saw one?"

Gustave grinned. "Uh-huh. Was in New Orleans. My cousin used to take us there ever' Carnival, an' this is where I seen the toilet an' the bathtub inside—not a big washtub like we usually used." He eyed the floor, embarrassed, then he laughed. "I musta been ten or twelve years old, an' I was afraid to use it because I was kinda . . . I was ashamed because I was in the house an' also it was a strange place. I didn't know exactly *what* to do. Should I go on an' do what I had to do right there, an' then knowin' I was in a big city—where else could I go? It was very awkward to me. It was a very excitin' thing *afterwards* to think about."

Back in the living room, I asked Gustave if he felt the only solution to the fieldworkers' plight was to unionize, and he said it was, or at least it was necessary for them to work together to improve their lot. Frustration filled his eyes as he surveyed his shabby belongings, and when he spoke, he was angry, indignant. "Black preachers always tellin' me how to die! I don't need no-body to tell me how to die. I wants to live before I die! Long as you can get to church on Sunday an' put up a good donation, the Lord gonna bless you, you goin' to Heaven when you die—stuff like that. I wanta go to Heaven, but also I wants to *live* before I die! They say ever'day is Sunday when you get to Heaven, but I would like to run into more a these Sundays right here."

The Way to Town

*The cane blended with the sky, and all was dark except for
a few windows and a streetlight. Gustave gazed fondly at
the road, toward where it met the wider road that led to
Napoleonville. By day, it was earthy orange; in the dark, gray.
Pools of rainwater, in which on other days cars and trucks
stuck and stalled, shimmered under the lone streetlight.* "Certain times of the afternoon that road always was full a people
goin' to an' fro. They had no other way to get to town but to
walk. Mostly it would be the women people because they the
ones had to go to the store. The mens an' all would walk out
in the evenin' if they was goin' out. They'd be on the corner or
go get a beer or somethin' with the rest a the guys. But when
we'd go, we couldn't go with them. We always had to go with
the mother, not the father, an' we would go not, say, to play
but jes' most a the time walk with 'em like for company. It was
a big thing, goin' to town. Goin' to the ice factory—that was
the biggest thing. That's when we'd go by ourselves, go without the mother or the father. Jes' a bunch a kids. We'd go like
in the afternoon or early in the mornin' before the sun get too
hot, an' we'd pick up a block a ice—a ten-cents piece, or some

hadda get a nickel piece, an' others gettin' twenty-five cents.
We had a li'l red wagon we'd have to carry the ice on. Now
the womens had these large, real heavy handbags they would
carry they stuff in. Sometime they had so much they'd walk
a piece an' they stop an' they rest an' they change hands until
they get home. This one lady, Miz Bertha Dowell—the man got
his legs burnt off? This was his *mother. An', well, she would*
carry so much on top her head an' steady it an' didn't have to
hold onto it. She was the onliest one. The rest the womens they
couldn't do it. Some of 'em would put their bags on their head
but they also hold it with their hand. But she didn't have to do
that. She jes' put it up there an' walk for miles on that same
dirt road."

The Wake

The clock over the pulpit—round, with big numbers like at a Greyhound bus station—said eight-thirty, half an hour before time for the wake to start, and except for muffled coughs and whispers, Bright Morning Star Baptist Church was quiet. The women of the family huddled on the first pew, the one nearest the casket resting her head in her hand, her body trembling. Mostly women and children—some in Sunday clothes, others in frayed cottons and sweaters—sat on the left side of the simple sanctuary. The right pews were empty except for Gustave and Beverly and me and a few others. The men still milled outside, talking in twos and threes, re-creating, reliving the accident—this one and others they had witnessed or experienced.

Now and then someone would walk down the aisle to the casket to look inquisitively at Cleveland Benjamin's body and then quietly take a seat. Laid out in a dark suit and tie, Cleveland seemed peacefully relieved of the rigors of his work and his way of life. The metallic casket was perhaps the most expensive thing that had ever belonged to him. A painting of the Last Supper lined the inside, and a small spray of carnations lay on the closed half. Several floral arrangements, more ribbon than flowers, stood to either side.

One by one the men made their way into the church, gradually filling the pews to the right. Even the younger men seemed permanently weary: their shoulders were stooped, their eyes bloodshot, their faces defeated. The congregation watched as a tall, graying man entered, paid his respects to Cleveland, and sat near the pulpit on a bench reserved for deacons. He took a handkerchief from his coat pocket, rubbed his eyes, then tucked it back in place. Gustave watched intently. "That's Deacon Crowley," he explained. "He's a student in the Plantation Adult Education Program. He tried to put out the fire with dirt when the other guy's legs was burnt off, an' he was close by when Cleveland was killed." He excused himself and eased past the mourners, toward the deacons' bench. Deacon Crowley looked up. His tired eyes became animated as the two men talked and gestured with their hands. The other deacons listened, occasionally interrupting. Then Gustave returned and whispered to Beverly and me that Cleveland Benjamin had been driving a tractor pulling a wagon loaded with cane when the tractor jackknifed, crushing him between it and the wagon.

Shortly before nine a light-skinned man with slicked-down hair began playing the organ. The women on the front pew sobbed and their veiled heads bobbed, their whimpers and moans sometimes competing, sometimes blending with the whiny organ. Deacon Crowley made his way to the pulpit and waited until the women quieted. From the large Bible opened before him, he recited John 3:16, occasionally saying the wrong words, as though relying more on memory than on his recently acquired reading skills. "Gawd soooooo love the world He give us His only son that whoever believe in Him won't die but have life everlastin'."

He ended and signaled the people to rise as the organist pressed the keys. *Must Jeeeesus bear this cross aloooone* . . . Their voices and the organ quivered. *. . . and alllll the world go free. No, there's a cross for ever'one, an' there's a cross for me.* The music stopped and Deacon Crowley singsonged the Lord's Prayer while the people hummed and the other deacons punctuated the prayer with *Ooooooh Lawd!* and *Yeah!* and *Well!*

Again the people sang, slowly and from memory, for there were neither hymnals nor racks to hold them. And then Deacon Crowley introduced a Reverend Augustine, from a nearby church. The visiting minister was a man in his late thirties, sportily attired in a plaid jacket and slacks.

"Good evenin' beeereaved an' all concerned," he said, gripping the podium and looking out over the congregation. "I'm here on behalf of the mother of the deceased—a member of my congregation." He paused and switched to a more doleful tone. "To us a tragic thing has happened."

The deacons and some of the people interspersed, *"Aaaaaamen!"*

"It is somethin' we cannot get use' to!"

"Aaaaaa-men!"

"Nooooooooo matter how much we pray or try, we can't get use' to death . . ."

"Hmmmmmmmmmm!"

"Death!—it mean you are finished! It mean it is *complete!*"

"Yes!"

"There is no more movement!"

"That's riiiight!"

His voice grew higher, forceful, as he preached on. "As Moses looked at that bush it was not con*sumed.* It was stiiiiiill green!"

"Still green!"

"Noooow, somethin' keep that bush *alive!* Somethin' keep that bush *green!*"

"Yesss!"

"We have this *physical fitness,* but that somethin' inside make us move around. You could fill me *fuuuullll* a bullet holes." His voice trembled. "But you couldn't kill this here soul. You could stab me from behind an' I'd still be alive!"

"Aaaaaa-men!"

"I wanta say to this bereaved family, to suffer a little with 'em. A *looooong* time ago a minister use' to come an' scream an' try to make you cry. Now we have become a little more educated. We've come to try to dry your tears a little. We've come to make you laugh." His voice soared. "He's a-*live!* I *knoooooow* he's *alive!*"

"Yesssss!"

The minister paused, and when he resumed it was in a somber tone. "You are gonna die, too! I'm gonna die, but we don't know when, an' that's good."

"*Aaaaaa-men!*"

"Doomsday is *ever*'day. For this young man doomsday has already come, but his day of reckonin' hasn't. I want you to dry those eyes an' open up the sunshine window! It's happened to others!"

Reverend Augustine returned to his seat and the music started again, fast and lively like roller-skating rink music, the organist swaying from side to side as he played. A heavyset girl in the fourth row—Cleveland Benjamin's stepdaughter, Beverly whispered—jumped to her feet and reached her arms toward the casket, sobbing, crying over and over, "*Goodbye, Cleveland, we gonna miss you!*" Several women in white uniforms and caps hurried to her side and began removing her coat and patting her hands. A young man stood behind her, massaging her shoulders until the sobs became whimpers. Then the women in the front pew began screaming Cleveland's name, and his wife wailed "*Ooooooooh, Lawd! He's gone!*" The uniformed ushers rushed to hug and comfort them, and two helped the wife from the sanctuary, past a sign—THE TITHE IS THE LORD'S.

Some of the voices were hoarse and tired, yet the singing neither slowed nor stopped. *No! never alooooone. He promised never to leeeeeave me* . . . A deacon on the side bench nodded to the spirited beat of the music, and some people tapped their toes. *. . . never to leave me alone!* The choir filed out of the sanctuary, and the organist turned some knobs, closed the keyboard, and left. Still the singing continued, except when the people bowed their heads as Deacon Crowley prayed.

"Gawd, as I come at this hour, wanta thank You for our life. I know You look high an' I know You look low an' look at my house, an' if You see anything look like sin, would You please to have mercy!"

The people chorused, "*Have mercy!*"

"Some day they gone lay ou-ur child in the clay. I'm not worried an' I'm not upset because I *knooooow* Jesus our Redeemer an' He is looking down. Gawd knows they done put our child in the clay. Gawd *knooooows* You been good to us. Bein' Negroes You brought us a mighty long way, an' for this, oooooooh Lawd, we wanta say thank You. *Pleeeeease,* Sir, would you *pleeeeease* to have mercy!"

It was past ten-thirty, going on eleven. Most of the men would be in the fields by six the next morning. Yet the singing went on as though they didn't want to leave Cleveland Benjamin alone.

In the Morning

"*Huet-P! Oh, Huuuet-P! Get up!*" The raspy voice was followed by the sound of a rock slamming against the tin roof—Millard Barnes's second alarm. Huet lay quietly in the dark listening to Millard trudge through the mud, each step alternating with the scrape of his lame leg. *Step . . . scrape . . . step . . . scrape.* Then more shouts. "*Murphy, come on, get up! Ooooh, Murph!*" And more. "*Oooooh, Danny, get up!*" The wakeup calls grew faint as they progressed down the road. Huet turned his attention to the rain pelting the roof, a gentle, soothing rain that, another time, would encourage sleep. But not today, not during grinding. By eight he would be in the soggy fields, on a tractor—rain or no—hoping not to bog down, to be spared Cleveland Benjamin's fate. He looked at Viola and, between them, three-year-old Jada Janise. They, like the rest of the household, were still sleeping, their silhouettes slowly rising and falling, their breathing barely audible. Huet watched them, and he worried. Soon Jada would be in school, soon he would have another pair of shoes, more tablets and pencils to buy. With what? And what *if* he were to lose his job, be fired because of the lawsuit? What would become of him, of his family? Where would they go? Why hadn't he listened when Ned Jackson had tried to talk him out of quitting school? *"One of these days they'll have a machine to do that work. You won't be able to do shovel work no more,"* the science teacher had warned. *"You need to have some kind of education, even to run a tractor."* Huet, thirteen at the time, had laughed at the notion that machines could do the work of men in the field, that one day he could be replaced by steel and gears and pulleys. Or that he would need to know any more than how, barely, to read and write and count.

His excitement over the court injunction had diminished with the growing realization that he could be fired and thrown off the plantation. When Henry Pelet and the others from Southern Mutual had explained the legal maneuvers, that the Department of Agriculture had appealed and the case wasn't over, Huet had shrugged it off, confident of a victory for the fieldworkers. But now, in the last darkness of morning, fear overcame confidence. He had heard rumors that several growers had complained to his boss: "You ain't got rid of that Freeman boy?"

He strained to hear Millard Barnes as he neared the last houses in the quarters and for a moment imagined it was his grandfather out there in the road. After the old man was no longer able to tend the mules and transport workers to and from the fields, he too had been given the job of waking the people. But now he was past doing even that. Huet tensed. *They don't care. None of 'em care. Jes' like when a mule get too ol' to work they shoot 'em in the head or turn 'em out.*

It was quiet except for the rain. Across a vacant lot a light brightened Tillman Dickinson's place. Down the road another lighted rectangle appeared, then another, as the people arose and readied for work. Huet put one foot on the cold linoleum, hesitantly, then the other, and stretched his arms toward the ceiling, yawning. Viola eased out of bed and pattered toward the kitchen. Then Huet stepped out of his pajama bottoms and sluggishly pulled on his graying long underwear and worn khaki trousers. Jada Janise lay still, and as he passed through the second room he saw Ann Marie, Rose Nell, and Leonora asleep on the double bed, and on the roll-away, Shirley May and Stacey.

On the kitchen stove, a pan of water heated while lard melted and sizzled in a black iron skillet. Viola emptied flour into a bowl, added water, cooking oil, and baking powder, then worked it into dough. She reached up and pushed aside her hair with the back of her flour-whitened hand as Huet kissed her on the cheek. He poured the heated water into a dishpan and splashed his face. Viola pulled small wads from the kneaded dough, patted them, and placed them in the hot grease.

"They're gonna bury Cleveland Benjamin today," she said.

Huet nodded.

And outside it was raining, hard.

The Burial

*The people came and they carried Cleveland Benjamin to the
cemetery. Six men in suits—three on each side of the casket—
surrounded and trailed by a procession of umbrellas. The
hearse pulled away from the church and the people followed,
the women and children not needed in the fields. Two blocks
over and around the corner, through the chain-link fence, past
simple vaults and mounds of earth. There they lowered the
casket into the ground and, on top, placed the half-dozen or
so wreaths and ribbons.* For dust you are an' to the dust you
shall go. *And the people prayed,* Oh, Lawd! Have mercy!

Back on Hard Times

Huet P. Freeman sat in dirty jeans and an unbuttoned khaki work shirt, wearing one blue sock, one brown. Leaning forward with his hands clasped between his knees, he talked with more concern than anger, and neither looked nor sounded like a troublemaker, not even when he insisted it was time people—meaning fieldworkers like himself—started doing something. He was a tall, sturdy twenty-nine-year-old with a neat mustache and a hint of a goatee. His mother had named him for Huey P. Long, even though she had not known how to spell it or what the initial stood for. She knew only that she wanted her son to bear the name of the man who had championed the cause of poor people like herself.

Just inside the front door Huet's rubber boots dripped muddy water onto the linoleum, next to a mop Viola had been using to wipe up puddles where the roof leaked. The rain that had been coming down all day—so steadily I could barely see the houses on Hard Times even in daylight—was still beating on the roof.

Jada Janise climbed onto her father's knee, and the other five girls, in thin cottons in spite of the cold, gathered around him on the couch, listening but not understanding what he was saying about the lawsuit.

"I was afraid when we filed that suit," he said. "I coulda lost my house, my job. Still could. But it hadda be did. I hadda take the chance. If no one speaks up, no one will know. The money's not enough to look forward to. It's jes' enough to have the strength to go out the next day. Even if I be fired, lotta people would be better off."

But Huet wasn't thinking only about money. He was thinking about paid sick leave and a pension plan—something more for the people to count on besides Social Security and welfare and one week's paid vacation. In the next room, Viola searched through some papers and returned with the most recent W-2 forms she could find, for 1971 when Huet was earning a $1.55 an hour. It reported $2,549.17 for the year. She had also found several pay stubs. One for a week in 1971 indicated he had worked eighteen hours; another, for a week in 1970, that he had earned $33.83 for twenty-four hours' work and that he owed the grower $39.03. This year he was making $1.95 an hour during grinding and $1.90 the rest of the year. Wages had gone up, he admitted, but so had prices.

"Really, I don't think we have a chance at life," he said. "I've talked to some boys that left the fields an' got other jobs. They say they shoulda been out the fields before. But if the price was equal I rather the farm. I like farm work."

"How do you—" I started, but Huet interrupted me politely. "You better move that chair 'cause I think it's gettin' ready to leak." He watched the ceiling until I had moved my chair.

"How do you get by?" I repeated.

He shrugged. "Without food stamps I couldn't do it, plus they're not gettin' the proper medical treatment they need." He glanced at his daughters, then at Viola. "If they be sick, well I have to do somethin', go to my boss an' get a paper an' take 'em to the doctor. But not jes' for a cold. They have to be *very* sick."

The paper Huet referred to was a form the grower would provide when a worker or a member of his family needed to see a doctor or dentist but had no money to pay. The medical bill was sent directly to the grower, who deducted it, along with bills for utilities and cash advances, from the worker's pay, sometimes leaving little or nothing to live on.

"Right now I have two kids I want to take to the dentist but can't," he said. Then, looking at his seven-year-old, he added, "Rose Nell had a tooth that hurt bad. It hurt for a week. Viola tried to doctor it, but finally we hadda bring her in to the dentist because it was abscessed. He was able to save it, but he sure raised sand. Said I should take my chil'ren for checkups, but I jes' can't afford it." He drew Lenora, his five-year-old, closer, to where I could see the inside of her mouth. Both front teeth and several in back were broken off at the roots.

Viola said, "She shoulda gone when she was three or four years old."

"Do they hurt?" I asked.

Lenora shook her head, and Viola answered no, and then, gesturing at Shirley May, who was nine, "She has a toothache," and at Ann Marie, the ten-year-old, "an' that one there." Viola already had a false upper plate, and her bottom teeth were bad and needed to be pulled.

Last January after grinding, Huet remembered, he had to borrow thirty-four dollars from a finance company to buy food stamps. But this year, he brightened, "I'm savin'—I have a hundred twenty-five dollars."

Viola corrected him, "Hundred twenty-one."

"It's the most I ever had saved," he said. "I never had a savin's account before. I cashed in my insurance policy—a ambulance policy—an' put it in the bank in case one a my chil'ren get sick I'll have somethin' to fall back on. My wife work two days a week. That's ten dollars, an' I put that in the bank, an' if I have a couple dollars left over I put that in too."

Huet surveyed the room—the rat-chewed wallpaper, the secondhand furniture, the damp ceiling. "The farmers say by us not payin' rent we gettin' a fair an' equal wage, but I don't think so. After a lifetime we still don't own the house," he said. "When you get too old or too sick to work, the farmer hires someone else to do the work an' you gotta get out the house you stayed in all your life, workin' for the same man, same company, them not payin' you enough money to buy you a house, a piece a property, *anything*. You jes' makin' enough to try to buy a little food. The day come you reach retirement age, when you disabled to go out there, an' here you gotta move. Where is there to go?" He shrugged. "You can't go to another farm because nobody's gonna hire you. You have relations. You can go there but you be crowdin' them. So what you gonna do?"

His own grandfather was eighty, his grandmother seventy-eight, and now that neither was able to work, the old man had to pay rent for the house across the way—about twenty-five dollars a month, Huet said, and it had been in no better condition than his until he and his brother installed a bath and a kitchen sink and hot water. He admitted that he himself had been offered a better house just last year but turned it down because he felt he couldn't leave his grandparents alone.

Like them and his uncle, Huet had spent most of his life in one or another of the houses on Hard Times. "I was born on St. Thomas, the next plantation," he said. "I was so small when we moved from there I don't remember. I started about thirteen workin' part-time in the field an' going to school. I dropped out in eight grade. I can read a little, but I wouldn't say well. I woulda like to gone more but I couldn't. I *had* to go to work to help my mother an' my stepfather. There was two sisters an' two brothers home besides me. I remember goin' to bed without eatin'. One time—I musta been ten or eleven—I had a penny in my pocket an' I went to this store. Really, I didn't go to the store to buy nothin'. I was gonna rob it. I was hungry. But when I got there I jes' couldn't do it. Jes' couldn't."

The girls eyed their father as his embarrassment turned to indignation. "If Secretary Butz do have kids I'm sure he'd want to see 'em happy, with things. How come he don't want that for ours?" he asked. "I would say he's selfish."

No one spoke for a time, until I asked one of the girls if they went to the movies and Huet answered for them. "My kids never been to a movie, an' last time I went—" He scratched his head. "When they close the movie house in Napoleonville—fifteen years ago?"

Viola nodded.

"Then it be fifteen years. We jes' watch TV an' go visitin'."

When I was on the porch getting ready to leave and the children were inside, I asked Huet and Viola about Christmas—less than three weeks away. I had seen no Christmas trees, no decorations, during my plantation visits, and most workers told me they seldom exchanged gifts. Viola said their two youngest girls would each get dolls; the four older ones would share one large gift, such as a toy piano.

"What about you and Huet?" I asked.

"We've never exchanged gifts. Can't afford it," Viola answered. Her smile was wistful. "I'd love to. I guess probably I'd give him a nice piece to put on, some clothes."

"She been axin' me for a watch, but look like she gonna be disappointed again this year," Huet said. He hugged Viola and kissed her on the cheek. "But, baby, you got me!"

Tomorrow . . .

*From the road, the shabby brick paper, even the rotting porch
and steps, were not discernible in the dark. And Huet studied
the shack's silhouette. "I always did want to get a house,
my own house," he said. "Seem like a world a dreams. Like
we livin' in a dream world. You always figger that tomorrow it's gonna be better. Next day come, an' it's the same
thing. But you jes' believe in that. Believe that tomorrow is
gonna be better. An' tomorrow is the day that never come. It
never come."*

*There was no moon in the sky, no stars; still Huet searched
the dark sky.*

"I guess," he said thoughtfully, "that's what keep us goin'."

A Few Miles Away, in Thibodaux

Father Vincent O'Connell was, in temperament and appearance, as Irish as his name. His round, pink face and his eyes were alternately tough, tender, and jovial, and even in his clerical collar he seemed as ready to resort to fists as to prayer in settling differences. Sitting in his office above the now-dusty Nixon-Agnew headquarters in Thibodaux, he smiled mischievously as he remembered how, as a young priest trying to unionize the fieldworkers, he had been "kicked upstairs"—the term he used to describe his transfer to St. Paul, Minnesota. It had taken him almost twenty years to maneuver his way back to Louisiana, and although he was cast in a new role, director of the Plantation Adult Education Program, he was no more welcome among the growers and antilabor interests now than he had been before.

"Back in the forties people told me the day collective bargaining came to fieldworkers, Bayou Lafourche would run red with blood and part of it would be mine. *Now* they're fearful of 'What's he up to next?'" he chuckled, pleased that although the fledgling union he helped form had collapsed with the 1953 strike, the growers feared the workers might again organize, this time more solidly. "I was told by the pastor at St. Joseph's Church word was out among the growers *and* the politicians that, quote, *a* priest and *a* nun were setting up headquarters in Thibodaux in order to start a campaign for labor organizations, and that we were using as a contact point this educational program on the plantation. Rumors were *all* over the place. That was one reason we had difficulty with attendance at our adult basic education classes, because these people were warned that we were attempting to get them involved in a union and '*you remember what happened in 1953!*'" His voice deepened, and he pounded on the desk to emphasize each word. "This nightmare has been in the background. We have dissipated it to a degree, but it's still there."

The balding priest leaned back in his chair and propped his feet up on his secondhand desk, painted the same institutional green as the floor and littered with studies on the fieldworkers. Next to the desk, on a metal folding chair, a briefcase bulged with more papers. In one corner a large sign read SUPPORT SOUTHERN MUTUAL HELP ASSOCIATION—the organization that had set up the education program with federal funds.

So far, the growers and the politicians had not been SMHA's only opponents. It had also met with resistance from Maurice Schexnayder, the bishop of the Lafayette diocese who in the past had given in to growers' pressure to oust priests and nuns involved with cane workers.

"If the bishop could do anything to remove SMHA from his diocese, he would," Father O'Connell said. "He's a very warm, friendly human being, but he's the son of a grower and he either owns or owns with his family a plantation. So he can't see this organization."

A Few Miles Away, in Thibodaux

Although SMHA had been established in 1969 while Father O'Connell was away, he had kept in contact with its founders, farm labor activist H. L. Mitchell and Sister Anne Catherine Bizalion, a French-born nun who served as executive director. He and Mitchell, an organizer of the Southern Tenant Farmers' Union, had worked together to unionize the fieldworkers during the 1940s and early 1950s. Sister Anne Catherine, recruited by "Mitch," had frequently sought Father O'Connell's advice while he was in Minnesota. In 1970, when he first returned to Louisiana as rector of Immaculata Seminary in Lafayette, she asked him to serve on SMHA's board. Then, after a temporary assignment in Ohio, and at Sister's urging, he had convinced the Washington provincial of his order, the Society of Mary, to allow him to come back as head of the education program in March 1972.

For all the innocence of its name and goals, the program had met with growers' opposition from the start because its interim director, Henry Pelet, had been involved in the 1940s unionization effort. When Father O'Connell arrived, many felt their suspicions had been well founded. While the program was not a union front, he made no effort as we talked to conceal either his personal hope that fieldworkers would one day be organized or his anger that they had been denied the right to collective bargaining in Louisiana.

"Just as I have advised men to belong to the bar association, the manufacturers' association, the American Medical Association, and to be active there, I have also advised all workers—whether they be Teamsters or fieldworkers—that they should belong to *their* appropriate organization," he said. "Now I have gone *beyond* this. I use moral power. I'm not talking about rights anymore. I'm talking to heads of families as fathers, and I say to them, 'You have *an obligation* to belong to an organization that can provide these things that are necessary for the education, health, and welfare of yourself and your children.' This is the thrust of what I say, and this frightens the antilabor interests."

"You made reference to a deal between the governor and Victor Bussie," I said, recalling an earlier charge leveled by Father O'Connell against the Louisiana AFL-CIO president.

"Let's put it as Vic would, because, you see, I'm prejudiced," the priest said. "I didn't go along with this type thing, but Vic is hard-nosed and practical. He realized in 1954 that the organized labor movement didn't have enough votes in the Louisiana legislature to prevent a so-called right-to-work bill from being passed across the board. It would have applied to *all* workers in the state. So in order to guarantee the bill would not be passed on its dues-paying factory and industrial workers, he decided not to fight passage of the legislation as it applied to farm workers. In other words, he and organized labor agreed not to push for the organization of fieldworkers. It was a question of half a loaf was better than none." Father O'Connell's face reddened, and he spoke forcefully. "The state grants professional and economic groups which are rich and powerful the right to organize and to represent their interests professionally through an appropriate organization, such as the American Sugar Cane League. To do this and yet deny that same right to the weak and the poor is not *bad,* it is, in the words of Pope Pius the Eleventh, *criminal!*"

Probably, he speculated, his interest in labor organizing had started when he was ten and his paternal grandfather was trying to keep the union out of his hosiery mill in Philadelphia. "When the textile workers started to organize in the twenties, they threw up picket lines and my grandfather just couldn't understand. This was a personal insult to him because he was a very paternalistic man who, in his own way, thought he was doing good for *his* people. *These* were *his* people." Father O'Connell chuckled, remembering. "My father came home one day and he said, 'Who the hell do you think was carrying the picket sign? Goddamn Johnny Murphy! We gave him two hundred dollars last month because his wife was having a baby and he couldn't take care of her, and there that sonovabitch is out there carrying the picket!' And my mother was the daughter of a longshoreman who fought for organization of the dock workers—*how* my father married her, I'll never know!"

"So you had a union and an antiunion," I observed.

Amused, he nodded. "And my mother's rattling things on the stove and she says, 'Dad O'Connell's a fine man but he thinks he knows better what's good for these people than they know themselves. Who does he think he is, God Almighty?' And, of course, she and my father went back and forth—they really got into it! *This* was my introduction into industrial relations." Father O'Connell laughed at how his mother apparently had influenced him more than his father. Then, growing serious, he recalled encountering, over the years, the same thinking as his grandfather's—*How could these people do this to me after all I've done for them?*

As a young man, Father O'Connell had worked with laborers in France while earning a degree in social action and studying for the priesthood. He had also witnessed the Abyssinian and Spanish civil wars and the rise of fascism in Italy, Austria, and Germany. After coming to teach at Notre Dame Seminary in New Orleans in 1940, he had headed the Archdiocesan Social Action

Committee's efforts to organize garbage workers, domestics, carpenters, and communications workers. He had not, however, become concerned about the sugar workers until 1943 while he was on temporary assignment at a church in cane country. That concern heightened after a large number of Europe's displaced persons were assigned to Louisiana plantations.

"After the 'Polish invasion,'" Father O'Connell recalled, "the chairman of the National Catholic Rural Life Conference got the idea of bringing five thousand refugees to Louisiana and putting them to work on the plantations. Within a week to ten days they were out on the road, thumbing. They couldn't even speak English, but they got the hell out of there, and that put the spotlight on the terrible situation. The pressure came from all over, even from priests in this area, to our organization. We had worked to organize this and to organize that; what—people asked—were we doing for poor cane workers?"

Father O'Connell loosened his clerical collar and spoke of whizzing past the cane fields and not being able to get to the workers. "We just couldn't get behind that cane curtain. We just couldn't. Finally, we figured the best way we could get at them was through the farmers, and so we started organizing the strawberry farmers as a base from which we could operate."

By the late 1940s, he recalled, he and his committee and leaders from H. L. Mitchell's National Agricultural Workers' Union had organized the strawberry farmers and moved on to the shallot and pepper growers. "Then we said, 'Let's get down to the cane worker and get it through his head that when he's working out there in the heat, all he's worth is two dollars and eighty cents a day.' By 1952 we had eleven hundred of them, but we had a hell of a job doing it. Often we met in pigpens, because if you met anyplace that was known it was broken up. They would go by with a shotgun and fire and just keep going."

"Was your life ever threatened?" I asked.

"Oh, yes, several times. I'd get phone calls, and they tried to run over me with a truck once." He leaned forward. "You see, politically we had them whipped. All these people together with the labor organization of the state could stand up against the opposition. Congressman Eddie Hebert was scared to death. We wanted him out more because of what he represented in Washington than what he represented in the state, and Allen Ellender was beginning to shake. He definitely would not have gone back to the Senate because we had enough votes. And the opposition knew this. They sensed this, and this is when they started to move in with the growers. I was one of the first to go because the people who had the money, the influence—the sugarcane and oil people—put the pressure on the local bishops."

"Did they tell you that?"

"Oh, yes. Our dear friend Eddie Hebert said publicly he would 'git me, git me.' One of the bishops was in such bad financial state—he was twelve million dollars in debt, which involved the schools, the old folks' home, the hospital, the orphanage. The opposition got to him and said, 'We'll shut your water off.'"

As Father O'Connell talked, I recollected a conversation with Thomas Becnel, a history professor at Nicholls State University who was writing a book about the Catholic church's role in organizing the fieldworkers. Although Archbishop Joseph Francis Rummel had supported the workers' cause financially and through letters to churches in cane parishes, many of the Catholic growers and even priests had opposed him. Becnel told of some Assumption Parish planters who tried and failed to have the white pastor of an all-black Catholic church ousted for taking a bus load of workers to a meeting to organize a local of the National Agricultural Workers' Union. Still another cleric, outspoken from the pulpit, had to be guarded by union volunteers. During the summer of 1953, when the national union men—with the help of Henry Pelet and Frank Lapeyrolerie, a black sugar refinery worker—were attempting to set up locals and gain collective bargaining, the archbishop wrote letters to the refineries urging them to recognize the unions, but in spite of management's Catholic heritage the refineries sided with the growers and refused. After all else failed, union leaders called for a vote, and on October 12, 1953, approximately three thousand workers went on strike—mostly along Bayou Lafourche, the same place at least thirty striking Negroes had been killed in the Thibodaux Massacre of 1887. Although the striking workers slowed production, they were never able to halt grinding altogether. The determined growers swapped workers and hauled their own cane, stubbornly refusing to give in. For the union stewards, the strike was equally wearing. Each day they transported the workers and their families to and from nearby churches and lodge halls to prevent the growers from pressuring them to return to the fields. Funds posed a severe problem, even with the contributions the archbishop slipped to union organizers. By November 10, when the union ran out of money to feed the workers and hastily set up picket lines at several refineries were crossed, the strike was over and the workers were back in the fields with no more money, no more benefits.

The afternoon I met with Henry Pelet in the small frame union hall of Local P-1422 of the Amalgamated Meat Cutters and Butcher Workmen, he had remembered those last, sad days. "There was no more food, no more money, so we had to send them back to work," he said regretfully. "Some of them, even after four weeks of being on strike, would have stayed out longer, but the spirit had gone out of the people—the fight was gone."

Slight, with gray hair and a Cajun accent, Henry Pelet had worked in a sugar mill in Labadieville thirty-four of his fifty-two years and had devoted almost as many years to helping the field-workers. Yet he remained gentle in his speech and in his ways, with a love for books and writing that equaled his concern for the workers.

"Actually, it was a very peaceful organizing," he said. "There was little pressure put on the workers until the strike. Before then, I don't think the growers took us seriously. They figured 'That's a bunch of wild-haired lunatics—we don't have to worry about them.'"

Henry Pelet told of an incident that had occurred in nearby Franklin when he and another union representative became embroiled in a heated argument with several growers after the workers failed to appear at an organization meeting. Following the exchange, the growers trailed the union men's car out of town. Once the strike began, workers were fired and some were put out of their homes.

"Still," he said, "there were a number of small farmers who I think would have been willing to sign a contract, but the cane establishment brought pressure." He remembered one particular farmer, a good Catholic who would have gone along because of Archbishop Rummel's influence if nothing else.

"Why was the Catholic church so interested when most of the workers were Baptist?" I asked.

Henry Pelet shook his head slowly. "Anybody who looked at the conditions was ashamed, and the Catholic church was ashamed. To me, it was a condition beyond anything I could live with. Today is a paradise compared to the early fifties."

Since the strike there had been only a minor effort to organize, in the mid-1960s, but Pelet insisted that organizing the fieldworkers was something he had to see through. Organized sugar workers in the mills and the refineries were talking about merging into one large unit. That would make them about twenty-five thousand strong in the state, and one of their first jobs would be to unionize the fieldworkers.

"Organizing the workers is not going to change the farm structure, but for the time being, it's the only thing that can give some type of dignity to these people," he said with hope in his voice. "It's the only chance they have to build up a life so they can at least be a part of the community. They won't ever join the mainstream of American life until they have something to live for."

*A Few
Miles
Away, in
Thibodaux*

Learning the Basics

By most standards, the conference room was unorthodox. The secondhand furnishings were as unpretentious as the people the Plantation Adult Education Program was striving to reach and teach, and the signs taped to the walls were equally simple. DO YOUR WHOLE DUTY REGARDING MAKING OUR WORK KNOWN TO INDIVIDUALS AND ORGANIZATIONS AND DO NOT WORRY ABOUT THE RESULTS, one poster quoted Booker T. Washington. Another, small and hand-lettered, labeled an apartment-size range, NICE LITTLE STOVE.

Out of place in their conservative suits and ties, the Department of Health, Education, and Welfare representatives squirmed on the metal folding chairs. "But where are the equivalency certificates? The progress tests?" they asked, bewildered. Again, Father O'Connell explained what he and his staff were attempting to accomplish: A man must have functional literacy. He must learn how to understand the gauges on the machinery he operates. He must learn how to go about registering to vote and how to qualify as a driver. He must understand the Sugar Act—that's of vital importance to him. We must put down in simple language what these legal terms, these laws, say with reference to his rights and also his obligations.

The men from Washington presented their theories and procedures; Father O'Connell outlined his—the two sides agreeing only that the program's objective was to help the plantation people. The government men were firm: The federal funds were designed for the traditional kind of education. Father O'Connell was equally adamant about what the workers and their families needed and wanted. His voice trembled with anger over the inability of these men and others before them to understand the special needs of these people. "I get emotional," he said, "because I see a program that, had it been followed in the forties, we would not be in the state we are." His eyes shot from man to man, and, dwelling on the past, he warned, "A damned big part of my life has been spent in this state, and *no*body is powerful enough this time to push me out again."

Later, after the arguments for new funding had all been made and the men from Washington were gone, I joined Father O'Connell in his office. He was drained after the emotional outburst, and except for a typewriter in the next room and the low hiss from a small gas heater, the office was momentarily quiet.

"The health, education, and welfare of these people are all tied together, and underneath it all, a man's income is what determines these three things," he told me. "We're interested in functional literacy, the kind of literacy that changes the lives of people—not 'see the dog run.'"

He handed me a mimeographed prospectus for the program, drawn up by a student intern from Antioch College and Joyce Hadley, a community organizer who until recently had lived on a nearby plantation. In preparing the prospectus, the two had visited plantations in Lafourche and Assumption parishes, talking to the workers and their families about their educational needs and wants. Now, Father O'Connell watched as I scanned the sheet. "We have found that it is not enough to merely establish a center and offer educational services to the settlements as past programs have done," it read, referring to a state-run program that had failed a few years earlier. "To be effective in attracting people's interest, it must have the mobility to reach out and involve itself with the everyday lives of people. The program must be concerned not only with literacy, but with health, nutrition, consumer education, food stamps, and other areas that affect their everyday lives."

Father O'Connell said, "Most of the grownups have no more than fourth-grade educations. Sixth at the very most. Many were pushed along whether they passed the second or third or fourth or fifth grade—it didn't make any difference. That's why you have people like Gustave—and I say this because now he's not too ashamed to admit it—but he went as far as fifth grade and did not learn how to read or write. If the child does not know how to read or write and you are the parent of the child, you say, 'Well, what good is the school doing, therefore let's put him to work.' Some of that psychology hangs on now with the older folks."

Father O'Connell thoughtfully reviewed the program's objectives: not only to upgrade the workers' education but also to encourage the children and at the same time raise the public's consciousness of their plight. "The people at times work so hard and so long that when they come home they would rather sit down and have a can of beer than learn their ABCs," he said. "Also it's difficult to prove to them effectively that their situation is not hopeless, that they can change this, because in the back of their mind runs the thought, 'If it can be changed, why hasn't it been changed before?' The other difficulty is the fear that exists among the people. Any type of meeting outside of the church—even if you call it a class—is immediately suspect in the plantation community."

Most workers and their family members were tutored in their homes; small classes were also held at Bright Morning Star Baptist Church and St. Peter's Baptist Church hall, the attendance varying with the number of hours the men spent in the fields. Since Father O'Connell's arrival, the program had worked with 150 people ranging in age from seventeen to seventy. The staff of three teachers and four community organizers was mostly black and from the area. Student interns from Antioch, Oberlin, Harvard, and nearby Southern University served as a link to the outside world.

"We have some students whose lives are over, finished," Father

O'Connell said. "They are just living out the rest of a life that has been a drab, unrewarding experience." The progress, the improvement in literacy, was slow, barely observable. And yet there was a brighter side: the reward of seeing a mind open, a person learn to write his first letter. "Take Gustave and Huet Freeman, who two years ago would have been afraid to stand up in a public meeting and say anything," the priest illustrated. "Now, Gustave is capable of chairing a meeting and Huet has no fears of standing up before a group of over a hundred people and explaining what his situation is and why he did what he did. These men have developed confidence along with backbone to make them stand straight before their brothers."

It had been this growth within the two men that had been responsible for the lawsuit and for the workers' thirty-cents-an-hour raise this grinding—a break from the dime-an-hour pattern of the past thirty or more years.

The Lesson

Fillmore and Mattie Jones and three of their four children—all except a married daughter—lived second from the end in a shack so old the Historical Society could put a plaque on it. Just old boards turned gray as the sky by decades of wind and rain and sun. A rotting porch sagged under the weight of an antiquated Sears Roebuck washing machine, a one-piece porcelain sink and drainboard, a small wooden cage, and an upturned bicycle without wheels. A clothesline scattered with wooden pins stretched between the posts that supported the rusted tin roof. A few feet out back, a path was worn to a privy of the same rough boards, an empty pigpen, and a pile of trash.

Inside, a bed with the shredded remains of a quilt pulled over its lumpy mattress took up most of the living room. Into the remaining space was crowded a collection of tired furnishings: a redwood chifforobe, a television set, a section from an old sofa, an end table laden with empty jelly glasses, and an organ like you buy at the five-and-dime. Two straight-backed chairs and a broken child's rocker were drawn close to a small gas heater and turned toward the television. The only ornamentation was a framed print of *The Last Supper* and one of Martin Luther King, Jr., between John and Robert Kennedy, nailed up over the bed. From behind a checkered curtain that separated the front room and the kitchen came the smell of white beans cooking.

Mattie and Eula, her seventeen-year-old, were piecing cotton scraps into quilts when I arrived with Elnora Mack and Jo Ann Morris, instructors for the Plantation Adult Education Program. A TV soap opera was in progress, but neither Mattie nor Eula was watching. It seemed to be on for company, to interrupt the monotonous drone of tractors in the nearby fields.

"We makin' covers, new covers for them quilts," Mattie explained, removing a faded green dress from the box of scraps and holding it up. "These ain't no more fittin', that why I taken 'em to make quilts."

Mattie was a wiry woman with cheeks sunken in from missing jaw teeth, her graying hair drawn into a ponytail over each ear and an elastic band circling her head Indian style. She could have been forty or fifty years old; it was difficult to tell, and she apologized, "I don't know. I done forgotten my age. I got a birth certificate, but my daughter—one live in town?—she got it. An' my husband, I couldn't tell you how ol' he be either."

Nor could she remember how long she had been married or life ever being any different. "I been jes' like this," she chuckled, placing her long, skinny fingers over her mouth. Remembering her years with Fillmore, she sighed, "Oooh, it be so *long,* an' there's a year comin' ag'in! 'Member I got married on a Thursday. It was the twenty-fourth—like Thursday comin' up. It be *so* long now, but me an' that boy married!"

The smell of burning food brought Mattie to her feet, and flinging aside the curtain she hurried to the kitchen, rattled pans, then returned to her rocker. "Rice," she said simply, again digging into the box of scraps. The clothes she and Eula had on didn't look much better than those they were stitching into quilt covers. Mattie wore a wrinkled pink cotton dress over a long-sleeved white blouse and flimsy turquoise slacks; Eula's black-and-white knit dress was shapeless and raveling at the seams.

Eula was a pretty girl who displayed little emotion. She had dropped out of school, and while she studied occasionally with the Plantation Education Program, most of her time was spent watching television or sewing or sitting with the vacant stare she wore through most of our visit. Mattie's own schooling was even more limited.

"Schoolteacher put me in the fields when I was sixteen. She stopped me in the second grade," she recalled, ripping apart a print dress. "I didn't learn no readin', an' I count but it may be right an' it may be wrong. My husband, he count out the money an' he tell me, he teachin' me how much it be. All my brothers an' sisters got the learnin'. They got *good* learnin'. I have ten brothers an' sisters—I guess," she said, not really sure. "Mama had twelve, an' one died an' that lef' ten."

"So your husband's teaching you, too?" I asked.

Elnora explained, "Mr. Jones went to the old adult education class. He used to be a student in this program, too, but he had to stop for grinding."

Putting aside the print dress, Mattie removed a workbook from a dresser drawer. Page after page was filled with unsure *O*s and *P*s—more the work of a first-grade child than an adult. Yet Mattie smiled proudly as she showed me that and other pages with words like *BUS* and *ICE* penciled in under simple drawings.

Elnora Mack complimented her, "Mattie never knew anything of reading and writing before, but she's doing fine."

"I didn't write even *all* this time," Mattie said.

"Do you like it?" I asked.

"What, the writin'?" I nodded, and childlike brightness flashed across her face. "Oooh, yeah!"

"Why did you want to learn?"

"It jes' was in my mind. It was in my mind an' I jes' went on an' did it. I jes' wanted the right words when tellin' 'em to people."

Eula, still by the heater, watched as Elnora sat on the edge of the bed leafing through another workbook until she came to this week's assignments. Pointing to a row of simply drawn objects, Elnora asked, "Which one's name doesn't start with an *F?*" When Mattie didn't answer, Elnora placed her pencil on the picture of a fence and hinted, "What do you put around a house?"

Leaning close to the book, Mattie squinted, then looked up, unsure. "Uh . . . uh . . . uh, rack?"

"Now, Mattie," Elnora started again, "what do you put around a house to keep children from running into the road?"

"A fence?"

Elnora moved on to the drawing of a book, then a fork, then a finger, waiting patiently for Mattie to identify each and prompting her when she couldn't. "Now which one doesn't start with an *F?*" she asked again. Mattie hesitated, then finally said, "Book," and awkwardly made an *X* under it, grinning like a child who had earned a gold star.

"That's good!" Elnora told her. Then, moving on to the next lesson, a review of the alphabet, she pointed to a word beginning with *E* and asked, "What letter is that?" Mattie studied the letter, then answered, "*H.*" Elnora turned to a page with the entire alphabet and asked Mattie to start from the beginning. Reciting more from memory than from knowledge, Mattie waited for Elnora to point to each letter before she named it: "*A . . . B . . . C . . . D . . . E . . .*—" Elnora stopped her. "*E,* Mattie; see, that's an *E,*" she said, returning to the original page to show her the letters were the same.

"Oooh, I forgettin' 'em awright," Mattie chuckled, putting her hand to her mouth.

When it was time to check the rice, Mattie invited us into the kitchen. One wall was papered with pages from magazines, and black-bottomed pots and pans dangled from nails. A washboard was propped in the corner, and a number 3 galvanized tub—for bathing and doing the laundry—caught drips from a spigot that stuck through another wall.

"I got a sink but I ain't got nobody to make it," she explained, "to put it in." She stirred the scorched rice and offered to show me through the rest of the house. "You is welcome to see 'cause I don't hide nothin'," she apologized. "If we ain't got nothin', we ain't got nothin'. That be goin' on ever since we married."

Her furniture—the greasy stove, rusted refrigerator, and the mattresses in the bedroom shared by Eula and Annie, her fourteen-year-old who was at school, and in fifteen-year-old Leroy's room—"was all give me," she said. Leroy's room was actually intended to be a bath. Before grinding, the owner had laid the foundation and constructed walls and a ceiling, but there still was no tub nor toilet nor lavatory.

Mattie rubbed her shoulder and winced. "What I got, this here, I never get rid a it. I got like a rooma—like osteritis—an' I never get rid a that. I gotta go to the dentist, too." She opened her mouth, exposing her few remaining teeth—brown, rotten, and some loose enough to wiggle.

"Do they hurt?"

"Yeah, they hurt. Hurt when they pull 'em too." Opening her mouth wider, she showed off large gaps in back. "They pull those an' now they gonna pull these."

When we returned to the front room, Leroy was watching television. He had stayed out of school that day, and Mattie confided, "He wanta work, but they say he ain't ol' enough."

A tall, lethargic boy, Leroy didn't speak or even look up until the conversation turned to Christmas—just weeks away.

"We had a tree someone give us, but I done got rid a it 'cause it wouldn't set up," Mattie said nonchalantly, "an' we ain't never had one nohow."

Outside, the steady drone of tractors was drowned out by one pulling into the yard. Then someone squished through the mud to the porch and scraped off his boots, and the door opened to a broad-shouldered man in work clothes.

"This my husband, Fillmore," Mattie said without getting up from her rocker to fix him lunch.

The man nodded a greeting and then went into the kitchen and returned with a bowl of hot beans and rice, taking a chair near the heater. "These houses," he complained between bites, "you catch death a cold in these places, an' in the summer they burn you up if you don't have no fans. An' do it leak? You jes' come here when it rain! Outhouse is so bad you can hardly stand to go in there, smell so bad when it hot."

He grimaced, as if he could smell it now.

"I get a dollar ninety-five an hour durin' grindin'—that be October to January—an' I make out pretty good then, for as far as it goes. I buy clothes for the kids an' food, get a little food stamps," he said, and then rehashed Mattie's menu: "Eat mostly beans, spinach, mustards. Chicken, I'm gonna tell you how often I have it—on weekends, that's all."

"Ever have a beer?" I asked.

Fillmore shook his head and smiled, a longing kind of a smile. "About years, I guess it's been since I did. Can't afford it. I do buy a pack of cigarettes now 'n then, but like I say, when the work is gone, it gone, an' you jes' don't get nothin' comin' in."

When Fillmore had finished his beans, he brushed off the knee of the orange rubber overalls he wore over his work clothes and wondered, even to himself, why he stayed on the plantation, why he worked year after year for nothing more than a shack and an outhouse and three thousand or so dollars.

"I got no choice," he shrugged. "People hardly hirin' anybody now, an' at my age—I'm fifty-one—it be kinda hard to get any kind a job. If I was young, I be off a long time." He nodded toward Leroy. "That's the reason I keep my boy in school, so he can get off the farm an' get a good job. My daddy took me outta school an' I *hadda* work, an' I'm sorry for that. My brother in New Orleans an' my sister, one who stays in Houma, an' the brother that got killed—well, they didn't quite finish; one went high as tenth, an' two up to 'leventh—but the rest a us had to work."

He leaned forward with his elbows resting on his knees. "When I went to school, I had to walk," he said, as though he were enjoying remembering that he had once gone to school, even if it been for such a little while. But then the smile faded. He still couldn't read and write, but he sure wished he could.

"Maybe some day," he said, putting on his cap and heading for the door, to his tractor, "maybe I might jes' take it back up."

Later, in the car, Jo Ann shook her head sadly as she thought about the family. "So far, Mattie is the only one in the program who doesn't know the alphabet. Most of them know that and numbers, up to fifty at least. I've been working with Mattie using pennies and stuff—not play money but real money out of my wallet—to teach her how to count. I'm also teaching her colors. She didn't know them either."

"Do you think she's retarded?" I asked.

Elnora said yes, but Jo Ann was not so certain. "I think part of Mattie's problem is she can't see," she said. "She had an old pair of glasses from TG&Y, but she lost them."

Jo Ann, a slender woman of twenty-four, had grown up a few miles away on the other side of the Mississippi River and had attended Southern University in Baton Rouge. At first glance she seemed carefree, but her eyes reflected the hurt she felt for her students. "It's still like it was a hundred years ago, maybe worse," she said. "Can you believe one woman I teach has sixteen people living in *two* rooms? I was surprised, then I was hurt, and then I was angry."

Elnora nodded understandingly. Older looking than her forty years, she was both quiet and outgoing in a warm, wanting-to-help way. Although her parents had moved off a nearby plantation soon after her birth, she was painfully aware of the field-workers' plight. Like Jo Ann, she had dropped out of Southern to raise a family. Now, with a husband, thirteen children, and a home to care for, she somehow found time to use her schooling to help the people left behind.

"It must be depressing," I said.

She shook her head. "I enjoy it. My husband's a janitor in the bank, so life really is hard for me too. I enjoy working with these people, seeing can I help them. We teach them what they want to learn, what they need to get along. Some on a higher level are working for GEDs—to pass their General Educational Development test," she said. "Some we're teaching the alphabet, and for some it's learning how to count or to handle food stamps and welfare problems. And some just want to learn to read the Holy Bible. That's all they want. They'll tell you that—'Just teach me to read the Bible.'"

Mattie and Eula were by the heater again patching together scraps when Elnora Mack and I stopped by a week later with new workbooks. The temperature was forty degrees, at most, and the sky a threatening gray, yet Mattie met us at the door in her stocking feet, wearing the same pink cotton dress and blouse, and Eula, barefoot, was in the black-and-white knit.

"That her ever'day dress," Mattie told us. "This here's her good one." Opening the cedar chifforobe, she removed a blue knit dress and a green one trimmed with ribbon. Eula smiled—the first time I had seen her show any expression—and Mattie said the green dress was Eula's favorite. She held up a brown plaid dress. "That mine, that my fancy dress. I haven't worn that yet. When I goes out mostly I wear pants. I go to the sto', but I don't never buy no dress for me. What I got was give to me."

Mattie's mouth was swollen, and she complained, "I can hardly talk, can hardly eat wit' it. It jes' hangin' there." She pulled back her lip to show the dangling eyetooth, explaining that she would have to wait until someone could drive her into Thibodaux to the dentist, maybe on Saturday.

Thibodaux, less than five miles away, was about as far as Mattie or Eula or even Fillmore ever ventured. "I been to Baton Rouge once, when I was sorta li'l," Mattie said, "an' I jes' go down there to New Orleans for treatment, down to Charity, but never jes' like for to visit." She stopped. " 'Cept one time when they was small. I got a brother down there, see, an' I taken 'em down an' they stayed up *all* night." She smiled, tripping over words in her excitement. "They jes' stayed out *all* night. We was a li'l sleepy but they wouldn't go home."

"You remember that, Eula?" I asked.

The girl didn't answer so Mattie probed, "You 'member that?" Finally Eula shook her head, then a faint smile came to her face. She *did* remember traveling to Baton Rouge with her class before she dropped out of school. *That* was the "furtherest" she had been from home. Then the smile vanished, and she shook her head *no* again—*no* she didn't have a boyfriend, and *no* she didn't go out.

Mattie tapped Target tobacco into a small square of paper, rolled it into a cigarette, and licked the paper's edge. "Neither me," she said. "That what you see me do right here, chile. I don't even go to church lessen it's a wake. An' movies, well, Eula been once, an' I use' to go all the time. I use' to like to see—what they are, cowboys?" She lit the cigarette and waved the burnt match toward the television. "I mostly like—what I tell you?—westerns. Durin' the day, though, I jes' hear what they talkin'. I don't look much."

When I asked who played the organ, the one from the five-and-dime, Eula nodded slightly and continued sewing together scraps.

"Can you play for me?" I asked. When she didn't move, I said, "Would you mind?"

"She gonna play," Mattie assured me as Eula rose lethargically to her feet, turned off the television, and plugged in the organ. "I give her that last year an' she taught herself. Bought all three of 'em—bought my oldest a pinana but somebody stole it. Wasn't no count no way."

Eula began to press the keys slowly, the wrong ones mostly,

and played a discordant dirge that dragged on and on until I complimented her. Then, unplugging the organ, she immediately switched on the television and again sat near the heater as though she had never moved.

There was a knock, and Mattie opened the door to a short, squat man in a cheap suit and new felt hat.

"Life insurance man come to collect," she explained.

As she rummaged through a drawer searching for the payment book, the man eyed Elnora and me suspiciously. "Who y'all with?" he asked in a nasal Cajun accent.

"Plantation Adult Education Program," Elnora offered.

"Well, we insure anything but a broken heart an' automobiles, heh, heh," he said, then abruptly turned off the chuckle. "Y'all outta Thibado'?" he pressed.

Elnora nodded.

"That's a good thing, bringin' up that illiteracy. Louisiana's about, what? third in the U-nited States. I *read* about that," he boasted.

The man, momentarily silent, continued to study Elnora and me until Mattie returned with the payment book and several worn dollar bills. As he wrote in the book, I asked if the workers paid by the month and he answered, "All depends on whether they have the money. Some pay by the week, some by the month, six months—somethin' like that."

"Do they pay you themselves?"

"Right. *Well,* some places the employer deducts. It's better to take it that way, from the employer—you know what I mean? But we do what they want, let's put it that way."

After making entries in the book, the man handed Mattie several receipts and explained she was still behind, paid up only to November 13. The book bore weekly entries of three dollars until July 24. Then the payments stopped—ending with Fillmore's work, when the summer rains came, and resuming November 6, after grinding. Two receipts were for ten dollars, with the notation "can't write" in the signature blank; one was for eight dollars, and another, for twenty-four.

After the man left, Elnora assigned pages in the workbooks for Mattie and promised we would come back in a few days to check on her progress. Mattie walked us to the door and then watched as we walked to the car, as though she wouldn't see anyone but Fillmore and their children until we returned.

Opposite the houses, cane-laden trailers were lined up waiting their turn to unload. The mill's huge smokestack sent up steady blasts of white. Some of the drivers sat in the truck cabs, others stood in groups talking, restlessly shifting from leg to leg, waiting. They watched as Elnora and I got in the car and started down the stalk-strewn road, back toward the main highway.

At the last house, Elnora said to pull over. She needed to drop off some workbooks for a white student named Lily Mae Smith. Thus far in my travels I had found white workers to be a rarity in cane country, and, according to Elnora, in the education program they were even rarer. "One other white family was very, very interested in the program, but they moved off the plantation," she said. "Now we just have this family. We have worked with others, but the younger members of the family got embarrassed so they didn't want to be a part of the program anymore."

As we approached the house, a tan, rib-thin dog nosed through garbage scattered in the yard. From outside, the house looked no different from the others, but Elnora insisted that it was in better condition, though she wasn't sure if it had anything to do with the family being white.

Inside, the walls were paneled, but, as in most of the houses I had visited, the furniture looked secondhand. The first room was cold, and Lily Mae apologized, "We ain't got no pipe to the heater in this room."

She was pretty and girlishly giggly, yet her eyes, and sometimes the giggle, betrayed her embarrassment over her belongings, her education, herself. Her shoulder-length hair was home cut and uneven, and she was missing a front tooth. Like the black families I had met, she had spent most of her twenty-six years on a plantation.

"Before I married I was livin' on the plantation," she explained. "See, I got married, an' then I ended up on another place." She clasped her hands between her knees. "My daddy worked in the sugar house doin' all kinda stuff, fixin' things an' all that."

"Did you have a house like this?"

"It didn't have panelin'. It had beaverboard inside, but it was better. Had more rooms, an' it had a toilet inside, a bathroom.

We jes' have an outside toilet here." She scrunched her shoulders and giggled. "I got a sink, but the water don't run to it. I jes' got one pipe runnin' in the house, an' that's in the bathroom, but that jes' has a pot, a ordinary pot to bathe in."

Her husband worked in the fields hauling cane and repairing equipment. "He use' to work at the shipyards weldin'," she said. "He was makin' *good* money, too, but he jes' like his field work. He was born 'n raised on a plantation, an' he don't wanta leave it. He *love* to drive tractors, mess 'round with tractors. Jes' give him that."

Two small boys and a girl ran in and out of the room, squealing and falling and scrambling to their feet again. "We got three children," Lily Mae said, introducing the youngsters. "He—Eddie— goin' on seven." She nodded at a blond-haired boy.

"Eight!" he corrected her, and she continued, "Eight, an' Suzanne is six, an' he's goin' on four, Bobby is."

Treats like Cokes and candy were rare for these children. Every two weeks, on payday, Lily Mae bought six half-gallons of milk; when that ran out, then it was gone. Watching Eddie kick a rubber ball, Lily Mae recalled the embarrassment of the children asking for toys when she would take them shopping with her. "Most of what they got my sister give 'em," she said. "She can afford anything, her. Her husband load gas trucks. She makes Suzanne's clothes, and she got two little boys older 'n Bobby, so she pass down clothes on to him. But I never bought any clothes for them kids, all except Eddie, an', well, I scratched to get for him."

Lily Mae had quit school in eleventh grade to get married. She had worked briefly at Morgan & Lindsey until management learned she was pregnant with Eddie and let her go. Three months ago she had signed up with the education program. When I asked why, she gave one of her shy little giggles.

"For when he was gonna get big, you know, when they all in school an' I could find me a good job," she said earnestly. "That's what I told my husband—then I have more education."

The Day the Floor Fell In

Look who it is, Cinderella, Cinderella!
Look who it is, Cinderella, Cinderella!
What caaan you do, Cinderella, Cinderella!
What caaan you do, Cinderella, Cinderella!
Weeeeee can do it too, Cinderella, Cinderella!
Choose you-ur partner, Cinderella, Cinderella—

The circle of giggling youngsters watched as I parked my car.
From the porch of a frame house, Viola Freeman motioned for
me to join her. Unlike the other houses on Hard Times, this
one was painted white and the porch was screened.

"Huet-P an' his brother did this," she explained as she in-
vited me inside. New linoleum lined the walls and floors, and
there was a bathroom with a tub, toilet, and washbasin.

In the front room, she introduced Florida Preston—"Mama
Shug," as her children and grandchildren and most planta-
tion residents called her. The old woman nodded her recogni-
tion. She was plump, her round body squeezed into a rocker.
Her eyes were both sad and strong, and her mouth firmly set.
A faded rag was tied about her head with only a gray ringlet
showing here and there.

"I'm the mother for five livin' chil'ren," she said by way of introduction. "The mother a eight, altogether. They didn't all live on account a miscarriages an' all like that."

"Have you lived on Hard Times all your life?" I asked.

"No, I been all up an' down the bayou. I was born up around about Belle Rose." She reconsidered. "Not Belle Rose. Lemme see. Somewheres back a there, but it been so long. I'm seventy-eight, an' my husband, he a old man. He be eighty—eighty year old."

"How far in school did you and your husband go?"

"I went up to the third or fourth grade. I can read an' write a little."

"And your husband?"

She shook her head. "Oh, no, an' he can't hear neither."

"Do you like living on a plantation?"

The old face wrinkled into a smile. "Oh, yes. I like it, been on it all my days."

"You don't want to go anyplace else?"

"Nooooo," she answered slowly, "not till I jes' have ta go."

Later, when Viola and I crossed the road to her house, Huet's mother, Mabel Williams, was there visiting from Dorseyville Plantation. She was a short woman, in dark slacks and striped knit shirt, with her graying hair combed back. Her bright eyes peered through gold-rimmed glasses, and when she smiled, more gold showed between her teeth.

"We had the same houses," she said, recalling her own days on Hard Times. "I lived in this house about ten years ago. Huet-P was five years ol' when it was built. Now when this house was built, honey, it wasn't built outta new lumber. Like you tear down an ol' buildin' an' use the best a the lumber to build another house? That's how this house was built."

She looked at the linoleum and chuckled. "See this floor, it's been repaired because it fell, jes' went down. We was havin' a weddin' an' the floor part went down."

"You mean the bride and groom went down?" I asked.

"Ever'thing in the house, honey."

"Did it go all the way down to the ground?"

"Flat!" she answered, and everyone laughed.

On the Way to Rienzi

The shortcut to the home of Joyce Hadley's grandparents was really just two ruts cut by tractors driving back and forth through the fields. If you followed it a mile or two in the opposite direction, it led to Coulon Plantation, where her father, a brother, and her other grandfather lived, and where, until two years ago, it seemed she too would spend her life. But at eighteen she had married, moved with her husband and year-old son into a house that had hot and cold running water, and found a job with the Plantation Adult Education Program as a liaison between the staff and the fieldworkers, building trust between the two.

"Long as I can remember, my grandfather's been working on one plantation or another—Orange Grove, Coulon, Rienzi, where we're on our way to now," she recalled as the car bumped over the muddy road. "He can't work anymore, but my grandmother works for the owners so she can hold the house. She gets paid something like twenty dollars a week. She milks cows, cleans house, irons, babysits, stuff like that."

As the Rienzi workers' houses loomed larger, Joyce's frustration mounted. "It's a cycle," she said. "My grandmother lives here, an' she has two sons an' a granddaughter here. They *all* live here in their own houses an' work. One son is thirty-nine an' another is twenty-four. The granddaughter is even younger, about twenty. There's a daughter living with 'em too, during grinding. They just *don't* get off. It's just 'Mama did it, an' if Mama could do it, it's good enough for me.'" She sighed. "Mostly, it's being afraid. It's hard enough living here. Just think about going into town where you have to pay rent. That be just one more bill you have to worry about."

We turned onto a dirt-and-gravel road that led to the houses, some of them painted and in better condition than most I had visited. An old man waited eagerly in the doorway of one, his grin widening as we neared the house, and him. At sixty-three, Willie King was lean and stooped, his chin spiked with gray, his voice husky and worn out, yet his spirit seemed unbent. As he recalled the past, he chuckled often—the way so many plantation people did, as though humor was their answer to a difficult life. After we were introduced to him and his wife, Lulu, he relaxed contentedly in a rocker and we talked.

"I worked on the plantation thirty-some years," he said. "I butchered till I was thirty, till I start workin' in the fields. That was in twenty-eight, somethin' 'round then. It was hard work, yeah."

He rocked and chuckled good-naturedly.

"Why did you leave the butcher's and come to the plantation? The pay wasn't very good, was it?" I asked.

"Well, I jes' did. 'Round town, things was so tough. It was the Depression, you know."

I asked how much he made when he started working in the fields, and he chuckled again. "I don't wanta tell you no story— we was gettin' *eighty* cents a day. Then we got a raise, we got a *dollar* a day. An' after that, we got a *dollar ten cents*—the price is goin' up, li'l bit, li'l bit," he said, his voice rising with the wages. "An' after that, we got a dollar an' twenty cents. Well, that stayed until Governor Long win—the *first* Long—an' he raised us to a dollar an' a half. He cut all them long hours, from dark in the mornin' to dark at night, an' start payin' a li'l bit more, but they kilt him. Then they start us off at twenty cents *a hour,* an', well, it jes' kep' on up, kep' on up till where it is now." He fell silent, and when he resumed there was disappointment in his voice. "But now they makin' more an' I can't get none a it."

He and his wife had raised twelve children. Now the two of them and a grandson lived on the $115 Willie received from Social Security, plus another $24 he got from "old age" and the $24 Lulu made babysitting and keeping house. Rent was free, but still there were the utilities to pay for.

"I tell 'em that's all I'm workin' for is gas an' water' an' medical bills," Lulu said good-naturedly. That and the house was why she kept going. "When you ain't able to work," she explained gravely, "they put you out."

Two women in yellow rubber overalls and jackets entered the house and edged up to the gas heater. Joyce introduced the older one, in her mid-thirties, as Aunt Golena, and the younger, twenty, as her aunt Lois. Even with layers of sweaters and slacks and the rubber overalls, the women shivered and Golena complained, "That wind go right through you!"

"What do you do?" I asked.

"Scrap cane behind the cutter," she answered.

Willie King interpreted simply, "That's when you foller the cutter an' pick the cane up an' throw it on the other side a the road where they be puttin' it at."

Golena warmed her hands over the heater. "Rest of the year I do housework," she explained, "but durin' grindin' I can make more money in the fields. I make but six dollars a day cleanin', an' durin' grindin' I *clears* about a hundred fifty-seven dollars ever' two weeks."

"The womens get the *same* price as the mens! They get a dollar eighty cents a hour! Now *that's* the common labor like I was!" Willie King shook his head with finality. "An' I can't get none a it. I worked till last year, but my legs give out an' my wind got short—I jes' couldn't make it no more."

It was drizzling by the time Joyce and I made our way back through the fields to Coulon. Grayness sat heavily on the living quarters, and all that was around. And we, too, felt the infectious lethargy, the damp chill that cut through to the bone and wouldn't be warmed. To our left, the cane, eight or nine feet high, teemed with tractors and cutters and men reduced in size by the distance; to our right, the quarters—a shabby house here, a gap of land there, then a sagging shack with only parts of the walls and a roof.

From the car, Joyce studied a crude batten-board house one room deep and a washed-out red. The windowless front had four solid wood doors, all of them shut against the cold. The porch was almost gone, its edges were ragged and some floorboards had collapsed. Two small benches and a straight-back chair sat empty, and a bare wire stretched between the supporting posts. The only signs that life still existed within the shack were turnips stacked at one end of the porch and wisps of smoke coming from the chimney.

"It's just as worse inside," Joyce said. "I stayed here when I was quite young. The house doesn't even have water. The people who live here have to walk over to the shed where all the tractors are or down to my daddy's house, about a block." She pointed to a green-and-white house on the same road. "They just cart the water down, an' most of 'em bathe in big tubs."

Although drab in color, her father's green house appeared solid and out of place among its decrepit neighbors. It was larger than most of the shacks crowded with families of nine and ten or more. The porch bore no signs of decay, and the familiar outhouse was missing. And Joyce agreed, "That's one of the better houses. My father's been here a long time, an', well, he gets all the breaks."

In the square of land between the green house and us, a yellow vehicle with a claw-like arm lifted blackened stalks from a pile of cane and lowered them into a long truck, its latticed sides high and sloping in at the bottom. More cane filled a cart seven to eight feet long. Nearby, a derrick once used to load the trailers stood idle, like a one-armed cross.

"The big one's called a trailer," Joyce explained, "an' that's a wagon. They use the wagons to haul the cane from out the fields to a more convenient place to put it in the trailers." She nodded toward the heap of blackened stalks. "See, this was burned out in the fields—the shucks were burnt off—an' it was brought here by a wagon. Now it's going into a trailer. Then it will go to the mill to be ground." She pointed to a machine with a short claw. "That's a cane loader. It picks it up out the field and puts it in the wagon. The other one's a transloader. It transfer the cane into the big trailer. The extension is so it can reach up over the sides. They use the wagons during planting time, too. They put the cane in a wagon, an' a man throws it down in the row as a tractor pulls the wagon along."

As we got out of the car and started toward the red house, Joyce remarked, "*Two* families live in this one house."

"How many rooms are there?" I asked, surveying the narrow structure.

"Only two on each side. It's all old people that live there now. They can't work anymore, but they practically lived all their lives here an' have kids, children, relatives here."

Joyce rapped on the end door, which in turn banged against the wood frame. From inside came the sound of a latch being freed, then the door swung open and an old man wearing baggy trousers over a union suit looked out quizzically. He was small, his face puffily wrinkled and his neck ridged like the trunk of an aging oak.

When Joyce asked if we could come in his house, the old man grinned, showing toothless gums. "Sure indeed!" he said in a Cajun accent reflecting a lifetime on the bayou. Closing the door behind us, he complained, "That wind col'!"

The room was small and dark, the drab walls barely brightened by a single lightbulb suspended from the ceiling and the glow from the fireplace. The furnishings consisted of an iron bed, a dresser, and two chairs pulled close to the fire. A Coca-Cola bottle, a clock, and a bottle of Vicks sat on the mantle. Tacked to the walls were religious pictures and calendars yellow with age.

Percy Green nudged the chair closer to the flames and sat, rubbing one stocking foot over the other as we talked. Each time the fire dwindled to coals, he doused it with kerosene, warming his hands over the rejuvenated flames.

"I like my chair 'cause it be warm by the fire," he said, rubbing his hands together, then holding them palm side toward the fire. "Nice an' warm. I got a heater, but I only turn it on when it get real, real, *real* col' 'cause we gotta save the li'l butane hyere. That's *really* expensive!"

Joyce nodded sympathetically. "Gas is expensive enough just if you have a regular pipe from a main gas line to your home. By having tank gas, it's much more expensive. When these people go into the harvesting season, they're kind of happy because it gives them a chance to pay the bills they owe, but by the time harvesting is over, they're in debt again because of the gas. You know, a hundred dollars a month to keep a house warm. Add that up, and you don't have much left. So they go in paying an' come out owing, an' that's *always* the case."

Percy Green squatted beside the fireplace and added two worn boards, then poured kerosene over the pile. The flames roared high.

"Is that what you do most days?" I asked.

"That's right."

"Do you ever go out visiting or anything?"

He shook his head. "Never go visitin' hardly ever. Jes' sit hyere by the fire. I go hunt me a li'l wood to cut 'cause it's 'spensive but hardly go an' visit. Hardly go out when it's col'. Can't stand the col'. Summer, well, I stir 'round, walk a little. That's my garden out there, an' sometime I walk about in it."

He ambled over to the room's lone window at the end of the house. Through it I could see rows of cabbages and mustards.

"What do you eat besides greens?" I asked.

"White bean, red bean, an' chicken an' fish sometime when white folks bring me fish. But mostly beans—hardly any meat. Can't buy meat. Cost too much."

He grinned, again showing smooth, pink gums. "All my teeth is gone," he said, as though aware of that fact for the first time. "I *been* havin' my teeth gone fer years, *years* aback. Doctor had give me order to get all 'em pulled. I got false teeth, but I jes' don't wear 'em."

Percy Green was sixty-five, he said, and retired. Before, he had worked in the fields—plowing, planting, helping with the crops. He had worked fifty years on Coulon and was born on still another plantation. Now he lived with a son who operated the cane cutter. Two more lived in New Orleans. When I asked if they visited him, he answered, "Sometime," his tone defining the "sometime" as not often.

"Do you get lonesome?"

Still staring at the flames he answered, "Uh-hmmmm, I be lonesome," and then looked back over his shoulder at Joyce and me. "See, when my wife was livin', well I had company, somebody to talk wit', you know, to keep yo' mind together." He shook his head slowly. "To keep yo' mind together."

Several days later, when I returned to Coulon with Joyce and a newspaper photographer, wash hung on lines propped high by boards, whipping in the brisk breeze. The photographer focused on the shirts and dungarees and khakis of all sizes and on a nearby outhouse while Joyce went into one of the houses to ask if we could take pictures of the woman and her children. I waited in the car, watching distant tractors slice wide, flat expanses in the towering cane. It wasn't until Joyce returned to say we should come back later that I noticed a dusty white automobile parked at the turn in the road, about half a block away. The driver's eyes were trained on us.

"That's the plantation owner," Joyce said nervously as she climbed into the backseat. "We better go."

The photographer was putting the key into the ignition when the white car sped up behind us, blocking our path to the road. Slamming his door, the driver rushed toward us and planted himself beside the photographer's window.

"What y'all doin' here?" he asked, glowering. "You know this is private property?"

The man was stocky, with dark, tousled hair and a scowl that seemed more permanent than temporary aggravation provoked by us. He dug both hands deep into his pants pockets, frowning, impatient for an answer.

"We're doing a story," I called out.

He leaned his head through the open window. "You from Channel Eight?"

"No, from the *States-Item* in New Orleans."

"What's your name?" he snapped at the photographer. His eyes swerved briefly to Joyce, then back to the photographer. "What kind a story you writin'?"

"I just do pictures," the photographer answered. "She's doing the story on the sugarcane industry in Louisiana."

Leaning farther into the car, the man scrutinized me. "Who you talkin' to?"

"We're going to talk to everyone," the photographer intercepted. "She's coming back and we're going to do the people around here, the workers, the fieldhands—"

"And I'd like to talk to you," I broke in, reaching across the seat to hand him a business card. "See, he can't stay, so we're taking the pictures before he has to leave. We want to get them before the cane is down. I understand it'll all be gone in a week or two."

The man stood silent as I chattered frantically, inwardly panicked. In 1969, three college students doing volunteer work in the area had been arrested on a nearby plantation and charged with trespassing when they met at a worker's house to discuss forming a union with him and several neighbors. The U.S. district court, still considering the case in 1972, had issued a temporary injunction restraining the growers from interfering with the workers' right to have visitors. Nevertheless, I worried that the growers might pressure the people not to talk to me.

I persisted, "If you give me your name and number I could call before I come back."

"Name's John Caldwell," he said. He gave me a telephone number, but suspicion filled his voice. "We've had some union trouble down here, people stirring up trouble."

"We're just doing a story. We're not with a union," I assured him.

"Well, I just wanted to know, because we had a Catholic priest down here stirring up trouble at one of the houses over there."

More relaxed, he stepped back from the car.

"Would it be okay if we get pictures of some of the kids and stuff?" the photographer asked.

Caldwell shrugged. "We don't have anything to hide." He got into the dusty car and drove away. And Joyce and the photographer and I sat there, not moving, not speaking until the car was out of sight.

Lulu's Story

Lulu King crossed her swollen ankles as she rocked and reminisced. She had never been more than an hour and a half away from home, no farther than her ancestors had ever traveled from Rienzi after the first one came as a slave. Once a month she made a trip to Charity Hospital in New Orleans and back—always back, as though a giant magnet was pulling her, as it had her parents and even now pulled her children and theirs. One time she would have liked to see outside Louisiana, what the world was like, to see it or to read about it. But now, she reckoned, she had "done got too ol'."

A large woman, her face fatly wrinkled, her eyes still bright with hope, she sat rocking and watching the red-faced Pepsi-Cola clock over the doorway and, through the window, the dirt road that led past the house where she was born and into the fields.

"That's the time I use' to always pray, when I was out in the fields. I could talk to Him better. Wouldn't be nobody to bother me, an' I could ask Him to save me an' to he'p me keep on agoin'.

When I got religion, it was out in the fields. Them same fields right outside the window. It was in 1922, on the seventeen day a May when I was thirteen. I never forget that day. Look like it was a *dark* road wit' a fork in it. One road goin' this-a-way. One like that. A voice, a hymn, was a'comin' to me, singin' 'Poor Mona Got a Home at Last.' Seem like the mo' I'd get to that fork, the mo' that voice'd come to me. There was a *big* man standin' in the middle a that road, so I said to him, 'Mister, could you tell me which-a-way to find Jesus?' He say, 'Go this-a-way.' But look like somethin' say to me, 'No, don't go that-a-way.' So I went t'other way, an' look like the more I'd go up that road, the bigger that light would get. When I got to the end of that road that light, look like it jes' lit up the *whole* world. An' then that hymn jes' come out, 'bout 'Poor Mona Got a Home.' I don't know how I didn't feel. I jes' felt light. I was happy. I was cryin'. An' then I got baptized that third Sunday in July up there at the church on Main Street. It was a pool at the back a the church, an' we all was in white. An' well, look like religion what kep' me goin' all these years. The he'p a the good Lawd, that what he'p me to make it. They say the Lawd always makes a way, so I didn't see no harder day in my sixty years than what I'm seein' now.

"I been right like this, livin' on this same plantation, all my days. Born last house down the street. It's no more fittin' to live in now, but that's where I was born an' where me and King got married. Ever since I knowed, my family was on this plantation, till fifteen, twenty years ago—till they move, they scattered an' moved away. They all was cane workers: cut cane, ditch, plow with mules—like that. My mama was 'bout sixty when she stop. She jes' fell down sick an' had her kidney taken out, an' she never did work no mo'. My daddy worked till he died. He died when he was fifty-nine, but he worked *all* a it. He always did work mules. My grandfather did the same thing. An' my great-grandfather— well, I reckon he did too, but I never did knowed him. Reckon he mighta been a slave. My chil'ren, they be married an' gone now, but they all did work on the farm at one time or 'nother. Start when they was fourteen years old, most of 'em. Junius an' Turner an' Oliver, the one live next door still do work in the fields, an' two my daughters from in town come in durin' grindin' to scrap cane.

"I started workin' when I was nine, 'side my mama. Worked *all* my life in the fields pickin' up rice an' scrappin' cane, till this arthritis got me in the hip. Scrap cane, cut cane, cut rice, load rice, sack it up—done *ever*'thing. Now I can't do too much. I'm not able. Jes' some babysittin' in town. An' King, he don't work no mo' neither. When I started in the fields it was eight of us in the family. Seven sisters an' one brother. I was the oldest. We jes' was poor. We didn't have nothin', an' the chil'ren then had to work. They had a bunch a us kids workin' on the place. We was workin' for forty cents a day. From five in the mornin' till five at night. We'd work five days in the field, an' the six we'd stay an' clean up us house an' wash the clothes. There was no time for playin' in the fields. The boss man'd be on your back, an' if you wouldn't work, he'd whip you. I never was whipped, but I was afraid of 'im. At that time, colored folks wasn't good as a good dog to the white folks. An' they always was callin' you a nigger. 'Get out there, *nigger*.' '*Nigger,* do this, 'n *nigger* do that.' An' you be scared to say anything. They never did hit me, jes' talk rough, an', well, I jes' thought that was our name, nigger.

"All what money we made we would give to Mama, an' on Sunday she'd give us a quarter. There was a nickel for me to spend an' one to put in church, an' if I had my monthly church fee to pay that was fifteen cents. I thought I had aplenty with that nickel. After church we'd go to that fruit stand in town, an' I'd buy me the most candy I could get. I'd buy me a *big* peppermint candy 'cause it was mo'. It lasted longer. That be what I always got. My mind would be on it 'fore I'd get to that fruit stand. 'Gonna get me a peppermint candy.' Sometime we use' to take the overripe fruit, them bananas an' oranges an' things that'd be rotten. We'd get a big pile for fifteen an' twenty cents. We jes' come up so poor we was glad for anything we could get.

"I only had one Sunday dress I always wore to church. It was navy blue with little white star dots on it an' lace on the collar. For the week I had different clothes, but never too many. Jes' a change a suit. When one get dirty, we'd wash it an' put it back on. Christmas, Mama use' to buy us a doll, an' that was all we was gonna get till it was Christmas again. Only time I got a birthday present was when I was growed up an' my chil'ren give me somethin'. Like when people celebrate their birthday, well, we never did when I was small. It jes' was a day you knew you had, but it wasn't anything special. The week I married King I worked in the fields. I had sixteen chil'ren. Raised twelve an' the other four died. Outta all I had I only lost three wintertimes from workin' in the fields—that's the three born in October. That one next door, he was born New Year's Eve day, an' I worked the day before that, out in the field cuttin' cane.

"I would keep the older ones home to see to the little ones durin' grindin', an' before the first one was big enough my sister'd mind 'em. It was hard workin' an' bringin' up kids. I use' to work all day in the field, come home an' have to wash an' cook. I use' to bathe my chil'ren an' put their day's clothes on 'em before I'd go to bed, 'cause I wouldn't get up time enough in the mornin' to dress 'em, an' the older ones wasn't old enough to put the clothes on 'em. They jes' could keep changin' diapers. Sometimes I jes' sleep 'bout an hour, then I had to get back up an' go to work again.

"By me workin' 'round white people, they use' to always give me a little clothes an' stuff for my chil'ren. An' furniture, it was the same thing. All what I got was give me. Ever' time I wished for somethin' the white folks'd come along an' give me a little piece better than what I had, an' I throwed away what I had. I never bought nothin' new but that stove an' TV. Paid for 'em on time. An', well, the TV's so old now till it don't even show the picture. Sometimes it goes out an' it comes back again, but I sure wish I could get one I could sit down an' look at.

"We lived in one them ol' houses cross the way till nine or ten years ago when we moved to this one. First time I ever had a bathroom was in this house, when they put one in three years ago. Before that, we bathed in a tub. One of those wood tubs that be made out those barrels. Ever' night we had to heat fourteen tubs a water, on the stove. Still do have to heats water, but now it's jes' King and me. We use' to have a shack out back, too. A little tin buildin'. Rain, snow, storm, anything else, you had to go outside. I remember it rained like I don't know what in that ol' house across the road. If it start rainin', we had to get up from sleepin' an' start pullin' the bed from under the leak. An' jes' like you see through that glass, you could see the road through the cracks in the wall. The rug on the floor, it be raisin' up like I don't know what. Plenty time we use' to have to put rags on the floor to stop the col' from comin' in.

"Still, I reckon I rather go live back in that ol' house than move in town. I been on the plantation so long till look like I ain't gonna feel right if I ever get off. I know I'd miss it. All my life I been knowin' these people. I likes it hyere. I knows it hyere. An' I could go anywhere with my eyes shut. I don't know. I never did like no town. I jes' got that fear feelin' 'bout it. Hyere we don't have to pay no rent—an' I worry 'bout that, 'bout havin' to move to town an' pay rent with the little bit a salary an' security we get. Lotta time they make you move when you can't work no mo'. But the boss tol' me, 'Lulu,' he say, 'if you wanta stay in there, stay. Jes' keep it up. Keep the grass an' the trash out the yard.' An', well, he ain't never bothered me. I been knowin' him an' his wife both since they was babies. I lived in the house next to his mama. When they move on the place, the boss wasn't big as this boy hyere, an' I 'Mister' *him*. I 'Miss' his wife, too, Miss Caroline. An' I got chil'ren older than what they is. But I always did 'Mister' 'em all. Look like it jes' more manners to me. That's jes' my way. When I was comin' up, you *had* to say 'Yes ma'am,' 'No ma'am.' Didn't care who you was. If you didn't, you jes' was gonna get punished. Sayin' 'Yeah' or 'No,' you was too sassy. Now they tell 'em anything they want, but I still say 'Yes ma'am' an' 'No ma'am,' an' that's how I taught my chil'ren. Even now, people I'm babysittin' for, they be after me to come sit to the table. But I'm so use' to bein' out in the yard—like a dog—I tell 'em all time, I'll eat when I get done doin' my work.' Look like I jes' can't make myself go sit down there with 'em. I tell 'em all time, I tell 'em, 'I jes' feel like a fly in a bowl a milk. That jes' the way I come up. Not say I hate y'all or scorn y'all, but it's jes' the way I was brung up.'

"Sometime I sits down hyere now an' thinks 'bout how white folks use' to do us. When my chil'ren was growin' up, there'd be a slavery picture on TV an' I'd say, 'The way you see those people, that jes' the way we was.' 'Cause in a way we was treated like them slaves. Not the way them people use' to go buy 'em from different people an' they couldn't go from one place to another. We could leave on our own. If you didn't like this place, you could move an' go to somewheres else an' stay, but it wasn't no better. The boss man might treat you a li'l bit better than what the other man did, but you might be in a worser house. There was really no place to go. Things was pretty much the same ever'where you went.

"I never thought I'd live to see things change like they did, the way white folks treat blacks. An' I'm glad for my chil'ren they did, 'cause I reckon I be more worried. When they started goin' to school together, that's one thing I kicked against my chil'ren doin' because I knowed how they treated us when the blacks wasn't mixed up with 'em like that. I was scared. But it turned out awright. There's some care more 'bout you. They treat you nicer than what the others do. Still, them what treats me nice I be scared. I don't trust 'em. I think they be like the ol' ones use' to be. Because you got some of 'em, they hate you still. They cut your guts out if you ever' walk cross their door. They got some right hyere in town now. I *knows* of 'em. If you go an' ask 'em for a drink a water, if you ain't got a paper cup, they ain't gonna give you no glass. If they give you a glass, they rather to throw it in the garbage an' break it up to keep from puttin' their hands on it. But I ain't got nothin' in me against 'em now. I forgive 'em what they did me 'cause look like that jes' the way they was livin'. I don't regret that. In a way, I'm glad, because I never been in a jailhouse in my life. Never been on no witness trial. An' I know how to go amongst the white folks. So I'm glad I lived that life I did 'cause I was out of trouble.

"To me, I had a good life. I was able to work, to get mostly what I needed—not what I wanted, but what I needed the baddest. An' if the Lord'd wanted my life to be better, He would a made it better. Still, I talk to Him sometime, 'bout Heaven. I *know* I'm goin' there. I'm fightin' *hard* to go there. I thinks about it, an' I asks Him to let my best day down hyere be my worst day there. I don't know what'll be up there. All I wanta do is be happy—be happy an' sit down 'n rest."

Teche Country

From Thibodaux I drove west to Abbeville, a town of eleven thousand that had changed little in the last hundred years except for the appearance of gas stations, television repair shops, and fried chicken stands. In this town of well-kept frame houses, screened porches, moss-draped oaks, and strong Cajun accents, the brick building with SMHA lettered across the front appeared to be the newest addition. The small, unpretentious structure was located at the edge of Bayou Vermillion, on a lot covered with shells and weeds that separated it from the rest of town. The interior looked still-new but lived-in. A collage of colored-paper bulletins and children's artwork bore testimony to the process of people working with people, to lives touching and being touched. There were the sounds of hurried footsteps and voices talking at business pace, and the phone rang more frequently than the Catholic church bells across the bridge as Sister Anne Catherine Bizalion kept in contact with Father O'Connell, the health clinic in Franklin, and Father Frank Ecimovich.

The latter, SMHA's president, had been transferred to Pine Bluff, Arkansas, the year before, after growers complained to Bishop Maurice Schexnayder about the priest's involvement with the fieldworkers and his testimony at the Houma hearings. Father O'Connell had shown me a recent article from *Saturday Review* mentioning Father Frank, whose parishioners had been mostly black fieldworkers. The story described how he had received a letter from Bishop Schexnayder of Lafayette, warning: "Your role, Father, is to convert people and teach catechism to little children." Then, the article continued, Father Frank had been summoned to the bishop's office, where he was confronted by a group of growers and instructed to mind his own business. Shortly after that, his superiors in Mississippi had transferred him out of state.

Several people around Thibodaux had mentioned Bishop Schexnayder as one of those who had pressured Father O'Connell and other pro-union priests during the 1950s, and *Saturday Review* had quoted the elderly cleric as pronouncing, "There's no suffering among sugarcane workers. Under the Sugar Act, the Department of Agriculture sees to that." The bishop had also attempted to oust Sister Anne Catherine after she and Lorna Bourg helped organize blacks and whites into HeadStart during the 1960s, but the superior of her order, the Dominican Rural Missionaries in France, had thwarted that attempt. As Sister Anne Catherine showed me into her office, she apologized for the bishop: He was a kind man who simply didn't understand what was happening—he needed educating.

She was a short, petite woman who wore a navy blouse, pinstriped slacks, and a nubby cotton-print jacket instead of a habit. Her salt-and-pepper hair was secured in back by a leather barrette. She had come to Abbeville from Grenoble in the mid-1950s and spoke with an accent undiminished by the years. Members of her order had always performed nontraditional kinds of service, she said, even working in bars and railway stations in their native country. Only four others remained in the United States, including another one in Abbeville and still another in nearby Jennings. When she herself first arrived, she had studied at grammar schools in order to learn English and familiarize herself with the people and their way of life. Nevertheless, she had remained unaware of the cane workers and their problems until three years ago, when she had become immersed in their world.

The surface of her desk was covered with papers and photographs, and, glancing down at it, she apologized for the mess. It was hectic keeping abreast of phone calls, she explained, especially since Judge Pratt had issued the injunction withholding grower subsidies.

"I wrote this letter, and now we are getting this kind of thing," she said, taking a sheet of paper from her desk and handing it to me.

The mimeographed letter attempted to explain the injunction to small growers and to assure them that SMHA was concerned about their problems as well as the workers' plight. Across the bottom of the sheet, a note was hand-printed in ink: "Is this Sister Anne a Catholic or what? Have you heard of her? Do you know her? I wish you'd burn a candle on her!!!"

Still another copy of the letter bore this brusque notation: "Sister, please keep your political propaganda; I am not interested."

"He is pastor of a Catholic church in New Iberia," she explained. "The priests get pressure from both the bishop and the white Catholic growers."

When the telephone rang, Lorna Bourg, SMHA's assistant director, took up the story, detailing the beginnings of Southern Mutual. At thirty, she was of medium size with short brown hair and sharp brown eyes framed by thick brows. Her manner was direct and set-in-her-ways firm. She held a bachelor's degree in psychology and was working part-time toward a master's at the University of Southwestern Louisiana in nearby Lafayette. She and Sister Anne had met in 1964 when they worked together first in a War on Poverty effort known as Acadiana Neuf and then in the local HeadStart. Although a native of Baton Rouge with a Cajun heritage, she too had been unfamiliar with the fieldworkers' plight until May 1969, when H. L. Mitchell solicited help from her, Sister Anne, and eight others in making a survey of plantation conditions for the Houma wage hearings. After spending six weeks in cane country, the ten—including Father Frank—decided something needed to be done. That fall, using expense money Sister Anne had received for a speaking engagement, they drove to New York and Washington, D.C., where they approached foundations and agencies and some of Mitch's contacts to ask for funding.

Reflecting on those first trips onto the plantations, Lorna remembered, "It was twentieth-century slavery still in existence. So we decided to carve out that area—that seventeen-parish area—and began putting all our skills and energy and whatever expertise we might have into solving the situation. We had come to realize that working at the local level we were extremely vulnerable, that if we could form an organization across the board in south Louisiana, then we would get very strong. So Mitch, Sister, Father Frank, the Broussards, and I decided to form SMHA."

Having hung up the telephone, Sister Anne rejoined the discussion of the plight of fieldworkers and those who try to help them, of the pressures to kill potentially beneficial programs like the one in Thibodaux and the health clinic operated in Franklin by Rose Mae Broussard. When I asked to visit the clinic, Sister Anne shook her head slowly. Since newspapers throughout the state had printed an Associated Press story about the cane workers a few weeks back, something had happened around Franklin. Sister Anne didn't know what. She did know, from talking to Rose Mae Broussard, that one of the clinic's most reliable employees and two fieldworkers had called in sick and made other excuses for not coming in the day a photographer was to take their pictures for an SMHA brochure.

"People who are normally pleasant individuals and communicate easily suddenly close up when they think what they say or do may have some unfortunate reaction," Sister Ann said, drawing on her own experiences. "The fear may be of the unknown—of what *might* happen—with bad recollections of things that *have* happened, like losing your job or being thrown out of your house or a life just made harsher when it's already harsh enough."

Two years ago, she illustrated, SMHA had managed to get a large group of fieldworkers to attend the Houma wage hearings,

but the next year there was no one because of the interim coercion. "The pressure can be extremely subtle," she said. "It doesn't have to be 'You're going to lose your job'—and I'm sure that in ninety-nine percent of the cases, it's *not* that you're going to lose your job, but there are other ways. Pressure can be like if a guy is beginning to be a leader and getting the people on the settlements to work with him in trying to get better housing for the group there, then his house is the only one fixed, and so he is ostracized by the others because everyone thinks he is the boss's favorite."

But she could not even speculate about what had happened in Franklin.

On the desk were photographs of Gustave and Huet and other workers made for the pamphlet SMHA planned to distribute around the United States. Handing me the photographs, Sister Anne promised to encourage Rose Mae Broussard to allow me into the clinic, and that afternoon when Father O'Connell arrived in Abbeville for a meeting, he too offered to help. The two tried repeatedly via long-distance telephone calls to persuade the clinic director that my visit and story would help the workers' cause. The next day, as I awaited Mrs. Broussard's decision, people trekked through the SMHA offices—among them a white nun and her companion, a striking black woman, and, surprisingly, Rose Mae Broussard. When we met unexpectedly I made my own appeal. She promised to bring the matter before her advisory committee, composed of fieldworkers, but I knew by her expression the answer would be no.

The clinic director was a white woman in her forties. She and her husband, Bernard, had experienced their own problems bucking the establishment. In the 1960s, after they started the Human Relations Council and HeadStart in Franklin, Bernard had been fired from his newspaper job and their daughter expelled from the local Catholic school because of the family's association with blacks. When Rose Mae was unable to get a job as a secretary with HeadStart and the program would not hire Bernard even as a janitor, he finally took a paper route. But when people began canceling their subscriptions, he soon lost that job, too.

The day after the advisory committee met, Rose Mae Broussard telephoned to inform me that I could not do a story. "You can write about what the clinic offers," she said, "but not what you see, not the health conditions of the people. Even then, the advisory committee will insist on reading it, and I'm not sure they will let you print it."

I thanked her, but I already knew what the clinic did. It had been funded by the Migrant Division of HEW for $200,000 for five years; it had a full-time doctor and a part-time dentist, and it operated on an out-patient basis. The cases the doctor could not handle were sent to a private physician, with the clinic footing the bill, or to Charity Hospital in Lafayette. I knew also about the health conditions from talking to Sister Anne and the field-workers themselves and from reading SMHA studies such as the one conducted in 1971 by a Tulane University medical student and several other young people. The study indicated that out of thirty-seven adults examined by physicians on two plantations, only two were medically normal and only eight did not need immediate care. Only sixteen of the seventy children examined were completely healthy.

"You can tell the people aren't healthy just by looking at them," Sister Anne said. "It is not unusual for children in the clinic to look much older than their age. Adults, too. You find a lot of obesity from eating beans and rice. The children have sores, and worms are a commonly accepted thing."

She hoped clinics like this one, which serviced only St. Mary and East Iberia parishes, would be available someday to the other plantation residents, who now had to scrape up money for a private doctor, pay bus fare to Charity Hospital in Lafayette or New Orleans, or do without.

Because of its outreach workers and part-time employees who had grown up on plantations, the clinic could identify with workers and their families in ways the area's public health units could not. And that was a real advantage. "The people in professional health positions don't speak the same language as the workers on the plantations," Sister Anne Catherine explained. "Immunizations, for instance. The fieldworkers don't see why, if a child has gotten one shot, he needs to go back for the second one."

"Communications." Sister Anne repeated the word, weighing its implications. "There is a lack of understanding between the grower's culture and the worker's culture. So there is no communication between those two worlds, despite what people may say.

Maybe the worker will say 'Yes, Sir' and the farmers will have the feeling their message has gotten across, but there is no real communication between them."

For Sister Anne, the cane workers' plight was heartrending, especially in a state so rich in natural resources. She was angry, she said, not so much at the individual growers as at the federal and state governments, which she held responsible.

"Do you think the industry has prospered off of cheap labor?" I asked.

"Yes, but that is not the whole story," she said. "It's a fact there is cheap labor in the fields—cheap labor not only because of low wages but because of the lack of other fringe benefits taken for granted in other industries. But there is also the other aspect: The sugar industry is a very protected industry, protected by the high tariffs against outside sugar and protected against problems at home by high conditional payments, which is a nice word for subsidies. If the federal government is taking responsibility for the sugar industry, if the industry needs that sort of protection, then that protection should be afforded the workers in the industry."

Sister Anne's eyes again fell on the photographs of Huet and Gustave and of the shacks they and their people lived in. The room was quiet as Lorna and I too glanced across the desk at them.

"Is this a vestige of slavery?" I asked.

"The people on the plantations don't feel free," she said. "I'm not trying to say they are or they aren't free. I think they don't *feel* free." She paused and considered the photographs. "I don't blame the growers, because it is part of the vision of the world, and to that extent they can't help it. I think for the most part when they say they are concerned about their workers, they are concerned, which doesn't mean they understand. I think there are a lot of unknown prejudices. We've heard it at hearings, that if they did give the workers better housing, the people wouldn't take care of it, that if they let the workers pay their own medical bills or their own utility bills, the workers aren't dependable enough to do that—they aren't capable. That's the whole attitude toward the farm workers, and the growers don't realize that by doing this—it's probably out of good concern—they are preventing them from growing up, from becoming truly independent."

What SMHA aimed to do was give workers the opportunity to do for themselves, she said. That was, in fact, the aim of a self-help housing program SMHA hoped to get under way by spring. At the moment she was unsure just what form the project would take, whether it would help fieldworkers buy or build new houses or renovate old ones. But she was certain of the objective: to help them move out of housing owned by the boss man.

"This is the only way they are going to get out of this vicious cycle," she said with conviction. "By owning their own homes they will have more pride in taking care of them and they will be better workers. Really, if the farmers would just realize that if the workers were happier they would be better workers. It would be to the advantage of the farmers. They would get a better day's work."

No Trespassing

To the left, outside Houma, plantations lined Little Bayou Black Road. Crescent Farms. Iodine. Belle Grove. One after the other, with nothing to distinguish which was which—just POSTED NO TRESPASSING SOUTHDOWN, INC. signs marking dirt roads that led to the living quarters hidden from the highway, out of sight. One settlement looked much like another, much like those that populated the rest of cane country—the shacks gray and paintless and paired with outhouses. The signs stood like sentinels, barring the present and the future—change. The newspaper photographer and I ventured past them, curious, nervous, taking pictures, talking to residents, then hurrying to avoid a confrontation with the boss or the law, because in these parts the two were often related, by blood or marriage or a mutual interest in the sugar industry. And although Southdown Lands, Inc., was a Delaware-based corporation, it was, in the end, tied to the plantation system and the area.

As the photographer and I wound our way through cane country, meandering with Bayou Teche through Broussard and New Iberia and Jeanerette, on to Franklin and Houma, traveling down "No Trespassing" roads and others, there was a sameness in the conditions, the attitudes, the wasted lives. Yet around a bend we often found something to again shock us: a grower still referring to the fieldworkers as "darkies"; elderly women lugging wood; whole families whose lives seemed as little valued as the shacks they existed in—families like Moses West and his wife and three children, left behind when Hollywood Plantation moved its workers into new houses with tile floors and baths and built-in kitchens.

The five of them—all retarded—lived in one of two battenboard shacks that stood on the site of the old quarters, just down the road and over the railroad tracks, near Houma. The Wests' was the one nearest the road. Surrounded by mud and weeds, it too would have seemed deserted had it not been for the porch assortment of rockers and sofas and a line of dripping clothes. As soon as we pulled into the yard, Moses scurried out of the house and over boards that straddled the mud. He had close-cut gray hair and was dressed in a white turtleneck sweater, a vest, and dark, baggy trousers as though he were expecting, or hoping for, company.

"We don't have to buy dem pi'tures, heh?" he worried after we asked to photograph him and the house. When we explained they were for a New Orleans newspaper and wouldn't cost him anything, he invited us in.

The house was dark and dank. There was no ceiling to hide the underside of the tin roof, and the outer batten board was visible through large holes in the Sheetrock walls. Three unmade beds occupied most of the first room. A teenage girl sat on one, and between the other two, on a lawn chair, a stout woman stared at and through us, dazed.

"Dat my wife," Moses said, ". . . an' my daughter Pearlie." He turned to another girl seated near us, just inside the door. "An' dat Ida, the one I takes to de hospital."

"What's wrong with her?" I inquired, and he explained, "Apalapsy spells."

The girl—who looked to be in her mid-teens although Moses said she was twenty-one—held a bowl of rice mixed with a smattering of beans. Her arms were twisted, and she struggled to move the fork from the bowl to her mouth. She looked up at me and in a slow, erratic voice announced, "I'm—awwwww—right."

"You're all right?" I asked.

She nodded. "Y-y-yes—ma'am." Her arm outstretched, her eyes offering, she handed me the bowl.

"Don't you want to finish?"

"Y-y-yes—ma'am," she repeated, finally returning the bowl to her lap.

Moses stood near, anxious to talk. When Ida stopped, he excitedly told about himself, that he was fifty-six, retired, and made regular trips to Charity Hospital in New Orleans for checkups. He showed us three prescriptions: One was his—he took it three times a day for the "TBs"—and the other was for Ida's "apalapsy."

"I'm not able to do anything," he said, "but dey lets me live here without havin' any rent to pay. I gets security—I done forgotten how much—an'," he gestured to Ida, "she gets welfare."

"How long did you work in the fields?" I asked.

He scratched his head. "I work about—I guess anywheres around three years before I hadda go to de doctor an' dey found I had TBs."

"But how many years did you work altogether before you had to stop?" I repeated, thinking he had misunderstood.

"Three years."

I tried again. "How old were you when you started?"

"I done forgotten," he said, shrugging.

Still seated in the lawn chair, his wife stared trancelike through an open window, into the distance. I aimed my voice at her. "How old are you?"

"Twenty-five," she answered absently.

Moses interrupted, "She ain't twenty-five! She was born in 1919—now you kin figger what she be!"

"Dat my mama," Ida broke in. "Dat—m-my—mama—an' s-she—m-my—sister. Y-y-yes—m-ma'am." She swallowed a forkful of beans. "K-know—w-what—I-g-got?"

"Apalapsy," Moses spoke up, attempting to proceed with the conversation when Ida interrupted. "Tell 'er some'in else n-now. G-gotta ra-dio!"

"You got a radio. Who gave it to you?" I asked.

Moses interceded. "A lady up dere in town bought her a radio wit' de check she gener'ly gets."

"Who was the woman who gave it to her?"

Wide-eyed, Ida watched, listened as her father explained for her. "She didn' *give* it to her. She got money outta Ida's check an' bought it."

When I asked about the house, Moses verbally laid it out: "Dis room, middle room, an' a kitchen. Bath's outdoors. I'd show it to ya except my boy Jay's takin' a bath." He called to the girl on the bed. "Jay got his clothes on?" She started toward the next room, cracked open the door, and over her shoulder answered, "Yeah, he got his pants on." Moses motioned, and the photographer and I followed. A teenage boy wearing dungarees but no shirt sat in a straight-backed chair, a bucket of soapy water and a rag at his feet. He glanced up as we entered, then bent over to wring out the rag. Old clothes were stacked against one wall, and along another was a single bed. That room and the kitchen—dark until Moses opened the back door—smelled worse than many outhouses I had inspected along the way. And the kitchen floor was wet and rotted through where the faucet dripped.

When we returned to the front room, Mrs. West and the two daughters were still seated, looking as if they had blocked out the world just as it had them.

"Do you get lonesome?" I asked Mrs. West.

"Ma'am?"

I repeated the question, and she answered, "Yeah, since dey move." She pointed to the house next door. "No one back here 'cept us."

Moses West's expression became forlorn, and his eyes lingered on his wife. "We jes' makin' out, dat all." He shook his head. "Dat all."

The photographer and I drove away, and Moses and the house stood alone—discards, of no more value, no more use to the owner.

"Somethin' to Lean On"

Millie Bordelon was a white woman in her thirties; nevertheless, she understood the workers' problems just as she did those of the farmers, for she had grown up knowing both. Her father and brothers themselves grew sugarcane, although they did so without fieldhands, and her job with a nearby neighborhood service center often took her into the workers' homes. At times, her concern for the workers had been construed by her grower acquaintances as betrayal. In fact, she was an opinionated woman, never hesitant to speak her mind. As we drove, she observed, "There are so many people around here with an attitude of, 'The nigger can't learn—you show him, you teach him, you gotta come back and show him again.' I don't think it's ever said in so many words. It's just an accepted attitude."

It was because of her contacts with the workers and her familiarity with the cane industry that the neighborhood center's director had suggested I seek her help in researching my articles, and so together we had set out on the back roads of Iberia Parish, deep in Cajun country.

With Christmas past, grinding had peaked and all phases of it quickened: the cutting, the burning, the loading and unloading, the trips to and from the mill. The already level horizon grew flatter by the day as the cane disappeared and the land again revealed the shacks and manor houses and mills. The land we passed through now was like that—mostly fields of stubble with patches of tall shoots rising here and there. The roads were littered with stalks crushed by the trailers and wagons parading back and forth to the mill.

A rare patch of uncut cane still obstructed our view when we approached a dirt road that intersected the paved highway. Millie Bordelon instructed me to turn right. Before us, trucks and tractor-drawn wagons lined the road two abreast, from the point where it met the highway all the way to the distant mill— a rust-colored monster that belched smoke. We followed the road and then, as we neared the mill, cut through to the other side. Two black boys perched on tractors looked down as we slowed and stopped.

"Y'all drive all the time?" I called to them.

One answered, "Uh-huh," and the other snickered.

"How old are you?"

"Fifteen," said one.

The other, "Seventeen."

"You don't go to school?"

"Unh-unh," the first assured me. They giggled as we drove away, rumbling over the tire-ridged road toward a row of tired houses. The roofs and porches sagged dangerously, and the houses themselves seemed ready to sink into the mud they sat on. A taxi was parked in front of the end house, where a small crowd had gathered. Some watched and others helped as a young black woman and an elderly man struggled across the mud. With his arm resting on the woman's shoulder, the man held one foot off the ground and hopped uncertainly on the other. She was not a large woman, and her body tensed to support his.

"What happened?" I asked after Millie Bordelon and I had edged into the group.

The woman looked up. "My father-in-law had stuck a nail in his foot an' it got bad on 'im."

"You didn't go to the doctor for it?" Millie Bordelon asked.

"He went but the doctor was outta town," the woman replied, without stopping.

Someone yelled, "Taxi's waitin'!" and the two attempted to hurry.

"Is that your only way to get to town?" I asked, aware the nearest town was fifteen or twenty miles away. "You've got no car?"

She nodded, helped the old man into the backseat, and then turned toward us. "At first I couldn't get him to no doctor because I couldn't get no cab to come out here in the mud."

"It's a five-dollar round-trip," Millie Bordelon interjected. "*Plus* what the doctor costs."

"Does your husband work here?"

"He drive tractor on the next place," the woman informed me. With seven young children, she and her husband—like most plantation families—were in debt to the boss.

"How much do they take out of your pay for what you owe?"

"Jes' what you owes, that's what they takes," she fussed. "My mother-in-law gets paid by the month. She had two hundred and something dollars on a payday an' they took *all* of it. Left her with somethin' like sixteen dollars. *That* was last week. Same thing's happened to me an' my husband."

The cab driver honked, impatient, and she hurried into the taxi and it pulled away. The crowd scattered, with the children slushing through the mud, some scurrying toward a dilapidated car—their playground. A small girl lagged behind. On one foot she wore a tennis shoe; on the other, a white buckled mary jane. Her dress was ripped at the sleeve and the hem was out, yet she grinned widely.

At the house, a woman stood in the doorway watching. When we looked her way, she waved to Millie Bordelon and smiled, and the sun touched a glimmer of gold in her mouth. She was short, bouncy, and friendly and at the same time apprehensive as Millie Bordelon explained my presence.

"I don't want no trouble," the woman said fearfully.

"I won't use your real name," I promised. "Why don't I just call you 'Elsie'?"

The woman nodded.

"Are you afraid something might happen?" I asked.

"Yeah, because, see, my husband not able to work," she explained as she led the way into the house.

"Oh, that was your husband who just drove off?"

"Yeah, he stuck a nail in his feet an' I sent 'im to the doctor." She gestured for us to sit in one of the worn sofas or chairs that lined the room and then chose a platform rocker for herself. Legs crossed, she rested her clasped hands in her lap and twiddled her thumbs, first in one direction, then the other.

"He hasn't been able to work for must be about, I'd say close to ten years." The thumbs stopped, and she leaned forward. "See, he took with a bad heart, plus he had a little sugar diabetes, an' he wasn't able to go back to work. That's the reason I have to pay rent, because he's not able to work no more."

I surveyed the darkened room, disheveled and cluttered with broken-down furniture. The rain-stained wallpaper hung loose, and one wall had buckled—even the painted-on-velvet portraits of Christ and the Virgin Mary were askew. Through a doorway, the adjoining room appeared equally run-down. Outside, the porch was missing entire boards and the steps had collapsed onto the mud.

"You pay rent?"

"Twenty-two fifty."

At fifty-nine, Elsie could no longer scrap cane. She supplemented her husband's $160 Social Security check and the $40 her son in New Orleans sent monthly by cleaning house for the grower's wife.

"It don't be much I get, but this little bit is better 'n nothin'," she said. "I jes' cleans an' dust three days a week, an' sometimes I cooks. Sometime by ten o'clock I be back home. Right now I get seven dollars a day. I get paid by the month, an' like this month have thirty-one days, so it come to about two somethin'."

"I understand you got only sixteen dollars last week," I said.

Her thumbs stopped and Elsie chuckled uneasily. "My daughter-in-law tol' you that, huh?"

I nodded.

"See, I was behind in my rent, my light an' gas, an' then my husband doctor bill was on there—it was eight somethin'."

"Was that one of your worst paydays?"

"Well, I remember one month I cleared I think it was fo'teen dollars," she said, seemingly not upset. "But in a way, I don't mind. I tell y'all why. See, when I don't have it, I got nobody to go to. My chil'ren not able to help me, an' my husband's people not able to help him, so I don't have nobody else to turn to *but* them."

A teenage boy seated nearby interrupted, "I make more 'n you, Mama, cleanin' our church. I get seven dollars a week dustin' the pews an' sweepin'."

Elsie glared at him and at a girl of about the same age. "If I listen at my grandchil'ren, they been wantin' me to leave." Her glare softened into pleading as she tried to make them—and me—understand. "But listen, baby, you gotta have somethin' to lean on. If I need somethin', I know them white folk will give me money. My chil'ren, my grandchil'ren don't understand. I'm not gonna lie. If I walk in that office an' say I need such-an'-such thing, they not gonna ask how I'm gonna pay 'cause they know how I'm gonna pay—"

"Yeah, take it out your salary," the grandson sneered.

Conceding that he was right, she reasoned, "If I leave out an' can't get no work, jes' gettin' the money from security an' no job or nothin'—I *know* it would be pitiful."

"Pearl an' them could get jobs in town," the granddaughter insisted, referring to Elsie's two daughters who lived at home.

"You're not sure of that," the grandmother argued. But the girl ignored her and, to me, explained, "If she would leave, she wouldn't have to work. She jes' want to do it because she been workin' all the time." She faced her grandmother. "You could stay home an' knit quilts."

From outside came the squeals and clatter of children scampering across the porch, jumping to the ground, then climbing back onto the rotten boards.

"Would you like for them to be cane cutters?" I asked.

"No," Elsie said softly. "I want 'em to go to school an' get a good learnin' so they won't have to work hard as their grandmother worked."

Although the room was dimly lit by a single bulb suspended from the ceiling, I could see Elsie's gold-capped tooth. On each side were wide gaps where only roots and stubs remained.

"Do you ever go to the dentist?" I asked.

"No'm," she answered, "an' I ain't had a doctor for sixteen years, since my baby was born. I had my first thirteen by a granny lady—you didn't go to no hospital. You'd take sick at the house an' a doctor would come, but it'd be a lady. We called her a granny lady. Well, with my baby that's the time the rule went 'round if you wouldn't go to the clinic, you couldn't have your baby at home. I thought they was foolin' me, an' I didn't go to the clinic. So when I took sick, my husband went after the granny. She tol' him, she say, 'I'm sorry but I can't come.' She say, 'You gotta take your wife to the hospital, 'cause that the rule.' Well, I went to the hospital an' stayed the night an' that's the onliest time I saw a doctor."

She leaned forward and in a confiding tone explained, "I woulda been goin' for these checkups, but when you got a gang a chil'ren an' nothin' ain't hurtin' you—now this the way I look at it—I said that was money I was losin', I could put it on somethin' else. An' look like the Lawd jes' kept me up an' I didn't get sick or nothin'." She massaged her knee and admitted it acted up occasionally, but not enough to see a doctor. And her children, the ones still at home, rarely ever had to go either. "I'm lucky on that account," she said, relieved. "They don't never hardly be sick. *Very* seldom. An' when they suffer with their head sometime, I give 'em aspirin or Alka Seltzer."

The granddaughter contradicted her. "She tol' you her knee don't hurt but it do."

"How you know that?" Elsie asked.

"Remember last time I was here—"

"Now you don't know that!"

"Then why you can't walk?"

Tired of arguing, Elsie changed the subject to the house. Nine people slept in the living room and two bedrooms. There was a bath, but the toilet didn't work and the tub drain was stopped up, so the family continued to use an outhouse and bathe in a washtub.

"The owner say this house's too bad to fix. He say he gonna tear it down an' build me another," she said, believing.

"And *how* long has he been saying that?" Millie Bordelon chided, chuckling.

Meekly Elsie replied, "Two years," then added confidently, "but he tol' me again *this* year. He say the porch can't be fixed but he tol' me, he *promised* me this summer he gonna take this house down an' build me one."

"Has he promised you that before?" I asked.

She shook her head. "All he used to say was he was gonna build me a house, but he never did promise."

For a time she was quiet, staring through the front door out at the mill and the ground and land that had been her world and her husband's for as long as they had lived. It had been the grower's world also, and yet his horizons extended beyond the big road.

Interrupting Elsie's thoughts, I asked what the boss had done for her over the years. Her eyes closed, she ran her index finger down the length of her nose, over her mouth, to her chin. "Some-time—I remember once he had give me, ever' two weeks he'd give me twenty-five pounds a rice," she answered.

"Free?"

"Uh-hmm. He done it about for three or four years. After I started gettin' little checks from my son, well, he cut it out. But I think, I *believe* if I would ask him for somethin' he would give it to me. If I ask him, though, I always ask him to borry an' I always tell him I'm gonna pay 'im back."

"Do you think that's fair, that you should work so hard and not get enough to live?"

"No, it's not fair in a way, but you see that's their money. You can't do anything." She laughed uneasily.

"Yes, but *you're* the one doing the work," I reminded her.

Elsie shrugged, "You can't do nothin' about it."

"Are you afraid to say anything?"

Her eyes widened and her voice lowered to a whisper. "You can get your feelin's hurt 'cause you gotta move an' you got nowheres to go. If you maybe sass them or tell 'em, they tell you to move. I knew this couple—they wasn't, say, a friend a mine. They was a young couple—young people these days ain't gonna take what us ol' folk take—an' they had to leave. The boss never said nothin' to me, but ways an' actions shows. They don't say, but you can tell mostly what a person got on their mind the way they talk."

"Do you think the grower treats you with respect?"

A young man crossed the porch and stood in the doorway, lis-tening. He wore boots and muddy work clothes and was strong and virile.

"That's my son," Elsie said, attempting to evade the question. But I persisted. "Do you think the grower treats you with the respect he should? Do you think he treats you as a human being?"

"Yeeess," she started uncertainly, "they treats me pretty good."

"Are you gonna answer that, Mama?" the young man asked.

"I *tol'* her they treatin' me nice, Jasper," she pleaded.

"You call *this* treatin' you right?"

"Well they say they gonna build me a house!"

The son retorted, "As far as I been knowin', they been tellin' my mother they gonna build her a house."

"They *say* they gonna build me one, Jasper!"

"Yeah, *when?* They ain't did it yet!"

I asked the man, "Would you like your mother to move off the plantation?"

"Correct," he answered, firm. "I'd like her to go to any decent place. I don't think they're treatin' her fair. This here's not even exactly a house anymore. It's a shack!"

Elsie sat forward in her chair, her words coming fast now. "Yeah, this a house! This a house here!"

I turned to the son. "Do you think *you* will ever leave?"

"Me?" he asked, surprised at first. "Yeah, I think so. Right now there's lotta things I'd like to do, but first I'd like to get them off."

Elsie listened quietly. When I asked if she ever became depressed, she started to say no, but the son answered for her: "Yeah!"

"How you know?" she asked.

"I can tell! You're my mother! What's the matter, you scared?"

"I ain't scared!"

The argument proceeded with Elsie growing increasingly excited and the son angrier. "Tell the truth, Mama, you don't call this a house!"

"Jasper, *what* it is?"

"It's a shack! Look, it's fallin' down! Look at that wall. It's fallin' to pieces. The whole thing could collapse at any time. That's true. Look over there," he told me. "That wall's cavin' in!"

Elsie wrung her hands. "This a house I'm livin' in! It's old—that's true—an' it's bad, but—"

"What about the wall?" her son interrupted her.

"She can see the wall bad, Jasper."

"It rains—"

"Unh-unh, it don't rain in here."

The grandson entered the melee. "That rain come down like outside."

I turned to Elsie. "Why do you feel you have to lean on the grower?"

"My husband—"

Jasper interrupted, "He worked night an' day in his time, an' her too. He'd only get about five hours' sleep when he was workin', an' what he was worth? Sixteen dollars!"

"Eighteen," Elsie corrected him.

"Eighteen dollars, all right. Like durin' the grindin' time, he worked from mornin' to night in the field. An' after he come from eatin' he'd go to the mill out there twelve at night, come back home about six in the mornin' an' get a sandwich an' cup a coffee an' go back in the field again. An' you think they shouldn't do better than what they doin'?"

"I *say* they could do better, Jasper!"

Elsie looked at me helplessly, hopefully, and I offered to go. She walked Millie Bordelon and me onto the porch, stepped carefully down to the ground, and followed us into the yard. When we were away from Jasper and the others, I again asked, "Why don't you want to leave?"

Now she was thoughtful. "I don't know," she said. "I guess I been here so long that I jes' hate to— See, I was raised up here, an' a lotta people 'round here knows me. If I stands in need, they'll help me. But if I move on another farm or somewhere, they gonna say, 'Well she wait till she got ol' an' can't work an' can't be of no more service,' an' they won't might not help me."

"What about moving into the city where your daughters live?" I suggested.

Again came the excuses: "Nobody there'd know me but my chil'ren. An' like my chil'ren would be able to help a little, but they have their families. I might could find me a job, but like my husband suffer with his legs an' he has diabetes an' his heart be bad, so I be afraid to leave 'im."

The three of us, all quiet, walked to the car. Then Elsie said thoughtfully, "I'm willing to stay here a little longer. See, if I was to move it might worries him. He been here all his life, an' if he was a well man, then it'd be somethin' else, but he's not, an' his age—the first of March he be sixty-one. An' as a sick man, he might jes' take it too hard. I wouldn't want him to grieve himself by movin' away jes' to satisfy me, 'cause I'd rather stay here till the good Lawd calls me or him." She looked beyond the mud and tractors, into the distance. "Yeah, I rather stay here an' be buried to the church."

The Departure

She seemed neither bitter nor sad when she told the story. She treated it more as a family heirloom she could treasure and keep, one she could pull out and reexamine from time to time and wonder and think about and know it would always be there. It was a belonging—her possession—and no one could rob or cheat her of it. And so, nostalgically, Elsie told the story about how her grandparents on her mother's side had lived on that same plantation and how they had come to leave. "My mother use' to tell me about her father was a slave," she started, her voice moving into the past. "She was a baby, but her sister tol' her she could remember when their daddy was a slave how they come got him in a little wagon. She called it somethin' like a buggy with horses. It had two seats an' two seats, like a car, an' they had 'im in back. An' far as her sister could see her daddy was leavin', an' her mother. But they didn't take 'em together. They took 'em separate. An' far as her sister could see 'em goin' the mother was wavin' to her chil'ren good-bye. That was on this plantation that happened. My mother say she never did know where they took 'em 'cause they never did hear from the mother or the daddy no more. Some-

*time we would ask my mother questions about it an' she'd
say, 'That was in the past.' She didn't want to think about it.
When she'd like talkin' about it, she'd tell us; if she didn't,
she wouldn't. It used to make her sad to think how they took
her mother an' daddy away an' how the kids was all small an'
each of 'em had to stay with different ones. I never did know
my daddy's daddy. He came from a place they called Sunrise.
That was another plantation. He was a slave, but I never did
know nothin' about him. But now my mother's daddy, they
use' to call him Young Tom. Sometime when I got nothin' to do
I sits down an' wonders about 'em, about my granddaddy an'
my grandmother an' how they looked.*"

The Big House

In the midst of the workers' shacks, just beyond the mill and mud and convoy of trailers, the Big House loomed in musty grandeur. Outwardly it had an aura of the Old South, of graciousness and good manners, of silver services and crystal, of lemonade and mint juleps. Two stories tall with columns and a veranda, the antebellum mansion was freshly white, and its immediate yard—the grass, hedges, and azaleas—was trim and well kept. A houseboy raked and edged the lawn. A bulky sweatshirt, khaki pants tucked into muddy boots, and a stocking cap concealed much of his body and his age. When the photographer and I drove up to the carport and parked behind a sports car and a sedan, he glanced up, then resumed raking.

A petite woman, gray-haired and genteel, held open the kitchen door, waiting. "I'm Miz Patout. Come on in and warm up a little bit," she called in a soft drawl. "Mistuh Patout will be along d'rectly."

In the kitchen, crystal, silver, and boxes from a bakery covered the countertops and tables, and as we walked through the house, Mrs. Patout apologized for her haste, elaborating on the preparations still to be completed for that afternoon's tea in honor of the New Iberia debutantes.

Admiring the polished floors and spacious rooms, the mantels and fine antiques, I complimented her, "What a lovely house. Does it have a name?"

"Enterprise," she said with pride, inviting us into the parlor. "Come on in where you can be comfortable. I'm going to go and get dressed, if you'll excuse me."

The house smelled of wax and fabric and wood, of elegance preserved and handed down. A fireplace dominated the parlor, and to each side a window looked out onto the yard and the distant workers' quarters. Overhead, hurried footsteps echoed across wood floors, and for a moment I envisioned hoopskirts and frilly petticoats and young officers dashing off to war in their uniforms. Heavier footsteps interrupted my fantasies, and a not-too-tall man entered the room. He shook hands, then sat opposite me in a gold-upholstered parlor chair. In spite of having worked at the mill office earlier that morning, he wore a white dress shirt and suit and tie. His voice reflected schooling and a proper upbringing; yet his manner was unpretentious, and he seemed to be a man of mild emotions.

"It's William *S.* Patout, Junior?" I asked as the interview got under way.

"Correct," he said stiffly. "The plantation is M. A. Patout and Son, Limited. M. A. is for Mary Ann, a grandmother of mine who took charge after her husband's death in 1911. It went under that name because the oldest son—there were eight in the family—helped her along. Now it's owned by a corporation."

"Who makes up the corporation?"

"Only the family. Two sons and a sister. I'm the majority stockholder. On the plantation proper we farm about 1100 acres, and then 750, 400, and 600, as I remember without adding it up. It's all in Iberia Parish, almost touching, just in various areas. This house has been in the family since the 1840s."

I observed, "So you were born here?"

He nodded.

"And your family has lived here in almost the same way the fieldworkers have on some plantations?"

"Oh yes, definitely," he acknowledged.

Through the nearby window the workers' shacks were visible, and even from a distance they appeared squalid. I asked if many of the houses dated back to slavery, and Patout speculated that they did. The family had acquired the property in 1825, he said. In fact, he even had records that showed how much sugar the mill had produced during the Civil War. The office dated back that far; surely many of the houses did too.

"At the Houma hearings some of the growers have said the housing is a reason for not paying more," I said proceeding cautiously, "yet some of the housing I have seen is in bad condition. Would you like to comment?"

"We've done our very best to have adequate housing," he said. "It's very discouraging because they just beat them up, break 'em up fast as we can fix them. The door falls off, a window falls off—it's nothing. It's never put back up as a rule."

"What about outdoor bathrooms?" I asked.

"I don't think we've got any *outdoors*. None at all," he was positive.

"None?"

He reconsidered. "I think every house, far as I remember, has plumbing. I'll be glad to take you to one or two."

"They *all* have toilets and bathtubs?" I pressed.

He shifted in his chair. "I would say most of them. Ninety-five . . ." He hesitated. "There might be . . . no, I think they all have them."

The day before, I had visited four families with outhouses on Patout property, and I wondered how he could be unaware of their existence. But this was my first interview with a grower, and, fearful of cutting off my sources, I decided to try diplomacy rather than risk a confrontation. I asked, "Do you have anything to say in defense of growers who *do* have outdoor privies?"

Patout ignored conditions on his own land and speculated, "It's an economic thing more than anything, I imagine. There's just not that much money to be made in the sugar business. Like this year, I think most of the mills will lose money. I know *we* are."

"But isn't sugar one of Louisiana's biggest products?"

"Maybe the second leading product in agriculture," he agreed.

"If it's such a big one, then why is it such a losing one?"

"It's not always a losing one," he conceded. "Some years are much less worse than others. But on an average, most mills barely hang on. There are two or three that may have to close." He sighed. "I don't like to think about it. We're going to lose quite a bit on account of the continual rains."

From the kitchen came the sounds of busy footsteps, the ring of crystal, and the opening and closing of the refrigerator door. Patout seemed to wait for the next question, and I brought up the workers' complaints about no work and no money in January and February after grinding.

"Well, on account of the weather—" He stopped abruptly, then quickly insisted, "But there *is* work. Especially this year. All the fields are cut up, in bad shape. We really need to get them out to work, but it's difficult because they have some money and they're going to take their time getting back to work until they really need it."

"But if the weather's too bad to work they don't get paid, do they?" I asked.

He answered, "No," but again insisted, "My goodness, there'll be more work than we can do in January and February."

This statement so contradicted my interviews with the field-workers and their families that I was stunned. "This is not typical, is it? Because I have seen pay stubs from last year for thirty-one hours for two weeks."

Patout tensed and sat forward, looking directly into my eyes. "You've seen those?"

"Pay stubs," I repeated. "A record that they've worked so many hours. Now would you say that's the workers' fault or the weather or that there was no work?"

"I would say both," he replied. "The weather, the fault of the worker, and sometimes the owner."

After offering to take me on a tour of the workers' houses, he continued to discuss the problems faced by him and other growers. He had been awake most of the night, he said, worrying that the steady rains would cause the cane to go bad before it could be cut and hauled to the mill. "Acidity gets it. It gets sour and you can't make sugar out of it. You get molasses instead, and there's no money in molasses." He shook his head and predicted, "The farmers are going to be hurt pretty much from it."

I asked when grinding would end, and he estimated, "About the twentieth of January."

"So it will be longer than usual this year. Is that because of the freezes?"

"No," he said. "Big crop, and rain."

In the kitchen he opened the door to the carport and yelled, "Carlton, go clean out the backseat of my car! Get the dust out!" The houseboy looked up from his rake, then hurried to a dusty blue Falcon.

As we drove toward the living quarters, Patout viewed the mill and the land around him. "There are some families whose fathers and grandfathers farmed this place before them," he said. "I feel very close to them, but I get awfully angry sometimes because of the things they do. They'll buy an old car, wreck it, buy another one, continue on in debt with automobiles and nothing in the house for them or their children. That's the bad part. They should be taught responsibility some way or another. I don't know how. It would be very difficult. It would take generations."

"Do you see any differences in the younger workers?"

"They're not as good as the old ones. The attitude is not there. The attitude is different."

"How?"

He shrugged. "They just don't want to work."

I thought about the reluctance of some to talk to me, the fear they expressed or that showed on their faces. "A lot of people have talked about being afraid of the growers. Do you think this is justified?" I asked.

"What do you mean by *fear* of the grower?" he challenged.

"Well, 'If I say anything, if I complain, the grower or the owner or the boss man or whoever will get mad and put me out of the house.' Is this true?"

"That's ridiculous."

The Falcon bumped over the tractor ridges and turned into a settlement of houses. Some of them were brick, some tarpapered, with the familiar galvanized tubs hanging outside the back door.

I asked Patout if he had a policy concerning repairs, and he assured me he got to them as soon as he could: "Sometimes within two days after it is reported," he assured me. "Sometimes three weeks, four weeks, six weeks."

We stopped in front of a newer brick house—the home of a black mill worker and his family. The interior was paneled, and there was a living room, two bedrooms, a bath, and a kitchen with built-in cabinets and a stainless steel sink. As we walked through the house, the housewife reminded Patout that the washbasin in the bathroom was pulling away from where the wall had rotted. I asked her how long it had been like that, and she complained, "More 'n a year."

Outside again, Patout pointed to one of the older houses and announced, "Now that house has a bath."

"What about that one?" I asked, pointing across the road to a brick-papered house where an elderly man sat on the porch dipping crackers in milk.

"Yeeess . . . I think that one has," Patout said.

"Can we find out?"

As we strode across the street, Patout yelled out, "You got a bath, don't you, Serge?"

"Naw, suh, Mistah Bill, we got no bath," the man called back.

"That other old house?"

This time the man nodded. "Yassuh."

After we returned to the car, Patout drove past more brick houses, several wooden ones, and a concrete building he called "the Shack"—where black fieldworkers from the cotton country lived four to a room during grinding. "There are ten rooms and a nice tile floor, central heat," he said, then grumbled, "We're on our third set of commodes in four years because they just break 'em up."

Opposite the mill, at the dormitory for white laboratory workers and chemists, each room included a closet and was furnished with a single bed and a heater. The kitchen smelled of white beans and frying chicken, and the black woman preparing lunch said the menu would include soup and cabbage.

When we passed a settlement of old houses, Patout insisted that most of them were abandoned and the others were rented to retired workers. They were beyond repair, he said. To replace them would cost six to eight thousand dollars—more than he could afford. I asked if it wouldn't be better to simply tear down all the houses and pay the workers a little more so they could afford to live in town, and Patout allowed as how there had been some thought along those lines. He doubted, however, that even if the workers had better houses, they would take better care of them.

By now, we had pulled up to the Big House, into the carport. A florist's truck was parked behind the sports car, and at the kitchen door boxes of flowers were stacked, ready for the debutante tea.

"How would you feel about the workers organizing?" I asked as I got out of the car.

Patout frowned. "I wouldn't like it," he said. "Anytime you fool with organized labor you're in for nothing but trouble."

The houses stood gray and alone
. . . and the sun was nowhere to be found.

Oaklawn, and Other Places

At the first house an old woman peered from around the barely opened door, only her head and spidery brown fingers venturing forth, slowly, warily. Her eyes focused on the car and us, traveling from the road, through the yard, never straying from our path. By the time we reached the steps she stood on the porch's edge. A rag was tied about her head, and she wore a sweater and a cotton-print dress that, like her, sagged from age. One hand rested on her hip, the other clutched a pipe to her mouth as she took inventory, her eyes rising from our feet until they were level with the photographer's, then mine. Still she stood firm, chewing on the pipe, not uttering a word until we explained who we were and asked to take her picture.

"Yassuh, but my pi'ture done been took," she informed the photographer flatly. Neither she nor her eyes budged; only her mouth moved, gumming the pipe. She waited.

"You live here by yourself?" I chattered, attempting to develop trust, to start a conversation.

"By myself," the old woman said. "My husband been dead a *long* time. Ain't got no chil'ren neither." She returned the pipe to her mouth and her gums worked.

"How long have you been living in this house?"

Again she cocked her head, her eyes finally moving past us to study the porch overhang. "Ooooh, 'bout thirty years, over thirty years," she said. Her eyes met mine, and she slowly lowered the hand from her hip. "Use' to work in the fields. That's where I went down, in the fields. I use' to cut cane."

When I asked if we could see her house, she backed away from the porch's edge and lowered her chin, uncertain. Except for the three of us the settlement seemed deserted. Two wagons hitched to tractors rested nearby, unattended, and the crude wood doors of all the houses were shut against the cold. Nevertheless the old woman's eyes shot up and down the road; then they searched mine, and the photographer's. Finally she answered, "I g-g-guess so" and watched intently as we climbed the steps.

Leading the way, she opened the wood door, then a screened one. Inside, a rocker sat close to a potbellied stove; behind that, an old brick fireplace was sealed with cardboard.

Surprised by the stove's presence, I asked, "Is that how you keep warm?"

"Yassum."

The photographer asked if he could take a picture, and the old woman's face clouded. "I don't know," she fretted, "'cause that don't belong to me. That belong to another man, to the boss man."

"We would love to take some pictures of the stove if you'd let us," the photographer pressed.

Raising her chin until the wrinkled skin became crepe, she ran her fingers down her throat to her dress collar. She lowered her chin, at last relenting, "Yass."

The photographer hurried to the car for his camera, and the old woman stood quietly as I surveyed the rest of the sparsely furnished room. Through a back window she pointed to a privy and a water pump set away from the house, in the middle of the yard. Then she shuffled ahead of me, to the kitchen. In front of another unusable fireplace stood a larger wood-burning stove with a kettle on the back burner.

"They ain't put no gas to it, so I have to cook on that," she said, remaining near the door with arms crossed against her bosom.

"I paid fifty dollars for that stove from a furniture sto' in town. I been havin' it a *long* time, ever since I been here. My brother from 'cross the bayou cut the wood."

"Does he work on the farm?"

She answered, "Yas, but he ain't workin' now. He's down to the sto'. He live over the bayou."

"I love the smell of a wood stove," I offered, taking an imaginary sniff. "What do you eat most of the time?"

"Well, most anything I gets close to I feel like eating," she chuckled, adding, "I gets stamps." The company store had been torn down, and she now shopped at a supermarket in town whenever she could get a ride with the plantation owner.

Her eyes followed the photographer as he entered the room and focused his camera on the stove. One hand returned to her hip, the other cupped her chin. She stood firm, guarding her possession until he had finished, then she again led the way to the front door and onto the porch. As she did so she muttered, mostly to herself, "Gotta stay here whether I like it or not." Her old head turned slowly from side to side. "That's right, whether I like it or not." All the way through the yard, to the car, I could hear her muttering, "Whether I like it or not."

From there, the photographer and I went to several neighboring houses, and then we returned to the main road and crossed a narrow bridge to another living quarters. Oaks surrounded the weathered houses, and a bayou meandered quietly behind. A tractor driver, home for lunch, leaned against the porch railing of one of the larger houses. Layers of denim contributed to his bulkiness, and a wool stocking cap was pulled over a billed one for extra warmth. Outdoor labor had toughened his face and his broad, thick hands, for he had worked in the fields since he was eight, he said, to help support his mother and seven siblings. Now, at fifty-six, he provided for his own wife and seven children by driving a tractor—his only skill. He could neither read nor write, and his sole possessions were hand-me-down furniture and clothing. Nothing more. Not even a battered car. To go to the grocery or to the doctor meant paying a neighbor two or three dollars for a ride to town. Yet he chuckled often, and his voice was firm and confident as he talked freely about his life, only his eyes betraying inner sadness and disappointment.

The parade of tractors and trailers along the main road had halted for lunch. Soon, when the fields were leveled, it would end for another year, until next grinding.

"What will happen then?" I asked.

The man gazed past the yard and lines of drying clothes to the deserted road. "Be no income at all, not after they finish with the harvest," he answered—positive, not predicting.

"What do you do during those months?"

"Best way you can," he said. "They'll lend you, but you pay it back when you start to work."

A whistle summoned the workers from lunch, and the man reluctantly removed his foot from the railing and said he had to leave. As he started down the steps I asked if he thought it would help if the workers organized, and he nodded.

"Would you like to see that?"

"I sure would," he said. Then, looking over his shoulder, he asked, "But, now, how you gonna organize 'em? Ever'body's afraid to say anything."

The next morning, an outreach worker from the St. Martinville Neighborhood Center drove with me to St. John, a sprawling plantation with a mill that served it and surrounding farms. From town, it was a pleasant ride, the road bordered by oaks and fields of grazing cattle as it wound its way past the stately manor house and the company store. From there, we followed a trailer truck loaded with cane onto a lesser road and continued on beyond the mill to a settlement of gray-shingled houses, where we parked the car. We studied the houses briefly before setting off down a dirt path through scrubby trees and over a narrow wood bridge that crossed what was now a trickle but in other seasons would swell to a creek.

At the largest house, a short, round woman, her head encircled by braids, waited on the porch. As we neared, she smiled and hurried down the steps with all the speed her size would allow. Her full bosom bounced with each step, stilled only when she reached the ground and us. A warm, radiant woman, she was introduced simply as "Sister"—not out of fear, but because that was the name everyone called her. Reversing her direction, she led us up the steps—her pace slower now than in her descent—across the porch and into the living room. The house, with fresh wallpaper and new linoleum, was modest but nicely furnished, and it had the only indoor bath on the plantation—because of the woman she worked for, not the grower, Sister explained.

Taking inventory of the well-kept living room, Sister emphasized that her family lived better than most on the plantation because of the things her employer had given them and because her husband now worked year-round at the mill. Besides four single children, a married son and his wife also lived at home, and his salary helped with the bills. Still, life wasn't easy.

"I been livin' here twenty-eight years, an' it's been rough. Still is," Sister said. "Yesterday, when I went to the company store, the edible food was thirty dollars an' fifty-nine cents, an' the unedibles, ten seventy-seven, an' I had *but* one cardboard box a stuff—not even enough for a week!"

Sister showed us into the kitchen and, opening a cabinet, read out prices: "Blue Runner Red Beans, thirty-one cents; Del Monte Sweet Peas, twenty-nine; Autocrat Spinach, twenty-four; a can of tuna, fifty-eight; a twenty-eight-ounce jar of Blue Plate Peanut Butter, a dollar four . . ."

A tall man in his mid-twenties had entered during the itemizing, and Sister introduced him as another son. He and his wife, married nine months, lived a few houses away. In the summer, he told me, he worked in the fields making $1.50 an hour. Now, during grinding, he was making $1.69 at the mill. That was the amount *due* him, but neither he nor any workers on St. John would be paid until grinding was complete—a holdover, I was to learn later, from Reconstruction.

"Not till after grinding?" I asked, amazed. "Has it always been this way?"

Sister nodded. "The reason they don't pay is they afraid the workers won't come back after they get their money."

"They pay ever' two weeks in the summer, but durin' grindin' not till after it's over," the son elaborated. "Like grindin's goin' on now, you don't get paid, but you borrow an' they take out interest when you pay it back. It's been sixty-two days since we got a check, an' they're sayin' now we not gonna get paid till January sixth."

It was the twentieth of December, and he estimated he was already in debt two hundred dollars to the plantation, plus what he owed the company store. "Pretty soon my wife an' me gonna have our first child, an' we needed to get baby clothes," he said.

I had heard about workers who received no money after all the deductions for medical bills and other debts were taken out, and about some who ended up with a minus, still owing the grower. Now, when I asked if he or Sister had had any paydays like that, she left the room and returned with her husband's pay stubs from last summer. One indicated he had worked thirty-two hours at a rate of $1.85. After taxes and $41.98 for utilities and groceries had been deducted, he had cleared $14.38 for a two-week period. She watched as I studied the figures, then she explained. "Sometime even in summer when you workin' an' you buy groceries—jes' groceries, *not* clothes—sometime you don't have *no* payday," she said with finality. "It all goes to groceries an' all these deductions."

At the Company Store

The buildings stood neatly in a row. All frame, painted gray, with porches and posts and overhangs. One was the mill office. Another, the one with the Bell Telephone booth out front, the Company Store. Men in khakis and hard hats lounged about, eating sandwiches and candy bars and drinking colas. Across the road in an open field their cane-laden trailers, lined up freight-yard fashion, waited to be unloaded. Within the store, the elderly clerk and his middle-aged assistant watched over their domain, over the rows of canned goods and cleaning supplies and the people who wandered in and out and up and down the aisles, looking, figuring, wanting, buying—and not buying. Seventy-seven cents for two pounds of spaghetti. Twenty for a can of mustards. *In and out, up and down, past overalls and bandannas, past sunbonnets and pantyhose. The storekeeper and his assistant followed with their eyes, craning, straining, keeping tabs. Items to live and survive on, and maybe a luxury or two. Items to need and want and not afford. Items to pay for later, on time—with a week's or a month's or a season's hard-earned wages. Boxes of grits. Sacks of rice. Cakes of Octagon and bottles of bluing*

and bleach. Bins of nails and potatoes and beans of all kinds.
Racks of mops and brooms and, all stacked up, some num-
ber 3 tubs. Giant jars of peanuts and pickles on the counter;
shelves of BC Powder and Bayers and Carter's Little Liver
Pills; and a look-through case of bacon and sausages and
ham hocks.

"Got any that good salt meat?"

"All out!" the fiftyish woman snapped. "Man'll be back
tomorra."

"What about the piece goods—could I see them, maybe?"

"Humph!" The woman bustled from behind the meat case,
through the aisles, and into a side room fragrant with fabric
and spools of thread, with zippers and rickrack and lace. Her
face tight, the woman shifted impatiently from leg to leg while
the customer fingered the cotton, admired the print, studied
the price.

"Well, thanks anyhow."

Now on to the margarine and eggs and milk. We gotta
have that.

"How much?"

"Dollar forty-two, for the eggs an' milk."

"Put it on the bill. Got no cash money now. I'll have ta pay
later. I'll jes' have ta owe the company sto'."

"The Boss Man"

Cane encircled the two-story home, and as we pulled into the driveway the grower strode toward us through the field across the road. He was a tall, broad-shouldered man, ruggedly handsome in khakis, a plaid flannel shirt, and boots. His manners were polished and charming, and he might more appropriately be called a planter. Like the workers, his life had been determined from birth: He too would remain on the land, close to his roots, and grow cane as his father and grandfather had. He would be "the boss man." He saw no inequity in the name-calling, or in a system that kept the workers subservient, for that was the way things had been and the way they were.

As he led us through the house to his office, he insisted I not use his name—the growers had received too much bad publicity lately—and then he began sketching his background. He had started out in partnership with his father when he was eighteen, with 60 acres of land, a tractor, and two mules. Now in his forties, he operated 1,650 acres. Fifteen men worked for him, living on the land. Some of their houses had baths; some, out-houses. Some had hot water; some didn't. But the conditions of the houses weren't really his fault, he argued.

"I rent every acre of land I work," he said. "Most farmers do. And the going rental rate is twenty percent of the gross. The landlord owns the houses, we don't, and they do very little to them. We spend a little money each year trying to maintain them, the essentials—screens, broken boards, things like that. But it really shouldn't be our responsibility."

"But don't you think outhouses and bathing in galvanized tubs is a little barbaric?" I asked.

Suddenly defensive, he answered with a question. "Suppose *you* were making two dollars an hour, you were living in this house *rent free,* you didn't pay income tax, you got food stamps, you had fifty dollars every week to blow on luxuries. Wouldn't *you* put in a bath? There's nothing stopping them if they want to con-tribute toward putting it in, and when they leave, the landlord or the farmer would gladly refund them the money."

"Do you think so?"

"I know *I* would," he said. "Besides, they aren't interested in it. They *don't* mind. So if they don't mind, I don't care." He shrugged. "Our people are completely satisfied. How are you going to change someone who doesn't want to be changed? Other people want to change them, but they don't want to change."

He eased back in his swivel chair and continued, "Besides, there's nothing tying them to this. Those that are here, they like it. They like the whole atmosphere—going to the saloon on week-ends, having a good time. And they don't take care of a thing. We put in new screens last summer and within *two* weeks they were all broke." He shook his head in bewilderment. "I guess it's inbred. I'm sure it goes back to lack of education."

From outdoors came the faint grating of the cutter across the road and the sound of distant voices.

"At the Houma hearings don't some of the growers say the free housing ought to be considered part of the workers' income?" I asked, aware from newspaper articles that housing conditions often triggered heated discussions at the annual meetings. Once a witness for the workers even attempted to enter a jar of roaches as part of his testimony.

But the grower objected. "We have *never* mentioned housing

at the hearings. Each year we ask the presiding officer *not* to allow testimony concerning housing because it is not germane. The Sugar Act specifically spells out the criteria that are to be considered in setting the wages, and it doesn't say housing. Right now our minimum wage for our *lowest*-paid worker is a dollar eighty an hour. *That's* twenty cents an hour *above* the minimum for industrial workers."

"But isn't the problem that you reach a point after grinding when there is not much work on some farms—"

"*Never!*" he broke in. "I don't know a farm that's yet caught up. There is a period when our workers don't work, but that's because they don't want to do the work that's available. I daresay there's not a farm that won't make available to every worker forty hours a week. Our absenteeism is terrible—as high as twenty percent." He edged forward and, with sarcasm in his voice, asked, "Suppose you're absent from your job twenty percent of the time and your pay is cut accordingly. You wouldn't be doing so well, would you? You'd probably be fired. We tolerate things no other industry tolerates." I started to speak, but he stopped me. "Wait—let me go back to the wages. A dollar eighty is our *minimum* for our lowest-paid workers. That is for cane scrappers, which are mainly women, old men, and young boys who have just reached the age of working. But the majority of our workers are tractor drivers who are in the category of a minimum of a dollar ninety an hour, and harvester operators and loader operators are a dollar ninety-five, and *most* make *more* than that. *Many* of our workers make as much as two and a quarter."

"Many? Where?" I challenged.

"Throughout the belt."

"Can the Sugar Cane League furnish me data showing what farms pay above the minimum?"

He hedged, "I don't think they have the statistics."

"What about in the summer during the rainy season when they can't work—"

Again he interrupted me. "There's *never* a time there isn't work available. We have equipment to maintain. We have work around the shop. We have draining work, we have—"

"But I have talked to a lot of people who say there *isn't* work. How can I document this one way or the other?"

Opening a desk drawer, the grower removed some papers and handed them to me. "You can look at my time sheets. When we go to work in the morning whoever wants to work can, and you can see the differences in the time that's made by these workers." His finger ran down a column of names and figures. "Here's one man who made eighty-eight hours and another who made twenty-three. Now this man's gonna practically *always* have the most number of hours. This is for a two-week period, and he worked eighty-eight, ninety-eight, ninety, a hundred and two. And here's another guy who didn't make but fifty-four."

"This was in March, which is a slow period—"

The grower sighed. "If you can find a slow period I wish you'd let me know!"

A trapped fly buzzed back and forth in the room. The grower glanced up at it, then looked at me, momentarily subdued. But when I asked if he loaned money to his workers, he all but shouted. "Do I lend money? They can make two hundred and fifty dollars on Saturday and by Monday need money for the essentials. They come in here with the saddest stories you ever heard." He opened a ledger to a listing of how much each worker owed. "I fill a couple pages each year on each employee, and as far as their gas and lights, we've found if we don't pay the bills for them they don't get paid." He flung up his hands. "That's what the workers want, they want paternalism! I would love to get out of it. *Every* farmer would. These, these liberal do-gooders say they can't leave because they owe you. That's a lot of bull! I can show you in this book how many have left owing me anywhere from ten to fifty to a hundred dollars. They do it all the time. They *love* to owe you money and then up and leave, and what can you do? I just wish every person could be in our position for one year to see what it's like. You have to live with this problem to see the way it really is."

"Then why stay in this business?"

He became quiet, then speculated, "I guess because I like it. I could make a lot more money doing something else, but I enjoy the challenge and I was born into this business. I'm the third generation of my family involved in the sugar business." He gestured toward framed photographs of silky-haired girls on his desk. I don't have any sons, but if I did I guess they would be like I am. It's handed down from father to son."

Some years he made money, some years he didn't. For the investment, he wasn't earning what he should. He rested his forearms on his knees and, in his own manner, echoed the sentiments, the hopes, voiced by Huet Freeman. "I always think, next year, boy, next year is going to be better," he said. "Next year's going to be that good year. But it's getting more and more difficult to make money in this business. In this parish we lose about ten farmers a year. So what happens? The big ones keep getting bigger and bigger. That's why I have grown to the size I am, people going out of business."

When I asked if the growers were concerned about the workers unionizing, he was confident organizers would have a difficult time. "It's hard to organize someone who's completely satisfied, and our workers are completely satisfied," he said confidently. "Union organizers come in here and promise, 'We gonna get you two and a half an hour. We promise you this, we promise you that.' But our workers are realists. They don't buy that pie in the sky. They are very, very suspicious of outsiders. They know with us they are getting a dollar ninety an hour. That's absolutely for sure. It's here. They have complete trust in us." He clasped his hands behind his head, tilted the chair backward, and propped his feet on the desk, relaxed, convinced of the workers' loyalty and contentment.

"I've had workers say, 'I don't want to say anything because I don't want to get in trouble with the boss man.' Would they really?"

"That may be true," he admitted smugly. "They don't want to get in trouble. They *know* where their bread is buttered."

"But *would* they get in trouble?" I repeated.

"Depends on what they did and what they said. If they said the truth, no, but if they lied about it, then they would be in serious trouble." He leveled his eyes with mine. "*We*, the sugar industry, are the only industry I know of that does for their employees what we do. We go and wake 'em up in the morning. We pick 'em up—those who live off the farm—at *their* house, bring 'em to work. At noon we bring 'em home, pick 'em up after dinner, bring 'em back to work. During harvest season we take a short dinner—a half hour—so instead of them bringing sandwiches we go to each house, pick up a hot dinner, bring *that* to them." He glared at me and snapped, "Is the *States-Item* going to pick *you* up in the morning and bring you home at night? There's *no* other industry that transports their workers around like we do."

The interview over, he accompanied me to the car. As we walked he questioned my objectivity and I assured him, "I plan

to be fair. I'm going to quote you and Mr. Patout, and in Thibodaux—"

"I don't know that Murphy Foster will talk to you. They burned
him so in the *Saturday Review,* that Peter Schuck did."

The reference was to the article written the previous May by
a young attorney from Ralph Nader's Center for the Study of
Responsive Law that attacked the Louisiana sugar industry and
the U.S. Department of Agriculture for their treatment of fieldworkers. The growers, not known for taking criticism lightly, had
issued a statement through the American Sugar Cane League
calling the story biased and inaccurate, and in a speech before Franklin's Rotary Club, Gilbert Durbin, the league's general
manager, had called Schuck "one of Ralph Nader's henchmen."
They had been particularly upset by Schuck's account of his
interview with Murphy Foster in an office festooned with *Play-
boy* nudes. "Niggers are the happiest creatures on God's green
earth," Schuck quoted the grower as saying. "I've worked with
these people for thirty years, and if they have a problem, they
know to come to me."

Now, when I asked this grower if he had talked to Schuck, he
shook his head, then chuckled. "And if you hadn't sounded so nice
over the telephone, I wouldn't have talked to you." As he opened
the car door for me, he jokingly warned, "And if you don't do a
fair story, I'm gonna come after you!"

It was about five minutes past four by the time the photographer
and I got to Murphy Foster's house in the little town of Franklin—
five minutes after we said we would be there—and Foster and
his wife must have been waiting right at the door because they
opened it as soon as we rang the bell. He chuckled that he had
just bet his wife that my call had been one of his friends playing a joke. When he saw it wasn't, he invited us in and insisted
we make ourselves comfortable in the den, by the fireplace, and
Mrs. Foster asked how we spelled our names so she could write
them in her guest register.

What I could see of the house was expensively furnished with
paintings and accessories from around the world. Outside, it
was white frame, surrounded by greenery, in what one would
call Franklin's "nice neighborhood." There were two late-model
Cadillacs in the carport—one a maroonish red, the other blue

and white. When we got ready to drive to Sterling Sugar to see Tom Allen, the executive vice president and general manager, we took the red one. In the front seat there were two mason jars of molasses that Foster gave us, and he said Tom Allen would give us some raw sugar at the mill and then he hoped we would come back and have a drink and visit with him and Mrs. Foster.

On the way to the mill, Foster explained that his father had been governor of Louisiana for eight years and a U.S. senator. He himself was vice president of Sterling Sugar and owned nearby Maryland Plantation. He was a dapper man, bald and in his late sixties or perhaps seventies, wearing a tweed plaid suit, suede hat, and a tie clip with a replica of Louisiana on it.

"I have the same people on my plantation we had in 1936, '37," he said, going down the road, "and the only problem we have is—not discontent, dissatisfaction with anything—it's the young ones just want to branch out. They want to go to Chicago, they want to go to New York.

"A lot has been written that's been distorted, about the way they are slaves," he said, and emphasized that the houses on his land had hot and cold running water, toilets, bathtubs and all. I asked him about those I had seen on other plantations that didn't, and he swore one could go to New Orleans or anyplace else and see the same thing. "Really, I don't know of hardly any plantations around here that don't have them," he insisted. "I really mean that. Now I'm only speaking for the major plantations—I can't speak for ever' little farmer—but I can speak for Sterling Sugar, I can speak for Oaklawn, I can speak for Caffrey."

Then he recalled a conversation he had had with Peter Schuck about why the workers didn't have a union.

"Well, I told him, 'It's quite simple,'" Foster said, like he was remembering the exchange verbatim. "'In the first place, the union is not interested particularly in this farm labor,' and I said, 'Also, the farm labor is not interested in having union dues.' In other words," he concluded as we pulled up in front of the offices of Sterling Sugar, "these people work because they want to. The wages are set by the government. If we don't pay them, we don't get benefit payments, and benefit payments are our profits."

Inside, he led us through a big room full of desks and women typing to another fair-sized office with a desk and a long table— the kind boards of directors sit around—and introduced us to Tom Allen, a man with a decided military air in starched khaki

Cleveland Benjamin's grave

The Huet Freeman house on Hard Times Plantation

Viola Freeman

Huet Freeman and his children

Willie Dowell

Gustave Rhodes

Beverly Rhodes

Taking a break from scrapping

Hauling the cane to the mill

Henry Pelet

Sister Robertine Galvin

Another generation

A plantation house

A retired worker

A woman with her cane knife

Peter J. deGravelles, Jr., and Kenneth Kahao at the sugarcane wage hearing, 1973

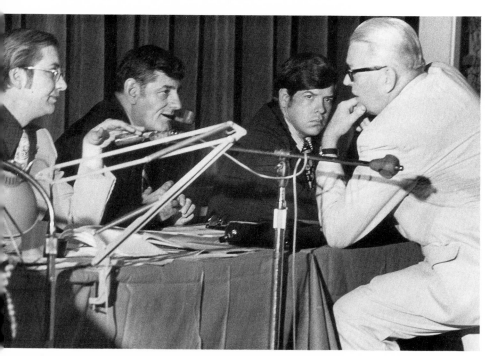

*American Sugar Cane League attorney Paul G. Borron, Jr., talks with
James Agnew, Marvin Gelles, and Donald Heitman at the wage hearing*

Sister Anne Catherine Bizalion

Father Vincent J. O'Connell

A child in cane country

Tillman Dickinson

The Huey Freeman family, 1978

Near Houma, Louisiana

trousers and shirt and a black tie, with gray hair parted down the middle.

"Sterling also grows cane and has laborers, so Tom sees both sides," Foster said as Allen shook hands and gestured for us to join him at the long table.

"We need friends in the press," Foster admitted as we waited for a secretary to bring coffee, "because we've gotten some publicity that really wasn't what it should be."

Allen agreed. "In so many instances, where you see good housing and bad housing together, the people living in the houses that are not in the best of condition in many instances are old pensioners," he said. "And these pensioners have been on the property for years. In most businesses they say coldheartedly when you're through, 'Leave.'"

Remembering the earlier argument I had heard, that a grower who leased his land wasn't responsible for the houses, I asked Foster's and Allen's opinions. "It's the responsibility of the people who hire the labor," Foster said without hesitating, and Allen agreed, "Absolutely."

"But what do you feel about the growers who don't?" I asked. "What about the outdoor toilets in 1972 and whatever?"

Foster looked at Allen and then insisted, "I just—Tom, correct me if I'm wrong on this—but I just don't know any growers or processors anymore who don't have these, not luxuries, but necessities for their labor."

"I've seen some," I insisted.

"You have?" Foster asked incredulously, and Allen wanted to know if I was talking about growers or processors.

"I'm talking about growers and the field laborers," I said to make myself clear. "And I *have* seen them. I've seen both houses with baths and without."

"But how many houses were there that you looked at?" Foster asked. "What I'm driving at is this: Was this some little farmer with just one or two houses around his place?"

I assured him I had been on some pretty big places that had outdoor toilets and mentioned one in particular that had nothing but that and faucets in the yard, and Foster said, "Uh-huh."

But it was Allen who spoke up to say that there had been tremendous improvement in these things over the past six or seven years. "Let me give you an example," he said. "We're spending five thousand, six thousand dollars a house, reworking the house entirely. We first started off on our Alice C division—you probably saw those gray houses along the highway. Now we're moving on to other places."

"They're all screened," Foster spoke up. "They're not sitting there with mosquitoes eating them up, and they're well insulated." He stopped a minute. "Oh, I know what I forgot to tell you; that they have, they've got gas—most of the houses have heating gas, either butane or natural gas."

Directly the conversation changed to wages, and Allen insisted that the growers' pay rates were competitive for unskilled labor.

"Remember," he pointed out, "sugar is the only commodity that has a separate wage scale over the Fair Labor Standards. The Fair Labor Standards Act says a dollar thirty. Our minimum is a dollar ninety-five for harvester operators, a dollar ninety for tractor drivers, and a dollar eighty for scrappers."

"And that dollar eighty is for men *and* women," Foster emphasized.

When I asked if they didn't think incentive raises—more money for those who had been working twenty years than for those who had been there two or three—were a good idea, Foster said he didn't really think the workers would like that system.

And loaning money, he said, was something you had to do, whether you liked it or not. "The thing is, just don't loan them stuff you know they don't really need, like buying an old wrecked automobile that some secondhand salesman is gonna—" he stopped midway and started in another direction: "And I try to keep my people out of the finance business. I had a man who unbeknownst to me went to a finance company and borrowed fifteen hundred dollars. Now the finance company finally took him to court and got this judgment, and by that judgment we were automatically forced to take twenty to twenty-five percent out of everything that man made. If he made two hundred dollars, it was forty dollars, and that forty dollars came out ahead of any debt he owed the company, any debts he owed anybody, and that poor devil paid back thirty-two hundred dollars." He pounded the table for emphasis. "There isn't hardly a payday that comes along that some darkie doesn't ask me to let him have twenty or twenty-five dollars, and then he'll come along the next payday and say, 'Please don't take it out.' Well, you don't take it out."

Nevertheless, Foster insisted he didn't have a man owing him a penny, and if I wanted to I could see that by taking a look at his payroll. "I think any man who gets in debt so heavily to the company is a darn poor laborer," he insisted. "If I got out there and I owed somebody four, five hundred dollars and knew I wasn't going to make over four or five hundred for that month, I wouldn't care whether my tractor had oil in it or whether it was properly lubricated or greased or anything else. I mean, the incentive wouldn't be there."

"What would happen if the growers paid two sixty-five an hour?" I asked, remembering the wage Sister Anne had suggested for cutters at the Houma hearings the previous summer. "Could the growers afford to pay more?"

"I think the growers have paid what they can afford to pay," Allen insisted, lighting a cigar. "Remember this, the federal government determines our wages, and the main criterion that is used is ability to pay. Now, sugar has been a cheap commodity. I imagine you've seen it in the grocery store. Sugar has probably gone up less than anything you buy."

Foster talked about the problems the growers faced—freezes, storms, too much rain, expensive equipment—but Allen insisted that the sugar industry in Louisiana was not in the doldrums.

"We have a wonderful future," he said flatly.

"What would happen if the growers got no subsidies?" I asked as we were preparing to leave.

"No subsidies? Well, now, that's a good word," Foster said to Allen. "She's brought up that dirty word *subsidies*. That's the word that Nader boy brought up to me, and I said, 'There's no such thing as subsidies.' I said, 'In 1936 or '37 when the Sugar Act started'—Tom, you correct me if I'm wrong, now—'the government, in order to keep the price of sugar down, put a one-cent tax on refined sugar, and that one-cent tax brings the government in around eighty or ninety million dollars a year. They then turn around and pay us what they call a "subsidy," which was put on when the tax was put on and that pays us back about thirty-five or forty million.' That's not a handout," he insisted. "When the government is getting eighty million and giving us thirty million, that's not a subsidy."

Later I interviewed J. P. Duhe II, who with his father and several uncles and cousins farmed Hope and Bayside plantations near Jeanerette. As we talked in the cramped offices of the oil business the family corporation also operated, the twenty-nine-year-old farmer insisted, "It's not fair to lump us all together. The only thing sugarcane farmers have in common is sugar."

His corporation paid its workers a nickel or a dime above the minimum as an incentive. It also provided paid sick leave, two weeks' vacation, and a retirement pension for some of its workers. Outwardly the houses looked terrible, he admitted, but all twenty-one had hot water and all but one, a bath. "It doesn't look like it, but we spent fifty-four hundred dollars fixing up the inside of one of those houses," he said. "Good labor is hard to come by, and a house is awful attractive."

Like the other grower, Duhe complained about landlords not wanting to put money into house improvements. But if they wouldn't, someone had to, he reasoned. Growers who provided their workers with houses that had outdoor toilets and fireplaces as the only source of heat gave the others a black eye. "I don't know if you've ever thought of the joys of an outdoor privy, especially in the winter," he said, "but this is 1972, and it doesn't look good. One reason it has persisted—hell, I guess if you're looking for a house, one with an outdoor privy is better than no house at all, and if nobody's bugging the farmer about installing indoor plumbing, he has no incentive to do it."

Duhe glanced out the window at the dreary winter day and studied the bare-limbed trees before continuing. "There's a point where you just can't spend a fortune on something you don't own, and you might not have that lease in another year or two," he said in defense of the growers. "A large number of the houses are abandoned because we're using fewer laborers every year. I've been agitating to put a match to 'em because they'll never be used again and they look bad. Besides, I think all farmers will eventually get out of housing. As the houses get too old, too dilapidated, and the more the public eye is focused on the whole thing, they're just going to abandon the houses, just tear them down, burn 'em up, get rid of them."

When I asked if providing good houses had paid off for him and his family in terms of keeping good labor, Duhe arched his eyebrow. "Honestly?"

I nodded.

"No. My observation—for whatever it's worth—is that good people, if you pay them well and treat them right, will stay with you, but to the drifters and fly-by-nights it doesn't make much difference."

"Do you think fieldworkers are treated right?" I asked.

"I can't make that statement," he said hesitantly. "I can tell you about several miles up and down *this* road; and several miles up and down this road, yes, they are. But farmers are no different from other people. You have rotten individuals who are farming, and you have good people. It's not fair to throw us in a big heap."

Duhe seemed troubled as he tried to assess the situation fairly and honestly. "One thing that bothers me is the impression that you get from reading various articles," he said. "I think the public has the idea that there are an awful lot of people sitting in cold houses without plumbing, that they're dying to work, and the big white man is sitting in his colonial mansion saying no, no, no. In many cases that's just not true. One of the biggest problems I have with labor is getting them to work, period, amen."

"But there are cases," I reminded him. "You said you can't make generalizations, and there *are* cases because I have been in some cold houses."

"Oh, yes," he answered quietly. While he and his family guaranteed their people forty hours' work a week year-round, he conceded that there were others who did not.

A graduate of Arizona State University with a degree in philosophy, young Duhe was lanky and sandy haired. Even in khaki shirt and trousers and work boots he didn't resemble "the boss man," and that was fine with him. "We've been trying to back out of this whole old-fashioned plantation system of managing personal affairs," he said. "We still loan money, but we are very cautious. If a person has a bona fide, genuine reason to borrow money I will loan it. But if it's just nonsense or if it's just the fact it's not payday, I won't. And it's made a big difference. Invariably the more money a man borrows, the poorer worker he is. There's a hundred percent correlation. And another thing," he added, "our employees pay their own utilities, and I haven't seen the lights turned off on anybody yet. I mean, if you manage your own life you're that much better person."

Back on Coulon

The Saturday before New Year's the photographer and I returned to the Thibodaux-Napoleonville area, to Leighton and Rienzi and Hard Times, to visit Lulu King and Tillman Dickinson and Mattie Jones. In the quarters, life continued as usual. Children playfully scuffled in the yards and on the roads. Women, the ones not scrapping cane, washed and cooked—the smell of beans was everywhere. And the men were in the fields, for the ravenous cutters were hungrily eating away at the remnants of still-standing cane. One machine was going through the field across from the workers' houses on Coulon when we pulled up behind the dusty white car of John Vernon Caldwell, the grower who had stopped us on our last visit. He stood at the road's edge, his windbreaker zipped against the cold, watching the giant machine struggle in the mud. The large tires slipped and spun, and the motor grunted and strained to free them. He winced until, freed, the wheels again proceeded down the rows. Caldwell was a formidable man, in his forties perhaps, of average height but solid, with a face resembling a bulldog's; his cheeks were fleshy, his dark eyes sharp and on guard, yet he spoke pleasantly, in contrast to his manner during our first encounter.

"Are you almost through?" I asked as we stood next to him on the road.

His eyes scanned the flat expanses and the patches of standing cane. "I imagine we have about six days left," he said, "but we're going to leave a lot in the fields."

"How much?"

"We're not sure. My tenant had to leave about thirty acres. He's hoping if it dries up some he may be able to get back in, but he's not real sure."

"What causes cane to go bad? By it being too late or the freeze?"

"No, the conditions, the mud. In some places you can't cut. In other places you can cut, but you can't haul it. That's when you lose it."

Suggesting we sit in his car, where it was warm, he opened the passenger door for me, then walked around to the driver's side and slid behind the steering wheel. Farther down the road, a large yellow vehicle rested beside the field. Caldwell gestured toward it. "We have that four-wheel-drive tractor pulling the equipment out," he said. "That thing cost thirteen thousand dollars, but without it we couldn't get some of the cane out. The harvester's going pretty good now, but we had to pull it out a couple of times this morning."

He traced the steering wheel's arc as he enumerated, as if by rote, the problems the industry faced: "Tractors increase in price about three hundred dollars every six months. Wages went up about twenty cents an hour this year. We furnish houses. Water. Pay these people's doctor bills, dentist bills. Loan 'em money and then take it out when they make a good check. I have a bookkeeper who spends about half his office time paying their bills."

"Don't you think it might better teach them to stand on their own feet if you didn't loan money?" I suggested.

"Not really. Psychologically they feel more secure, that you need them if they can borrow money. If I wouldn't loan to 'em, they'd quit right now."

From the field came the steady grating of the cutter. Caldwell watched it move away from us, felling the stalks in its path. His eyes lingered on the field and then swept the horizon, surveying the land that belonged to him and his brother and mother, land he had lived on all his life except for his years at Tulane University and a stint in the air force. His father owned still another plantation, and he and the family were members of the Caldwell Sugar Co-op, a sugar mill owned and operated by area farmers. In fact, both sides of the family had been in the sugar business as far back as his grandfathers, and on his father's side, back at least another generation. His maternal grandfather came by this particular plantation after working fifty years for the former controlling company, which had given him stock options instead of bonuses. After he worked his way up from bookkeeper to manager of five plantations and a sugar house, he had traded the stock for Coulon.

The work was not easy, Caldwell emphasized. "I'm over here seven days a week during harvest season. The rest of the time we try to work five days. It's a tremendous investment, and hard work."

He fell silent and again he surveyed his land and the equipment and houses on it. We were parked opposite the faded red one. Its doors were closed, and the only indication of Percy Green's whereabouts was smoke rising from the chimney.

"What about the housing?" I asked. "It has been a point of criticism, and I have been in some of yours."

He chuckled lightly. "Well, that's fine. I don't mind." Then the lightness left his voice and he became defensive, repeating the arguments of other growers I had met: that the workers and their families didn't take care of a thing, that they kicked in screen doors, literally tore the houses apart and used the lumber for firewood. He shook his head as though after all the years, all the generations his people and the workers had lived together on the land, he still didn't understand them.

Down the road, a man came out of the green house. Caldwell watched him walk to a car parked out front and continued watching as the car drove away, toward town.

"Most of the people working on a plantation live here because they like it," he said. "They like living here, they like working here—*this* is what other people don't understand," he said emphatically. "They like getting that money every two weeks, go in town and blow *every* penny of it, and know that when they lose it

I'm going to take care of them and they're not going to get thrown in the street. If they really need something, they're going to come see me and I'm gonna get it for them, which is something maybe *your* boss won't do for you," he sneered. "Would *your* boss loan you a thousand dollars *interest free?*"

"No, but I get other benefits—" I began, but Caldwell interrupted, "Would—your—boss—loan—you—a thousand dollars —*Answer the question!*—interest free?"

"No—"

"No," he mimicked, his face reddening. "But *I* have loaned these men over five hundred, some of 'em eight hundred dollars interest free. *Your* boss won't do that!"

I countered, "Yes, but I get paid when I'm sick."

"Well . . ."

"And I get retirement and a pension—"

"But supposing you don't live that long?" he argued. "There are certain things I will do that they won't."

"But you don't pay your workers when they are sick, right?"

"No, but we'll take care of 'em, definitely. We don't make a firm—I won't sit here and say that I'm going to do such-and-such thing, but I guarantee if one of 'em gets sick he's not going to starve. He's going to have food, and I will also advance him money *interest free!*"

Caldwell waved toward a dead car rusting on its rims in the grass near the green house. "That's what they invest in, automobiles! I can show you a hundred automobiles stacked up in a pile that's been there for years. That's all they live for—an automobile, a television set, and getting drunk. That's what they want! I can't tell them that's wrong, that they should take care of their families. This is the same thing that's going on in the ghettos. Most blacks have no family responsibility, and they're laughing at the public for giving them food stamps and welfare payments so the father has no responsibility. Yet the liberals in this country try to foster this to even a greater extent where they have less responsibility, and nothing good comes without responsibility!

"Look at this house," he called my attention to the green one. "That's where one of my best employees lives. It *was* a real good house. The inside was painted. It has beaverboard, a bathroom, kitchen facilities. I had it open for a while and he asked to have it. I said okay. They've been in there five years now. The posts fall off the porch, he doesn't fix it! He's a very good mechanic. He can do anything. But he lets it fall apart!"

His anger building, Caldwell criticized "do-good liberals" who had broken up this employee's family, sending one son through the Job Corps, first to learn to be a carpenter, then a mechanic, and then a welder. Another son wouldn't work, and his wife had left him. One daughter went to eleventh grade in Thibodaux— "the integrated school system," he emphasized—and then, because she didn't want to attend school with the whites, she went to Texas and had an illegitimate child, and he—Caldwell—had to send money to get her back home. Another daughter had gone to work for Southern Mutual Help Association. "And then," he went on, "some of the do-good liberals came down here and took his wife and threw her in a college in Texas to learn the basic food groups so she could teach the rest of the people. *Any* schoolteacher could teach that, but no, they gotta fly her to Texas. Since they moved in—the do-gooders—she's left him. The *whole* family has been destroyed. He's living alone. You saw him get in his car and leave awhile ago. He's going to get something to eat because there's nobody cooking in that house. He's by himself now and that house looks like a bomb hit it!"

He sighed, then added, "He's a fine person, but he misses about three or four days a week because he gets drunk. He's a good employee. We've never had a cross word since he came to work. But they came in here—those do-gooders—and they had hippies and longhairs sitting on that porch, white, black, a Catholic priest, nuns, and everything else, and they broke up that home. I don't know how they broke it up, but it's broken up. Now they're happy. They've destroyed this family. But they just pack up their bags and leave and say, 'Oh well, we messed up there.' They destroyed this family unit and they're going to destroy some more!" He jerked his head angrily. "Why don't they take one of these plantations and run it and show *us* how to do it? Why don't they go out and make a crop and hire some employees and fix all this up and get it perfect and run it and make money and then say, 'Hey, look.' Oh, no. *They're* going to tell *us!*"

In the field the harvester plodded up and down the rows, clattering, methodically leveling the cane. Caldwell checked its progress and then watched as a man in yellow rubber overalls climbed down from a tractor and walked along the road toward us. "There's a tragic case," he said, shaking his head. "That man is a confirmed alcoholic. He's a good worker, but he gets so drunk he can't walk down that road without falling in the ditch. Every once in a while he'll get on the loader drunk and I gotta go get him off. Sometimes he stays drunk for four or five days. It's pitiful. But people don't worry about that, see. They worry about bathrooms. Why don't they help the real problem, the drinking? And teach them how to use their money so it can mean something?" His tone softened. "Bathrooms aren't going to save them."

Mourning

After leaving Caldwell's, the photographer and I returned to Napoleonville and, accompanied by Beverly Rhodes, visited Cleveland Benjamin's mother. Almost a month had passed since the tractor accident, and the shock and mourning still rested heavily on her. A short, plump woman in her late fifties, she lived alone in a small, dark apartment just around the corner from the cemetery where her son was buried.

"It was a boy came an' tol' me that he had got hurt," she recalled, nodding her rocker back and forth slowly, its rhythmic creaks punctuating her story. "An' that was what I was leavin' out for to see, but when I got to the hospital it was all the way different. It was *all* the way different when I got there." Her voice rose and fell and faded, and for a time the room was quiet except for the rocking. Then she continued the obituary. "He jes' was thirty-four, born close around Napoleonville on Brule St. Vincent, another plantation. My husband was a worker too, worked in the fields, uh-hmmm."

I asked her when Cleveland started, and she rocked and thought. "I couldn't tell you that 'cause he was quite young when he use' to work for Mistah Lawrence. He went to school an' he got tired an' he didn't wanta go no more. I reckon he went to about third, an' then he stopped to help out at home with the chil'ren 'cause I had nine altogether. He was my oldest one an', my *goodness!* he was my *best* one!" Her voice, filling with pride, crescendoed. *"He* was the one I could depend on! When I'd be needin' a li'l change I'd go to Cleveland!" Her tone softened but the pride remained. "Yeah, he helped me out. Yes—he—did. He like to work. He worked aplenty."

"Before this, did you worry about accidents?" I inquired.

"Well, no. I never had my mind on that," she answered distantly. The rocking stopped. Then it and her grieving began again. She didn't cry, but you could tell she wanted to, that the tears were inside. "I feel bad about it! It hurts me! The *first* time with my chil'ren . . ."

Softly Beverly sympathized, "It's hard to lose a child."

"Yes, it's hard! the mother repeated, her voice swelled. "Ooooooooooh, it hurts me! I don't know no mo' to say or no mo' to do!"

After Grinding

*One day led to the next, and one was as cold and dreary
as another since the cane that shot up during summer and
lined Highway 1 all August and September was harvested.
The cutters and tractors—still caked with mud—rested
somewhere under sheds. And the long trailers spilling over
with stalks of cane no longer crept up and down the highway like a steady stream of ants after molasses. The shacks
stuck out on the land, barren now, just muddy rows of khaki-
colored stubble—leftovers from this year's crop, beginnings of
the next . . .*

1973

Gustave Rhodes on the cane cutter

The Series

On the map above my apartment desk Bayou Lafourche squirmed from the Mississippi River to the Gulf of Mexico. My eyes followed its meander from just above Donaldsonville, through Paincourtville, on to Napoleonville, Labadieville, and Thibodaux, where it intersected with the narrower Little Bayou Black. Mentally I placed Elm Hall and Hard Times on the map and revisited Gustave and Huet before returning to my typewriter to complete their story.

The sexton who unlocked the gate walked with us past some graves, dodging anthills, and pointed out the oblong concrete box that was Cleveland's. Unless you'd been to the wake and seen the six or seven sprays that still stuck to the styrofoam, you couldn't tell his box from the others.

There was no headstone or marker, nothing saying it was Cleveland Benjamin or that he died on a tractor when he was thirty-four or that he'd spent all his days in the Louisiana cane fields.

THE END

The final draft of the last article was completed, but had the story ended? During the time I wrote alone in my apartment my world had revolved around the fieldworkers and, like theirs, seemed fixed in time. What was happening now? Had anything changed? And what of the future? Would Gustave's and Huet's children and their children's children spend their days in the same fields, the same houses? Would Caldwells and Patouts always own the land and control the destinies of Rhodeses and Freemans?

That evening, after two months of immersion in the fieldworkers' story, I was preparing for guests, among whom would be a state legislator from cane country. One politician had already described the growers as a "very powerful" group, and a Louisiana congressman had confided to a *States-Item* editor that the workers' plight was too hot an issue to tackle. *He* had to run for reelection. Now I wondered what this legislator's reaction to my series would be, since among his constituents were both workers and growers. When we first met, the weekend before I began my cane research, I had been hesitant to discuss the assignment for fear he would alert the growers, but he had promised not to, and apparently he had kept his word.

After my guests arrived, the legislator inquired about the progress of my series and when it would be appearing. "The governor was asking me about you the other day," he volunteered.

Since I had never interviewed or met Edwin Edwards, I was puzzled. "The governor?"

"Yes. One of the growers wanted him to see what the *States-Item* reporter who's been snooping around the cane fields was up to, and so the governor asked me to find out. I told him not to worry."

In the past the growers had succeeded in getting other governors to block what they considered outside interference. Would they now ask this one to attempt to stop publication of the articles? Nothing else was said about the series, but for me, knowing Louisiana politics as I did, the seed of apprehension had been planted.

As the fifteen-part series reached the editing and production stages, my world shifted back to the newsroom, helping the makeup editor coordinate photographs and articles, selecting a title—"Behind the Cane Curtain"—and meeting with the publisher to discuss what stance we should take when and if we received critical response.

The first article appeared on March 19, and the reaction came quickly. The next day outraged calls and letters began to arrive. Some readers expressed shock that such conditions should still exist; others accused the newspaper of making them up. Some praised our courage; others blasted our bias.

> Your photographer is an artist. How does he get those pathetic expressions? He "oughta" be in pictures. Father Frank and Sister Anne should look at both sides. During the cane strike a *fat* woman with 5 illegimate children (each had their own private father) came to my son asking for a loan of $200. He offered her clothes and food for the children. Her reply, quote, "It aint for them. It is for my *car payment.*" As to the potbellied children and the unhealthy fatness of the adults—set your camera at the cars parked in front of the bars and nightclubs. You'd be surprised what that does to nutrition of the children and the unhealthy fat of the adults. If your camera is busy elsewhere taking pathetic pictures, I have some pictures to prove my point. Want them? My side of the story is true. I am as adamant as you!!!

The letter was postmarked "Napoleonville." I recognized the signer's name as one prominent in both the Louisiana sugar industry and New Orleans "old-line" society.

A New Orleans reader wrote:

> Replying to your series . . . this crap can be done without.
> I was born and raised in this city and to my estimation this blacks are not treated as bad as many try to claim. . . . Run a series on this apes that do nothing but drink and hold up citizens! A nigger will never have any sense if they live to be a thousand years old 98% of the robberies are done by blacks. . . . Them stupid creatures get help from the government through lies and false names. And illegitimate children 8 or 10 to a family they breed like dogs. . . . After 10 years of

the Civil Rights bill it seems that instead of them acting like white people they are becoming more savage by the day. All they want is everything free and have fun at the taxpayers expense. What is needed is more jails, the re-enactment of the death penalty and them either put on some island where they can live like a drump trow all they trash on the street in live in a cave.

Yours Truly
A Reader of your crap

Another letter appeared unpostmarked on my desk. It was short and to the point:

Re: Behind the Cane Curtain—the story about niggers: Could you arrange to have it printed on 6 inch wide perforated rolls. It would be much easier to wipe my ass with. Sort of shit for shit deal.

Wasp

Many letters expressed a thoughtful indignation, like that of one New Orleanian who wrote, "It is almost unbelievable that a condition like this occurs in our beloved Louisiana." Some were supportive of the workers and of my reporting:

Having grown up in the heart of Louisiana cane country I have seen the conditions under which these people are forced to live, and shocking as it may seem, the reports are not exaggerated. I hope that public opinion can accomplish what few good people have been unable to accomplish thus far—legislation to insure the cane workers a decent living wage and reasonable working conditions.

No official reaction came from the American Sugar Cane League, but James D. Graugnard, a St. James Parish grower, wrote in his capacity as president of the Louisiana Farm Bureau:

Miss Patsy Sims . . . perhaps is pointing the finger of guilt in the wrong direction. Why blame the cane grower for the workers' plight?

Under the present Sugar Act, the U.S. Department of Agriculture sets wages growers must pay workers. A check of the records will show during the grinding season harvester operators got $1.95 an hour and tractor drivers $1.90. Both dropped

to $1.85 when the season ended in January. Scrappers re-
ceived $1.80. These wages compare favorably with the $1.30
minimum for other farm labor and the $1.60 minimum estab-
lished by the Fair Labor Standards Act for commercial and
industrial workers. It might also be pointed out that the figures are minimum wages required, and many farmers pay in
excess of this amount. According to Miss Sims, cane workers
are not only underpaid, but are in poor health, have bad teeth,
live in substandard housing, are poorly educated, and in general, live at a standard far below the average American citizen. Specific examples quoted by Miss Sims I cannot disagree
with, but the sweeping generalization that all cane workers
live at a substandard level is not an honest assessment of how
things are behind the so-called "Cane Curtain."

Why not show the good with the bad? All workers don't live
in poor housing, nor are all workers in poor health, or under-
fed. Most have adequate housing, and the working conditions
are such that promote a good relationship between grower
and worker. There is not a constant state of fear on the part of
cane workers toward the grower, as Miss Sims would lead her
readers to believe.

Conditions are not perfect in the cane area, but neither are
they as bad as Miss Sims' articles portray. Conditions are
not perfect because the government can't set one's desires to
better himself, force the individual to finish his education,
increase his ambition, nor instill in him all those qualities
which make one man succeed and another fail. The government can only set a fair and just wage for workers and a price
for the grower.

Cane workers are not forced to work for a particular grower,
nor are they forced to live in housing provided by him. This is
still a free country. The individual charts his own path. If he
cannot feed, clothe, and educate his family at his present job,
there are other jobs in other areas. . . .

So perhaps Miss Sims should not point the finger of guilt
at all cane growers for the plight of some workers. Perhaps
she could be of greater service to those she seeks to help if she
took the positive approach. Instead of holding the cane worker
up as a pathetic individual, she should encourage him to take
that first step toward being more successful. She should, as

The
Series

should others apparently so interested, encourage him first to mow his lawn, fix his home to be more livable, and point out the importance of good mental and physical hygiene. The next step, quite obviously, is better money management and finally an education so necessary in today's world. But let's not place the blame on cane growers for individual shortcomings of some cane workers. But rather, let's help individuals to help themselves and this cannot be accomplished by promoting self-pity.

The newspaper responded with an editor's note:

The "finger of guilt" was pointed at no single individual or group in Reporter Sims' articles. In an April 6 editorial, the *States-Item* commented that the sugarcane workers' plight stems from a complex system of economics and other factors that, to be remedied, demand the cooperative action of public agencies and private interests alike.

Besides the letters, there was more tangible, active response. The Volunteers of America undertook special trips to cane country to distribute clothing, and students at Loyola University's dental school volunteered to clean the teeth of the workers and their families and teach them proper dental care. The National Sharecroppers Fund in Washington informed the paper of its plans to introduce the series the next week during hearings on the food stamp program before the House Agriculture Committee and later before the Senate Committee on Labor and Public Welfare and the Senate Oversight Committee on Implementation of the Rural Development Act.

The letters and phone calls were only the beginning of the reaction the series and I—even the mention of my name—were to stir up. Until I accepted a job in Philadelphia seven months later, I could not attend a cocktail party or a luncheon without becoming embroiled in a stormy discussion with a relative or friend of a grower. To them I was an enemy, a traitor, who had manufactured the conditions portrayed in the photographs and articles. After I won an Associated Press award for another series on race relations in New Orleans, I received an envelope with a return-address sticker from Napoleonville. Inside was a copy of the news story and photograph of me accepting the award. With a ballpoint pen, the sender had transformed me into a devil with horns and a goatee and had written over the headline: "I give you my version of Patsy Sims. Give her another award. The Biggest Liar!" I recognized the handwriting. It was the same as that on the earlier postcard from Napoleonville.

But even that was mild compared with what was yet to come.

The Victory

Father O'Connell was jubilant. "We won!" he announced. "Phil Larson just telephoned from Washington that Judge Pratt has ruled in favor of Huet and Gustave. The workers will get their back pay!"

While writing the series I had attempted to be objective, merely describing conditions and allowing both the workers and the growers to tell their sides. But now I could not help sharing his excitement. The court decision meant far more than whatever money the workers would receive. It meant that at last their rights had been recognized.

"That's fantastic!" I responded. "When did it happen?"

"April thirtieth. Judge Pratt ordered Butz and the guys at the Department of Agriculture to issue a new wage determination within fifteen days and to hold out enough from the subsidies to pay the workers the additional money owed them for the 1971 grinding."

"Do you want to make a formal statement?" I asked.

"This is people power," he boasted. Then his mood became more reflective. "With people in high places being able to be bought, it is a heartening experience to know there is still power in the hands of the people."

In Washington, the workers' lawyer, Philip Larson, was pleased yet cautious. The Department of Agriculture could appeal the decision, and the legal battle that had occupied him and two partners for fourteen months would certainly resume. He had been with Hogan & Hartson less than a year when the prestigious firm took the case without charge. The firm—which counted among its clients Chrysler, Howard Hughes, and Gulf Oil—had done so at the urging of Peter Schuck, the attorney who had written the *Saturday Review* article and whose job with Ralph Nader included monitoring the Department of Agriculture. Schuck had learned about the lost wages through Sister Anne Catherine and had himself written a letter in early January petitioning Earl Butz to apply the 1971 wage determination to all work performed on or after the beginning of grinding. When that effort failed, he suggested that a lawsuit was the best course and, knowing it would be long, costly, and difficult to handle alone, he began searching for help. He turned to Hogan & Hartson because of the firm's commitment to public interest law, and in February Larson, Arnold Johnson, and John Ferren, head of the firm's community service department, began preparation of the complaint. Ferren had been a law professor in charge of Harvard University's public interest program when Hogan & Hartson lured him to Washington in 1970 to set up its own department. Larson, a recent Duke graduate, had been assigned briefly to the department as part of his orientation to the firm's various practice groups. Working closely with Schuck, the three attorneys had spent the next six months familiarizing themselves with the Sugar Act and the wage-determination process: analyzing the workers' legal rights, determining what claims could and should be made, speculating as to what defense the Department of Agriculture might raise and how it could be countered. *Freeman, et. al.,* v. *United States Department of Agriculture, et. al.,* had been filed on July 25, 1972, in the U.S. District Court for the District of Columbia, naming as defendants the Department of Agriculture, Secretary Earl Butz, and three subordinate officers. The plaintiffs were Huet, Gustave (as president of

SMHA's Plantation Adult Education Advisory Committee), and "all others similarly situated."

For the next nine months, most of the action was played out in Washington between Larson, Johnson, and Ferren and the Department of Agriculture attorneys. But in Napoleonville the time, the waiting, had been equally difficult. Now, when I telephoned Huet, excitement and a new hope filled his voice. "I'm very, very happy! Very, very glad! I feel good!"

"What do you think will happen now?"

"I think more people on the farm will help themselves," he predicted. "They'll realize they have a right to be heard. Far as the farmers are concerned, they'll look to us more as a man instead of jes' a field hand. I think they'll realize we are human, that we have a right to live jes' like they do even though we're poor."

Gustave was equally exuberant. "We had so many people sayin' we weren't gonna win, but I always was livin' in hope that we'd get it. It's a big step forward because never before has a worker gone to Washington an' been able to pour out they's feelin's an' been listened to."

"Do you think this will help get the workers together?"

"It'll help a lot," he said optimistically, "'cause like I believe plantation workers now should know that if jes' two people had enough nerve to stand up an' do what is right an' accomplish this, then much more can be did for us by havin' a lot more workers involved. We have a voice, an' we should stand up an' make it heard. Jes' because we're poor, we don't have to be forgotten. You have to think you're somebody. If you think you're nothin', you're nobody. If you think you're somebody, you're poor but you're somebody right on."

The complaint had charged that the Sugar Act required the secretary of agriculture to issue an annual wage determination prior to the beginning of harvesting in October of each year, and that by failing to do so and then refusing to make the 1971 rate retroactive, he and the other defendants had erred in using President Nixon's Economic Stabilization Act guidelines to set the wage rates, because these guidelines were not included in the factors the secretary was supposed to consider under the Sugar Act, and because the plaintiffs and members of the class they represented had been exempt from the restrictions imposed by the Economic Stabilization Act. The complaint asked that the defendants be restrained from making further subsidy payments to growers until the case was decided, that they be required to make a new wage determination based solely on the Sugar Act, and that it be made applicable to all work performed on or after October 1, 1971.

The defendants retaliated with a motion to dismiss the complaint because the court lacked jurisdiction over the matter, because "indispensable parties"—the growers—had not been named defendants, because the Sugar Act required only that the secretary of agriculture hold annual hearings, not that he redetermine the wages annually, and because the Sugar Act was broad enough to encompass the Economic Stabilization Act.

On October 27 Judge John H. Pratt sided with the workers and handed down an injunction restraining Earl Butz and the Department of Agriculture from making further subsidy payments until the case was decided and ordering them to issue within thirty days a new wage determination that would be based only on the Sugar Act provisions and that would apply to all work performed on or after October 1, 1971. The defendants filed a notice of appeal with the U.S. Court of Appeals for the District of Columbia and then issued an amended wage determination making the 1970 rates applicable from October 1, 1971, through December 31, 1971, with the explanation that these rates "continued to be fair and reasonable for the harvest of the 1971 crop." The original, higher 1971 harvest wage rates would apply only to labor performed on or after January 2, 1972, which amounted to nine days, since grinding had ended on the tenth.

The legal skirmish continued with the plaintiffs asking the court to compel the defendants to establish a second amended wage determination, arguing that "only when they [the defendants] were compelled to issue the amended 1971 determination . . . did defendants first attempt to buttress their prior conduct by asserting that the 1970 harvest labor wage rates were fair and reasonable during the 1971 harvest."

When both parties appeared before the Court of Appeals for oral arguments, the court requested that they try to reach a mutually acceptable modification of the preliminary injunction. As a result, a tentative agreement was drawn up to allow the Department of Agriculture to immediately pay subsidies to producers who had employed no workers during the 1971 harvest, or to release that portion of a producer's subsidy which exceeded any additional wages he might owe if the original 1971 wage determination were applied to all labor performed on or after October 1, 1971. The payments were to be made only after a review of each producer's wage records by the department's Agricultural Stabilization and Conservation Service (ASCS) and by a representative of the workers.

To Larson, Ferren, and Johnson, the negotiations seemed to proceed smoothly enough. Even in telephone conversations with the defendants' attorneys there had been no hint that the slight differences in the two sides' proposals could not be worked out. Then, to the Hogan & Hartson trio's surprise, the Department of Agriculture lawyers filed a supplemental memorandum with the court, insisting that the differences were such that the matter could only be resolved in court. The memorandum also insisted that Hogan & Hartson's demand that worker representatives be present during the review of wages was unreasonable and asked that the court issue an order lifting the injunction against the payment of $8.6 million in subsidies—an amount, the motion said, that would leave enough money to pay the wage claim if the case were decided in the workers' favor.

The workers' attorneys replied to the court that the review process was merely a refined version of what both parties had agreed to and would not impede the department's processing and payment of subsidies. They advised the court that the workers had at least six representatives who could begin the wage review as early as the next week. But Department of Agriculture attorney Edwin E. Huddleson III, in an affidavit, maintained that his side had never agreed that the workers could have representatives in the ASCS offices or that subsidies would be paid only after such a review. His arguments, however, were to no avail. On February 22, the Court of Appeals ordered the preliminary injunction altered essentially as the Hogan & Hartson team had suggested and sent the case back to the district court for immediate consideration of the issue of the amended rates and the claim of additional back wages.

Before the case could be decided, however, the Hogan & Hartson lawyers went to court to challenge the defendants' ongoing efforts to have the case dismissed because the growers had not been named as defendants. The workers' attorneys noted:

The record . . . will accurately reflect the Louisiana sugarcane producers' continual and extensive—albeit veiled—participation in the defense of this action. The ultimate relationship and cooperation between the producers and the defendants was vividly demonstrated during the recent proceedings in the United States Court of Appeals for the District of Columbia Circuit. . . . As the attached affidavits and letter clearly demonstrate, Louisiana producers were represented throughout these negotiations by a representative of the American Sugar Cane League. . . . On February 15, 1973, one day after counsel for plaintiffs and defendants reached their tentative agreement . . . the League's Louisiana office mailed a letter to numerous persons in Louisiana including sugarcane processors and defendants' own "ASCS County Parish Office Managers." Signed by Mr. G. J. Dubin [Durbin], Vice-President and General Manager of the League, the letter related the status of pending negotiations in the court of appeals concerning modification of this Court's preliminary injunction. More importantly, the letter specifically noted the participation of Mr. Horace Godfrey in those negotiations. Mr. Godfrey, who maintains an office in the District of Columbia, is a Vice-President and the District of Columbia representative of the League. . . . Plaintiffs respectfully submit, therefore, that the League and other producer representatives have refrained from intervening only to enhance the joinder issue on appeal.

Several days after my telephone conversation with Father O'Connell, I received a photocopy of the court decision. In his legal opinion, Judge Pratt reprimanded the Department of Agriculture defendants for responding to his earlier order for an amended wage determination by applying the 1970 wage rates for work performed through December 31, 1971. "We can only conclude," he charged, "that the amended wage determination is a thinly disguised 'subterfuge or device' to evade the purpose and intent of the Court's order of October 27, 1972."

The Wage Hearing

The morning was hot and humid, typical for June in south Louisiana, and the cane along the highway to Houma thrived. By October it would be ready to cut. Even now it was tall enough to hide what I knew was behind it and what the Department of Agriculture officials would again miss as they had year after year driving from the New Orleans airport to the annual wage hearings. They would come and go but never see the workers' shacks and their meager existence. The growers would present their side, and the workers—or the workers' representatives—theirs. The growers would depict a money-losing business; the workers would plead for more money and understanding. The Washington officials would listen, but could they even imagine what lay behind the cane? Could they go beyond the quality of the crop—*this is a good year; this is a bad one*—and understand that for the workers every year, every crop, yielded the same?

Actually, the expanses of cane along the fifty-five-mile drive were limited to the stretch between Raceland and Houma, and even the approach to Houma, from the east, gave the impression of a town dominated by the oil and fishing industries. Nevertheless, sugar had long been one of the community's mainstays: Southdown, Inc., based its Louisiana operation here, and privately owned plantations—including that of the late Senator Allen Ellender—abounded. The Sugar Act did not require that the hearings be held in Houma, but in recent years they had been staged here with such regularity that many people referred to them as "the Houma hearings." The setting was always Municipal Auditorium, a typical small-town meeting hall built of brick and surrounded by saint augustine grass and oaks. Inside, the arrangement of metal folding chairs was tailored to the event: a graduation, a beauty pageant, a regional festival. Today, when I arrived, a number of seats were already occupied in a pattern that had evolved over the years: the growers on one side of the center aisle, the workers and their representatives on the other. Hushed discussions of sugar prices and wage rates and the cost of living rose from each side and converged in the middle in a cacophony that increased in volume as the audience grew.

Shortly before 9:30, twenty or so black men, women, and children filed into the auditorium. Their clothes were worn but freshly laundered; their faces, scrubbed. Some walked with eyes lowered; others glanced timidly at the already seated spectators. But Gustave looked straight ahead as he led the group to the rear of the workers' side. There were far from enough of them to fill the school bus that had brought them. Still, Gustave's face and Huet's, just behind him, glowed with satisfaction. The turnout of fieldworkers was encouraging after years of mustering no more than a carload, and, once, traveling alone with only their two families on a bus. This year, thirty. Next year, maybe fifty or sixty? Even this many workers willing to sacrifice a day's work, a day's pay *must* have an impact on the growers. Perhaps it was the beginning of the end of the workers' willingness to step back and accept without question what was handed to them. Perhaps "I" was becoming "we," and the growers would have to contend with a union, a group, a force. Maybe not today or tomorrow, but *one day*. And so the growers watched the procession. Some watched with amusement, but many looked on with concern.

Over the years, testimony at the hearings had been largely one-sided, restricted to the growers and the American Sugar

Cane League. The workers had seldom been represented because of their fear and their inability to speak for themselves, because they were rarely notified of the hearings, and because, if they did know the hearings existed, many felt that to attend would be "stepping out of place." During the organizing efforts in the early 1950s, union representatives occasionally spoke of the workers' plight, but it wasn't until the formation of SMHA that their side began to gain impact. Even then, mostly whites testified on behalf of the blacks, who remained as silent as they were scarce.

Five men seated themselves behind a long table on the stage. One of them, in his thirties, leaned toward the microphone and waited for the workers to be seated. "Ladies and gentlemen, may we please get started." The rattling of chairs settled and ceased. "I'm James Agnew, from the U.S. Department of Agriculture. I'll be acting as presiding officer. With me are William Ragsdale, from the Sugar Division of the Agricultural Stabilization and Conservation Service; Earle Gavett, from the Department of Agriculture's Economic Research Service." He turned to the men on his left. "Marvin Gelles, from the ASCS Commodity Stabilization Division; and Donald Heitman, from the Department of Agriculture's office of general counsel." The audience applauded lightly. Agnew continued. "At this time I would like to call Mr. H. L. Mitchell."

A tall, white-haired man made his way to a small table placed to the side of the stage at floor level. While the veteran labor organizer had been mentioned frequently in the course of my interviews, this was my first glimpse of him. He was slender in a farm-boyish way, with thick hair that turned up at his ears as it must have in his youth. His face was determined and caring, that of a man who had fought for and felt human causes, one who did not give up when principles, beliefs, lives were at stake.

He was, he told the audience, a former international representative of the Amalgamated Meat Cutters and Butcher Workmen of North America, AFL-CIO, who had retired just three months earlier after more than forty years of attempting to organize agricultural workers. Then, with obvious pride, he said he was one of eleven whites and seven blacks who had founded the Southern Tenant Farmers' Union in 1934 in Tyronza, Arkansas.

"I wish," he glanced at his prepared statement, "to review briefly the record of shame in which the U.S. Department of

Agriculture—under every secretary of agriculture from Henry Wallace to Earl Butz—failed to protect the lives and improve the wages and working conditions of the plantation workers under the Sugar Act. We do not wish to imply that the sugarcane industry, the producers, and the processors are without blame. However, the Department of Agriculture had the power but failed to extend a helping hand to those at the bottom of the agricultural ladder."

Mitchell's eyes panned the audience, passing Father O'Connell and Henry Pelet and some of the growers the three had first challenged almost thirty years ago. His voice grew stern as he recalled the first wage hearings he attended in New Iberia in 1947 as president of the National Farm Labor Union. "The problems that existed in 1947 are still with us," he said. "The living conditions of fieldworkers are poor, the wages remain near and often *are* below the subsistence level. In 1952 a representative of our union appeared at a hearing and recommended that the wages be fixed at a dollar per hour. At that time the pay for skilled workers was forty-seven cents an hour. *Yet* it was not until nearly fifteen years later that the secretary of agriculture found that a dollar per hour was a, quote, 'fair and reasonable wage for skilled tractor drivers.'"

Chairs rattled as Mitchell, in deliberate silence, focused on the growers, who shifted uncomfortably under his gaze before he returned his attention to the panelists. "*Never*, to my knowledge, has the increased productivity of the cane-field workers been taken into account in settling wage rates. One man now does the work of about ten men, compared to twenty-five years ago, but he does not get the wages of the nine other men which he and his big machine have replaced. Now that the secretary of agriculture has been hauled into court by the plantation workers, he must begin fixing a living wage for workers in the field. Perhaps *some*where there is a black Cesar Chavez."

The room was silent as he concluded his testimony, then applause erupted from the workers' side. A gray-haired man approached a microphone in the center aisle and waited. He was the image of southern aristocracy in cord suit and dark-rimmed glasses. When the outburst subsided he introduced himself as Paul G. Borron, Jr., attorney for the American Sugar Cane League. "Sir," he began, "your dissertation was on the history of the administration of the sugar program during recent years, but *most* interesting you did not refer to the present wage rates." His tone was snide. "Are you familiar with the fact that under the present determination the minimum rate for most unskilled workers in Louisiana sugarcane is a dollar eighty an hour?"

Mitchell answered, "Yes."

"Are you familiar that the average wage of *all* workers in the United States, skilled and unskilled, is *only* a dollar sixty an hour?"

"I would question that."

Ignoring the challenge, Borron turned to Agnew. "Mr. Presiding Officer, we will put evidence in the record to establish that is a fact."

"The last I have seen it was higher than two dollars, and that was a Department of Agriculture—" Mitchell started, but Borron cut him off.

"The figure *will* be put in the record from the Department of Agriculture to show that a dollar sixty-seven is the average wage."

"That includes every type?" Mitchell asked. "From the pickers—"

The attorney was condescending. "*All* agricultural workers, skilled and unskilled."

Mitchell's jaw set firmly as he too faced the hearing officials and argued, "Mr. Borron says on the *national* level, which includes all these people who pick fruit and vegetables for a few hours. But their average earnings are not a true picture of the skilled workers anywhere in this country. Even fruit pickers are earning more. You can average it out and it shows very little, but if you take the rates which we are dealing with here, I think you will find it's somewhere between three and four dollars, average—"

"I merely want to ask Mr. Mitchell if he has statistical data to support his statement."

"I would be happy to submit some. I don't have any with me, but I recently saw a study of that type."

"I would be delighted to have it," Borron responded sarcastically.

The next witness, P. J. deGravelles, Jr., moved to the small table and adjusted the microphone as he awaited Agnew's go-ahead. Tall, handsome, in his early forties, Pete deGravelles had been the growers' chief spokesman for ten years, perhaps because his family had been planters for generations. He made an impressive appearance—articulate, knowledgeable, a man capable of winning elected office, which some suspected he might one day do. In navy blue blazer and conservative tie, he confidently identified himself as the representative this day for both the American Sugar Cane League and the Louisiana Farm Bureau Federation's Sugar Advisory Committee and began his lengthy statement.

"Since 1967 the cost of living has risen 30.7 percent. During this same period, the minimum wage rate, *as* presented in the wage determination, has increased approximately 80 percent in Louisiana. Thus it appears that since 1967 the increase in the minimum wage rate has been about 2.6 times the increase in the cost of living." He paused, allowing the officials time to sort and analyze the statistics. "From the 1947 crop Louisiana sugarcane producers were paid—exclusive of conditional payments—a price of $7.00 per ton of standard sugarcane. If we can assume a price for our 1973 crop at today's level, this would mean a raw sugar price of 10.21¢ per pound and a molasses price of 31.75¢ per gallon. These prices would result in the Louisiana producers receiving for their 1973 crop approximately $11.60 per ton of standard sugarcane, exclusive of conditional payment. This would be an increase of *only* $4.60 per ton over the price twenty-six years ago."

Audience attention was divided between watching the speaker and following his mimeographed statement. "Income to the sugarcane producer and his costs are influenced more by the elements of nature than any other factor," he said. "In recent years we have experienced very adverse weather conditions." His delivery was rapid as he reviewed the adversities—a hurricane, a freeze, heavier-than-usual rainfall. In the audience, the growers nodded their heads in agreement. "And because of the energy crisis, thirteen of our mills were required to suspend operations for three days, causing loss of cane and the products thereof having an aggregate value of $1,141,819."

DeGravelles sounded discouraged. Even after grinding, he said, the rains had continued, washing away drainage ditches and delaying cultivation. He looked directly at the hearing officials as he continued. "Undoubtedly our 1973 crop has been hurt to some unknown extent. In our opinion *no* increase is justified under these criteria."

Heavy silence fell on the workers and SMHA staff members. Shock moved across their faces, and their bodies stiffened. Gustave, his forehead creased, exchanged glances with Huet and Beverly. Across the aisle, the growers remained relaxed, their attention directed to deGravelles.

"The prices of sugar and the by-product, black-strap molasses, have increased and the cost of living has increased," he conceded. "If we consider the price of sugar and molasses and could forget the results of adverse conditions in prior years and can assume favorable weather conditions in the future with a reasonably good crop in 1973, then an increase in wage rates can be justified. So, after considering all pertinent data and criteria, we have concluded to recommend an increase of ten cents an hour for harvester and loader operators and for tractor drivers and operators of other mechanical equipment, and an increase of five cents an hour for other workers."

Sighs moved through the workers' side like a breeze rustling cane. Tense bodies relaxed and eased into their chairs, and Gustave closed his eyes, relieved. But Father O'Connell, Sister Anne Catherine, and Henry Pelet exchanged guarded looks as Agnew called for questions. The panelist to his right raised his hand.

"Mr. Gavett?"

The hearing official directed his attention to the witness. "Mr. deGravelles, you referred to rising costs of producing and rising wage rates. What has happened to the productivity of workers all that time?"

"We have not made any studies of this. However, I would say that there has been no appreciable increase in the productivity of the workers in the last few years," deGravelles replied.

"But you have no studies to document it?"

"No, sir."

Chuckles came from the workers' side, and, standing at the aisle microphone, Father O'Connell grinned as he awaited Agnew's recognition.

"Father O'Connell?"

The priest's grin vanished. One hand rested on his hip, the

other held a sheaf of papers at reading level. "I would like to ask Mr. deGravelles two questions," he said, glancing down at the papers. "On page six he makes this statement that 'Obviously, this situation increased the producer's cost per ton of cane and per acre of cane and reduced his return.' Now, Mr. Chairman, I would like to read some statistics from the Annual Rural Manpower Report and ask Mr. deGravelles whether he agrees or disagrees. Nineteen seventy-one was your peak season. Employment for the activity per month—the planting, October—required 3,125 employees, whereas 1972 required only 1,975 employees, which to me means more acreage and less workers. I also refer him to a report issued by the Rural Manpower Service of Louisiana. Quote, 'The number of mechanical sugarcane planting machines in operation in 1972 was approximately double the number used in 1971. Reports from the field indicate that the mechanical plants proved successful during the normal planting season in 1972, and it is predicted that their use will be more prevalent in the coming years'—end quote. According to this report, gentlemen, it was estimated that in 1972 Louisiana produced 9,315,000 tons of sugar to 2,345,000 tons *more* than produced in 1971. The total value of the 1972 crop was estimated at $117,740,000—or $44,495,000 *more* than reported in 1971. *Now, Pete*—Mr. deGravelles—how do you account for the discrepancy seemingly between your figures given here under oath and these figures by the Rural Manpower Commission of the State of Louisiana?"

DeGravelles sneered, "I lost you on those figures long before the court reporter did."

A smile sneaked across the priest's lips, and the audience tittered. "You want me to define them again, Pete? Where did you lose me?"

"When I started writing them down."

"This will be submitted in evidence," Father O'Connell assured him.

Pete deGravelles stiffened, and his eyes fled to Agnew. "It's—it's difficult for me to answer that, Mr. Chairman, because I don't have the figures in mind."

"I don't see any problem to recognizing a discrepancy," Father O'Connell was firm. "My question is, *is* there a discrepancy here?

You *have,* Mr. deGravelles, indicated a loss of $1,141,819. You have *over here* in this particular report that they have *made* $44,495,000. *That* is confusing."

At the officials' table James Agnew nervously looked from the priest to the grower. He was an average man in looks, size, and presence and would not have stood out in the crowd had it not been for his assigned role and seat. Now he seemed overwhelmed by the exchange between the two more dynamic speakers. Still, he attempted to mediate. "They are not claiming—as I understand—that they had a loss from the 1972 crop of $1,141,000 in total. They are saying that this much was lost because of the shutdown of natural gas for three days in the thirteen factories."

"I have no problem understanding that," Father O'Connell said, "but that aggregate figure together comes out with the same amount."

Momentarily at ease, the grower rearranged his massive shoulders under the weight of his jacket, then flinched as Lorna Bourg neared the microphone with a menacing air. Her thick, bushy eyebrows moved together as she tackled him first with her eyes, then verbally.

"Is it true the wages are based on one criterion, that being the growers' ability to pay?"

"Miss Bourg, I am only recommending the so-called criterion of the Sugar Act," deGravelles responded coolly. He nodded toward the officials' table. "Mr. Agnew and his department set the wage."

"But you *do* maintain that apparent criterion to pay the wages?"

"I maintain the criterion set forth for the secretary of agriculture by the Sugar Act. I said the cost of living, the price of sugar and its by-products, the ability of the area to produce—"

"And the employer's ability to pay?"

DeGravelles wearily conceded, "Employer's ability to pay, I guess that's right." He lowered his eyes.

"So it seems we should be able to examine the overhead operation costs," Lorna Bourg concluded. "If one's operation cost is personal cost, it seems we should be able to examine that personal cost. We know the wages of every worker in the state. We should have the information on *at least* one grower. Mr. deGravelles, what is *your* income, including sugar production and conditional payments?"

Behind her, the workers and the growers alike waited expectantly.

"Mr. Agnew, *sir,* is this question pertinent to the subject matter at hand?" the witness pleaded.

Paul Borron raced to the mike. "This is most highly impertinent!" the attorney snapped. "We are here to determine the level of sugar produced in the state. Mr. Pete deGravelles's income, by a loss or profit, has no relevance whatever!"

Lorna Bourg persisted. "Mr. Agnew, may I come before you to make a ruling on that?"

"Miss Bourg—" the chairman started, but she stopped him. "In order to see that wages are fair and reasonable, we think it is only correct that we have available to us the personal incomes of every grower in the state to determine the ability to pay."

This time Agnew moved in firmly. "When the Department of Agriculture determines wages or prices, no consideration is given to any operation of an individual. It's all done on the basis of state average. Therefore I rule that Mr. deGravelles does *not* have to reveal any of his personal operations. I maintain that *no one* has a right to know the personal business of any individual."

"Except that sugarcane is a federally subsidized and controlled industry in the United States," Lorna Bourg objected. "The wages of fifteen thousand people is based on the ability to pay, and we cannot determine the growers' ability to pay without knowing the personal costs involved. Do you *still* maintain that we have no right to know that? Is *that* your ruling, sir?"

Agnew refused to budge.

"I would like to note my objection, and I object vehemently!" she protested.

"Your objection is noted," he replied with finality, shifting his attention to Sister Anne Catherine.

Unlike her angry assistant, the gentle SMHA director seemed dwarfed by the crowd. She wore a simple cotton skirt and sleeveless blouse, and when she introduced herself and directed her questions to the witness, her tone was soft and deceptively pleasant.

"You are basing your testimony on the fact that you are a producer of sugarcane, am I correct?" she asked.

"That is correct."

"You have described a pretty grim sugarcane industry scene

in the last few years," she observed. "Mr. deGravelles, when did you start as a producer?"

"Nineteen forty-eight."

"At that time, how many acres did you have?"

"Approximately sixty acres."

"How many acres do you cultivate now?"

"One thousand, one hundred sixty."

"I am wondering," Sister Anne Catherine mused, "if the production of sugarcane is such a bad thing, how could you have worked up from 60 to 1,160 acres?"

Turning abruptly, she made her way back to her seat as a young priest edged his way through rows of chairs to the microphone. Just entering his thirties, he was formidable, with shoulder-length brown hair, a solid build, and black raiment. DeGravelles eyed him curiously, and the priest returned an impassioned glare.

"Father Bill Crumley, from Lafayette," he announced before aiming his first question at the presiding officer. "I believe you work for the federal government, don't you?"

Curious, Agnew answered, "Yes, sir."

"Your employer has put together certain statistics," the priest replied. "One is that the poverty level for a family of seven— which is pretty close to the average family—has been set at $6,200. And from what we have been able to determine, the workers are paid $3,200. Also, as far as we have been able to determine, they work 1,750 hours per year. Now if you care, I will give you the time to jot these down, Mr. deGravelles." The priest waited with mock patience. "Six thousand, two hundred dollars is what the government sets as the poverty level for seven people—"

DeGravelles interrupted, "Is that agricultural or rural or farm?"

"The government doesn't distinguish between types of work when they have a poverty level!" Father Crumley snapped. He gathered his temper and began again. "So whether they are farm workers or factory workers or government employees, Mr. Agnew, the government sets the minimum level at $6,200 at which you can survive and you are *still* on the poverty level. That's for a family of seven for the lowest average. You *did* say we have to deal with averages."

"Please, what is your question, Father?" Agnew asked nervously.

The priest proceeded slowly, deliberately. "We have determined that $3,200 is about the average income of a farm family here. So if you subtract $3,200 from $6,200, you have $3,000. Even if you took the wage rate Mr. deGravelles suggested, that would not bring the workers up to the poverty level—"

"Mr. Agnew," the grower broke in, "on this $6,200 poverty, as I said before, I don't know whether the level is for urban or rural or farms."

"There is no distinction! Mr. deGravelles, if you are poor, you are poor!" Father Crumley said sternly.

Snickers from the workers' side interrupted the sharp silence. Across the aisle, chairs rattled as the growers tensed. Agnew glanced from side to side, then at the harried Pete deGravelles, and back at the audience. "Are there any further questions of Mr. deGravelles?" he asked. "Then we'll break for lunch and re-open the hearings at approximately two-thirty." He stood and studied the crowd as it stirred with conversations. Soon he and deGravelles were surrounded. Shoulders shrugged, hands gestured, brows creased. Gradually the growers, accompanied by the hearing officials and local Department of Agriculture representatives, drifted from the auditorium, leaving the workers and their families to eat lunches brought from home.

Later, when the newspaper photographer and I returned, a grower ambled over to us. "I talked to a worker on Oaklawn. He told me he *never* said the things you quoted," he informed me with smug satisfaction.

The tractor driver who had talked so freely about the workers' need to organize came to mind. "But he *did!*" I insisted. "I taped the conversation. I taped *all* my interviews!"

The grower chuckled. "Yeah, but those people aren't ever going to tell you the truth."

From the stage, Agnew's voice rose above the crowd. "Ladies and gentlemen, take your seats." The folding chairs filled and conversations ceased. "We will continue with the testimony of the producers' witnesses. Mr. Borron?" The attorney stood before the aisle microphone. When the room was quiet, he summoned Dr. Joe Campbell to the witness table and had the aging, gray-haired agricultural economist from Louisiana State University state his position and then sum up the study he had prepared on the state of the sugar industry for the American Sugar Cane League.

When the professor was done, Borron addressed Agnew. "Dr. Campbell has prepared a comprehensive study bringing out data on costs and returns through the end of the year 1971. With the permission of the presiding officer I would like to ask that this testimony be incorporated in the record in full, just as though it had been given personally and verbally in the presence of this commission."

"That will be acceptable," Agnew ruled.

A bearded man in his forties, his graying hair thin across his head, waited until Paul Borron handed the study to Agnew, then introduced himself as Benjamin E. Smith, attorney for the Amalgamated Meat Cutters and Butcher Workmen of North America and subsidiary local unions in the area. "Dr. Campbell," he began, "were you paid to prepare this report?"

"I drew a salary from LSU and to that extent I was paid, but not specifically to prepare this extra," the elderly witness replied cautiously.

"And you say you prepared this report *gratis* for the American Sugar Cane League?"

"In a sense, yes."

"In other words, LSU is in the business of doing gratis work for the American Sugar Cane League."

Campbell squirmed. "Since I don't draw pay and since no payment has been received by me from the American Sugar Cane League specifically, I suppose the answer is that I have done this gratis in the public service to provide background information."

"What if the Amalgamated Meat Cutters came up and asked you to do work like that for them?"

"I suppose I would have to get approval for it. I haven't refused to cooperate with anyone."

Ben Smith shifted his weight. "Does the American Sugar Cane League pay your expenses here?"

"No, I drove down with the head of my department in a state car. We do all kinds of work like this. We visit with county agencies, farmers, and the like."

"Have you visited with farm workers or with Sister Anne?"

Campbell shook his head. "They have never asked me."

The questioning continued, with Father O'Connell, Henry Pelet, and Lorna Bourg taking turns. The professor stiffened when Father Bill Crumley stepped forward.

"Since we have not had a chance to read your report, what was your specific recommendation?" the flamboyant priest inquired.

"Concerning wage rates?"

"Yes."

"I have made none."

Father Crumley was adamant. "If it doesn't concern wages, it should be thrown out. This is a wage hearing."

Agnew attempted to explain. "This is a report by Dr. Campbell on the cost and returns in the production of sugarcane in Louisiana."

"Then it should be admitted in evidence for the price of sugar," the priest argued. "If it has nothing to do with wages, it isn't pertinent."

In the audience the growers grumbled as Father Crumley persisted. "As an economist, what do you think would happen to the economy of Louisiana if the price of sugar were increased to such a degree that the wages could be raised very considerably?"

"I would personally feel we have to consider the consumer a little bit," the witness hedged.

"That's not the question. What would be the effect?"

Campbell proceeded cautiously. "If the price of sugar were doubled, then they would be able and I think would be willing to pay higher wages, but you can price yourself out of the market."

"How much has the price of sugar gone up in the past thirty years?"

"I don't have that figure available." Campbell's forehead creased.

"Doctor, do you think this is a significant factor when you consider economics?" Father Crumley asked.

The witness answered meekly, "Yes."

Paul Borron broke in. "I am not going to stand here and have this witness abused by this man!"

"Well sit down, then!" Father Crumley shouted, then to Agnew, "I submit that this report isn't complete. He does not even know the price of sugar. How can he make a statement?"

Agnew entered the melee. "We are determining the wages for sugarcane fieldworkers, and the farmer gets the price from the sale of raw sugar, not from the sale of refined sugar."

"Then why not raise that price?" the priest argued.

"That's limited by a mechanism in the Sugar Act," Agnew replied. "And I would suggest next year when the Sugar Act comes up for legislation, if you think that mechanism should be changed to get a price up higher, it would have to be recommended to Congress."

"In what way is it figured specifically?" the priest pressed.

Agnew remained calm. "The price of sugar is run at this time on a base period from September 1970 through August 1971—I'm going from memory—the price for that twelve months. There is a price objective established each month and increased by the average increase in the wholesale price index and the consumer's price index. The consumer's price index is the cost of living."

"And this is rigid?" Crumley asked.

"This is rigid. If the price varies from that objective by more than three percent up or down, the secretary of agriculture then must adjust the consumption requirements of sugar in the United States in order to get the price back in line."

"In other words, Mr. Agnew, this is a socialized industry," the priest observed.

As the argument grew heated, the presiding officer shot back, "I won't answer that question!"

"Well you will have to answer it! You won't have to answer it publicly, but you will have to answer it in your own conscience!"

"I didn't write the Sugar Act, Father Crumley."

Marvin Gelles attempted to end the verbal skirmish, but the irate priest would not be stopped. "Is credibility of the federal government a pertinent question?" he asked.

Gelles hesitated, then replied, "Of course it is."

"Well it's pertinent because that's what my question relates to."

"How that got into this type of hearing—" Gelles groaned.

"I just want to say that it has been a past mistake, in my judgment. Let's not make that same mistake by leaving with doubts."

Gelles rolled his eyes and sighed. "Let's pray tonight!"

"It takes more than prayer," Father Crumley assured him. "*I* am a gentleman of the cloth. I pray. If I didn't *do* something, some of the parishioners would lose faith."

Outside, the summer sun slipped in the sky as the procession of witnesses continued. The audience grew restless, and gradually the crowd thinned. Several nuns testified before Vincent O'Connell moved to the witness table. The room grew quiet as he adjusted his glasses and shuffled papers. He glanced up, his round face impishly innocent as he introduced himself and apologized that he couldn't give a permanent address because the bishop of Baton Rouge had just seen fit to ask him to leave the diocese. The audience sat erect, its attention restored. "I was thrown out of the house where the Marist fathers have lived for seventy-three years on the pretense that I attended a meeting— *which* I did not—as reported by a man who would call himself *Mr.* Sugar in St. James Parish. You can understand, gentlemen, if I am, at the age of sixty-one, a little emotional—I don't even have a home."

Several growers applauded loudly. Father O'Connell wiped his forehead with a folded handkerchief, then went on. "Gentlemen, I have listened to the hearings many times, and I feel that what I have to say will have no effect whatsoever. I don't know what good it will do if I just quote figures and discuss economics. So I am addressing my remarks to Mr. Butz. He is the only man who will be able to put this industry in a condition where it has a moral right to exist, where the sugar will have a price from which a just profit will be earned and from which just wages will be paid." He paused. "Mr. Secretary, I am presenting the hearing officer a copy of some articles which appeared in the New Orleans *States-Item*." He held up a reprint of my series. "I direct your attention to the editorial on the back page. And I quote, 'Some of the reaction to "Behind the Cane Curtain" was disbelief. But the men, women, and children who peopled the series are, unfortunately, real. They are in a rut, much like the mud ruts in the horrible roads that crisscross the cane fields in which they labor. . . . As long as the Department of Agriculture and the growers set inequitably low wages those families will never reach the quality of life that is America's long-made promise, and even more importantly, the basic freedom of a man or woman to determine as best as possible his or her destiny. As long as parochial government neglects to enact or enforce housing and health codes, the sugarcane workers and their families will continue to live in squalor and sickness. As long as the workers are not educated enough to recognize their own misfortune The System will continue to hold them down.'"

After a brief pause, the priest continued his argument to the absent secretary for higher wages and better treatment, then he closed with a prayer. As he rose from his chair, Agnew stopped him. "Father, did you want to introduce the articles, 'Behind the Cane Curtain,' into the record?"

"I would, sir, if I am so permitted."

Paul Borron hurried to the aisle microphone. "As a matter of formality, Mr. Presiding Officer, I object to the introduction into the record."

Quiet fell over the audience. Agnew's eyes moved nervously to the first row where I was seated. I stared back, waiting. "Your objection has been noted, Mr. Borron," he said. "I asked Father O'Connell for an extra copy so I could introduce it into the record. It will be accepted as Labor Exhibit Number 1."

It was almost six o'clock when Sister Ann Catherine came to the witness stand. For a time, the hearing officials and the audience only half-listened, then suddenly they were jolted. ". . . We are informed by workers from at least one plantation that it is the practice to withhold wages until the end of the season, forcing workers to purchase necessities from the company store on credit." Marvin Gelles leaned forward as the nun continued. "I am wondering why the protective hands of the secretary of agriculture have not stopped this exploitive and illegal practice. It is difficult enough for workers to provide for their families without waiting two to two and one half months for their wages."

Without waiting for recognition, Marvin Gelles inquired, "Isn't it common practice in Louisiana to pay workers at least every two weeks?"

"I would suppose so," she answered, "but there is one exception. That is the case I know of. There may have been others."

At the aisle microphone, Paul Borron anxiously addressed the witness. "I would like to ask if she knows the one plantation that caused the withholding of wages forcing the workers to purchase food at the company store on credit?"

"I have proof," Sister Anne was firm.

A wave of *ah's* swept across the audience.

"You have proof?" Marvin Gelles repeated, stunned.

"Would you wish to read that into the record?" Agnew asked, stunned.

Sister Anne Catherine hesitated. Finally she answered, "Levert–St. John Plantation, in St. Martinville."

Gelles promised he would have the ASCS assign someone to look into the matter and had just eased into his chair when Lorna Bourg stepped to the microphone and demanded to know why the USDA had not uncovered the practice.

"We operate under the Sugar Act with respect to wages, prices, or matters similar to this," Gelles replied defensively. "There is no basis for us to even discover something like this unless it's brought to our attention."

The accuser's eyes hardened. "What we contend is that the local ASCS *did* have knowledge of this for several years and made no attempt to correct it."

His face flushed, Gelles was emphatic. "As I said, I will bring this to the attention of our local ASCS office and *they* will look into the matter."

When Lorna Bourg suggested the evidence be entered into the record, Sister Anne Catherine grew worried. "My only concern would be for the safety of the workers. I wouldn't like this information entered into the record where everybody can find out whose paycheck it was."

"You can give that to me in confidence," Gelles assured her. He walked to the edge of the stage, and the nun handed him a small slip of paper, which he placed in his jacket pocket without reading.

Agnew called for the next witness, Sister Robertine Galvin, and the woman who had been seated behind me approached the witness table. In her early forties, she wore a navy suit and veil and spoke in a soft but firm southern accent as she described her visits with families on sugarcane plantations. "We hate to think that such words as *servitude, oppression,* and *fear* could justly be used to describe the life-style of people living in the United States in the late twentieth century," she said. "But there *is* oppression. There *is* dependency-based fear."

Her voice was steady and accusing as she described the low wages and debts, the growers' almost total disregard for the workers' worth. She illustrated: "For more than forty years this worker had performed as a highly skilled machinist in the mill. Two months ago he suffered a stroke which left him partially paralyzed in his arm and leg. One week after this happened I asked his wife if any of the bosses ever came to see her husband.

She told me they had not and predicted that 'none of them are gonna come either, not even to bring him a can of juice! They don't want him the way he is now, only when he's well. They don't want him and that's the truth.' Six weeks later I asked her the same question. Her prediction was right. They still hadn't come the two blocks from the mill to see about him." The nun faced the panel squarely. "This condition of life is no one's intent; yet it has come about through a demeaning dependency on the plantation owner because of low wages. Increased wages, above any other single factor, can open this circle of poverty and despair."

Before she could return to the audience, Marvin Gelles stopped her. "One statement concerns me—that is when deductions are made from the worker's salary with no indication of why they are being made and for what purpose. Do you have a specific situation where this condition exists?"

"Yes, sir," Sister Robertine said. "I would need to know whether it would be safe for the workers." She glanced toward Sister Anne Catherine.

Marvin Gelles assured her, "Believe me, you can give me that name and it will stay within the ASCS family."

"It's the same plantation Sister Ann Catherine told about."

The audience murmured.

The hearings had entered their tenth hour, and the metal chairs rattled under the audience's restlessness. The bus load of workers had long since departed for Napoleonville, and the growers' side had thinned. Even adversaries tired of arguing and anxiously awaited the final witness, Henry Pelet. In spite of the long day, Henry appeared alert as he agreed to enter his bulky printed statement into the record without reading it aloud. He distributed copies of the charts and studies he had laboriously compiled to Agnew and members of the audience, then returned to the witness table. Throughout the questioning, he remained calm, even when Paul Borron appeared at the mike.

"Mr. Pelet, I would like to comment on the tremendous job you have done putting together all this data and facts," the attorney said condescendingly. "I *assume* you assembled and compiled all of this data yourself."

"Yes."

"You computed all the results shown in your report?"

"Yes."

"I believe you testified you are neither an economist nor an accountant?"

"That is correct."

"What is your position?"

"I work in a factory in a stock department."

Borron smirked. "In all good humor, Mr. Pelet, I would like to make one observation—and I am referring to page 14 of your statement where you say, and I quote, 'The problem isn't cost. The problem frankly is a contempt for the workers, an attitude that the workers are slaves and should be treated as such'—end of quote." The attorney's eyes narrowed. "My observation, sir, is that this is a figment of your very vivid imagination!"

His left eyebrow arched humorously, but Henry Pelet remained quiet as he watched the attorney walk brusquely back to his chair. When he responded, he did so gently but with an eloquent anger. "I do have a little imagination," he said softly. "I don't think it would be possible to live without one. However, let me say this: That this is not a figment of my imagination. It is, for instance, in the series of articles that were recently run in the *States-Item*. The whole thing comes out." His voice broke, and his eyes moistened. "My God, it all smells!"

Putting on the Pressure

Clusters of people lingered in the auditorium to continue the day's discussions and debates. In spite of the late hour, Father O'Connell still seemed energetic as he huddled with Henry Pelet and Sister Anne. Their concerned expressions had given way to triumphant glows as the three delighted in the verbal inroads made by the workers' side during the hearing.

As they edged toward the door, I called to Father O'Connell, and after an exchange with Henry and Sister Anne he joined me at the back of the hall.

"What's this about the bishop putting you out of his diocese?" I asked.

"I haven't heard directly from Bishop Tracy, but that's the word I've gotten from Charlie Barrett, the provincial for my order," he said. "I was up in Washington the other day and Charlie showed me a letter he had received from Tracy saying I *have* to be out of the Baton Rouge diocese and the rectory in Paulina in thirty days."

"Why?"

The priest shrugged. "Charlie says Tracy received a complaint from a St. James grower that I attended a meeting protesting the workers' housing on his plantation. I wasn't even aware of a meeting." He chuckled, then added, "But if I *had* known, I would have gone! I've been told the grower's a big contributor to the church."

Since his return to Louisiana Father O'Connell had lived at St. Joseph's rectory in Paulina and commuted by ferry across the Mississippi River to Thibodaux, which was part of the Baton Rouge diocese. The Marist fathers had assigned him as a delegate to the four-state New Orleans province, which meant he was free to work or reside anywhere in Louisiana, Arkansas, Alabama, or Mississippi.

He handed me a paper from his briefcase and watched as I read the letter written May 21 to the Very Reverend Charles J. Barrett in which Bishop Robert Tracy forbade Father O'Connell to either live or work in the Baton Rouge diocese. "I find no need to explain to Father O'Connell or to anyone else the rationale for this decision," the letter read. "I just do not believe, after much consideration, that Father O'Connell's ministry or residence in our diocese is in the best interest of our people. Any evaluation of the matter must rest between you and Father O'Connell. I cannot accept the position that Father O'Connell has any right to minister or reside in my jurisdiction without my consent. I refuse that agreement."

"It all goes back to the lawsuit," Father O'Connell said, explaining that because of the injunction, the court had been holding up subsidies until the suit was decided. The large growers could get all the credit they needed, so they didn't care whether they got the subsidies from the government or not, he said, but the small farmers who depended on them were being crucified. So in February, Hogan & Hartson and the lawyers for the Department of Agriculture had worked out an agreement with the Court of Appeals to permit the department to pay subsidies to the family farmers who had no workers and to release to the larger growers the balance of their payments after whatever wages might be due their workers were placed in escrow until the case was settled. The court had also agreed to let the workers' representatives examine the growers' records when they were submitted to the ASCS.

"Because I live in Paulina, I said I would take care of the

three parishes in that area, one of them being St. James," Father O'Connell explained. "So this grower had to come in and present all his records. And I'm sitting there with my collar on, and this woman says to him, 'Oh, y'all going in there and make confession to that priest, eh?'" He chuckled. "Of course that upset the grower, because he's Mister Big, you know. But that was when he called Tracy. Said I was interfering with his business, and Tracy wrote this letter. Barrett has advised me to move out of the rectory but to stay within the diocese so it won't appear we are giving in to this directive."

He glanced toward the stage and studied the group of agriculture officials deep in conversation with several growers, and his tone became defensive. "It's an invasion of my civil rights as to where I live and what I do. I'm not under his jurisdiction and never was. It should be clear now to the executives of the sugar industry that they aren't going to get me out of here by pressuring any bishop of any diocese. A damned big part of my life has been spent in this state, and *no*body is powerful enough this time to push me out again. They'll have to shoot me because I intend to die in Louisiana," he paused, and the impish little smile came to his face as he continued, "where the soil is so soft they could push me down standing up, so when the bugle blows on Judgment Day I'll get a head start on everybody else!"

A few days later I telephoned Father Barrett in Cleveland, where he was on business. The letter from Bishop Tracy was the first official indication he had had that everything was not all right, he told me. He planned to be in Louisiana the next weekend to discuss the matter with both Father O'Connell and Bishop Tracy. He denied knowing anything about pressure from a grower, and although the letter indicated that a carbon had been mailed to Father Joseph Buckley, Barrett's predecessor, Buckley also said he was unaware of the grower's complaint. Bishop Tracy declined to comment.

My article on Father O'Connell's eviction appeared on the *States-Item*'s front page the following Monday. That afternoon, a spokesman for Bishop Tracy telephoned with a statement denying that Father O'Connell's ouster was related to his involvement with the fieldworkers. "That is not the case," the bishop insisted. "The principal reason is that Father O'Connell is working in the diocese without request, consultation, assignment, or permission. Neither Father O'Connell nor his provincial has sought permission to work in the diocese, and he has never discussed his activities with any diocesan authorities." The statement was the first of several issued by the bishop in what grew into a heated exchange between him and Father O'Connell in newspapers and on television.

By the time Father Barrett and nine Marist priests from Washington met with the bishop and, separately, with the evicted cleric, Father O'Connell had already moved in with Henry Pelet and his mother. After the sessions, the group publicly announced that it was "fully behind" Father O'Connell, reiterating the priest's good standing in his religious community and the council's desire that he continue his work in the sugarcane areas of Louisiana.

The day after the council's statement appeared in the newspaper, the Associated Press reported that Bishop Tracy had rescinded his orders. The story quoted Father O'Connell as saying, "The bishop has now backed off. I'm told he no longer has any objection to my remaining here. I have now moved out of that house because it was under the jurisdiction of the Baton Rouge diocese, and I have moved in with a sugarcane mill worker." In the same story, the bishop again denied that his actions had anything to do with Father O'Connell's sugarcane activities and cited his own support of efforts to improve the workers' conditions. He acknowledged that Father O'Connell's move eliminated his jurisdictional objections but emphasized, "Because his efforts appeared to be harmful to the interest of the people, it was necessary to make it clear that he in no way represented the Baton Rouge diocese. All concerned are agreed that Father O'Connell's misguided efforts are a hindrance, rather than a help." The next week the bishop, through his spokesman, issued still another statement insisting he had not backed down on his stand that Father O'Connell could neither live nor work in his diocese.

The eviction was not the growers' first attempt to retaliate. Shortly before the Houma hearings, Father O'Connell had expressed suspicions that an SMHA request for $300,000 in federal funds to provide manpower training for fieldworkers may have been held up deliberately by the Louisiana Department of Education because of pressure from the growers. The program would have offered basic education and occupational training in gasoline engine repair, automobile mechanics, and farm equipment mechanics to forty-five workers, and to a second member of each trainee's family. To receive the funds, SMHA needed forms outlining curricula and expenses as well as signatures from both the Department of Education and the Louisiana Department of Employment Security. The project supposedly had received the backing of Governor Edwin Edwards, who on January 23 had written to Secretary of Labor Peter J. Brennan asking that he personally review the project and give "some indication of when we can expect a formal commitment . . . we are concerned that there be no additional delay." Brennan replied on March 12 that he appreciated Edwards's support and agreed "it is a project which would be beneficial in enhancing any further developing opportunities for rural poor in your state." Yet in spite of the governor's endorsement and repeated calls from Father O'Connell warning that SMHA stood to lose the grant if the forms were not expedited to Washington, the Department of Education failed to meet the deadline and the money was reallocated to another agency.

After a conversation with Father O'Connell, I spoke long distance with a source within the Department of Education who assured me he knew "for a fact" that Education Superintendent Louis Michot had been pressured to hold up forms required by the U.S. Department of Labor for the funding of such projects. "I know pressure was put on him by the growers, primarily from the St. Mary area," the source confided, "but I don't know if he succumbed. He didn't want to get in the middle of it, but I know he has delayed approval of the project as far back as the end of summer."

A few days later I drove to Baton Rouge to see Michot, who confirmed that he was opposed to the program but denied that his objections and the delays were due to pressure. The accusations, he said, were a complete falsehood. "I'm all for getting the poor blacks out of the fields, but the methods SMHA are using to achieve the results are very costly. In my judgment it's an unwise expenditure. We want to do the training. We have the experts and we feel it would be done in a professional manner by the Department of Education."

He was unaware of a letter written May 21, over his own signature, to Secretary Brennan—a letter describing the request as "exorbitant" and referring to SMHA as "Poverty Professionals." He attributed his unfamiliarity with the letter—a copy of which had been mailed to me by Colonel Sylvan Chaze, director of the Department of Education's Manpower Training Division, after an earlier telephone interview—to the fact that he had so much to keep up with. Father O'Connell and the Employment Security officials also said they were unaware that the letter opposing the project had been sent to Brennan after Chaze had already signed the forms approving it, just as they had not known that Chaze had typed over his signature on the printed form, "Only if the training is conducted by the Louisiana State Department of Education."

In the telephone interview, Chaze, a former business partner of Michot, also objected to the program because the projected cost was exorbitant and because he felt the training should be done by the Department of Education. Asked why he did not tell SMHA of his objections, Chaze replied, "They never asked me." The delay, he insisted, was due to the paperwork involved, and not the pressure. "The only person who put pressure—and I wouldn't call it pressure because *no* one puts pressure on me— was Father O'Connell, who said they would lose the money if the papers weren't sent in."

The Return

Little remained of the shack. Just the shell and even more cracks and cobwebs than when the photographer and I had first visited Moses West. Across the highway, the cane grew tall, but now there was nothing to hide. The shack that had been next to the Wests' was gone, replaced only by weeds, and Moses West's would soon disappear also. Its guts were gone, and so were the lumpy mattresses, the remnants of platform rockers, and the garbage cans on the rotting front porch, and, with them, Moses, his wife, and their three children. The only reminders of the retired sugar-cane worker and his family were an empty Dr. Pepper bottle, a pair of jockey shorts hanging on a rusty nail, and this epitaph crudely scrawled across the door:

J. C. W. WAS HERE AND WILL NOT BE BACK HERE AGEN

Dark clouds moved across the cane, toward the house, sending ahead of them a breeze that wandered carefree in and out of the glassless windows, swinging the door on its hinges. Outside, a rooster crowed and a nearby industrial plant hummed and grunted, but the house itself was quiet. A lizard creeping up the door frame stopped and stretched its neck and head toward us, then continued its even pace.

It had been seven months since the photographer and I had traveled through cane country, two months since the Houma hearings. We had set out this morning to retrace our steps for a follow-up story. Moses West's house was our first stop, and its emptiness stunned us, for it was as if he and his family had never existed. When we asked others in the area about the family's fate, nobody knew, nobody seemed to care.

The Wests moved ghostlike through our minds as we drove along Bayou Black Road, ignoring the POSTED NO TRESPASSING SOUTHDOWN, INC. signs and venturing down dirt roads looking for settlements we had visited before. Along road after road we found cane fields and weeds and occasionally a crumbling chimney, but no houses or people.

The photographer turned to me, puzzled. "Are we on the right road?"

"I'm sure this is it," I said, equally baffled. "I just don't understand. Maybe we were farther down."

We continued down the highway, turning off onto dirt roads only to find land so overgrown with cane or weeds that the recent presence of people and houses seemed impossible. It was a strange, unsettling feeling, almost as though we had imagined the shabby settlements. When we reached a fork in the highway, we agreed we had not traveled that far and headed back toward Houma, perplexed.

"Wait! Try this one," I suggested.

Patiently the photographer turned onto a road marked by the familiar No Trespassing sign. He shook his head, but neither of us spoke as we became surrounded by the green stalks. Suddenly he braked. To our left was a row of frame houses, neat and freshly painted. To the right, four fieldworkers—one of them on a ladder—were tearing down a shack, gray plank by gray plank. A heavyset black man watched as we got out of the car, then ambled toward us. His khaki shirt clung dark and damp to his body, and he removed his billed cap and mopped his forehead with a rag.

"What are y'all doing?" I asked after we had introduced ourselves.

"Tearin' down them ol' houses. Done tore down four over yonder." He gestured past the remnant to land now covered by weeds. "Them green ones 'cross the road? They jes' was moved here from off another place."

"Oh?"

"Yassum," the old black man answered. "They tearin' them houses down *all* along the way." He shook his head slowly. "Wonder where them ol' folks goin'? Jes' don't know what's to come of 'em."

As the photographer focused on the workers and the shack's gradual demise, a pickup truck pulled up behind our car and a gray-haired man in work clothes and a straw cattleman's hat strode toward us.

"Who y'all with?" he demanded. "You can't take no pi'tures of them houses without a permit!" He bit into a thick cigar and glared.

"We're just trying to show how you're replacing the old houses with new ones," I explained.

The man refused to listen. "You gotta destroy that film or I'm callin' the law!" he threatened.

I looked at an antenna sticking up from the truck's roof. "But—"

"Now!" He took the cigar from his mouth and spit tobacco shreds to the ground.

"Okay, I'll destroy it," the photographer said.

The man held out his hand. "I want 'em destroyed *now!*"

Reluctantly the photographer fumbled in his pants pocket, then released the camera's latch and placed a roll of film in the man's palm.

"Now gimme those names!" he ordered. He printed our names in a small tablet and then squinting toward the car jotted down the license plate number, the fat cigar rolling between his teeth. His eyes fixed on us menacingly. He lumbered over to the pickup, climbed into the cab, but didn't start the motor until we were in our car, headed back to the highway. When we were out of sight, the photographer chuckled.

"I switched film on him," he said.

We laughed, then fell silent. Should we have forced the issue? Would the man have called the law? And would we have been arrested? We were uncertain of our legal rights, yet we began to regret that we had not stood our ground.

By the time we had driven the sixty miles to Franklin, clouds masked the sky, as they do so quickly in summer in that part of the country. A drizzle fell as we left Highway 90 and turned onto a road that wound past Katy Plantation to Oaklawn. At a crossroads, outside a small frame church, a group of blacks—some solemn, some crying—stared as we turned onto the narrower road and slowed to pass them. Their eyes and ours shifted to a polished black hearse, its rear doors open, waiting. Then we speeded up, toward the mill and the living quarters. There, before us, the old houses that had not been painted in years—maybe never—stood bright as Easter eggs against the sky: blue, yellow, turquoise. We stopped in front of the first house, where the old woman with the wood-burning stove lived. Except for a new coat of yellow, the house—like its neighbors—was unchanged. The solid wood doors were shut tight, and no one answered when we knocked. We walked around back and found the old woman near the outhouse studying a pile of scrap wood, one hand on her hip, the other dragging an ax behind her. I called to her from the fence, and she jolted.

"How are you doing?"

Her eyes narrowed, then ignored us.

"When did they paint your house?"

Without looking our way, she muttered, "Got no time, got no time." She poked at the wood with her ax.

"Did they paint the inside?"

She limped a few steps, stopped, then glared at me over her shoulder. "Boss tol' me if y'all come here ag'in he gonna put me on the road! An' I ain't got nowheres else to go. Ain't got no chil'ren, no husband neither—jes' me by myself." She shook her head, then moved away.

The wife of the tractor driver I had interviewed cracked the door of her house, not opening the screen. Her eyes widened.

"We're the ones from the *States-Item*—"

Quickly she cut me off. "You talk with him. He's the manager of the house." She waved her hand toward her husband, who was sickling weeds. The photographer and I strolled across the yard.

"Hi, could we talk?" I called to him.

The man glanced over his shoulder. "I'm busy!" he grumbled, then resumed whacking, swinging the sickle forcefully. In December he had been open and friendly, talking freely about the need for a union and allowing us to photograph him. Perhaps he didn't recognize us, I thought.

"You remember us?"

"Yeah, y'all messed me up!" he lashed out. "That be why I don't wanta talk with you!"

The sickle sliced through the tall grass.

"How did we mess you up?" I asked. "Did we get you in trouble?"

"No!" he thundered.

I remembered the grower at the Houma wage hearings who claimed this same worker had denied making the comments I quoted, even though I had tape-recorded the conversation. Now I wondered what had happened. His house, although in better condition than many I had seen, was one of the few on this plantation that had not been repainted. Had there been additional pressure?

There were others, too, talkative before, silent now.

"I don't know how long these houses be painted. You gotta ask the boss," one woman evaded us.

Another insisted, "I got no time to talk," and closed the door.

In Napoleonville we found Hard Times almost a ghost town. When we crossed the railroad tracks, the deserted dirt road stretched before us; the shacks—even Huet's—were boarded up. Curious, we crept along the road, stopping at the house of Huet's grandparents. Only it, Tillman Dickinson's hut, and one other shack had no boards nailed across the windows and doors. By the time we got out of the car, Shug Preston stood on the porch.

"Where is everyone?" I called to her.

Holding open the screen door, the stout old woman sighed. "Oh, chile, they done move ever'body save us ol' retired folks to some new houses over by the highway. Place they call Little Texas. You know the store what they call Stiffin's? Well they be back a that."

"How long ago did they move?"

With her index finger she tapped her lips. "Must be two, three months now."

Nearby, Jessie Preston sat in a rocker. His eyes were clouded over and watery, and although he nodded agreement, he seemed not to hear as his wife directed us to the new settlement.

"Jes' us ol' folks," she repeated. "Jes' Tillman an' another family an' us all alone back here."

She stood on the top step waving as we drove away, until we lost sight of one another and the road again was left to the old people and the shacks called Hard Times.

The new houses, freshly painted, were gray and green, and at Huet's house zinnias bloomed. Grass carpeted yards from which privies and outdoor spigots were noticeably absent.

"First time in my life I had hot water except for heatin' it myself," Viola Freeman said as we admired the bathroom and its shiny white tub, toilet, and washbasin. "They move' these houses from off another plantation."

The house was neat and clean, and even the battered furniture looked better in its new surroundings: a living room, two bedrooms, and a kitchen with built-in counters and cabinets.

"Huet working?" I asked.

"No'm," she answered. "Been rainin'. He jes' been makin' two days a week for about the last three weeks, but he work regular long as it don't rain. He be out catchin' us some fish now."

Unlike Huet, Gustave was at work under a tractor shed when we stopped at Elm Hall, so we continued to other plantations we had visited during grinding. Except for the stilled mills and some painted shacks, things had not changed: the rotten teeth, the day-after-day diet of beans and rice, the tattered clothes, the fear. "It's the same thing—outdoor toilet an' all," Elsie's daughter complained, holding open the screen door that was busted now as it had been when I visited her last December. The rotten boards that once served as steps still lay on the ground, and the porch and its overhang sagged dangerously.

At St. John we learned that the Department of Agriculture had kept its promise to look into the plantation's practice of withholding the workers' pay during grinding. Now they were paid every two weeks, like the rest of the state's cane-field workers. And the houses had been painted white with green trim.

"They give us the paint an' we all did the paintin'. The men got paid," one woman, seated on her porch, explained. She chuckled and nodded at the outhouse. "I even painted that. Now if you wanta do the indoors you gotta buy it yourself."

"Is your husband working much this summer?" I asked.

She shook her head. "He came down with a stroke Good Friday, an' it'll be a good while before he be able to go back to work."

"Has the owner helped you out?"

"Oooooh, Lawd, the plantation don't do nothin' for you! Ain't nobody come see 'im or give us a nickel!" I recognized her story as one related by Sister Robertine at the June hearings. In the month following, nothing had changed. "We gonna get on welfare in August. First money we got was fifty-three dollars last week, but they say next week we get ninety dollars."

"How did you make it during all that time?"

"I bought to the store." She motioned to the photographer not to take her picture. "I gotta live here!" she exclaimed.

"Do you have any idea how much you owe the company store?"

She rolled her eyes upward, calculating. "Oooooh, almost a hundred now. They sell high there. An' I owe the grocery store in town an' the drug store."

"How will you pay them?"

"Well, I jes' pays little bit by little bit what I can," she said shaking her head. "Can't do no more 'n that."

The Ordeal

Broussard, population seventeen hundred, was quiet and peaceful, with a general store, a pharmacy, a gas station or two, and the usual small-town assortment of repair shops. Highway 90, the four-laner, missed the town by less than a mile, but the narrower Route 182 provided a lone traffic light. In the lazy late afternoon heat the tree-trellised streets and impeccable lawns were virtually deserted, and the sugar mill just beyond town stood idle, its shredders and crushers stilled. Even the convent across from St. Cecilia's School was outwardly serene when the photographer and I arrived. The comfortable frame house was scrubbed, and massive concrete planters edged the porch. Hurried footsteps, on wood, mingled with the door chimes. They grew louder, nearer, then Sister Robertine opened the door. The nun who had been energetically outspoken at Houma was subdued, and her eyes seemed troubled as she invited us in. She wore a white blouse and the navy skirt from her secular suit but no veil over her short, curly hair. Her slender, pockmarked face was drawn.

Earlier, Father O'Connell had briefed me on Sister Robertine's ordeal. For her, Broussard was no longer the nice southern town that had quickly accepted her when she arrived as principal three years earlier. Suddenly she had become an outsider, an intruder—even, to some, a traitor. Vicious words and rumors had led to violence. In the early morning darkness of July 3 the convent was pelted with tomatoes, and obscenities were scrawled in ketchup across the front wall. The concrete planters were shoved off the porch. That same morning, shortly after five o'clock, four shots were fired at the large window of her pastor's bedroom-study. The convent was empty, and Sister Robertine herself was away at the time. Nevertheless, she was shaken.

The incident occurred the day after the Agricultural Stabilization and Conservation Service mailed letters to sugarcane growers informing them of a statewide investigation—prompted by the testimony Sister Robertine and Sister Anne Catherine had given at Houma—into the growers' wage-paying practices. Now, she was reluctant to discuss the incident and others leading up to it, preferring I get the information from her pastor, Monsignor John Kemps, and from her mimeographed diary compiled at the request of the state's Council of Religious Women.

"They occurred as isolated incidents," Sister Robertine said positively. "We have two hundred children at the school, and I have never heard one of them talk about any vandalism at their house. It is not an ordinary thing to occur in this town. Certainly not here at the convent." She hesitated. "But I really prefer you talk to Father Kemps about this." Again she paused. "He has suffered very, very much from the whole thing, and he has stood firmly by me."

"When did you return?" I asked.

"July twenty-first. We got back a little after dark, and I was glad because I was scared to come back," she admitted. "I hated to get into it all again. It had been so heavy, so hard, so constant." Her voice cracked. "It was a little relief to leave for the summer, but I still had to come back and I hated it—Really, I'd rather you talk to Father Kemps." But slowly her story unfolded, and she seemed relieved to be talking about it at last. "I was making retreat about thirty miles from San Antonio, and I didn't know anything about it. Our superior general told me, and I called Sister Anne Catherine."

Except for the soothing hum of an oscillating fan, the room was undisturbed as I skimmed the diary. The first entry, dated October 1972, concerned the letter written by Sister Anne Catherine to small growers informing them of the federal court injunction to withhold subsidy payments until the Rhodes-Freeman case was decided; the second was a request to Sister Robertine by a Broussard farmer for information about Sister Anne Catherine and SMHA.

"Had you been aware of any feelings or hostilities or prejudices in the community toward the cane workers?" I asked. "Or were you even aware of the cane workers?"

Sister Robertine shook her head. "I had never been on the plantations. I think everything was just taken for granted. I don't think there had been any involvement on the part of other people into the cane worker situation, and so there was never any disturbance of the system. About six months after I came, I called the Neighborhood Service Center here in the black community and asked if I could be involved, and so I became more and more aware of the problems of the blacks. Then I became aware that many of the blacks were cane workers. It was just in that indirect way that I became aware of the situation. As far as direct involvement with cane workers as such, it wasn't until one of the farmers asked me if I knew anything about why they weren't getting their subsidies—I didn't even know anything about subsidies—and then he said they got a letter from Sister Anne Catherine."

Another nun entered the room with a tray and offered iced tea. Sister Robertine took a glass and sat back against the plush chair. She surveyed the room—its high ceilings, its polished floors, its elegant old furnishings—and seemed comforted by the convent's buffer from the outside. She sipped the tea and continued. "The farmer wanted to know if Anne Catherine was a real sister. I said, 'I don't know but I'll find out.' And then Frances Bernard, whom I worked with at the Neighborhood Service Center—a couple had asked her about it, too. So I made an appointment—" Her eyes traveled down the printed account. "That was December twelfth, and Frances Bernard went along—"

"I was there interviewing Sister Anne for my series, and I remember Frances Bernard coming in, but I didn't realize you were with her," I interrupted. We had not been introduced, but I remembered the pair, perhaps because of their racial difference. Now we were surprised at our simultaneous introductions to SMHA and the role that day was to play in our lives. Innocently, we each had incurred the growers' wrath.

Sister Robertine resumed her story. "Anne Catherine explained the lawsuit, and it was very clear to me that the farmers simply were not informed." She reconsidered. "As a matter of fact, they were *mis*informed, I'd say deliberately misinformed. So I said, 'If I set up a meeting for the small farmers, would you come and explain this to them?' She said yes, so I set it up." She shook her head. "*Did* I set it up."

Thumbing through the diary, she came to a copy of the letter sent to farmers by her and Frances Bernard. It was simple and impartial, identifying Sister Anne Catherine and alluding to the farmers' reaction to her letter. The meeting at City Hall, this letter explained, would be "to obtain clarification on points of the letter you received and to express your feelings and viewpoints regarding the court decision, as well as the problems you face as a small grower in this locality." It concluded, "One point which should be emphasized here is that SMHA is as committed to helping the small grower to meet his needs effectively as it has helped the farm workers meet theirs."

After I finished reading, Sister Robertine went on. "The same night the farmers received the invitations in the mail, Father Kemps called and asked to come over. When he got here, he said some farmers were threatening to withdraw support from the church. They were angry because I had called this meeting. Really Father Kemps was asking me to cancel the meeting and get out of the whole thing. He said two farmers had come to see him and they were very upset. So I asked him, 'Who are they?' He didn't want to tell me. And I said, 'You know it has nothing to do with the school, and what I do on my time is my business.' He said, 'Yes, but they hold me responsible.' I said, '*Who* are they and I will write them a letter, I'll tell them that *I'm* responsible for my actions and you're not.' So finally he gave me the names. So I wrote the two farmers a letter. The next night I saw Frank Garber at a PTA meeting, and I don't know how it came up, but he said, 'That letter made me angry.'"

As Sister Robertine reminisced, I browsed the written account of the PTA meeting and how her right to become involved in the socioeconomic and political problems of the area had been questioned because she was employed as principal by the local church parish. Her letter to the farmers had been polite but firm:

> I hope this letter will establish beyond the slightest doubt that Msgr. Kemps is in no way responsible for my involvement in any "extra-curricular" activities! Indeed, he had no knowledge of my brief and indirect involvement with SMHA prior to his having received the bulletin Monday. . . .
>
> I certainly have very definite obligations as a principal and teacher in St. Cecilia School, but I insist that none of my current involvements outside the school make me less effective in the area for which I am employed.
>
> Finally, I want to make it very clear that I refuse to be intimidated by any threats made against Msgr. Kemps, the Church or me. As long as my actions are moral and legal and are not in conflict with the exercise of my duties for which I am employed, then I cannot be denied by anyone the right to act according to my personal interests and concerns.

Sister Robertine's face darkened. "Then there was the meeting," she said. "Frances and I were the first ones there, and then the small farmers started coming. But even though only *small* farmers were invited, some larger growers showed up, and there was a man from the local Department of Agriculture, a Farm Bureau representative, and a police juror from here in Broussard. Curley Bernard—Frances's husband—was a farmer at that time. Had about fifty acres. When he arrived later, he saw the road was blocked off by police cars—two cars from the Lafayette sheriff's department—and the deputies were taking down license plate numbers. So he figured somebody better stay *out*side." She paused, then returned to the meeting. "Frances Bernard opened the meeting. I was the *lowest* key there. I just sat. Anne Catherine talked about the lawsuit and the subsidies and payment for the workers, and then the small farmers—she asked them to talk and they did. They started talking about their problems. And then Walter Comeaux came in. He's a big, big politician. He's president of the Lafayette Parish Police Jury, and the Comeauxs are very much involved in the sugar business. Anyway, he came in about forty-five minutes after the meeting started with Father Gauthe, the assistant pastor, and Gus

Guilbeaux, the town marshal, who was armed and in his uniform. Comeaux started a speech about Americanism, patriotism, SMHA badgering the poor farmers and making it hard for them, and they need their money—*all* this kind of stuff. He went on and on and on. So I raised my hand. I said, 'Before you came, the farmers were ably speaking for themselves and I think they should be permitted to continue speaking for themselves.' And he shot across the room. He was crimson. His teeth were clenched and his fists were doubled. His neck vessels were bulging. And he said, 'This is all your fault! It's all your fault!' I just sat there and let him say it. And then he tried to get control of himself. The farmers started talking again, but as soon as Comeaux got control, he started again. Nobody else could say anything, and that was the end of the meeting. He just controlled everything."

By the next day, rumors—the first of many—had begun: that Sister Robertine was being fired or replaced, that she was having an affair with a radical black priest, that she had spent the school's money for her personal use and had attended a week-long NAACP meeting at the school's expense, that she was a Communist. There was even talk of behind-the-scene maneuvering to encourage an area congressman to use his influence to cut SMHA's federal funds. Father Kemps was pressured to replace her, and finally a school board was hastily set up to undermine her effectiveness. Father Kemps and the new bishop, Gerard Frey, had been supportive. So had Sister Elizabeth McCullough, superior general of the Sisters of Divine Providence. But that was little consolation as the bitterness passed from parent to child into the school.

Father Kemps lived about a block away from the convent. The priest was short, stooped, and had sparse gray hair. He was visibly nervous as he showed us the pocked window in his bedroom-study. Although he had spent more than half of his seventy-eight years in Broussard as pastor of Sacred Heart Church, the accent from his native Holland remained strong, and it thickened as he related the incident, hesitant to make accusations.

"The third of July early in the morning, at five-twenty, I heard the shots," he recalled. "I didn't know what it was. It was a big metallic noise. I thought the record machine had fallen down. Then I pulled the curtains back and saw the holes and the glass on the floor." He pointed toward four quarter-size holes. "I called the police, and then during the day I found obscene words on the front of the convent." His voice lowered. "Four-letter words they write in restrooms. Like that. So I called the police and I've heard no more." Suddenly he seemed frightened. "But more than that I don't want to talk. Too many things happen."

"The police never did anything?" I asked.

He shook his head. "They picked the bullets up and wouldn't talk to me about it. They think there were two guns. There were pellets and one looked like a bullet hole."

I pressed, "Have you had trouble before?"

Hesitantly he answered, "No, I never had anything like that happen before. But I prefer not to—"

"Do you think it had anything to do with Sister Robertine's involvement with the fieldworkers?" I asked.

The elderly priest's eyes reflected childlike fear. "I don't want to talk. Too many—"

"Did you attend the meeting last January?"

He nodded. "It was very rough."

"Have you been pressured?"

He shuddered. "I have been pressured in this way, that the people said they were displeased that Sister was involved in things outside the school."

"Did they threaten to cut off money?"

"Not exactly." He wavered. "They have expressed they were displeased and it might affect support of the school, but more than that—"

"Growers?" I asked.

He answered softly, "A few farmers were among this. But it might have nothing to do with the shooting. I don't know. There have been narcotics arrests—" He looked helplessly toward his elderly housekeeper. "Sister's involvement, that is her privilege. Sisters can indulge in apostolic work. They're free as long as they take good care of the school."

I studied the four bullet holes. "And the police never did anything else about the shots *or* the vandalism?"

He shook his head.

"What about the newspapers?"

Again he shook his head. "You're the first one, and the *National Catholic Reporter.*"

He accompanied us to the door, relieved at our going. "I was startled, but I was not scared," he insisted stoutly. "I wanted to go after them!"

Later I talked by telephone with the janitor who had cleaned up after the vandalism and with Frances Bernard, who briefly repeated details of the stormy January meeting and how her husband, after noticing the roadblocks, had watched unobserved as the two sheriff's deputies recorded the license plate numbers of those inside.

Back in New Orleans, before writing the story, I telephoned the Lafayette sheriff's office and talked to Deputy Harry Saucier, the person in charge of public relations.

"The holes are not the type made by bullets," he insisted. "We found some pieces of gravel in the house."

"You don't think it was gunshots?" I asked.

"No," he was positive, "gravel."

"What about the vandalism at the convent and the obscenities?"

"Some potted plants were broken and something that looked to be tomatoes was smeared on the house, but as far as we are concerned there was nothing to it. We just patrolled the area for several nights to check to see if they would return. It was what we would normally call vandalism."

"But two people told me they *saw* obscene words written on the house," I said, referring to the janitor and Father Kemps.

Deputy Saucier remained firm. "I had two men who went out on it and neither said they found any writing."

Baffled, I changed the subject to the sheriff's cars that had blocked the street outside the January meeting and the deputies who reportedly had recorded license plate numbers.

"I don't know anything about that," he insisted.

Town marshal Gus Guilbeaux also denied the cars' presence. "I was at the meeting," he acknowledged, "but I was never aware of the street being blocked."

"There were no sheriff's cars?"

"Definitely not."

"I understand you were armed and in uniform."

"Sure, I'm on twenty-four-hour duty," he explained. "The

mayor couldn't attend, and since it was at City Hall he asked me to go in his place."

"Does someone from the mayor's office always attend meetings at City Hall?"

"Yes, usually."

Later that day Saucier called back. "I checked again with the deputies and they said there *were* some obscenities written in what appeared tomato juice or tomato paste. They recalled some four-letter words," he reported. "It was just some wild kids, I imagine."

"Oh?"

"Yeah. I also checked with the traffic and enforcement department, and they can't recall any of our cars blocking the road at that meeting last January. I asked around and no one here recalled it, and I couldn't find it in writing."

The story appeared on the *States-Item*'s front page, headlined PASTOR TARGET OF GUN. In the article I observed that while Father Kemps had been reluctant to cite a possible motive for the vandalism, he had noted that the incident had closely followed the investigation into payroll practices at nearby St. John, prompted partly by Sister Robertine's testimony at Houma. I also mentioned that the U.S. Agricultural Stabilization and Conservation Service memos regarding that plantation and others in the area had been mailed by the St. Martin Parish office on June 19 and July 2. The evening the story appeared, a state trooper repeatedly telephoned my apartment asking me to meet him that night—as late as nine-thirty or ten—to discuss the vandalism. I refused, insisting everything I knew was in the article. The next day he came to my office and asked me about names he had circled in the clipping. He insisted he was surprised no investigation had been conducted and vowed to do something, yet I heard of no further action.

A week later, Sister Robertine sent me a photocopy of two articles carried in the *Lafayette Advertiser*. The first, a wire story, was merely a rewrite of mine. The second, apparently staff written, quoted Father Kemps as denying any connection between the incidents and Sister Robertine's activities. Across the sheet, Sister Robertine had written: "Can't win! But please drop this matter; too much commotion here!!!"

The Investigation

Following my return trip to cane country, I received a note from Sister Anne Catherine and copies of the correspondence she had received from ASCS. Two days after the Houma hearings Marvin Gelles had written that he had begun looking into the legalities of St. John Plantation withholding fieldworkers' pay during grinding. He could find nothing in the current wage regulations that stipulated a time limit for the workers' pay periods. Nevertheless, he assured her that his agency would not tolerate any more single payments during grinding. "I have discussed this matter with my superiors," he wrote, "and they will approve an amendment to the regulations requiring that workers be paid at least every two weeks. While there is very little we can do for the past, much will be done to prevent any more inequities for future crops."

Later in June, Gelles had forwarded a copy of the memo sent by state ASCS director Willie Cooper to all offices in Louisiana's sugar-producing parishes notifying them of the complaint made at the Houma hearings and instructing them to contact a representative number of growers to find out if the practice was widespread. The notice emphasized that those contacts should include growers who owned or operated grocery and dry-goods stores. The parish offices were instructed to report to the state director on or before July 2 the number of farms checked and how many did not pay their workers at least every two weeks.

In a letter dated July 20, 1973, Gelles informed Sister Anne Catherine that the investigation had turned up one other case, in St. James Parish. He emphasized that on both plantations the money was withheld at the workers' request and that they could get interest-free advances by asking for them. From now on, however, the workers would be paid biweekly throughout the year.

The complaint made at the hearings had brought results, but in her note to me, Sister Anne Catherine was less than satisfied: "It seems that the workers have not been interviewed as part of the 'investigation' of their wages—Forest Reubin & Sr. Robertine visited on St. John last Thurs. and could speak to that."

After receiving the correspondence, I talked long distance with Willie Cooper at his office in Alexandria. "We made investigations on *all* plantations—not just St. John," he informed me, his voice reflecting pride at both the fairness and the thoroughness of the study. "In practically all instances the growers were paying on an every-two-week basis. In the instances we found where they were not, it was during grinding and it was optional with the employees as to whether or not they wanted to be paid on a two-week basis. On St. John, the general manager stated he would change the manner of payment during the harvest season. His plan is to pay the workers on a biweekly plan throughout the year."

"And what is his name?" I asked.

"Roland Hebert."

"Where were the other 'instances'?"

Cooper stalled. "Well, it was only in one other area."

"Where was that?"

"Uh—St. James Parish, but that was an agreement worked out between the grower and workers."

"What was the plantation?" I pressed.

"I don't think I could give you that information," he insisted.

After he had freely discussed the Levert–St. John situation

and provided the manager's name, his reluctance to elaborate on the St. James case was perplexing. Father O'Connell had been told on good authority that it was a St. James grower who had pressed Bishop Tracy to evict him from the Baton Rouge diocese. The parish was also home to both F. A. Graugnard, Jr., secretary of the American Sugar Cane League, and his brother, James D. Graugnard, president of the Louisiana Farm Bureau.

Next I telephoned Fred Cormier, ASCS director for St. Martin Parish, in which St. John was located.

"I did the investigation myself," he said. "In the case of Levert–St. John, any worker can go at any time and request an advance, and most of them do, *weekly*. This is an agreement the workers requested, *not* something Levert–St. John decided. The workers made the request three or four years ago."

"But when I visited St. John in December to research my series and again late last month, several workers and their wives complained about the practice," I said. "One guy insisted the pay was withheld so the workers wouldn't leave before the end of grinding. And a nun who has talked to at least half the workers told me that when she asked the workers if they could make one change what would it be, they all said they would like to get paid more often during grinding."

Cormier was defensive. "Well, if the workers have a complaint they can come to this office and it will be given *top* priority—whether wages, working conditions, whatever."

"How long have you been ASCS director?" I asked.

"Twenty-four, twenty-five years."

"And you didn't know the workers on St. John weren't paid until after grinding?"

"Not until this spring. We do check wages for child labor and to see if the workers are receiving the minimum wage. Through the years we have checked over twenty percent of the farmers' records, and this is not even required until we have a complaint or something irregular." He paused. "Like I say, the workers should come to me if they're not satisfied, but they're *hard* to communicate with."

1974

The Huet Freeman family

The Firing

When we drove into the settlement known as Little Texas that April day in 1974, the yards were empty except for a few children playing, and even the youngsters scattered and disappeared into their own houses as we neared the Freemans'. Holding open the screen door, Huet glanced up and down the deserted road and shook his head, dejected. Inside, cardboard boxes were everywhere, filled with mismatched dishes, battered pans, shabby clothes—the family's belongings. The lines around Viola's eyes and mouth were etched deeper by worry and by the day's packing; nevertheless, she smiled warmly as she greeted Gustave and a photographer and me.

I had moved to Pennsylvania in November 1973, and this visit was both a reunion and a chance to hear firsthand about Huet's firing. The news had been passed along by Father O'Connell and Henry Pelet and repeated by Gustave when he offered to accompany us to Little Texas. I had seen Gustave in Washington a few months earlier at hearings conducted by the House of Representatives' agriculture committee on extending the Sugar Act beyond its December 31, 1974, expiration date. Then and now I detected in him a confidence not exhibited during our earlier meetings. He seemed less shy, and he expressed himself with greater ease, perhaps because he felt more comfortable around me and because of his new role as SMHA's president. He never had been afraid to speak his mind, but now he did so with uneducated eloquence.

Huet, too, seemed more self-assured in spite of almost two months without work and his imminent uprooting. He gestured us toward the threadbare sofa, then sat opposite us on a straight-back chair.

After we were settled, I inquired, "When did they ask you to leave?"

"A little after grindin', in January," Huet said. "The grower came up to me, he axed me, 'You think you can find a job somewheres because I don't have much work?' I said, 'I'll try.' So I went out an' got a job with the telephone company. I was workin' there for a while an' they run outta business. So I came back to the boss an' I told him, 'I'm outta work, can I come back?' An' he told me, 'No, I don't have nothin' to do.'" Bitterness crept into Huet's gentle voice. "Still, he was givin' them other men work."

"The others were working?"

He nodded. "Some been workin' here for three years. Two of 'em. I been workin' for 'em *eleven* years," he said, the bitterness dissolving into hurt. "So last time I axed him for work—I was workin' in Thibodaux towin' boats an' I jes' couldn't get no ride, so I went back to the boss—I said, 'Look, I don't have no work, can I come back tomorrow?' He told me, 'No, Huet, I jes' don't have nothin' for you to do. *When* I find somethin' I'll let you know.' So then on a Wednesday he come 'round lookin' for me, an' I wasn't home—"

Viola broke in, "I had a mind what it was he wanted 'cause he looked so angry."

"Next mornin' he come to me an' say, he axed me if I have a job, an' I said, 'Yeah I done found a job,'" Huet went on. "He say, 'Well, see if you can find a house to live in.' I axed him why, an' he said, ''Cause the wind blowin' down the cane an' I got less land.'" Huet's voice became firm, accusing. "But I don't think that's the reason at all."

"Do you think it had anything to do with the lawsuit?" I asked.

Huet glanced at the floor, then back at me. "I think so."

"Did he ever say anything to you about the lawsuit?"

"No, but other people tol' me some farmers came to him an' axed him, 'You ain't got rid a that man yet?' That was right before all this happened."

Gustave interrupted. "I think it's comin' not jes' because a the lawsuit. I think it's a lotta talk on the place itself between the laborers an' the growers. That's my belief."

"What do you mean?" I asked.

He explained, "Like, you see the growers got some a the people still under this impression, 'Look, we doin' good for you.' A lotta people, they still believe this, an' it's a lie. It isn't true. The growers only doin' what they is *forced* to do. If the minimum wage is a dollar eighty, they pay a dollar eighty an' nothin' above that. But they'll tell the laborers, 'We helpin' you out,' an' some the people fall for it." Gustave shook his head, disgusted. "I guess they never was with Huet on the place. Like the lawsuit or either we try to get a meetin' together to try to better the condition of the workin' man, well, the workers'll never take part but jes' what happen at the meetin', they tell me the growers know it the next mornin'."

"So the workers go back and tell them?" I asked.

"I believe so, an' they really didn't know the purpose of some a the meetin's. It was nothin' against the growers. It was only to get the laborin' people together, fightin' for the same goal. Why should I hurt South Coast? Any job is better 'n no job at all." Gustave shrugged. "But also I wouldn't wanta know there was somethin' I could have—*suppose* to have—an' not be gettin'. If I'm supposed to get a dime or dollar more, I *want* that dollar more because they able to pay it, an' I don't think I'm doin' no harm against the growers. I'm only lookin' out for myself. Well, I don't think the laborers at Hard Times understand that."

When he ended, I turned to Huet. "When we stopped by earlier, one neighbor said he didn't want to get involved."

Viola spoke up, embarrassed, "That was my brother."

"None of 'em want to get involved," Huet said. "I'm disappointed. People I practically was raised up together with, they treat us col', real col'."

"Are they afraid it could happen to them?"

"Could be. I was the only one laid off outta six workers."

I turned to Gustave. "Your employers haven't said anything to you?"

"No, so *far* I haven't had any trouble."

"What about the people you work with, how have they reacted?"

"Some good, some bad," he said. "The ones that understand is all right. The ones that don't—maybe they *might* understand but they jes' don't wanta admit it, an' so sometimes I get called 'Uncle Tom' because a my workin' with Southern Mutual an' Sister Anne."

"Do you think the people are still afraid?" I asked.

Both men agreed, and Gustave explained, "The most of 'em use this excuse: 'This isn't my house. If I go such-an'-such place or if I do such-an'-such thing an' they put me out this house, what I'm gonna do?' But ever'body that was put off the place, it always was for the better. You can't do no badder because we're still at the point we jes' survivin'.'" He looked supportively at Huet.

I glanced at the cardboard boxes, at the old furniture, and beyond that, out the window at the fields. This had been Huet's world since his birth, and I wondered now about his future, his ability to survive.

"I hear you have a new job," I remarked.

Huet's face brightened, and he drew up tall. "I'm a swamper at Avondale Shipyards in Houma. I work on a winch truck movin' stuff. Make *two* forty-five an hour an' I get Blue Cross insurance an' a couple a weeks vacation. *After* ninety days I'll get paid for holidays."

"Do you think life will be easier?"

"I think so," he answered confidently. "I'm workin' much easier an' makin' a little more money. I work nine hours a day, five days a week. This week was my first check, an' I cleared seventy-nine dollars an' twenty-six cents for thirty-five hours. See, I had but four days because of the holiday."

"So you'll be making more than that," I observed.

His excitement showed through his cautious answer. "'Course I'll be payin' out a little more now. Rent's thirty-five dollars."

"But do you think it will be easier feeding the family?"

"I don't know," Viola said uncertainly. "I'm gonna have to wait an' see because I'm pretty far behind. He was outta work so long with no money comin' in."

"How did you make it?"

She sighed, bewildered. "I don't know myself. I ax my own self that. I jes' don't know. 'Course, we get food stamps—"

Huet added, "An' my grandfather, he helped me too. I owe him right now 'bout ten for the light meter at the new place, an' the gas meter was—" He turned to Viola. "How much?"

"Twenty-two fifty."

"Lotta time we had beans an' no meat so I'd go huntin', fishin'. I'd tell her, 'Baby, put my rice on, I'm gonna go out an' kill us a rabbit.' I'd go out, bring back a rabbit or maybe a coon or a possum or a squirrel—anything big enough to eat. An' me an' her'd skin 'em."

"Did you go every day?"

"Yeah," he answered, then chuckled. "Night. Use' to go at nights, which was against the law, but I'd go 'cause that was all the meat we'd have, me huntin' an' fishin'. Sometime I'd go with two shells, jes' two."

"You had to make sure you had a good hit."

"I've already had jes' one," he said with pride.

"Do you think you'll like having your own place and being off the plantation?"

Viola's face brightened. "It be kinda small, but I'll manage. I rather be somewhere I'm welcome."

In the doorway, the girls grinned and giggled. Huet looked at them and smiled. "I never was afraid on the plantation to say what I wanted, to speak like I wanted, because I'm a free man," he said. "That's one reason I lost my job. I really do think so." He paused, then added, "But I don't hold no grudge or nothin' against 'em. I was livin' in *their* house. Matter a fact, I went an' talked with one of the bosses yesterday. Me an' him shook hands an' he wished me luck. He tol' me, 'Huet, you're a good worker. I hope you understand I had to. If it was me—I understand ever'body want a better livin' condition. Anything I can do to help, let me know.' *That* was the older brother. I think really he understood. But his brother—" Huet shook his head. "He jes' couldn't understand. Look like to him it felt like I jes' took a shotgun an' put it to his head. Before the lawsuit, me an' the younger brother use' to talk around the farm sometime, an' we use' to play softball. He'd get a glove an' catch a few balls. But now he'll hardly speak to me. One time he ax me why I'm doin' this to him. I tol' him, 'I'm not doin' anything to you. All I'm tryin' to do is help my family an' myself. Look at your house. Look how nice it is. I got more kids 'n you, an' you makin' a lot more money 'n I'm makin'. You complainin', you talk about you ain't makin' enough. What about me?'"

"What did he say?"

"Nothin', jes' 'I never thought you'd do this to me.' Last summer when we wasn't workin' I axed him for a paper to take my wife to the doctor. He tol' me jes' like this, 'Oh, you need me now, huh?' I said, 'Look, I jes' need a paper to take my wife to the doctor.' He say, 'Awwww, you think I oughta give you one?' An' he kept on talkin'. So I say, 'Forget about it,' an' walked off. He called me back an' he give it to me, but I come home an' her an' me had a talk an' she say, 'I don't want you to use that paper. I rather stay here sick if you can't take me to the doctor without this.' But I did. Paid for it outta money I had for food stamps an' took the medicine out on credit. Monday mornin' I brought him back the paper. He said, 'Well you coulda used it.' An' I said, 'I didn't want to.' He lef' an' come back an' me an' him talked. He was talkin' about the newspaper—"

"The articles I wrote?" I asked.

Huet nodded. "He said, 'You know some a the things ain't true.' I said, 'Like what?' An' he tol' me, 'They had in the paper that one a my men came to me an' axed me for some money to get food stamps'—which I knew *then* he was talkin' about me, so when he finish talkin' I said, 'Wait, it's true 'cause *I* came to you an' axed you for some money to get my food stamps, an' you tol' me no, you ain't had no money.' I called the date to him an' ever'thing, but he tol' me, 'I'll never forget about that.'"

Gustave interrupted. "People that work, I don't think they should be on food stamps. Now I'm not *against* food stamps," he quickly clarified. "I'm for food stamps for like elderly people and disabled, but if I get out there an' I work forty hours a week, I should be gettin' money that I would be able to walk in a store an' buy what I want without usin' food stamps."

The room was quiet as he finished. Huet's and Viola's eyes met in agreement. In the doorway the older children listened, awed at the humiliation, the indignation expressed by their elders.

When I asked Huet if he regretted filing the lawsuit, he was honest. "There was a bunch a times I maybe thought that way. It seemed like I had caught myself in a trap. No work. No food for the kids. I kinda felt bad. A nickel a day is better 'n nothin'. I thought that way for a while, but it passed. I said you wanted to do it, you did it."

"Now you're glad?"

A smile warmed his face. "I have no regrets," he said. "It was somethin' that had to be did. If it had to be done again, I would."

"So you feel good about moving?"

Huet's brow creased. "I hate to move," he answered slowly, firmly. "I knew it'd happen sooner or later, but I hate to move. I'll miss the farm."

From outside came the sound of workers in the field fertilizing the cane, which, come October, would be ready to cut. In between, the ground around the stalks would be worked and reworked— when it wasn't raining—and in August and September the cane for next year's harvest would be planted. But Huet would no longer be part of that cycle.

The Move

*First the sway-backed beds, then the worn sofas, the odds-
and-ends chairs and tables, the old stove and refrigerator, the
jelly glasses and mismatched dishes. From the house on Little
Texas, into Woodrow Brown's pickup, and on to Napoleonville. Two trips was all it took: Huet and Elton Berry lifting
and loading, Viola and Huet's mother helping. Neighbors
peeked from curtains' edges, but no one ventured outside into
yards or onto porches. There were no offers to help,* no *lots a
luck,* no *good-byes as the battered old truck pulled onto the
highway and moved toward Napoleonville, toward the outside
world. Huet and Viola, silent, solemn, bounced in the truck's
cab, and in back, spilling over, were somebody else's castoffs—
all they had to show for ten years of marriage, thirty years of
living.*

1978

Woman in the field

The Reunion

Up and down Highway 1, shopping centers and subdivisions had eaten into the cane. In a corner of Rienzi, in the fields where Lulu King once played and worked, a TG&Y stood next to a Winn-Dixie supermarket and a record shop, and brick homes and paved streets backed up to the land on which Fillmore and Mattie Jones's shack once squatted, vacant now except for weeds waiting to be plowed under. The Joneses and their neighbors were gone. Some had been transplanted to the next road, to homes little better than the old ones; others—Mattie and Fillmore among them—had left for good. Yet for the most part, cane still ruled and the land and lives remained unchanged. Down dirt roads, away from highways and out of sight, shacks huddled in misery, boards and bones commiserating, creaking, bowing, breaking—growing older. Some workers had retired, some had died, others had moved, but many remained, geographically and economically, where they had been when we met almost six years before.

The cost of living had outdistanced wage increases; thus, pockets were poor and dreams unfulfilled.

So it was along Bayou Lafourche and the Teche when I returned in June 1978. Some houses had been painted or replaced, some bathrooms had been installed, and many workers now received paid vacations, but the improvements had come out of pressure, not a change of heart, for the grower remained "Boss" and the worker "Boy," with all that the relationship implied. Any attempt to alter the status quo still met with resistance and resentment. SMHA's presence was no less controversial. Although the Houma hearings had ceased to exist after the Sugar Act expired in 1974, SMHA staffers and the growers continued to clash in the press and sometimes face-to-face. Even some of its own staff members—disillusioned with what they saw as a diversion from SMHA's original aims and purposes—now worked independently among the cane workers. Nevertheless, the organization had gained the support of several agencies, enabling it to broaden its scope. Headquarters for Sister Anne Catherine and Lorna Bourg was a two-story building on Jeanerette's Main Street. Father O'Connell, limited by doctor's orders, worked out of New Orleans while Henry Pelet shuttled back and forth.

The turbulent existence of those involved with the fieldworkers was rewarded by the satisfaction of watching the workers grow into leaders. That growth was perhaps most evident in Gustave and Huet. Although the latter still worked at Avondale Shipyards, he—like Gustave—continued to speak out and to encourage the workers to stick together to better their conditions. The years since we last met had not been easy for them and their families. They had felt the hurt of being isolated and even ridiculed by the very people they were trying to help. But their struggles had paid off. Huet and Viola had bought a modest brick home up the bayou in Dorseyville; Gustave—promoted to mechanic's helper at Elm Hall's shop—had also moved off the plantation, into a house that had belonged to Beverly's parents and which he and friends had repaired.

On my first Sunday back in the area, Gustave was buoyant as he and Beverly hosted Henry Pelet and the Freemans and me. He greeted us proudly at the door of the frame house across from Beautiful Zion Baptist Church in Napoleonville and showed us through its living room, paneled and linoleumed, with new furniture bought on the installment plan. The smells of baked ham and frying chicken and garden vegetables filled the kitchen as the five of us and the Freemans' fourteen-year-old daughter, Shirley, sat at the table, talking, reminiscing, catching up. In the background, Beverly, with the help of her youngsters, finished preparing potato salad and stuffed eggplant. Matthew, nearing the end of childhood, poured tea into ice-filled glasses.

When I asked what was happening with the young people, whether they were going to work in the fields, Gustave answered no. "I can't say about other places," he said, "but here you're not findin' too many youngsters that are stayin' on the plantation. Most of 'em are leavin'." He glanced proudly at Matthew and David and Rodney. No longer the playful boys I had watched feeding the hogs, they now were tall and slender, neatly dressed in the vested suits they had worn to church. "The school board an' the system is now that a kid *must* go to school till he's sixteen years old. So, well, once he's sixteen, then he's got another mind. He don't wanta be workin' in the fields. I don't know about the rest of 'em, but I know mines 'cause they don't even wanta get out there an' cut grass in the yard!" He chuckled in a tone that conveyed pride.

During a lull in the conversation we could hear the scraping of spoons against pots and the opening and closing of the oven door—the air was as heavy with remembrance as it was with the fragrance of food.

"How long have you known one another?" I asked the three men.

Henry tilted his head, and his eyebrow arched. "I've known Gustave since the mid-sixties. Huet, I didn't know until the lawsuit."

"I'd say Huet an' I been knowin' one another a lifetime," Gustave said, and Huet nodded. "Now we become more closer together durin' the lawsuit because we had somethin' in common we could talk about. We could share our thoughts, our true feelin's among ourselves. It was kinda a tryin' experience for the two a us, an' also at the house with the wife. She say, 'One a these days these people gonna put you off the place because they'll think you goin' too far.'" He chuckled. "This is Beverly. An' at the time I say, 'Well, maybe I am goin' a little far, but if I have someone else to go along with me maybe we still can go further.'"

Beverly grinned self-consciously. "I was afraid the boss was goin' to ask us to leave, and then, after Gustave filed the lawsuit an' nobody said anything, well, I encouraged him. I *been* encouragin' him ever since."

I turned to Huet. "Did you feel badly toward Gustave for having asked you to do it?"

"No," he said positively. "I jes' felt badly because the people I was tryin' to help, look like they jes' ignored me, hardly wanted to talk to me. Things I was tryin' to tell 'em they'd go back an' tell the man I was workin' for. That hurted me. But I feel this way now: There's a lot more still needs to be did on the farm, but it can't be done by someone jes' sittin' down thinkin' about it. We have to all join hands an' take action."

Gustave agreed. "We need to be organized among ourselves, an' then I think we can be more stronger together. We are too divided. One person get out to do somethin'—one or two peoples— an' they are usually called 'Uncle Tom.' I had that called to me a lot of times. An 'cheese eater.'"

"I haven't heard that one," I observed.

"That mean you talk to the man that you is under an' he is over you—that mean I would go to him an' talk about Henry, say, to make my way good," Gustave explained. "But then all this would relate right back to some a the hearin's. I know many time when changes come, we sittin' out there on a tractor, we didn't know where the changes come from. We say, 'The growers *had* to do this for us, they got to do this.' They didn't have to do nothin'! It was pressure put on the growers that made them kinda change. All this come through Southern Mutual Help Association gettin' people to know what was goin' on. I think because a this the people begin to be treated a little better because the growers see somebody payin' close attention to what was happenin' to the people on the plantation, where before, it didn't seem like anybody was interested."

When I asked Huet and Gustave how much back pay they had received after the lawsuit, Huet couldn't remember, but Gustave was positive. "I *never* forget: I got eight dollars! Some a the workers got high was two hundred an' fifty dollars."

"Eight dollars, after all of that!" I exclaimed.

"If I'd been a man with the least little bit a money I woulda framed it," he said.

Beverly broke in, "You kept it a *long* time."

"Yeah, I tried, I really tried without framin' it to keep it an' the envelope they give it to me in." His eyes brightened. "I wanted to keep it for years an' years to come, but, well, I jes' had to use it, an' I can tell you *how* I used it. When things got *real* tight at the house an' we was lookin' all around where we could get some money, I thought about those eight dollars. I went an' got 'em out an' I said to Bev, 'Well we have no alternative, we have to use this.' That was to buy food—bread, milk, rice, beans, whatever, far as it went."

"How long did you wait?"

He cocked his head and thought. "Lessee, we musta got that money back in August or September, so we had a lotta work then 'cause like we was jes' goin' into cane plantin' an' right outta cane plantin' into harvest, so I didn't have no real dire need for it. So it was February, late February. I remember because I muscled out January."

"I remember you sayin' if you could jes' hold onto it till March," Beverly offered.

"Yeah," he agreed, "there's an ol' sayin' on the plantation if you can make it through January an' February you can march out on your own, because that's the time when work begin to open up. So I say if I can hold it jes' a *little* longer, but then the rains start pourin' an' it start to get colder an' I wasn't workin'. I think I had took with a sore throat also, an' the few days there was work I wasn't able. So that's when I had to spend it."

As Beverly set the table, Gustave smiled fondly at her. "We done have some really good times together, an' we done have some rough times. I hear people say 'the good ol' days'! Well, the good ol' days was good back then, but I more prefer these days." He shook his head slowly. "Some a the things I like to remember, but the most of 'em I like to forget. When you livin' in a planta- tion house you never become a man. You're always a boy-man. I really believe that by movin' into my own house, I'm beyond that boy-man. *I'm* a man. If somethin' happen today, onliest thing I have to do is look for me another job, an' that makes me jes' a little bit more above the guy that's livin' on the place."

Huet watched quietly, nodding agreement. Finally he said:

"Things is a whole lot different. Now I stand on my *own* feet. Before, when the grower use' to tell me somethin', I couldn't say what I really was thinkin', but now I can tell him right back. I don't have half the money he have, but I'm jes' as much a man as the grower are."

The Homecoming

Curtis and Margaret Singleton's house and yard were surrounded by cane fields, but they were not part of a plantation,
even though the house itself was shabby and reminiscent of
those on Hard Times. The porch and steps were unpainted
and in need of repair; the brick-paper covering was torn.
Faded cotton curtained the screenless windows and door. The
large yard was a patchwork of weeds and parched earth, cluttered with old appliances and automobiles. To one side, in
the shade of a tree, three men—one bare-chested, the others
in T-shirts—were occupied with the guts of a battered Ford,
while Viola and Margaret Singleton, Huet's younger sister,
kept an eye on nine or ten children of all ages and sizes as they
ran in and out of the house and through the yard yelling and
squealing. In the center of the yard, on two wooden benches
shaded by a large oak tree, I sat talking with Huet, his thirty-
nine-year-old brother Joe "Peanut" Freeman, and their uncle
Claiborne Preston. Peanut was small, wiry, and somewhat
brash, with short hair and a trim mustache. He had returned
on vacation from Oakland, California, where he worked for
Mack Trucks, and admiration for him shone on the faces of

his relatives, admiration for his fine clothes—the bright green slacks and color-coordinated print shirt—and for the way he talked so boldly about the growers' treatment of his people.

"They took my ass outta school 'cause I use' to have to take care of Huet-P an' Horace an' Valeria while my mama worked," he said, sneering. "She was workin' for Miz LeBlanc in the house. She'd go there an' scrub up clothes an' wash Carol an' Suzanne's ass. Ever' time they needed somethin' she had to go take care of 'em. I missed out on all *my schoolin' because a them, an' I have a attitude about it. Always had, from a young man. But I never had the opportunity to sit down wit' Carol an' Suzanne an' rap about this, you know. I really wanta tell 'em how I feel about their parents*, really."

"Do you feel bitter?" I interrupted.

"Bitter?" He laughed sarcastically. "Yeah, an' dig this: I mean they *really hurt me, because I have all the good opportunity, you know. Like I get the best of jobs without the education, but I coulda been the mayor or the president, I believe*," he boasted. "An' that kinda shit really, really freaks me out! Right now—today—my mother's still doin' it. I ain't seen her in about three, four years, an' I come here all way from California to see *her, an' she went to work for Miz LeBlanc half a day anyway. An' I'm out here to see her! She's still doin' it. An' you know what it is now?"* He became indignant. "It's Suzanne an' Carol's chil'ren! She's bringin' them *up, she's raisin' them."* He kicked at the dirt. "Shit! Ever'time I'd get to trippin' on Suzanne an' them I'd get to fightin' an' get put in jail. I mean I had a attitude—you can check my record down here in Napoleonville. Seriously, I hadda get from around here before I lose my thing an' jes' go up there an' get me one a them guns an' blow all of 'em away. Ever'time I come around here I get attitudes. I don't have a attitude behind whites. It's behind *these people that misuse my ma like this an' still doin' it. This is my attitude—yes, this shit here. When you look around an' see all this shit still goin' on. You'd expect there'd be a little bit a change, but it's really still goin' on.*"

On the Porch

The wheelchair raced down the narrow dirt road, a cloud of dust behind it. The young man's legs ended just below his torso, yet he appeared unfazed by the handicap. He pushed forcefully on the wheels, his face reflecting obvious delight with the speed and the breeze it created. When he was in front of the house, he waved and then returned his hand to the wheel, thrusting it forward, hard, for new momentum.

"That's Willie Dowell," Huet said softly. "You remember, the tractor driver what got his legs burnt off?"

I nodded.

"He an' his mama live next door. He work on lawn mowers sometime, but mostly he don't do too much."

Only gray light was left of the day. A slight breeze cooled the land and the people, and the peace and freedom that evening brings had settled on them. From farther down the road came the laughter of playing children and the barks and growls of a community of dogs trotting side by side, occasionally stopping for one to sniff another. And from nowhere, yet everywhere at once, a chorus of crickets heralded the approaching dark.

Those of us on Mabel and Andrew Williams's porch watched as the young man coasted past. Then Mabel leaned toward Jessie Preston, her knees touching his as she moved her lips close to his ears, to make him hear. The old man sat rigid against a straight-back chair, his palms resting flat on his thighs, his bony head and shoulders slightly bowed. He seemed oblivious to the others seated on the porch, for his eyes and ears had all but shut out the world around him. His upper lids were permanently closed, and the lowers drooped and watered. He strained to hear his daughter as she patiently struggled to make him understand my questions and then to translate his mumbles and grunts into answers. The process was slow and tedious, yet neither became impatient. Huet and his stepfather, Andrew, looked on quietly, sometimes assisting in the interpretation, occasionally contributing a recollection of their own.

Florida Preston also watched, speaking only in response to the questions asked her. She and Jessie Preston shared the cramped little house with Andrew and Mabel and their youngest son and his wife and children. To one side, their neighbors were Gustave's brother, and to the other, past Willie Dowell's, Gustave's mother and sister. Mama Shug had changed little since I first met her. Unlike her husband, she remained alert and spry at eighty-three. Her body and face were full and fat, and her heavy bosom sagged from nursing eight children. Fuzzy knots of white hair sprinkled her head like dotted swiss, and she wore a faded print housedress, yellow bedroom slippers, and gold loop earrings. Her mouth was firmly set, and her eyes were piercing and determined.

Mabel Williams had inherited that same strength. She was short and bouncy, yet she stood erect and held her head high. Even before the Civil Rights Act gave her permission, she had spoken her mind with a forcefulness that surpassed her size. She was the mother of eight children—four by Huet's father, four by Andrew Williams—but at fifty-six she remained girlish in appearance. Her graying hair was neatly braided in cornrows, and her eyes were vivid and intense as she peered at her father through gold-framed granny glasses.

"Patsy—" she started.

"Huh?"

"*Patsy,* this her name, Patsy—she wanta know *when* you first start workin' how *ol'* you was?"

"How ol' I was?" the old man repeated, his voice husky and bewildered.

"Yeah, how ol' you was when you begin in the fields?"

Jessie Preston grunted.

" 'Bout thirteen?" Mabel asked.

"Thirteen or fo'teen," he rumbled. "Was a water boy."

With an air of importance, Mabel turned to me. "You want me to tell you how it was?"

"Yes."

"You see, they had what they call a water cart. Then they had a barrel on the cart, you know, with a faucet on it, an' they had tin cups. They use' to make most of 'em outta milk cans. They use' to shave a stick an' bore a hole in that can all way through at the top, an' that was the handles, an' you dip your water, draw your water from that barrel. No ice, you understand. Jes' water," she explained. "Well, that was a water boy, an' they go around the quarters an' pick up the people's breakfast. Like the women fix their husband breakfast in the mornin', they'd put their breakfast in a little ten-cents bucket an' carry that out to the field to the workin' people."

"Did he ever work in the fields, did he do cutting?"

"Now wait, I'm gonna get it good for you," she said. She moved closer to Jessie and placed her hands on his. "Look—you ever cut cane?"

"Did I ever cut cane? Yeaaaah." The answer rumbled from deep within. "Yeah, I cut cane."

Pleased, Mabel continued. "All right. What other kinda work you did?"

"Ever'thing to be did in the field!" he answered forcefully, the corners of his mouth curling. Huet and Andrew Williams laughed, and the old man's grin swelled into a chuckle. "Ditch, shovelin' ditches—done ever'thing!" Again he gave a deep, gravelly chuckle, and the rest of us joined in.

"Did he work with mules?" I asked.

"Yeah, you want somethin' on that?"

I nodded.

"What kinda work you ever done with mules?"

"Cut a little cane an' mind the stable," he said, then the words dwindled to mumbling.

Mabel prodded. "What about the teamster's job? *Teamster* —carried the people to the fields to work? Use' to carry the people—"

"People?"

"In—the—field," Mabel emphasized each word.

The old man's words become more distinct. "That's my business, fieldwork. I can remember at Wildwood. That's my biggest fieldwork I can remember. I was eighteen, seventeen."

"How *long* did you work in the fields? How ol' you was when you stop?"

"How ol' I was?"

"Yaaass, how ol' you was when you stop workin'?"

"I can't remember how *ol'* I was when I stop," he started uncertainly, "'cause I got on security when I was sixty-five—I *know*— but then I kep' a-goin', I kep' on a-goin'."

Mabel turned to me. "You got that?" I nodded, and she continued. "How ol' you was when you stop it all?"

Jessie Preston cocked his head, thinking, straining to remember. "Seventy-two, seventy-four—when I stop altogether. They was givin' me a *dollar a day* to wake the people up—that's the last work I did. They was givin' me that to pay my light bill. Got up at fo' an' went 'round an' call the people."

"They gave him that to hold the house?" I concluded.

Together, Huet and his mother answered "Yeah."

"Why did he stop working the fields?"

"He wasn't able to," Mabel said, her voice flat. "I can remember that. He jes' wasn't able to go no more." The flatness left, and she became indignant. "Now listen, after he wasn't able to work in the field no more, the boss man give him this job jes' for him to be doin' somethin', to go an' wake up the people. Now the man was payin' Papa's light bill—it was five or ten dollars; it doesn't matter *what* it was. He was payin' this bill for him an' givin' him one dollar a day. That was six dollars. Now when somebody *else* come along an' say Papa was too ol' to do it, to give *him* that dollar a day to do it, well, Papa didn't have anything else to do on the plantation but make his garden."

"Then did they charge him rent?" I asked.

Andrew Williams answered for his wife. "Yeah, C.J. an' them charged him rent. That's when Mister Bill died."

"Yas," Mabel agreed. "They charged him rent, an' he had to pay all his utility bills outta whatever the government was givin' him. Had to pay for gas an' lights. The water was pump water, a 'lectric pump on the place."

"Can you ask him how he felt about working all his life in the fields and then having nothing when he got through?" I asked.

Mabel leaned near her father. "Now listen, how you felt when you had to move?"

The old man's face and his voice grew sad. "I didn't wanta move!"

"After you done worked, after you done spent your *lifetime* on the plantation—how you felt about movin'?" Mabel pressed.

"I *hadda* move!"

"But how you felt about that?"

The old man's sadness spread to Huet and Andrew. They waited and watched.

"I felt like— I didn't wanta move! But I hadda go wit' you 'cause I wasn't able to take care a myself anymo'!" His words deteriorated into an emotional jumble.

Andrew Williams broke in. "The boss man tol' him *that* was his house long as he live!"

"Why, *why* you didn't wanta leave?" Mabel asked.

As though he was going through it again, Jessie Preston pleaded for understanding. "Well that place, I been there *so* long. You un'erstand? I been there so long, feel like I'm leavin' ever'thing. An' I got nothin'. An' I didn't wanta leave. But I hadda leave. I *hadda* leave. Been there *so* long. I couldn't take care myself. What was I gonna do? They gonna tear the house down, an' they turn off all the 'lectricity an' I *gotta* leave."

Huet explained, "To get 'em to leave they cut all the 'lectricity off back there."

"He didn't wanta leave *then*," Andrew repeated bitterly. "They went down there an' took the heaters to be sure they leave. An' it was cold *that* night!"

At fifty-six, Andrew Williams was himself unable to work as a result of three hernia operations and his deteriorating eyesight. But ironically, those same impairments had enabled him and Mabel to make the down payment on their home with money from his veterans' disability pension. He was tall and handsome, with graying hair and mustache and blue-tinted glasses that enhanced his stately manner and shielded his blindness. Although he had been raised up the bayou on Belle Alliance Plantation and had gone to work at age ten, he had never liked fieldwork. As a youngster, he kept up his studies at night, and at seventeen he went to live in New Orleans for three years before enlisting in the military. He returned to the cane fields in 1946 after meeting the recently widowed Mabel and remained until 1972, when his health forced him to quit. Since then, he and Mabel had lived on the veterans' pension, his Social Security payments, and Mabel's earnings from housework.

Shaking his head sadly, Jessie continued to mutter, "They cut the meters, the light meter, an' the water pump. They cut that off. No water an' no lights, nothin' but the house if I stay."

"They did that before they left?" I asked.

"Oh, no," Mabel said quickly. "*When* I got the news that they was gonna do it the next week—they warned 'em about it—I commenced to hustlin'. They axed 'im to leave, but he said he *weren't* goin' *no*where!"

Andrew Williams again explained, "Mister Bill had give him that place for a *life*time."

"You see, the man what own the place, he *told* Papa that was *his* home jes' as long as he live," Mabel continued. "But this man died, you understand, an' he didn't tell that to his brother an' them 'cause I guess he figgered his brother would do the same 'cause the life was from one plantation to the other—all in the family. So the brother took over, and he leased this plantation what Papa was livin' on to another man, and well, Papa couldn't work, so he jes' hadda search for his own self."

Four years had passed since the workers were moved off and the shacks on Hard Times boarded up, yet every detail of the uprooting was vivid in Mabel's memory. "Huet-P stayed till he made sure Papa had somewheres to go. An' well, Papa commenced to gettin' worried when he seed ever'body goin'. He told me, 'Well this stuff must be real.' I say, 'It *is* real.'"

As Mabel spoke, Mama Shug rose slowly from her chair and scurried across the porch and into the house, her slippers brushing against the floor. The day's grayness had thickened to dark, and from inside she turned on a porch light, then her footsteps faded farther into the house. Attention drifted from Jessie Preston, and for a time he sat alone with his thoughts. When I glanced his way, Huet had edged his chair close to his grandfather's. With both hands he caressed the old man's head, then drew it close to his chest and hugged him. Neither spoke; neither had to.

I turned to Mabel, not wanting to intrude and yet anxious to talk more with Jessie Preston. "What did your father think about Huet's lawsuit? Did he know about it?"

"Wait, let me see how could I ask him that." Mabel's forehead crinkled. "Patsy wanta know what you thought about Huet-P when he sued the agriculture—" She turned to me and asked, "That the right word?" I nodded. Again she moved her lips close to his ear. "She wanta know what you thought about him—"

"Huet-P?" the old man interrupted.

"*Yas,* when he sued this place for the people to get more money —*what* you thought about it?"

The old man nodded slowly, slightly. "Huet-P? Sued? He can't sue nobody!"

Mabel tried again. "You 'member when Huet-P hadda move?"

"Yeah," he answered, then waited expectantly.

"All right. The wages went up—well, Huet-P sued the people. What you thought about him doin' that? How you felt?"

The old man mumbled, and Mabel translated. "He ought to ask for more? He oughtn't to have done did it? He did! He axed him for more."

Andrew cut in. "Let me explain it to him a little bit different way." He moved close to his father-in-law. "Look, how you felt when this man Earl Butz, he was *for* the farmers, the farmers was payin' him some hush-mouth money, see. The farmers suppose' to fix those houses, but they didn't fix 'em, an' they wasn't payin' the laborers what they was suppose' to. So that why Huet-P sued the secretary of agriculture which was Earl Butz. How you felt about that?"

Jessie Preston chuckled.

"Yeah, how you felt about that?" Andrew Williams pressed.

"Huet-P was tryin' to better his conditions. He bettered a many,

many more conditions by doin' that. Now how you felt about it?" He waited. "How you felt about your grandson pickin' up enough guts, enough nerve to sue the secretary of agriculture?"

Jumbled sounds streamed from the old man. They seemed to have no meaning, yet Andrew continued conversing with him, nodding his head and repeating what he heard. "You didn't like that? That caused you to get more money . . . Naw, unh-unh, you didn't have to pay no more." Shaking his head, Andrew proceeded in a different direction. "You remember that back time what the farmers was supposed to pay the laborers? They wasn't gonna get that, but by Huet-P doin' what he did, that's why the laborers got theirs. Now you *still* felt he shouldn't did that?"

Finally, slowly, Jessie Preston, answered, "He did right."

Andrew and Mabel smiled.

"What about when Huet was fired?" I asked, but Jessie talked on without prompting.

"It bettered him conditions."

Andrew added, "An' many more. Now how you felt when Huet-P got fired from his job?"

"Off his job?" Jessie Preston echoed. "I felt *bad*. Had to work it through."

"He worked it through. He won!" Andrew said, to the rest of us on the porch as much as to Jessie Preston. "It woulda been bad if he hadn't got it through, but he got it through."

A smile came to the old man's lips.

"Yeah."

"That's My Son!"

The porch light defined the roundness of Mabel Williams's cheeks as a smile of motherly pride brightened her face.

"Yes ma'am, I'm proud of him! I don't know what it's all about on account a the readin' an' writin' stuff, but I'm proud of him." *She leaned forward confidingly and placed her hand on my knee.* "Now while we're talkin', let me tell you what happen, honey. Those ol' houses on Hard Times—You know about them houses. After I got this land with the he'p of the Lawd, I axed the boss man to sell me one of those ol' houses. He tol' me he couldn't. I say, 'You mean to tell me you can't sell me one a them ol' houses?' He say, 'If I could do anything with 'em I'd give you one.' I say, 'Why you can't sell me one?' He say, 'Do you know that Freeman boy?' " *She sat up straighter.* "Then I got real proud, I'm gonna tell you that. Well he say, 'Do you know that Freeman boy?' I say, 'That Freeman boy?' He say, 'Yeah.' Now, honey, I done work for this man when Huet-P was a baby, an' he know Huet-P is a Freeman. I say, 'Yeah, I know him.' He say, 'Well that boy got ever'thing here all tied up.' I say, 'That's why you can't sell me one a these houses, because

*a the Freeman boy?' He say, 'Yeah.' I say, 'Mister Sonny,' I
say, 'you see that Freeman boy?' I say, 'That's my son!' He say,
'Well I be doggone. That's your son?' An' I say, 'Yas, sir!' He
mighta thought he was hurtin' me, but I felt proud to tell him,
'Yas, I know that Freeman boy. That's my son!'"*

The Prayer Meeting

Moaning—a woman's, faint and without words—drifted from the living room, gradually swelling into a hymn so permeated with emotion it became a prayer, Mama Shug's prayer. "*Oh, Lawd! Oh, Lawd! Ooooooooh, Lawd! Oh, death laaaaay down for me.*" Her full, rich voice reached into the darkness, drawing Andrew Williams into the house. His deep bass hum accompanied her voice, yet never overpowered it. "*Oh, Lawd! Ooooh! Oh, Lawd!*" The duet swelled into a chorus as others from the porch joined them, until only Huet and Mabel and I remained outside.

"Mama's ready to have prayer meetin'," Mabel announced. She led the way, motioning me to a chair just inside the doorway. Mama Shug sat in a metal folding chair, her ankles crossed and her hands clasped in her lap. Next to her, Jada Janise swung her short legs back and forth under her chair, her eyes pursuing an occasional roach across the floor. Andrew Williams knelt before a sofa, resting his elbows on its seat and bowing his head in his cupped hands. As Huet sat next to him, his stepfather recited the Lord's Prayer. The others watched but no one stood to help as Jessie Preston entered from the back of the house. Slowly he felt his way into the room, tapping his cane along the linoleum, his feeble left hand tracing the door frame, the television, and finally a simple wooden rocker. Steadying himself with the cane, he turned around and eased into the seat. He rested the cane against the wall, gripped the rocker's arm, and bowed his head slightly. Then the twisted old lips parted and from them came a mournful "*ooooooh*" that rose and fell and rose again.

Andrew Williams's prayer became almost a sermon as the others merged their voices with Jessie's—wailing, moaning, pleading, sometimes echoing. "Oh, Gawd, my heavenly Father, wanta thank Thee for last night You watch over my body *all* night long . . . whilst I slumber an' slept. An' sometime this mornin' You touched me with the button a nature, an' my eyes was open an' I seen a *brand* new day which I never seen before! Lawd, I thank Thee! Oh, heavenly Father, when I rose up I found my bed was not my coolin' board, my soul was not required into Your judgment, my body was not consumed to the cemetery. Oh, Father! I thank Thee!"

"*OOoooOOOOOHhhhhhh!*"

"Father, I know You have heard me pray days that have passed an' gone. An' You told me whensoever I bow down on my knees an' pray an' pray right, You'll be a pray-healin' savior. An' You're no shorter than Your word. Oh, heavenly Father, beggin' You to search in me, search my heart, an' if Your eyes behold anything around my heart like sin, I beg You bid it depart!"

"Yes, Lawd!"

"Oh, Lawd, cast it *way* out in the seas of forgiveness!"

"*Well, yes!*"

"Beggin' You please to have mercy!"

"*Mercy!*"

"Father, keep my feet on the narrow path a righteousness! Keep my hands *close* to Your gospel plow. Some day sooner or later I'll be able to plow a straight furrow from earth onto bright glory. Beggin' You please to have mercy."

"*Have mercy!*"

"*Ooooooooooooooh!*"

In the background, Mama Shug began to sing softly, ". . . *If I can't goooooo home, Lawd, if I can't go home . . .*"

"An' oh, heavenly Father, when it be all over, Father, when I did *all* You commend to my hand to do, come to testify. Oh heavenly Father, You tol' me You were to be a lamp to my feet an' a light to my pathway. Jes' shine Your light upon the road that I travel. For Christ, our Redeemer's sake, a-men, an' thank Gawd."

As Andrew Williams rose to sit on the sofa, Mama Shug led the spirited singing. "*Sail oooon, my Gawd, sail on . . .*" The voices moved strongly through the spiritual as Stacey mumbled a quick, dutiful prayer and then returned to her seat. Only when Mama Shug labored to her knees and intoned the Lord's Prayer did the voices gradually fade into a soft hum. The old woman's fat hands covered her eyes as she chanted: "Oooooooooh, Lawd, You said ever' knee must bow an' ever' tongue must confess for to give account of the days that are done an' gone—have mercy, Lawd. *Ooooooh, Laaaawd!*"

"*Lawd!*"

Mama Shug's voice soared. "Oh, our heavenly Father, I am weak, Jesus, but You are strong, askin' You to hol' me, Jesus, with Your powerful hands, if it is Your holy will. Have mercy! Ooooooh, our heavenly Father, You say that You was a man a war an' the Lawd Gawd is Your name. You have been in many battles an' You have lost ne'er a one, askin' You to fight my everlastin' battles if it is Your holy will, Jesus."

The chorus swelled.

"Oh, our heavenly Father, You know the secret a my heart an' You know the content a my mind, Jesus. Askin' You when me, Your servant, will be done goin' an' comin', when this ol' world can't afford me a home no longer, askin' You, my Father, go down to the chilly borders of Jordan wit' me."

"*Please!*"

"Askin' You, our Father, please command Your understudy an' tell me Your servant to cross over."

The room was quiet as the old woman's voice lowered. "Hear my prayer, for Christ sake, our Lawd, a-men, thank Gawd! Have mercy."

"Mercy, Lawd!"

Now Huet knelt, chanting as he did. ". . . far from home an' all this world go free." The others picked up the cue and sang, their voices discordant and dragging, "*Must Jeeeesus bear the cross alo-ooone . . . an' all the world go free?*" The pace quickened. "*No!*

There's a cross for everyone, an' there's a cross for me." The singing continued, the tempo at times lively, at times mournful— almost drowning out Huet's animated conversation with God.

"Father, I know that I have a time too. I'm jes' here temporary. Father, while I'm here, able me to take care of my family!"

"Yes, Lawd!"

"Jes' give me wisdom. I want You to teach me, Lawd. *Teach* me so I may be able to teach my kids. I jes' wanta be able to raise them in a Gawd-fearin' manner." He pleaded, "I don't want them to be brought up like I were, Father, I'm doin' my best!"

"Yes, Lawd!" the others vouched.

"Give me the power to carry on!"

"Give him power!"

"I realize sometime it's gonna be hard, but jes' able me, jes' bear with me, jes' to go through it, Father, *please!*"

"Please, Lawd!"

His voice softened. "Father, when I die, I don't wanta go to hell!" he begged. "I wanta enter Your kingdom. When I come to die, jes' fix my heart—please, please! to give me life! In Jesus Christ name, thank Gawd, a-men."

The room stilled again. Jessie tossed a small pillow to the floor near his feet, and his voice wobbled, "Oh, how I love Jesus. Ooooooh, how I *love Jesus*." A family of voices joined in. "Oh, how I love *Jesus,* be-cause He first loved me. I heard the vo-ice of Jesus say, come unto Me an' *rest*. Come on thou wear-y an' lie down, thy head upon My breast."

Mabel clapped twice and raised her voice to start the refrain. *"Sinnnngin'—ohhhh, how I love Jesus. Oh, how I looooove Jesus! Ooooh, how I love Jesus, because He first loved me."*

Still singing, Jessie strained to raise himself from the rocker, at times his voice rising above the others, echoing or punctuating the verse.

"I oncet was lost but now I'm found, was blind but now I seeee."

"I see!" he echoed, lowering himself to his knees.

"I heard the voice of Jesus say come unto me an' rest. Oooooooh, how I love Jesus."

The singing softened as Jessie muttered a prayer. "Lawd! Jes' set me free," he pleaded, "so I can go home! Have mercy!"

"Oh, how I love Jesus!"

"Ooooooooooh, Lawd! I neeeeeed you sooooooo much! Ooooooh, Lawd, JeeeeeeeeSUSSSSSSSS!"

"*. . . because He first loved me!*"

The old man struggled to his feet and raised his closed eyes upward.

"Thank You, now."

Paying His Respects

Late one afternoon, that summer of 1978, Huet visited the cemetery. He squatted beside the grave, a plain, oblong concrete box. A spray of plastic flowers and a simple cross marked its head. Silently, thoughtfully, he studied the cross and its primitively printed epitaph:

CLEVLAND BENJAMOM
BORN   10-4-38
DIED   12-2-72

1992

A worker's home

Epilogue

When the book was published in the autumn of 1981, the cane
workers and I marked the occasion with a party at the black
Masonic Hall in Napoleonville. Each person was presented a copy
with a marker at the place where he or she was mentioned so
that even the illiterate could see their names in print. There
was cake and punch and speeches, and then I invited the audience to accompany me to the cemetery to place a yellow wreath
on Cleveland Benjamin's grave. Huet and Gustave led the way,
and when I looked back, the entourage was a block long and we
were halting traffic. Even at that moment in history, the people
in the stopped automobiles must have found us a curious sight:
a crowd of black men, women, and children and three whites:
Henry Pelet, Sister Anne, and me. What I remember most was
the pride on the people's faces, especially Moser Benjamin's. Re-
splendent in white, a turban swathing her head, she was on this
day a noble mother.

More than ten years passed before I again visited cane country, though the people were seldom far from my consciousness. From time to time I would talk by telephone with Sister Anne or Lorna Bourg or Father O'Connell, and we would meet when business brought them to Washington, but it was not until June 1992 that I returned to south Louisiana for a firsthand look at what had happened since my first visits.

I landed in Lafayette and for three days traveled the familiar network of dirt roads. Outside town, I veered right and cut through Broussard, where a For Sale sign stood in front of the convent—Sister Robertine had long since left town. As her involvement with the fieldworkers continued, the sugar establishment had become increasingly hostile until she finally resigned as principal and devoted her time entirely to the cane workers, assisted by another member of her religious order, Sister Imelda Maurer. The latter had shared her friend's anguish long distance, by telephone, before moving to Broussard in August 1973 to work in SMHA's Plantation Adult Education Program. A year later, she too found herself immersed in the controversy when their own order abandoned them because the two insisted on remaining in Broussard. For the next couple of years they supported themselves and their plantation work with Sister Imelda's SMHA salary. When that position ended, they worked at odds-and-ends jobs, at times resorting to food stamps, until their order again offered to support them financially. With time, the two nuns, like Henry Pelet and Father O'Connell, became increasingly anxious to see the fieldworkers organized. While maintaining their concern for the people's overall plight, their efforts moved toward achieving that single goal. First, they would concentrate on the mills. Then, with that as a base, they would move on to the fieldworkers. In January 1976 they succeeded behind the scenes in orchestrating a contract between the Teamsters and mill employees at Cajun Co-op. But in the early 1980s, beaten down by the struggle, Sister Robertine and Sister Imelda moved on to South Carolina to champion the cause of textile workers, abandoning their dream of seeing Broussard's Billeaud Mill organized.

Past Broussard the cane fields began, and for a time I was lost in a great sea of green. It was lay-by time, and the fields were empty, the tractors idle. The cane itself was chest-high, but there was little to hide—most of the shacks had disappeared, replaced by weeds or cane or, along that stretch of Bayou Black Road, by industrial parks and subdivisions. In Patoutville, all but a dozen of the houses had been leveled or boarded up, and when I stopped to inquire into the whereabouts of the workers, a tractor driver told me most had moved to town, into low-income housing, many of them taking other jobs. One machine nowadays could do the work of several men, he explained, and the young folks didn't want to stay on the farm anyhow. He himself loved the farm: he had lived on the same road all his life, as had his parents and his grandparents, even his great-grandparents, and he was content to stay. He had a bathroom and running water, and after forty years in the fields he earned six dollars an hour. "Yes," he said, "they been good to us. They help us out."

On Oaklawn, the company store was closed and only five of the thirty houses still stood. A fieldworker insisted he was still there, on the farm, because he loved the work and his boss treated him well. But when I asked if he would want his children to do the same, he shook his head vigorously. "I don't want 'em followin' behind me," he said. "No way. I want 'em to get more education. Don't let 'em do like their daddy done. No, I never want 'em to be like me." The week before he had worked twenty hours due to rain, and after eighteen years in the fields he earned five dollars an hour—seventy-five cents over minimum wage. While he insisted the pay was fine, his cousin complained, "It's no livin' out here."

Along Bayou Lafourche, one grower had sold his workers a parcel of land and let them move their old houses onto that, but for the most part life continued there as it did on the Teche, with a handful of faithful workers—many beyond finding jobs anywhere else—tending the land. SMHA estimated that less than a third of the once twenty-two thousand work force remained. The rest had essentially disappeared: dead or retired or lost in the anonymity of town—replaced by giant machines, just as Huet's old teacher had predicted.

Gustave was among those who had left the fields. He and Beverly still lived in their little house in Napoleonville, and for the past thirteen years he had worked on the river, as a longshoreman. Before he made the switch, he had first tried working in the fields by day and on the river at night. "What I was making in two weeks, I made in two days," he said. "So I say, 'This is where I'm gonna be at.'" The Sunday Henry and I dropped by, there was the usual parade of people in and out of his house. On this day, the occasion was the baptism of his son David's seven-week-old namesake, and Beverly and Gustave proudly showed off their family: Rodney, now a deputy sheriff, and his three children; David, a pipe fitter, and his two; Cookie, just home from Atlanta with her three-year-old son; Wanda, who lived across the street, with still another grandchild; Tim, retired now from the military; Charlene and Matthew remained single. Three had attended college, and not one had worked in the fields.

When we stopped at the Freemans', Huet was equally pleased with his offspring. Rose worked as a nurse, and Shirley was studying to become one. Jada Janise had just earned a degree in sociology from Dillard University in New Orleans. Only he and Viola and their youngest, seventeen-year-old Greg (born in the interim of the series and my book), were left at home, in the house they had bought after he was fired in 1974. These days Huet was a gardener, and for the first time in years he had worked in the fields during grinding and was full of awe over the ease of the work, thanks to the new technology.

For a time, he and Gustave and Henry and I sat at the kitchen table, recollecting the old days and the folks who had passed on: Mabel Williams, Mama Shug, his grandfather, Tillman Dickinson. We laughed about the leaky roofs, the rotten porches—the way you joke about bad times you no longer have to endure. I asked what had made the two of them different from the other workers, how it was that they always knew they wanted something more and worked toward getting it rather than accepting things as they were, and Gustave answered. "I had some people in New Orleans, an' I use' to visit them," he said, "an' you could see so many other people were livin' so much different from the way I was livin'. I was workin' jes' as hard, I guess, as anybody else, but the livin', the bein' comfortable, wasn't there. I had to live in somebody else's house, an' they could tell me when to go an' when to come an' what I could an' couldn't do. I wanted jes'— even though it could be somethin' small, even this little house, this is mine."

Huet said he had learned something from the experience. "I learned to teach my children how to get the best out of life," he said. "But also sometimes we have to think back to those times in order to make it better now. I tell the children, I look back there an' I say, 'Wow, y'all don't wanta go back there, y'all don't wanta be like this, like I have been.'"

Nevertheless, he conceded that there were times he got homesick, and he vowed if he ever won the lottery he was going to buy Hard Times. We all laughed and asked if he meant the whole plantation or just his old house, and he said, with conviction, the whole plantation. "What I meant was I wish I was livin' with the people I was back there livin' with," he said. "I really miss that. They was good people, my neighbors."

In Thibodaux, from the highway, I could see across the fields to the settlement where Lulu and Willie King had lived. There were fewer houses than before, but against the bright morning sky it could have been twenty years ago. When I came to the tractor ruts that had served as a shortcut between Coulon and Rienzi, I turned and followed them to the houses. I asked a man in the road if the Kings still lived there, and he pointed to the next house. Lulu's son Oliver opened the door, and when he saw me his big, wonderful face widened into a smile and he called over his shoulder, to the others, that the lady who took the pictures was there, and before long the room filled with people: his wife, their two sons, a nephew, a young neighbor. Willie had died in 1978, after my last visit, he told me, and Lulu had passed in 1983. He hurried from the room and returned with a Polaroid of the old woman in her casket, a reproduction of "The Last Supper" lining the lid. Golena was dead, too, and Joyce had grandchildren and was living nearby in Raceland. If only they had known I was coming, more of the family would have been there to meet me. I agreed to come back later, and when I did, two more siblings and a smattering of grandchildren were in the side yard waiting. Lois, the young scrapper who had come in out of the cold the day I interviewed Willie, was forty now, divorced and working in Houma as a clerk-typist. Oliver was the only member of the family still living on the farm—he was retired and paying rent to remain on the place, and the others were glad he did so that they could bring their own children back. He and Lois and their brother Junius talked about growing up on the plantation, not with bitterness but nostalgically. It had taught them how to survive. They were better people for having had the experience. This was their roots.

After forty years of trying to organize the workers, to improve their lot, Henry Pelet had given up on the ones who were left. While their living standards had improved, he doubted they were any better off economically. Most earned thirty to thirty-five dollars a day, and who could live on that? "Practically all of them are getting food stamps," he said. "That's why their living standard has improved, because the federal government since the sixties has increased its programs." If it weren't for that, he didn't know what would happen. The drive for more was gone. "Basically there's nothing to stir the workers up," he said. "There's nobody to work for change. So they just accept it."

Father O'Connell's poor health kept him pretty much confined to New Orleans and out of touch with the situation, but Sister Anne and Lorna Bourg did not share Henry's pessimism. Along the Teche, their efforts were at last beginning to bear fruit. Lorna had just been awarded a MacArthur Fellowship for her work, and the Four Corners Self-Help Housing Project she and Sister Anne had helped found among former plantation women had successfully renovated more than two dozen dilapidated old houses. Even more gratifying was a developing spirit of cooperation between them and a new generation of growers in creating a more viable and environmentally responsible agricultural community where all sides would benefit. Since their colleague Sister Helen Vinton (who joined SMHA after this book was written) organized a thirteen-state conference on sustainable agriculture, local farmers had begun seeking out SMHA. "This is a new generation," Lorna said. "They come in here saying, 'You realize my father won't talk to me because I'm sitting here talking to you, but I've got to find out what you're talking about, because I think you may be on to something.' And they'll say, 'Y'all did us wrong with that "60 Minutes" piece,' and so we have to go all the way back to '60 Minutes' and we have to begin to say that we told our story and if you didn't tell your side of the story, maybe it's because you didn't understand it or maybe it's because you didn't have the right person telling your side, or maybe it's because you're beginning to see another side of the story. We're having to work all that out, and it's painful and it's kinda hot at the meetings we've had. But one of the commitments that we have is that everybody stays in the room and everybody can say whatever they want to say until it's said, and we're gonna just be kind and listen to each other, because this confrontation crap isn't going to work anymore. We're gonna have our differences, but let's see where we have some common ground where we might be able to begin to work."

Sister Anne was equally optimistic. While SMHA's progress had come slowly, she insisted they were never discouraged. "I never did think it would change in one or two years or three years," she said, "and so we had to count success in very, very small steps, and we could not be discouraged when we saw those small steps happening because we knew where it was going. I think the essential thing was that we had a long-term vision and an understanding that what we were dealing with was not just a situation of poverty, but of long-term oppression. Also, I think, an understanding pretty early that a people had been damaged, that their pride, their self-respect, had been taken away; and you can give back a better house to somebody, but you don't give self-respect to somebody. They have to take it back."